SOUTHERN
ELECTRIC

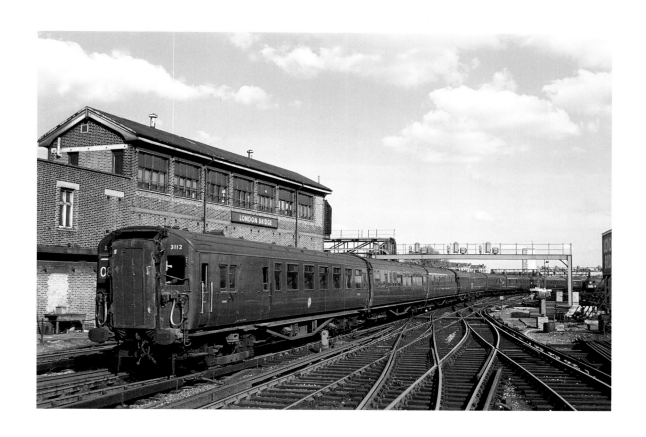

First published 2010

ISBN 978-185414-340-2

Published by Capital Transport Publishing
www.capitaltransport.com

Printed by CS Graphics, Singapore

ACKNOWLEDGEMENTS

In the preparation of Volume 2 of *Southern Electric – A New History*, I am once again particularly indebted to Laurie Mack, founder member of the SWCS, who not only freely provided vast amounts of information from his extensive researches over more than fifty years, but who also greatly assisted with the final editing task. The book would also be poorer without access to the detailed notebooks of G.T. Moody dating back almost to the beginnings of the Southern Electric, kindly lent by the late R.C. Riley, who also freely provided photographs from his extensive collection. Others who looked at the text and made valuable comments and/or other useful contributions include the late Alan A. Jackson, Gregory Beecroft, Laurie Bowles, Keith Brown and Tony Dyer. For the supply of photographs I am grateful to staff from the National Railway Museum / Science and Society Picture Library and the RAF Museum and also to James H. Aston, John H. Bird, Colin Boocock, Dick Coombes, E.W.J. Crawforth, the late Denis Cullum, Alex Dasi-Sutton, Steve Davies, Chris Heaps, Andrew French, Fred W. Ivey, the late David Jenkinson, Mike King, Colin Marsden, John H. Meredith, David Scouler, The Railway Correspondence and Travel Society, the Railway and Canal Historical Society, Joseph Sietta, John Scott-Morgan, Bryan Rayner, John Scrace, the late John L. Smith (Lens of Sutton), Brian Stephenson, Richard Stumpf, Peter Swift and John Wills. I am also indebted to Gordon Rushton, who provided the very fine maps for this Volume. Finally, I would like to thank my wife Alison and children Jennifer and Iain for their patience and support over the many years this book has been in preparation.

David Brown

Front cover Portsmouth express stock motor third brake 11159 from 4 RES unit 3064, in original condition without the power jumper below the windscreen, poses for its official photograph when newly-built in 1937. On vehicles constructed for the Portsmouth No.1 electrification, lining was restricted to the waist only, but still formed into 'panels'. *SR Official*

Frontispiece A twelve-coach formation of 'Nelson' stock, led by 4 COR 3112, weaves past the impressive three-storey signal box at London Bridge with the empty stock of an evening coastal express. The leading unit has roller-blind headcode panels but retains its whistles and has not gained yellow warning panels, which dates the photograph to 1964 or 1965. *Chris Heaps*

Back cover Until the late 1950s, few families went on holiday by car, and even fewer by air. This cover illustration from a 1958 issue of John Bull Magazine shows a typical family of the time on its way to a Southern Region resort. The young boy – in his school uniform as he may not have had much else considered smart to wear for the journey – holds a toy boat, while the girl is attracted to the machine selling chocolate. Dutifully the man carries three suitcases while his wife carries one. He is smartly dressed for the occasion. Only when in holiday clothing is he likely to be seen in public without a tie.

Opposite Still looking good after thirty years, 6 PUL 3019 leads the 10am Victoria to Brighton non-stop through the inner London suburbs at Wandsworth Common on 26th May 1963. *Brian Stephenson*

SOUTHERN ELECTRIC

VOLUME TWO

Main line electrification, the war years
and British Railways

DAVID BROWN

Capital Transport

CONTENTS

INTRODUCTION

Volume 2 of *Southern Electric – A New History* covers the main line coastal and middle-distance electrification schemes completed by the Southern Railway between 1932 and 1939, and provides what is thought to be the most detailed description and history of the electric multiple unit (EMU) rolling stock built for these schemes yet published. It also includes developments through World War Two and its aftermath until nationalisation in 1948 and then gives a survey, in rather less detail, of the British Railways era up to September 1983, including rolling stock introduced from 1952. This seemingly random cut-off date has been chosen because it marks the withdrawal of the last of the second-generation 4 SUB suburban units from regular passenger service. These units, which entered service between 1941 and the end of 1951, are considered by the author to be the last of entirely Southern Railway lineage. Additionally, by the early 1980s many features of the 1930s main line schemes were being swept away with resignalling and track remodelling on the Brighton line and elsewhere.

(Volume 1, published in 2009, covers the suburban electrification schemes of the Southern Railway and its pre-Grouping predecessors between 1909 and 1939. It also describes the rolling stock provided for these schemes and introduced up to the end of 1951, including the 4 SUB class mentioned above. Additionally, as well as giving a fuller introduction, it provides general information regarding design, construction and operation of the SR's EMU fleet, including electrical and braking equipment, almost all of which is also applicable to the rolling stock described in Volume 2.)

Although a cut-off date of 30th September 1983 has generally been adhered to in this book, I have considered it necessary to make a few exceptions. In Chapter 6, where Southern Railway-designed stock withdrawn from passenger service and then converted for further use as departmental (service) stock are described, I have continued their story beyond this date until finally taken out of use. Departmental vehicles converted from coaches built in the BR era from 1952 are not covered. A surprising number of coaches from the pre-war main line fleet have survived into preservation to this day (including all but one of the fifteen splendid *Brighton Belle* Pullman cars) and their story has also been continued to the present. Again, currently preserved vehicles built from 1952 and withdrawn by BR or its successors after 1983 are not included.

The fascinating, but unsuccessful, experimental double-decker units have also been problematical regarding their true position in the history of SR electric stock. While they were originally intended to be part of the suburban renewal programme, the concept was quickly abandoned and thus they became an evolutionary dead-end. Also, construction was not authorised until after January 1948 and so it could be argued that they correctly belong to the BR era. It has therefore been decided to include them, together with other miscellaneous SR electric stock that does not fit into convenient 'compartments' (the Bulleid/Raworth electric locomotives and departmental conversions), in Chapter 6.

It is fortunate that the multiple unit stock built by the SR for express, semi-fast and longer-distance stopping services in the 1930s was well documented over its entire life by interested contemporary observers such as the late G.T. Moody and members of the Southern Carriage and Wagon Society (SCWS). By combining their notes with contemporary published literature and with the many official records still existing at the National Archive (Kew) and elsewhere, it is possible to provide a detailed survey with relatively few questions unanswered. To describe the electrification schemes themselves, much use has been made of the supplements issued with the professional trade journal *The Railway Gazette* as each succeeding scheme was completed, as well as other contemporary railway magazines. Many other sources used, including articles published in the Southern Electric Group's journal *Live Rail*, are listed in the Bibliography at the end of Volume 2.

As with Volume 1, it has been a challenge to collect together the necessary photographs for this book. Electric trains were generally considered uninteresting by amateur enthusiast photographers until the 1960s and the negatives of many official views commissioned by the Southern Railway in the pre-war era have since disappeared. However, access to those images held by the National Railway Museum is much simpler since the establishment of their excellent 'Search Engine' facility, and with perseverance and luck it has been possible to gather together (nearly) every subject required, from a wide variety of sources. Decent pictures of SR catering vehicles, in particular, have proved very hard to locate. Many of the photographs unearthed have either never been published or have not been seen for many years. I hope readers find them interesting and useful.

While a surprisingly large number of main line Southern Electric coaches have been preserved, it is at the time of writing not so easy to get a flavour of what it was like to travel from London to Brighton, Portsmouth, Hastings, Reading, etc, in a pre-war electric train. Unfortunately the last such unit to work electrically on the third-rail network, 2 BIL 2090, has not operated since 1990 and is now a static museum exhibit. For the well-heeled, a ride in Pullmans *Audrey*, *Vera* or *Gwen* in the *Venice Simplon Orient Express* gives a good impression of first class travel in the *Brighton Belle*, and it is hoped that composite car *Bertha* (arguably the luckiest accident in EMU preservation) will soon return to service on a preserved line. In my personal opinion, however, the best impression available in 2010 can be gained from preserved vehicles residing on the Bluebell Railway in Sussex which have little electric history at all. These are Maunsell steam-hauled thirds 1336 and 1309, contemporary with, and virtually identical internally to, 6 PUL and 4 COR open motor coaches respectively. In fact, their seating units were recovered from electric vehicles of these types. Both have been outstandingly restored, 1336 having been upholstered in replica 1930s blue 'jazz' moquette and 1309 in one of the SR post-war patterns. The only ways in which all these vehicles fail to provide the full flavour is their lack of the characteristic SR electric train 'smell' and their well-behaved riding, due to vastly improved bogie design in the case of the VSOE Pullmans or otherwise to the pedestrian speeds allowable on preserved lines. The alarming thumps, bangs and lurches experienced in a PUL motor coach as its leading wheels hit the points at (for example) Streatham Junction at speed, remaining on the track in defiance to all known laws of physics, could only be replicated today by a specially-designed 'white-knuckle' ride at a theme park!

Third class was renamed second class on 3rd June 1956 in a change agreed by railways of Western Europe, but there was of course absolutely no change in the standard of accommodation provided. References to motor coaches before that date refer to 'third' succeeded by 'brake' eg motor third brake (MThB), reflecting Southern Railway usage; while references afterwards refer to 'second' preceded by 'brake' eg motor brake second (MBS), as in BR documents.

The 24-hour clock was adopted by British Railways from 14th June 1965. Times quoted before that date are in the twelve-hour format suffixed am/pm as appropriate, while times quoted after that date are in the 24-hour format.

Sums of money quoted in the text relate to values at the date given. The value of money has declined over the years. An approximation of 'what it would cost now' can be taken by using a retail price index factor. This indicates that prices have more than doubled since 1985, risen ten-fold since 1970, fifteen-fold since 1960, 23-fold since 1950, about 45-fold since 1935 and forty-fold since 1925 (there was deflation in 1930-35). Where the costs of projects undertaken in the period 1932-39 are quoted in the text, an approximate equivalent for 2010 can be calculated by multiplying the figures quoted by fifty. This factor is based on values for purchasing power and retail price indices. Because of significant annual inflation since 1950, equivalent values for costs of projects after 1950 need to be identified individually; for these, the website *www.measuringworth.com/ppoweruk* is recommended.

In a book of this size and scope some errors and inconsistencies are bound to arise, however carefully the completed manuscripts are checked, and for these I accept full responsibility. Any reader who feels moved to comment on any aspect of the book is invited to contact me via the publisher.

David Brown, Chichester, January 2010.

In 1939 the Southern Railway postponed indefinitely electrification of the Tonbridge–Hastings line, and it was not until 1986 that it finally became part of the third-rail network. 2 BIL 2090, retained as part of the National Collection following withdrawal in 1971, pauses at Robertsbridge with the 'William the Conqueror' railtour during the late afternoon of Saturday 10th May 1986. It is now a static exhibit at *Locomotion*, the NRM outpost in Shildon, County Durham and, while safe for posterity, is sadly unlikely to run on its own power ever again. *David Brown*

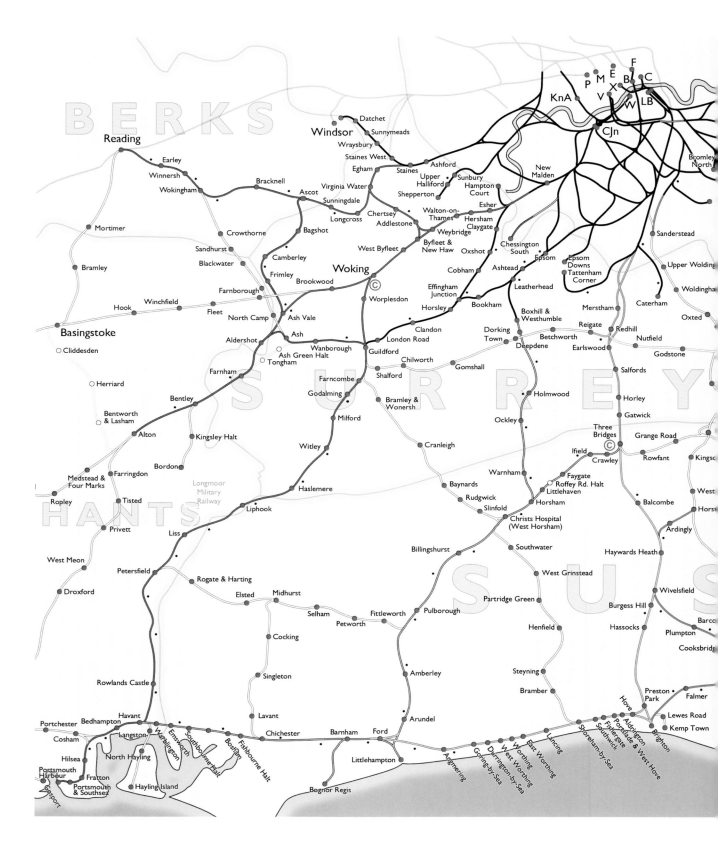

B E R K S

Reading

Datchet
Windsor
Sunnymeads
Wraysbury
Staines West
Egham
Staines
Ashford

Earley
Winnersh
Wokingham
Bracknell
Ascot
Sunningdale
Longcross
Virginia Water
Chertsey
Addlestone
Upper Halliford
Shepperton
Sunbury
Hampton Court
Walton-on-Thames
Esher

Mortimer
Crowthorne
Bagshot
Weybridge
Byfleet & New Haw
Hersham
Claygate

Bramley
Sandhurst
Blackwater
Camberley
Frimley
Brookwood
West Byfleet
Woking
Oxshot
Cobham

New Malden
Sanderstead

P M E F C
KnA V X B
W LB
CJn
Bromley North

Chessington South
Epsom
Epsom Downs
Tattenham Corner
Upper Wolding
Woldingha

Ashtead
Leatherhead
Effingham Junction
Horsley
Bookham
Boxhill & Westhumble
Merstham
Caterham
Oxted

Worplesdon
Farnborough
Winchfield
Hook
Fleet
North Camp
Ash Vale
Clandon
London Road
Dorking Town
Deepdene
Betchworth
Reigate
Earlswood
Redhill
Nutfield
Godstone

Basingstoke
Aldershot
Ash
Wanborough
Guildford
Chilworth
Shalford
Gomshall
Salfords
Cliddesden
Ash Green Halt
Tongham
Farncombe
Bramley & Wonersh
Holmwood
Horley
Gatwick
Herriard
Farnham
Godalming
Milford
Ockley
Three Bridges
Grange Road
Rowfant
Kingsc
Bentley
Bentworth & Lasham
Witley
Cranleigh
Warnham
Ifield
Crawley

West
Alton
Kingsley Halt
Haslemere
Baynards
Faygate
Roffey Rd. Halt
Littlehaven
Horsham
Balcombe
Hors
Medstead & Four Marks
Farringdon
Bordon
Rudgwick
Slinfold
Ardingly
Ropley
Tisted
Privett
Liphook
Liss
Christs Hospital (West Horsham)
Billingshurst
Southwater
Haywards Heath
West Meon
Petersfield
Rogate & Harting
West Grinstead
Wivelsfield
Droxford
Elsted
Midhurst
Partridge Green
Burgess Hill
Barco
Selham
Fittleworth
Pulborough
Henfield
Hassocks
Plumpton
Petworth
Cooksbridge
Cocking
Amberley
Steyning
Bramber
Preston Park
Falmer
Singleton
Rowlands Castle
Lavant
Arundel
Hove
Aldrington
Portslade & West Hove
Fishergate
Southwick
Shoreham-by-Sea
Lancing
Lewes Road
Kemp Town
Portchester
Bedhampton
Havant
Langstone
Warblington
Emsworth
Southbourne Halt
Bosham
Fishbourne Halt
Chichester
Barnham
Ford
Angmering
Goring-by-Sea
Durrington-by-Sea
West Worthing
Worthing
East Worthing
Brighton
Cosham
North Hayling
Littlehampton
Hilsea
Fratton
Portsmouth Harbour
Portsmouth & Southsea
Hayling Island
Bognor Regis
Gosport

Longmoor Military Railway

S U R R E Y
H A N T S
S U S

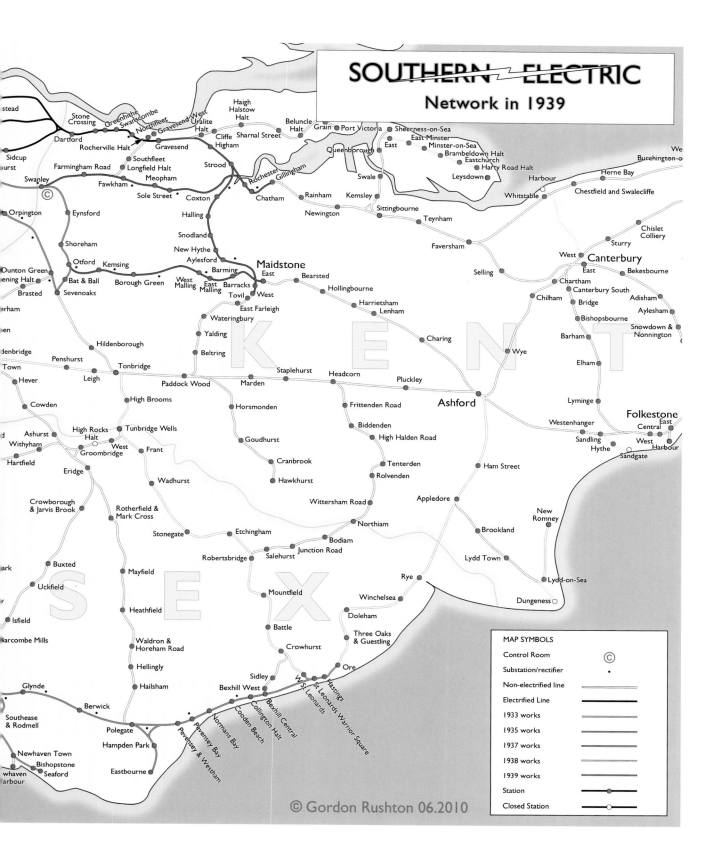

SOUTHERN ⚡ ELECTRIC
Network in 1939

KENT

SUSSEX

Hampstead
Sidcup
Swanley
Orpington

Stead
Stone Crossing
Dartford
Rocherville Halt
Farmingham Road
Longfield Halt
Southfleet
Meopham
Fawkham
Sole Street
Coxton

Greenhithe
Swanscombe
Northfleet
Gravesend West
Uralite Halt
Gravesend
Higham
Strood

Haigh
Halstow Halt
Cliffe
Sharnal Street
Beluncle Halt
Grain
Port Victoria

Rochester
Gillingham
Chatham
Rainham
Halling
Snodland
New Hythe
Aylesford
Barming
Maidstone East
West

Kemsley
Sittingbourne
Newington
Swale
Teynham

Sheerness-on-Sea
East Minster
Minster-on-Sea
Brambeldown Halt
Eastchurch
Harty Road Halt
Leysdown

Queenborough
East

Faversham
Selling
Chartham
Chilham
West
Bishopsbourne
Barham

Whitstable
Harbour
Chestfield and Swalecliffe
Herne Bay
West
Burchington-o
Chislet Colliery
Sturry
Canterbury East
Bekesbourne
Canterbury South
Bridge
Adisham
Aylesham
Snowdown & Nonnington

Eynsford
Shoreham
Otford
Kemsing
Dunton Green
Dening Halt
Brasted
Sevenoaks
Bat & Ball
Borough Green
West Malling
East Malling
Barracks
Tovil
West
East Farleigh
Wateringbury
Yalding
Beltring

Bearsted
Hollingbourne
Harrietsham
Lenham
Charing
Wye
Elham
Lyminge

Hildenborough
Penshurst
Leigh
Tonbridge
High Brooms
Hever
Cowden

Staplehurst
Marden
Paddock Wood
Headcorn
Pluckley
Horsmonden
Frittenden Road
Biddenden
High Halden Road
Tenterden
Rolvenden

Ashford

Westenhanger
Sandling
Hythe
Sandgate

Folkestone
Central
East
West
Harbour

Ashurst
Withyham
Hartfield
High Rocks Halt
West Groombridge
Frant
Eridge
Goudhurst
Cranbrook
Hawkhurst

Ham Street

Crowborough & Jarvis Brook
Rotherfield & Mark Cross
Wadhurst
Wittersham Road
Appledore
New Romney
Brookland

Stonegate
Etchingham
Bodiam
Junction Road
Northiam

Lydd Town
Lydd-on-Sea
Dungeness

Buxted
Uckfield
Isfield
Barcombe Mills
Mayfield
Heathfield
Robertsbridge
Salehurst
Mountfield
Rye
Winchelsea
Doleham
Three Oaks & Guestling

Waldron & Horeham Road
Hellingly
Hailsham
Battle
Crowhurst
Ore

Glynde
Berwick
Southease & Rodmell
Polegate
Hampden Park
Newhaven Town
Bishopstone
Seaford
Newhaven Harbour
Eastbourne

Sidley
Bexhill West
Cooden Beach
Collington Halt
Bexhill Central
Normans Bay
Pevensey Bay
Pevensey & Westham
St Leonards
West St Leonards
Hastings
St Leonards Warrior Square

MAP SYMBOLS	
Control Room	ⓒ
Substation/rectifier	·
Non-electrified line	
Electrified Line	
1933 works	
1935 works	
1937 works	
1938 works	
1939 works	
Station	━●━
Closed Station	━○━

CHAPTER 1: MAIN LINE ELECTRIFICATION 1932-39

By 1930 the majority of the suburban lines of the Southern Railway had been successfully electrified, and the company then turned its attention to the conversion of its longer distance routes, starting with the main line to Brighton. While much of the technology was tried and tested, electrification of the Brighton line was much more of a pioneering venture than the suburban schemes, as nothing quite like it had been attempted before in this country. However 'Britain's First Main Line Electrification' proved to be just as great a success and encouraged the SR Board to embark upon on a rolling programme of main line electrification covering its shorter routes to the south coast through Sussex and Hampshire. By the time that this came to a halt in the latter part of 1939 concurrent with the outbreak of war, the conductor rails had snaked outwards from London covering the most important lines inside a rough triangle to the South Coast as far as Portsmouth in the west and Hastings in the east. Also converted during this period were the intermediate-distance routes from London out to Reading in the west and Maidstone and Gillingham in the east, the latter forming a stepping stone for electrification to the Kent Coast for which provision had been made and which would no doubt have been proceeded with had war not intervened.

Hand-in-hand with electrification went significant timetable improvements, and thus the effect of the SR's main line programme was to create a network offering frequent, convenient and relatively fast services which attracted passengers in ever-increasing numbers and which was able to compete with the expanding Green Line road coach network over comparable distances. Not only did the attractive peak-hour services encourage longer-distance business travel with a consequent rise in season ticket revenue from towns such as Haywards Heath, Haslemere and Horsham, but increased off-peak frequencies encouraged shopping expeditions and day-trips to London and the coast. Electric traction was also better able to deal with the heavy summer holiday traffic which then existed, particularly on the sinuous Portsmouth Direct line.

Having said all that, it is important to remember that the 1930s were a period of considerable economic hardship for industry and society generally, even though these difficult times affected the south-east less than elsewhere in Britain. The Southern's main line electrifications were therefore carried out with utmost concern for economy and, with a few inexplicable exceptions, no money was spent unless it had a specific purpose. For example many lines retained semaphore signalling where it was still adequate, and station rebuilding was not undertaken unless absolutely necessary to ease operating restrictions and handle increased traffic. As will be seen, much of the capital for the longer-distance schemes was procured by taking advantage of cheap Government loans and other financial provisions whose purpose was to stimulate the British economy and reduce unemployment. One result of this careful financial control was that all the schemes were completed for less than their authorised budget.

This chapter covers, in chronological order, the main line and other longer-distance electrification schemes outside the suburban area completed between 1933 and 1939, and subsequent developments up to the outbreak of World War Two. It also deals with relevant personnel and administration changes which took place during this period. Much of the detail comes from supplements to *The Railway Gazette* which appeared through the 1930s as each successive scheme was completed. As before, only outline details of rolling stock, of which there were two distinct and incompatible fleets, are given here; they are covered fully in Chapters 4 and 5. As with the later suburban electrifications, there was some seemingly peculiar apportioning of rolling stock costs, such that units financially attributed to one scheme were really intended for some other line. This exercise was basically to satisfy the company accountants and shareholders, and details are given where known. Numerical headcodes were introduced for the main line electrifications, in some instances using different numbers to distinguish stopping patterns as well as route and destination. This complexity has made including these headcodes in the main body of the text in most cases too unwieldy, but a complete list of letter and numerical headcodes was included in Volume 1.

BRIGHTON AND WORTHING

It will be recalled how, in 1903, the erstwhile London, Brighton and South Coast Railway obtained parliamentary powers to electrify the whole of its route mileage, mainly to head off proposals for rival electrically-worked high-speed lines from London to Brighton. Although any such scheme (and there had been several) failed to reach the statute books, the LBSCR decided to adopt a high-voltage ac system with current collection from overhead wires as being more suitable for long-distance main line routes than the more usual low-voltage dc conductor rail system adopted by other British railways in the early years of the twentieth century. With threats of competition on its prime routes coming to nothing, the Brighton company instead embarked on electrification of its inner-suburban lines, a process fully described in Volume 1.

A pair of homely and comfortable 2 BIL units, led by 2075, pauses at Liss while forming a morning stopping service from Waterloo to Portsmouth and Southsea, c. 1938. The Waterloo – Portsmouth via Guildford route was electrified in 1937 and this photograph encapsulates much of the philosophy of the Southern Railway's main line schemes – little has been done to improve or rebuild still-adequate station facilities, but better, cleaner, rolling stock and a much more attractive, reliable and frequent regular-interval service provided. *Box Collection (NRM/SSPL)*

By the end of 1929 all of the former LBSCR 'overhead' lines had been converted to the 600V dc conductor rail system originally adopted by the LSWR and chosen by the Southern Railway in preference to the ac system. They now formed part of the SR's electrified suburban network, at that time the largest in the world. The furthest extent of this network towards Brighton was Coulsdon North, barely 36 miles from the south coast. It was therefore natural that extension of the third rail southwards should have been considered by Sir Herbert Walker and the SR Board of Directors as a logical progression of the suburban conversions already carried out. Furthermore, two significant developments, one financial and one technical, had occurred which no doubt helped to persuade the General Manager that electrification of the Brighton line was a feasible proposition.

Firstly, as part of the 1929 Budget the Chancellor of the Exchequer, Winston Churchill, announced that Railway Passenger Duty was to be abolished. This tax, levied on the four main line railway companies in respect of first and second class fares, had cost the Southern Railway £112,476 in 1928. Abolition was on the condition that 80% of the value of the duty paid was capitalised at 5% and used to finance improvement and development schemes, in order to reduce the unemployment which had arisen as a result of the 1926 General Strike and subsequent slump. Details of such schemes were to be submitted to the Treasury for approval. The Southern's share of this bonanza amounted to just over £2 million; apart from providing a considerable sum towards the electrification of the Brighton line, there was also enough to pay for 200 much needed new corridor coaches for steam services.

Secondly, development of the mercury-arc rectifier (which had no moving parts) in the late 1920s did away with one of the major running expenses of direct current electrification, the manning of the rotary converter substations. Although some of the electrified suburban lines made use of remotely controlled substations in a minor way (in the 1925 Dorking and Guildford scheme for example, where Leatherhead and Clandon substations were unmanned and controlled from Effingham Junction), the widespread use of unmanned rectifier substations enabled all on a particular section to be controlled from one location. This technical development improved the financial case for a longer distance direct current electrification scheme, such as that to Brighton.

However, one the most important factors influencing Walker's decision must have been the undoubted success of the suburban electrification schemes. Traffic levels had soared and the electric trains demonstrated a high degree of reliability. Improved receipts had resulted not only from a huge increase in the number of workers making daily journeys between their suburban homes and London which the new electric services encouraged, but also from the development of lucrative off-peak traffic. The non-stop Waterloo – Surbiton runs of the Cobham line trains also showed that the running of electric multiple units at sustained express speeds would be a viable proposition.

Walker first broached the subject of a possible Brighton electrification scheme at an officers' meeting in July 1929.

After a brief feasibility study had been carried out, the proposed plans were presented to the SR Board in October of that year. With their consent, detailed planning was started, and the finalised scheme put before shareholders at the Annual General Meeting of 23rd January 1930 by the Chairman, Brigadier-General the Hon. Everard Baring. By the end of the year, half a million pounds worth of equipment had been ordered.

The electrification to Brighton and Worthing was announced as involving 52 route miles and 162½ single track miles. Routes to be included were Coulsdon North (via the Quarry line) and Purley (via Redhill) to Earlswood and on to Brighton; Preston Park and Brighton to West Worthing; and Redhill to Reigate. The basic system to be adopted was the same as that on the suburban lines, but with all power purchased from the Central Electricity Board and supplied through unmanned rectifier substations rather than generated by the railway company. Use of similar voltage and pick-up arrangements meant that suburban units could be used for excursion and extra holiday traffic, which was to be a feature of the Brighton line up to the 1960s. All services were to be provided by electric multiple units, and the expresses would continue to include catering vehicles owned and operated by the Pullman Car Company. Those traditional prestige Brighton line services, the all-Pullman *Southern Belle* and the mainly-first class *City Limited* business trains, would continue. The proposed timetable showed an increase in loaded train miles of roughly 150%; 1,971,983 steam miles per year were to be replaced by 4,921,200 electric miles. Resignalling of much of the route mileage with colour-lights and remodelling of certain key stations and track layouts were to be carried out. Total cost of the scheme was estimated to be £2.766 million of which about half was charged to capital, and an increase of 6.6% in receipts would be required in order to maintain the profit margin. The works involved were to set the pattern for subsequent main line electrification schemes up to 1939.

The Brighton line was the first electrified route in Great Britain to take its power directly from the new National Grid. Alternating current at the standard industrial voltage and frequency of 33KV, 50Hz, was supplied by the Central Electricity Board to feeder stations at Croydon, Three Bridges and Fishersgate (on the Worthing line). From these the electricity was distributed via lineside cable to eighteen substations, which rectified and transformed the current down to a nominal 660V direct current for supply to the conductor rails, which were of 100lb/yard flat-bottomed rail mounted on porcelain insulators. The average voltage was slightly higher than that supplied by the rotary converters in the suburban area (660 instead of 600), but this did little more than to improve train performance marginally. The 33KV cable was effectively continuous from Purley to West Worthing, and between the outermost feeder points at Croydon and Fishersgate formed a ring-main whereby each substation on its route could be fed from either direction. However, the substations west of Southwick could only be supplied from one direction. These lineside cables were boxed-in by wooden boarding (which sloped at the top to allow

The interior of Three Bridges Electrical Control Room, showing part of the mimic diagram on the semicircular far wall. To the left is Three Bridges substation and its connection to the adjacent CEB feeder station, while on the right is Keymer Junction substation.
Charles Brown Collection (RAF Museum)

rainwater to run off, and also carried the substation remote-control pilot cabling) and mounted clear of the ground on short concrete posts. Concrete conduit was used where it was necessary to carry the cables under occupation crossings or other obstructions.

Located about three miles apart, the substations were situated at Star Lane, Merstham, Redhill, Salfords, Gatwick, Three Bridges, Balcombe, Ouse Valley, Haywards Heath, Keymer Junction, Hassocks, Pangdean, Preston Park, Brighton, Portslade, Shoreham, Lancing and West Worthing. Each was enclosed in a fenced compound and consisted of a building housing the rectifier plus cooling equipment, and external reinforced concrete framing on which the static transformer, switchgear and circuit-breakers were mounted. The flat-roofed buildings had a raised section at one end to provide clearance for the rectifier and were designed to be in keeping with the line's surroundings, the brown brickwork being tastefully set off by green-painted doors, window frames and drainpipe. Inside the building a 2,500KW mercury-arc rectifier was enclosed within a steel tank, the necessary vacuum being maintained by a pump which also circulated cooling water. The rectifiers were supplied by the Swiss-owned firm Brown Boveri and Co. Ltd, but most other equipment was of British manufacture. Delivery, installation and maintenance of the substation equipment was aided by an access siding and a large doorway with roller-shutter.

Roughly midway between each substation at the southern end of the line were sited track parallelling (TP) huts. These contained connections to parallel the four conductor rail sections supplied from the substations either side; this helped to reduce voltage drop between substations (another problem with low-voltage dc electrification) and hence allow fewer of them. They also contained circuit breakers, enabling a particular substation to be isolated if a fault occurred, and were designed to trip if the current draw exceeded 4,000 Amperes. In the event of an incident, power could be isolated from the offending section in half a second.

Workmen fitting out an unidentified Brighton line substation, possibly Star Lane on the Quarry line, on 5th October 1931. The reinforced concrete frame carrying the switchgear is prominent, with the brick building housing the mercury-arc rectifier behind. Note the pile of ubiquitous concrete trunking in the foreground.
Charles Brown Collection (RAF Museum)

The whole electrical installation and control arrangement was devised by the Southern Railway's own Electrical Department (New Works) under the direction of Alfred Raworth. The remote supervisory equipment for this and succeeding schemes up to 1939 was supplied by the Swedish-owned Asea Electric Ltd, with whom Raworth had been in discussion since 1927. The substations and TP huts were controlled centrally from Three Bridges Control Room, in its day a widely-visited technological wonder. Situated on the west side of the line at the bottom of the embankment south of the station where the Horsham route diverged, it was a two storey building with a flat-roofed rectangular ground floor on which was superimposed a semi-circular upper storey. The windowed ground floor contained the control equipment cubicles, switchgear and accumulators. The upper storey contained the control room, all lighting inside this bunker-like emporium being artificial to give the operators inside a clear view of the warning lights on the mimic control diagram without being dazzled by sunlight or reflections. The operators sat at a desk in the centre of the floor, lit by a pair of pedestal lamps on columns, observing this control diagram which occupied virtually the whole length of the curved wall, with Purley on its left and West Worthing on its right. Its physical dimensions were determined by the size of the warning light fittings, which were located in their correct relative geographical position for each substation. Warning buzzers were additionally provided to indicate substation malfunction. The building also housed the control room for the adjacent CEB substation, and a private telephone exchange communicating with all railway substations under its control.

Simply, the substation remote-control system worked by sending low-voltage control signals at 60V dc from transmitters located in the control cubicles to the substations through special five-core pilot cables carried in the same lineside wooden boxing or concrete conduit as the current distribution cabling. Each cubicle controlled two substations which were not adjacent. Current was supplied from the accumulators located on the ground floor, which were normally continuously trickle-charged. Return signals were powered by 50 Amp/hour batteries located in each substation. The control system was so arranged that any two substations could do the work of three in an emergency.

As with the suburban electrification projects, considerable modification and simplification of station and junction layouts was carried out, both to facilitate an increased service and to remove redundant facilities. Track alterations took place at Redhill where provision was made to divide and combine stopping trains, a widespread practice on the suburban lines, into Three Bridges/Brighton and Reigate portions. Similar provision was made at Hove, where the platforms were also extended to 800ft. In the London area, platforms 14 and 15 at London Bridge were lengthened to accommodate the new trains.

Hand in hand with track alterations went resignalling, using three aspect (red, yellow and green) colour lights, although this was only done where considered necessary. It was installed over the whole route from Coulsdon North into Brighton station via the Quarry line. The coastal section from Brighton and Preston Park (via the Cliftonville curve), as well as the Purley – Redhill – Reigate/Earlswood section, retained semaphore signals, largely because it would mainly be slower stopping services using these routes and because the signalling equipment on them was still serviceable. Anyway, even the fastest Brighton line services were still being signalled by semaphores through the complicated junctions around East Croydon as late as 1954.

The new signalling was brought into use on various dates in 1932. Starting at the northern end of the route, the first stage was completed on the night of 4th-5th June, when colour-lights replaced semaphores on the Quarry line and southwards to Balcombe Tunnel Junction, where the four tracks all the way from London converged into two. The double-track section thence to Copyhold Junction, north of Haywards Heath where the route from Horsted Keynes joined the main line, was converted as from 6th October, followed by Haywards Heath to Preston Park three days later. Finally, the Brighton station area was resignalled on 16th October, the work this time being hampered by pouring rain. When completed, the 36 miles from Coulsdon North to Brighton was the longest continuous stretch of colour-light signalling in the country, and the entire route was controlled from just seven signal boxes. Only two of these, at Brighton and Haywards Heath, were entirely new. The new box at Brighton Central was built into the wall of the Works building on the Down side, and contained 225 electrically-interlocked levers: it replaced six smaller signal cabins which had previously littered the station area. Haywards Heath was provided with a sixty-lever mechanical-framed box of traditional design, situated opposite the Up platform.

Southwards from Balcombe Tunnel Junction the route was mainly double-tracked only, in spite of several abortive schemes to widen it (the last being in the 1920s). Between Copyhold Junction and Haywards Heath however, there was a one-and-one-half mile stretch of quadruple track, originally arranged as two pairs (Up-Down, Up-Down). On electrification, the junctions were rearranged so the lines became paired by direction (Up-Up, Down-Down) with the fast lines in the centre and the slow lines on the outside. This arrangement facilitated cross-platform interchange at the remodelled Haywards Heath station, and reduced possible conflicting movements at Copyhold Junction. This was necessary in view of the frequent services planned, particularly after the 1935 Eastbourne electrification which included the branch to Horsted Keynes. The reconstructed station at Haywards Heath consisted of two 800ft long island platforms, the standard length where twelve-coach trains of the new electric express stock were to call. The platforms were connected via a subway to a frontage of *Moderne* style in brick. Waiting rooms, staff accommodation, canopies and other platform fittings were designed by the engineering department and, although serviceable, showed little of an architect's hand – they were similar to some of the rebuilt suburban-area stations such as Epsom (1929). At Brighton, the approach layout was much simplified, with seventeen crossovers being abolished. One short platform (formerly no.4) was obliterated, and four centre platforms were extended to 800ft. Little work was required to improve the passenger facilities here, as these had been rebuilt as recently as 1929. The station departure board, dating from 1908, had been moved from Victoria to Brighton in 1927.

Elsewhere, structures originating from the SR concrete works at Exmouth Junction were much in evidence, helping to give a recognisably Southern house style to the stations on the line, as did the green and cream enamel station name plates liberally applied to lamp posts. Prefabricated concrete platform extensions and fencing were provided at such locations as Coulsdon South and Balcombe, the latter also gaining a footbridge of the same material.

A total of 275 new coaches were built for the new electric services on the Brighton line, formed into multiple units of four cars (given the SR electric stock code 4 LAV), five cars (originally 5 PUL) and six cars (originally 6 COR). The 33 4 LAV units, initially numbered 1921-1953, were for London – Brighton semi-fast and stopping services. These had reasonably comfortable seating of main-line standard and one vehicle of the four equipped with a side-corridor and toilets, but otherwise were not unlike the suburban units.

Twenty 6 COR units (2001-2020) were provided for most of the fast trains between London and the coast. These were based on the latest SR steam-hauled coach designs, and had a mixture of compartment and open seating with gangways between coaches (except at the driving ends) to give all passengers access to lavatories and to a Pullman refreshment car. A further three 6 CORs (2041-2043) were similar, but had a greater proportion of first class seating for use on the *City Limited* business service between London Bridge and Brighton. Finally, the three 5 PUL units (2051-2053) were composed entirely of Pullman cars, the first such electric multiple units in the world, and worked the *Southern Belle* non-stop services with full at-seat refreshment facilities. (Note that in 1935 the 6 COR and 5 PUL types were reclassified to the more familiar 6 PUL, 6 CIT and 5 BEL, and in 1937 they were renumbered by the addition of 1000 to the unit numbers – further details are given in Chapter 5.)

New maintenance facilities were provided to service all this new stock, although use was also made of the existing suburban depots at Peckham Rye, Selhurst and Slades Green (4 LAV stock only), particularly for repair and heavy overhaul. The former paint shop at Brighton Works (on the Up side of the main line) was converted into a twelve-road maintenance and inspection shed. Seven of the tracks were provided with centre inspection pits and a plug-in power supply at line voltage to enable electrical equipment in the trains to be tested without the hazard of live conductor rails. Interior cleaning was facilitated by the provision of vacuum cleaner sockets, and external cleaning by an automatic carriage washer. This was situated at the north end of the depot, almost level with the works of the Pullman Car Company near Preston Park. A large number of electrified berthing sidings were also provided in the Brighton station area. An 800ft long, three road carriage shed was provided at West Worthing, the limit of electric working westwards along the coast from Brighton between 1933 and 1938. This was of standard SR prefabricated design of which examples could already be seen on the suburban lines (eg Orpington) and was constructed of a steel framework mainly clad in corrugated asbestos sheeting.

Work on the scheme started early in 1931, and by the middle of the following year was far enough advanced to allow an interim timetable of electric trains to commence from London as far south as Three Bridges. On 17th July a half-hourly stopping service was introduced, starting alternately from London Bridge and Victoria and running through to Redhill, where trains split into Reigate and Three Bridges portions. The Up service was arranged similarly. From this date Salfords Halt (hitherto for the exclusive use of staff at the nearby British Monotype Works) was open regularly, and Earlswood on all seven days of the week. The first 4 LAV units to be delivered were used for these trains, having already been run-in in service on the Waterloo – Guildford via Cobham line. Test running into Brighton itself began only on 2nd November, barely two months prior to the scheduled opening date. On a return proving trip between Victoria and Brighton on Sunday 20th November, express unit 2018 completed the Up journey non-stop in 46 minutes and 45 seconds. As testament to Raworth's forward planning and attention to detail, it appears that there were few commissioning problems with either the new rolling stock, signalling or electrical supply equipment.

As advance publicity, examples of the new electric trains were exhibited to the public. At Victoria 6 COR 2002 and 5 PUL 2051 were on display between 26th and 31st December 1932, while a similar exhibition took place at Brighton. The electrification received a very favourable reception from the press of the day at both local and national level, no doubt at least partly due to the efforts of the Southern's go-ahead publicity office. For example, a reporter from the *Brighton Herald* found the electric train, '. . . in every way an improvement on the steam-driven train. Both inside and out the coaches are far pleasanter to the eye . . . The electric train is bright. It has a sense of lightness and neat simplicity.' The same journalist also sampled the Pullman and was even more expansive in his praise: 'In the steam-driven Pullmans', he wrote, '. . . one was housed like a rich man. In these electric Pullmans one is indulged like a princess in a fairy tale. The only drawback one can conceive . . . is that people will find them so luxuriously comfortable that at the end of the journey they will decline to get out.'[1] Similar praise came from a report in *The Times* of 29th December 1932, in which the obviously impressed writer concluded his piece thus: 'After this foretaste of electric luxury let who will creep at their own and others' peril along the highway: sensible and self-regarding persons will stick to the train.'[2]

The official inauguration took place on Friday 30th December 1932, when a *City Limited* 6 COR unit (one of those with additional first class accommodation for business trains) carried various railway company officials and invited civic dignitaries from London on a special run. Starting at Victoria, the train travelled via the Quarry line and Cliftonville curve directly to Worthing, where it was met by the Mayor of that town. The entire entourage then returned to Brighton, where an inaugural luncheon was held in the Royal Pavilion. The full public service commenced two days later, on 1st January 1933. This was a Sunday, helpfully giving the trains, staff and timetable a chance to bed down before the first Monday morning rush hour. The first down *Southern Belle* run featured a concert by a group of female madrigal singers, to enable the Pullman Car Company to show off the smooth riding and quietness of the new electric cars on this service. One passenger on this inaugural run was the railway author and commentator R.W. Kidner who later wrote that, in his opinion, the test failed[3]. Anyway, the company's illusions were sadly all too soon shattered, the third class motor brakes in particular soon developing an embarrassing reputation for rough riding.

The new timetables for the service provided a massive increase in train-miles when compared to the superseded steam service. It offered six electric trains per hour between London and the south coast all day, with the usual extras at peak hours, including Saturday lunchtime. The description below refers to the Monday – Friday service, but there was little difference at weekends. The centre-piece was the non-stop Victoria – Brighton service, leaving London on the hour and taking sixty minutes for the journey. The 11.00am, 3.00 and 7.00pm workings were the all-Pullman *Southern Belle* using the 5 PUL units, while virtually all others were formed of express 6 COR stock with a Pullman refreshment car. An exception was the 4.00pm working, which was formed of semi-fast 4 LAV units and took 63 minutes. Express stock was also used for the xx.25 Victoria – West Worthing fast service, which made calls at East Croydon, Haywards Heath, Hove, Shoreham-by-Sea and Worthing Central. Hourly semi-fast trains ran from Victoria, calling at Clapham Junction, East Croydon, Redhill, Haywards Heath and Preston Park, and from London Bridge, calling at New Cross Gate, East Croydon, Horley, Three Bridges, Haywards Heath and Preston Park. Stopping trains also ran from both Victoria and London Bridge, calling at either Clapham Junction or Norwood Junction, then East Croydon, Purley and all stations to Brighton via Redhill, where a Reigate portion was detached. In the late evening, some London Bridge trains were extended to start from Charing Cross for the benefit of theatre-goers. Corresponding services in the Up direction were arranged similarly with, for example, the non-stops leaving Brighton at xx.25 from 10.25am until 10.25pm, those at 1.25, 5.25 and 8.25pm being all-Pullman *Southern Belle* workings.

A long-standing feature of the Brighton line rush hour service, originating in the Victorian era, was the provision of a fast train from Brighton to London Bridge arriving just before 10.00am and returning to the coast at 5.00pm. Patronised largely by first class season ticket holders, it quickly became known colloquially as the 'stockbrokers' special' and was later formally christened the *City Limited*. This important train always commanded the best rolling stock, culminating in LBSCR days in Panter's magnificent semi-gangwayed 'balloon'-roofed set, built specifically for it in 1907 and superseded by a new rake of 'ironclad' vehicles (set 471) by the SR early in 1926. For the new electric timetable, the Up *City Limited* left Brighton at 8.45am and the Down working departed from London Bridge at 5.00pm. These services, together with the 8.30am West Worthing – London Bridge and 5.04pm return to Hove, were each worked by one of the special units with extra first class seating (2041-2043) coupled to a standard corridor unit, the resultant twelve-coach formation having 210 first and 356 or 358 third class seats, including 24 first and 32 third in the Pullmans. The *City Limited* name was lost from the timetable in 1934, but the services themselves remained basically intact until September 1939.

For the first time numerical headcodes or 'route indications' were used for the new services (rather than letters), the number denoting whether the train was fast, semi-fast or stopping (Walker insisted that there were no 'slow' trains on

1   Cooper, B.K.: *Railway World Annual, 1979*, Ian Allan Ltd, 1978.
2   Gray, Adrian: *The London to Brighton Line 1841-1977*, The Oakwood Press, 1977. p87
3   Kidner, R.W.: *Pullman Cars on the Southern 1875-1972*, The Oakwood Press, ISBN 0 85361 356 7, 1987. p35

New 5 PUL (later 5 BEL) *Southern Belle* all-Pullman electric unit 2051 on display to the public at Victoria in December 1932. The crowds have a ghostly air due to the time exposure necessary to film under the gloom of the station roof in mid winter. *Lens of Sutton*

Ladies clearly enjoying their day out to Brighton in the third class section of an unidentified Brighton line Pullman car on 15th February 1933. One hopes their pleasure was not spoiled by the weather. The period details, including the ladies' clothing, 'jazz' style seat moquette and the obsequious white-coated Pullman attendant, give an evocative flavour of the 1930s, at least for the better off. *Charles Brown Collection (RAF Museum)*

the Southern Electric) and whether it was routed via Redhill or the Quarry line. Odd numbers were used for services to/from London Bridge, even numbers for Victoria trains. Generally, the higher the headcode number, the greater the number of stops.

The full Down service in a typical off-peak hour was as follows (* denotes a service including a Pullman Car):

xx.00: Victoria – Brighton non-stop* (headcode 4)
xx.00: London Bridge – Brighton semi-fast (headcode 5) calling at New Cross Gate, East Croydon, Horley, Three Bridges, Haywards Heath, and Preston Park.
xx.16: London Bridge – Brighton stopping (headcode 15) calling at New Cross Gate, Norwood Junction, East Croydon, Purley and all stations via Redhill, where a Reigate portion was detached.
xx.25: Victoria – West Worthing fast* (headcode 16) calling at East Croydon, Haywards Heath, Hove, Shoreham-by-Sea and Worthing Central.
xx.28: Victoria – Brighton semi-fast (headcode 12) calling at Clapham Junction, East Croydon, Redhill, Haywards Heath and Preston Park.
xx.46: Victoria – Brighton stopping (headcode 14) calling at Clapham Junction, East Croydon, Purley and all stations to Brighton via Redhill, where a Reigate portion was detached.

Due to the poor economic situation of the time the original plans to provide both fast and stopping electric services between London and Worthing did not materialise, and consequently the original 4 LAV order had been reduced from forty to 33. However, in addition to the fast service between Victoria and West Worthing, a local service operated to and from Brighton (headcode 1) every fifteen minutes, with alternate trains missing the halts. These halts were manned once electric services started, and were therefore provided with a small corrugated iron hut for the use of the booking clerk-cum-porter. Ex LSWR '1201' class suburban units, transferred from the London area and most with their first class accommodation reduced (see Volume 1), were initially used on these trains.

On the Brighton and West Worthing expresses, the individual Pullman composite cars in the 6 COR (PUL) units were staffed by two uniformed attendants and a cook, while this provision was doubled in each 5 PUL (BEL), giving a staff total of fourteen in a ten-car *Southern Belle*. The Pullman Car Company collected revenue not only from food and drink sales but also by charging a supplement for occupying a seat in the car, this being slightly higher for first class passengers. The cars were victualled from stores at Victoria. In the corridor units, Pullman staff could also serve limited refreshments to non-supplement passengers in other parts of the train, this originally being aided by bell communication between compartments or motor coach seating and the Pullman car, and also by an additional pantry with tea-urn at the opposite end of the car to the kitchen. When a composite Pullman car ran closed, the internal doors inboard of the entrance vestibules were locked to prevent through access.

By the time of the Brighton electrification, the Publicity Office at Waterloo was in full swing, although John Elliot had by this time been promoted to the traffic department. Slogans such as 'Five and nine – the Brighton line' (referring to the day return fare[4]) and 'Every hour, on the hour, in the hour' soon became well-known and helped to sell the service, both to regular travellers and to day-trippers. Although Brighton itself never quite became a London dormitory suburb, increasing numbers of City white-collar workers made the return journey each weekday from there or from other towns at the southern end of the line. The advertising particularly stressed the frequency of the service, although timetable consultation was not perhaps quite as superfluous as for London suburban services.

The Brighton line electrification was an instant success, the novelty of the new service attracting the public to the seaside even if the weather did not. Traffic increased by an encouraging 5% compared with the last New Year's Day of steam working. Easter 1933 showed in a spectacular fashion what electric trains could do. On the Easter Monday alone receipts rose by 127% compared with the previous year, and no fewer than 28 trains conveyed day trippers back to London in the four hours between 4.00 and 8.00pm. This could only have been achieved with multiple unit rolling stock. Overall, in the first year of service, an increase in traffic of 33% resulted, fully justifying the decision of Walker and the SR Board. Two years later it was possible to look at the overall costs of the Brighton line electrification and it was found to have come out under budget by half a million pounds, an encouraging trend which was to be repeated for later schemes.

At the end of 1934 the suburban stock working the Brighton – West Worthing local service returned to the London area, being replaced by the first eleven 2 NOL units, 1813-1823, specifically designed for coastal workings. Like the units they displaced, the NOLs were of non-corridor layout with wooden bodywork of LSWR origin. As the Brighton line electrification had already been paid for in 1932-33, their cost was actually charged to the Sevenoaks electrification account (see Volume 1) as a paper exercise to satisfy the company accountants.

Changes to the Brighton main line and its services in the early years of the electrification were few, and mainly involved the gradual substitution of remaining steam services by more frequent electric trains as successive main line electrifications were completed, as related later in this chapter. Trains to Eastbourne and Hastings used the Brighton line as far as Keymer Junction, whence they diverged eastwards towards Lewes; these were electric as from July 1935. Similarly, Mid-Sussex line trains were electric as from June 1938. In both cases local steam trains along the coastal routes from Brighton were replaced by electric units. One result of this was that different types of electric stock regularly appeared

---

4   Five shillings and nine pence in 1933 was roughly equivalent to £15 at 2010 prices. As a comparison, the off-peak day-return fare (without any railcard discounts) to Brighton in 2010 was £13.40.

on trains into Brighton, particularly the 6 PAN units built for the Eastbourne electrification, but also 4 COR, 4 BUF, 2 BIL and 2 HAL types.

Ever with an eye for good publicity, the SR Board and Pullman Car Company decided in 1934 to change the name of the *Southern Belle* all-Pullman service to the more popular-sounding *Brighton Belle*, partly to match the similar (but steam-hauled) *Bournemouth Belle* service introduced that year. Thus on 29th June, on the occasion of the opening of a large indoor swimming pool in Brighton, the train was renamed as it arrived at the coastal terminus with the 11.00am from Victoria. The renaming was carried out by the Mayor of Brighton, Miss M. Hardy, accompanied by several officials of the Southern Railway Company.

One of the more far-reaching developments to occur was the opening of Tinsley Green for Gatwick Airport station, intended to serve the new passenger aerodrome at Gatwick. Situated between Gatwick Racecourse and Three Bridges, it consisted of two side platforms and a central island, connected by a roofed concrete footbridge. The unpretentious station buildings were situated on the Up side, connected to the airport building (known due to its shape as the 'beehive') by subway. The Victoria/London Bridge – Brighton stopping services called there from 30th September 1935, even though the airport was not yet operational. Following a formal opening on 6th May 1936, the first air services to use the new airport were transferred from Croydon eleven days later. The railway station was renamed Gatwick Airport from 1st June, and from 5th July until the outbreak of war in September 1939, the hourly semi-fast trains between Victoria and Brighton also called there.

The wooden-platformed halt at Bungalow Town, between Shoreham-by-Sea and Lancing, had been closed on 1st January 1933, coincident with the introduction of electric services. However, renamed Shoreham Airport, it was opened again on 30th September 1935, the same day as Tinsley Green. It was intended to serve the new Brighton, Hove and Worthing municipal airport, to which it was adjacent, and half-hourly Brighton to West Worthing stopping services called there from about 8.00am until 9.00pm seven days a week. Air services were operated from Shoreham to Jersey, Birmingham and Liverpool, the latter two routes being run by Railway Air Services Limited on behalf of the GWR and SR jointly. Following the outbreak of war and the use of the airfield for military purposes, the halt was closed for reasons of security on 15th June 1940. Never reopened, all traces of it have since disappeared.

Shoreham Airport Halt, photographed on 11th May 1938 with a through Brighton – Plymouth steam train passing. Originally opened in 1910 as Bungalow Town Halt, it was closed on electrification but reopened with a new identity to serve the Brighton and Hove municipal aerodrome on 30th September 1935. As can be seen, interchange facilities for those intrepid (and wealthy) passengers travelling by air to and from Jersey, Birmingham or Liverpool were somewhat primitive. *H. M. Madgwick*

The 1931 station at Hastings, looking east towards Ore. A pair of 2 NOL units, led by 1822, runs in with an Ore to Brighton service in 1958, when the type was becoming due for withdrawal. Spending virtually their entire lives on the coastal stopping services for which they were intended, they lacked lavatory facilities and were constructed using existing bodywork of LSWR origin on new underframes in the same manner as much contemporary London suburban stock. *F. W. Ivey*

EASTBOURNE AND HASTINGS

With the financial success of the Brighton line electrification readily apparent in the first months of 1933, it is unsurprising that further main line schemes were soon being considered by Sir Herbert Walker and his team. The most obvious of these was really an extension of the Brighton line scheme, involving the conversion of the routes eastwards from Keymer Junction and Brighton to Lewes, and thence along the coast to Eastbourne and Hastings. Preliminary surveys were carried out in the spring of 1933, but Walker then had some difficulty in persuading the SR Board to authorise the scheme, and a decision on it was deferred a number of times. The report of the Government-sponsored Weir Committee on future railway electrification in Britain, published in 1931, had endorsed the findings of the 1927 Pringle Report in recommending large-scale conversion at 1,500V dc overhead in the interests of more economical working. These findings had prejudiced the Boards of the main-line companies against major electrification programmes due to the high capital costs involved; without Government assistance (not at that time forthcoming) they generally had neither the will nor the finances for such an undertaking. Although members of the SR Board of Directors probably had fewer financial interests in coal production than those of the LMS and LNER, it nevertheless required considerable effort on the part of Walker and others, as well as some cost-pruning, to ensure that the proposed scheme did not sink without trace. Fortunately it was finally and belatedly approved at the SR Board meeting of 1st March 1934. As authorised, the Eastbourne and Hastings electrification scheme involved the conversion of 60½ route miles and 133½ track miles at an estimated cost of £1.75 million.

The lines involved were Keymer Junction (between Wivelsfield and Burgess Hill) and Brighton to Lewes, Lewes to Hastings and Ore, Southerham Junction (east of Lewes) to Newhaven and Seaford, the branch to Eastbourne, and Copyhold Junction (north of Haywards Heath) to Horsted Keynes. The decision to terminate electric trains beyond Hastings at Ore, an insignificant halt on its eastern outskirts, was taken to avoid congestion at the busy Hastings station, whose four platforms also had to accommodate Eastern section steam trains via Tunbridge Wells. The Horsted Keynes branch, in entirely rural surroundings and with little potential for traffic development, was also a strange choice for electrification. It was allegedly converted for much the same reason as Ore; to avoid the reversal of local trains on the main line at Haywards Heath. However, it was probably also intended to be the first stage of an electrified loop off the Brighton line via Oxted and East Grinstead, which would have formed a useful diversionary route. Unfortunately for those responsible for maintaining Rastrick's imposing but troublesome Ouse Valley viaduct, subsequent events have ensured that this will never now happen.

In most respects the works involved were similar to those on the main Brighton line, the same contractors and teams generally being responsible. One difference was that the mercury-arc rectifiers came from the British company Bruce, Peebles and Co., who went on to supply this equipment for all succeeding Southern Railway electrification schemes up to 1939. Power was again supplied by the CEB from the National Grid, via feeder stations located at Eastbourne and Ore which between them fed current to sixteen new rectifier substations via lineside cabling. At Southerham bridge (east of Lewes), which could be lifted to allow vessels to pass up the River Ouse, the trackside cabling was carried through a concrete duct on the river bed. Of the substations, twelve were supervised from the existing electrical control room at Three Bridges, where the additional mimic diagram was installed on the flat wall of the semi-circular upper storey. These were at Plumpton, Cooksbridge (both on the main line from Keymer Junction), Lewes, Southerham Junction, Glynde, Selmeston, Folkington, Willingdon Junction, Eastbourne, Southease, Newhaven and Falmer. The latter three, all between Brighton and Seaford, were not on a direct cable run but were fed from Lewes. All had single mercury-arc rectifiers except Newhaven substation which had two. The remaining five substations, located at Pevensey, Normans Bay, Bexhill, Bopeep and Ore, were supervised from a new electrical control room at Ore. All pairs of substations had a track parallelling hut between them. Substations were of basically the same design as those on the main Brighton line, but the buildings housing the rectifiers and auxiliary equipment were now faced with concrete.

A pair of amusing anecdotes involving the electrical installation on the Eastbourne line are related by the late Charles Klapper[5], and are worth repeating here. The first concerns Cooksbridge substation which was constructed, like all those between Keymer Junction and Newhaven, by SR maintenance bricklayers (probably as part of the cost-cutting exercise). Although their design was largely standardised, individual plans for each substation location were prepared. Now the architect who drew the plans for the rectifier building at Cooksbridge failed to include the usual access door, an omission not noticed by the men erecting it! The train which came to return them to Brighton at the end of the day's work (a Stroudley D1 0-4-2T and Marsh 'balloon' coach) sounded its whistle but received no answer. It was therefore assumed that, as the substation looked complete, they had left 'under

5   Klapper, C.F.: *Sir Herbert Walker's Southern Railway*, Ian Allan Ltd, ISBN 0 7110 0478 1, 1973. pp215-217

their own steam'. When the foreman later checked off his men at Brighton, he was perturbed to find himself fifteen short. It just so happened that Walker was present on that occasion and, making one of his quick decisions, insisted: 'We must return to Cooksbridge'. Muffled cries from within the substation building made it clear that, as the GM had suspected, the fifteen had incarcerated themselves. A quick exercise with pickaxe to free them was followed by a return to Haywards Heath station where Jones (then still Chief Electrical Engineer) and Raworth received a dressing down from their boss. What happened to the hapless architect is not recorded!

The second story concerns the official switch-on of power on the Eastbourne and Seaford lines, a Saturday afternoon occasion at Three Bridges Control Room attended by the usual impressive array of senior officials including Walker, as well as the control room operator. On switching on Newhaven substation, the 'electrification' telephone instantly rang, with a distressed signalman on the other end pleading 'Switch off, for God's sake, me levers is all alive!' This was a result of exceptionally fine weather resulting in the drying out of the pier timbers and drastically increasing their insulation, causing the running rails (to which the signals were earthed) to be at nearly the same potential as the conductor rail when no trains were running. The junior from the Electrical Engineers department sent to solve the problem found that the General Manager had arrived at Newhaven before him and sampled the problem for himself. Walker's suggested solution was to run a thick copper wire from the buffer stops at the end of the pier down into the sea water to improve the earthing.

Minimal alterations were carried out to the signalling on the lines concerned, manually controlled upper-quadrant semaphores generally remaining at most locations. The main advance was that track-circuiting was provided throughout.

Lewes: the new takes over from the old, as a new 6 PAN unit on test approaches from the Eastbourne line, and is about to pass the new rectifier substation. An LBSCR locomotive and carriages, shortly to be redundant, stand waiting for one of the new SR signals, mounted on posts made up from old rails, to clear.

The long block section between Hampden Park and Eastbourne was divided by the provision of intermediate signals, a new West cabin was erected at Lewes, and a new power frame was installed in the existing signal cabin at Eastbourne. Regarding track alterations, the east end of Lewes tunnel was widened, enabling the curve through the London platforms to be eased to permit the use of 9ft wide Restriction 4 rolling stock and the platforms themselves to be lengthened. The station at Hastings had been reconstructed with two island platforms serving four lines as recently as 1931, and was therefore already suitable for an electric service. As part of this rebuilding however, much of the trackwork had been relaid with steel sleepers, and these had to be replaced with wood before conductor rails could be laid. Other trackwork alterations included the provision of electrified berthing sidings at Eastbourne, and an 820ft four-road carriage shed at Ore. This was similar to that at West Worthing, and was connected to the running lines east of the station, making it necessary to lay conductor rails a short distance towards Three Oaks (on the line to Ashford).

Other major incidental works were few. A new station replaced the former halt at Cooden Beach, between Pevensey and Bexhill Central, in the optimistic hope of housing development. The line here was on an embankment, and the concrete platforms were reached through long sloping passageways up from the very urban-looking red brick frontage in *Moderne* style at street level. Here and elsewhere the usual crop of concrete fencing, platform extensions and by-now standard green enamel 'bullseye' signs made their appearance. At Horsted Keynes, in the wilds of rural east Sussex, only the line into platform no.4 was electrified. This platform was completely devoid of shelter and remained so following electrification – one supposes intending passengers for the hourly service to Haywards Heath and Seaford were expected to hide in the subway during inclement weather.

Rolling stock provision was largely similar to that for the Brighton line scheme. Prior to electrification, services on the Eastbourne line had been provided by stock of mixed vintage, with some modern Maunsell corridor vehicles interspersed by older ex-LBSCR coaches. As on the Brighton line, refreshments on the expresses were served in Pullman cars. However, after the purchase of the cars for the Brighton electrification (which had been more expensive than originally intended) the Pullman Car Company was in a weak position financially and largely because of this the new electric units for the express services did not continue this facility. Instead, railway-owned catering vehicles (ROVs in Pullman parlance) were provided, but still staffed by Pullman personnel under the existing contract. These vehicles, known as pantry cars, were never really satisfactory as catering coaches, being basically compartment firsts with a small kitchen and serving area at one end from which tea and biscuits (and not much else) could be served. Apart from this feature, the seventeen 6 PAN units, numbered 2021-2037, were largely similar to the earlier Brighton corridor units, (now reclassified 6 PUL). From the onset of electrified services on the Eastbourne route, the majority of expresses to the coast were formed 6 PUL+6 PAN, so at least some passengers had the opportu-

nity to use the Pullman car. For other services, two types of two-coach unit were provided, both of which could work in multiple with 4 LAV and suburban stock if required. The 39 2 NOLs, numbered 1824-1862, were identical to those provided for the Brighton – West Worthing line, and inter-worked with them from the beginning on coastal stopping services. Most were funded as part of the Eastbourne electrification but 1856-1862, like 1813-1823 before them, were budgeted from the Sevenoaks account as part of the Eastbourne scheme cost-pruning exercise. The ten 2 BIL units, initially numbered 1890-1899, had side corridors and toilets in both coaches, and seating was the same as in the express stock. These features made them suitable for longer distance work, and the SR perpetuated the design (with a few modifications) in quantity for later electrifications up to 1939.

As was usual with SR electrification schemes, no time was lost in introducing the new services once conversion work was complete and the new rolling stock delivered. Trial running with newly-delivered 6 PAN units commenced in May 1935, and the formal opening was arranged for 4th July. This was the (by now) usual grand civic affair involving the Lord Mayor and Sheriffs of London, who travelled down from Victoria in CIT unit 2043, accompanied by Southern Railway officials. They were met at the appropriate resort stations by the Mayors of Eastbourne, Bexhill and Hastings.

Public services commenced on 7th July, with a new time-table offering a vast improvement in frequency and convenient connectional possibilities. The Down service was based around a train to Ore leaving Victoria at xx.45, calling at East Croydon, Haywards Heath, Lewes, Eastbourne, Cooden Beach, Bexhill Central, St Leonards (Warrior Square), Hastings and Ore. Normally, the twelve-coach train split at Eastbourne, only the rear six coaches (normally a 6 PUL) continuing to Ore. Up services were arranged similarly, and there were the usual alterations in peak hours with some trains serving London Bridge rather than Victoria. In the summer, services were augmented by extra expresses leaving Victoria at xx.15. Local services comprised an hourly train between Horsted Keynes and Seaford, which also provided the stopping service between Haywards Heath and Lewes, and half-hourly trains along the coast from Brighton to Eastbourne/Hastings and to Seaford. Together, these gave the Seaford branch a lavish twenty-minute interval service. The timetables were arranged so that the various services connected without long waits for passengers changing trains, facilitated by island platforms at Haywards Heath and Lewes allowing simple cross-platform interchange. Virtually all these local services were initially worked by non-corridor 2 NOL units, the ten 2 BILs starting life mostly supplementing the LAVs on the Brighton line or being loaned to the Eastern section (Chapter 4 refers). Conversely, some rush-hour semi-fast workings between London Bridge or Victoria and Eastbourne/Ore were worked by LAV stock.

Although the new services were a great improvement on what had gone before, not everyone was happy with the revised arrangements. In particular, there were many complaints from Hastings passengers that virtually all trains

Bishopstone station, opened in November 1938 for housing developments which didn't materialise at the time. This was a typical new Southern Railway station, made up largely from standardised prefabricated steel and concrete components. The tall octagonal booking hall was designed to be easily seen from surrounding streets. *Stations UK*

ran in and out of Eastbourne, whereas previously there had been separate Eastbourne and Hastings portions, dividing or combining at Polegate. With their lack of toilets, the use of 2 NOL units on the lengthy Brighton – Hastings run also caused disquiet. The pantry cars in the 6 PAN units gave rise to complaints from staff due to their cramped kitchens. The latter problem was remedied by the eventual closure of the catering facility in the pantry cars after about 1950, but many Brighton – Hastings services continued to be operated by NOL stock until 1958 and regular direct Hastings services by-passing Eastbourne were never restored.

Other developments on the electrified Seaford, Eastbourne and Hastings lines prior to World War Two were few. Another over-ornate brick and concrete station in *Moderne* style, this time with a covered steel footbridge, was erected on a new site at Bishopstone (between Newhaven Harbour and Seaford), again in anticipation of housing developments which never fully materialised. The new Bishopstone station opened for traffic on 26th November 1938. The former Bishopstone station at Tide Mills was renamed Bishopstone Beach and opened between Easter and the end of September 1939 only. (It was officially closed permanently on 1st January 1942.)

PORTSMOUTH VIA GUILDFORD, INCLUDING WEYBRIDGE – STAINES (PORTSMOUTH NO.1)

The very satisfactory financial results of the electrification to

Brighton and Worthing, by this time in operation for over two years, together with the successful completion of the Eastbourne and Hastings extension at less than the estimated cost, encouraged Sir Herbert Walker in placing further plans before the SR Board. Now that the busiest Central section main lines had been dealt with, it was time to consider electrification down the Western section main line south-westwards from Surbiton, first reached by suburban electrics to Claygate and Hampton Court in 1916. The Direct line to Portsmouth via Guildford and Petersfield was an obvious choice, not least because its sinuous and steeply-graded nature made it ideal for electric traction from an operating point of view. More importantly, it had developed into an important holiday route (particularly for the Isle of Wight, but also for Hayling Island and Southsea), and included several well-heeled provincial towns such as Guildford, Haslemere and Petersfield along its route, from which increased business traffic could be expected. This was easily the longest electrification so far attempted by the Southern Railway, and its completion was to be the culmination of Sir Herbert's outstanding railway career.

Following the usual preliminary surveys and discussions, the decision to electrify to Portsmouth was made public on 27th June 1935. It was proposed to convert the ex-LSWR main line from Hampton Court Junction (west of Surbiton) to Portsmouth Harbour, from Woking to Pirbright Junction and onwards to Farnham, and the outer-suburban Weybridge – Staines line. This gave a total route mileage of 89. As with earlier schemes, in addition to the electrification work itself a judicious amount of resignalling and track rearrangement was to be carried out to facilitate the passage of a greatly-increased train service, and a number of stations would be improved or rebuilt. Originally the work was to be financed in the same way as the Eastbourne scheme, that is from the SRs own resources, and detailed planning was commenced on that basis.

In July 1935 a far-reaching financial arrangement was announced between the Treasury and the four main line railway companies. Similar in its intention to the abolition of Railway Passenger Duty in 1929, under the terms of the Railways (Agreement) Act, money was to be made available at a lower interest rate than on the open market, provided it was spent on large-scale infrastructure improvement schemes designed to boost the British manufacturing industry in order to relieve the slump and unemployment which continued to be a feature of Britain between the wars. In fact, as mentioned elsewhere, the south east enjoyed a period of relative prosperity at this time, and there is no doubt that these loans were of most benefit to the travelling public of this region. Schemes financed in a similar way had included the electrification of the LNER Liverpool Street – Shenfield line (not completed until 1949) and extensions to the London Transport Central and Northern Lines into the suburbs over tracks owned by the GWR and LNER. The 1935 Act led to the setting up of the Railway Finance Corporation Ltd at the beginning of 1936 to administer the loan, of which Southern's share was just under £6 million. A list of possible schemes to be carried out was drawn up and, with the agreement of the Minister of Transport and the Treasury, it was decided to use most of this sum to initiate a rolling programme of electrification. The loan was to provide the necessary new capital to finance all such remaining schemes completed up to the start of World War Two.

Unsurprisingly, the Portsmouth Direct line, electrification of which had been estimated to cost about £3 million, was placed at the head of the list. The final route mileage to be done was 95, giving a total of 242 track-miles, although this did include the somewhat rural six-mile route between Farnham and Alton, not part of the original plans. It was realised that this section needed to be included firstly because Farnham did not have the capacity to reverse the complete intended peak-hour service, and secondly because onward connections were needed to/from the Bordon branch at Bentley, and the Meon Valley (to Fareham) and Winchester lines at Alton. The entire scheme became known as the Portsmouth No.1 electrification, to distinguish it from the conversion of the Mid-Sussex line and western coastal route, or Portsmouth No.2 scheme, which immediately followed it. Physical work on the electrification commenced in October 1935, and proceeded at a rapid pace.

The electrical installations followed previous practice exactly, and work was carried out by the same electrification teams and using largely the same suppliers. New Central Electricity Board feeder stations at Byfleet and Wymering

(Portsmouth) obtained power from the National Grid, and also from the Southern's own generating station at Durnsford Road (Wimbledon) in the case of Byfleet. To provide the necessary increase in the electricity supply, a new 12,500KW turbo-alternator replaced one of the existing 5,000KW machines at Durnsford Road. The feeder station at Wymering was actually located some distance up the non-electrified Fareham line towards Cosham. From these feeder stations, high tension current at 33KV 50Hz ac was distributed to substations via the usual lineside cables, generally carried in wooden ducting on short concrete posts, except where local conditions required it to be buried underground in concrete conduit at level crossings etc. Twenty-six new substations and fifteen TP huts were provided, remotely supervised from two new control rooms, strategically located at Woking and Havant. Those substations at Walton-on-Thames, Weybridge, Byfleet, Woking, Worplesdon, Guildford, Farncombe, Milford, Grayswood, Shottermill and Wheatsheaf on the main line, plus Brookwood, Pirbright, Ash Vale, Farnham, Bentley and Alton on the Alton branch and Chertsey and Egham on the Staines line, were controlled by Woking electrical control room, situated adjacent to the substation on the Down side at Woking Junction. The remainder, at Liss, Petersfield, Ditcham, Finchdean, Havant, Farlington and Fratton, were controlled from Havant control room, located on the Up side where the Direct line to Petersfield diverged from the coastal route to Brighton. The new Guildford rectifier substation replaced the original 1925 installation, the redundant rotary converter equipment from there being relocated at Durnsford Road (Wimbledon) substation to boost the supply in the inner-suburban area.

The substations were again of brick faced with concrete, with the rectifier, cooling system, low-tension line switches and remote control equipment located internally and the transformer and high-tension switchgear outside. Fratton substation was provided with two 2,500KW rectifiers rather than the usual one, while various others had additional switchgear where they included a junction of the 33KV feeder cable. Both control rooms were flat-roofed rectangular concrete-faced buildings with no architectural pretensions. That at Woking was much the larger, containing forty panels, each controlling a feeder station, substation or TP hut, and was also designed from the outset to control the Reading extension (completed in January 1939) requiring an additional 26 panels. Havant control room initially had fourteen panels, but space was included to control the equipment on the projected Portsmouth via Horsham scheme (completed in July 1938).

The civil engineering works for the Portsmouth No.1 electrification were extensive, involving the complete rebuilding of Woking and Havant stations and major alterations at Portsmouth Harbour. Much of this work would have been necessary to cater for increasing traffic anyway, even if electrification had not taken place. The new layout at Woking comprised two side platforms and one centre island, all 800ft long, to serve the four through lines. There were also Up and Down bays at the country end and a parcels bay on the Down side at the London end. Platform buildings were in brick, but both Up and Down side booking halls, together with a wide covered footbridge, were concrete or concrete-faced in the Southern's characteristic *Moderne* style. 500ft glass and steel canopies were provided on all platforms. Extensive alterations were made to the track layout here to facilitate the working of the flat junction on to the Portsmouth line, controlled from a new 'glasshouse' signal box located at the country end of the central island platform. Replacing three manual cabins, this new box had a power-operated frame with 131 electrically interlocked levers. (Evidently the LSWR's plans to provide a flyover at this junction were by now discarded as unnecessary and uneconomic.) The work at Woking was completed in time for the commencement of Portsmouth line electric services, as was Surbiton in the suburban area, first call out of Waterloo for the Portsmouth/ Alton stoppers, which was reconstructed in very similar style at the same time.

At the southern end of the line, the main civil engineering tasks were the reconstruction of the junction station at Havant, where the Portsmouth Direct line and coastal routes joined, and enlargement of Portsmouth Harbour terminus. In the case of Havant, the new track layout comprised two through lines, off which there were loops serving 800ft Up and Down side platforms. A bay for the Hayling Island branch trains was located at the London end of the Down platform. A covered and glazed steel footbridge connected the platforms, which had the usual steel-framed canopies. The platforms and fencing were constructed entirely from reinforced concrete, as was an additional pedestrian footbridge passing over the station. There were entrances on both Up and Down sides but the main booking office, another concrete-faced structure in *Moderne* style, was located on the Portsmouth-bound platform and was not completed until the autumn of 1937. A level crossing at the western end was replaced by a bridge carrying a new arterial road, but that at the eastern end remained. Located between the platform ends and the junction, this unusual crossing also incorporated the Hayling island branch track curving at a sharp angle away from the main lines. A new signal box of traditional design, with a ninety-lever mechanical frame, was located here.

Portsmouth Harbour station itself was mainly perched on steel piers over the waters of the Solent, and was approached from the Town station (later Portsmouth and Southsea) on an embankment which curved sharply at the platform ends. At the seaward end, progressive improvements over the previous ten years had made transfer between train and Isle of Wight ferry as efficient as possible for passengers within the limited space available, but otherwise these factors made extensive reconstruction and enlargement difficult. However, by widening the approach viaduct, involving construction of a new retaining wall on the north side and extending and strengthening a number of the steel girders and screw piles on which the station stood, it proved possible to extend four of the five platforms to the required 800ft. The station throat layout was entirely rearranged, and the platform-end curves eased. An electrified siding was provided on the south side adjacent to No.5 platform road, and the junction for the

Admiralty siding down to the dockyard relocated to the landward end of platform No.1. At platform level, the existing canopies were extended by 200-250ft to cover 620-650ft of the platform lengths, and a new covered steel footbridge was erected to enable passengers to access all platforms without having to walk around the concourse. In the same area, the island platform at Portsmouth and Southsea (High Level) was extended to 800ft, while the throat layout was altered and a former siding between here and Fratton was made into a Down relief line.

Elsewhere, alterations were similar to those of previous main-line electrifications, with minor track rearrangements and platform extensions carried out to facilitate the greatly increased train service. As well as Woking, Havant and the two Portsmouth stations already mentioned, twelve-coach trains of the new express electric stock were also planned to call at Haslemere, and so here the single Down platform and Up island were lengthened to 800ft also. The track layout was modified by the addition of a Down-to-Up facing crossover at the London end of the station and an Up-to-Down trailing crossover at the country end, enabling the inside face of the island to be used as a Down loop to allow fast trains to pass stopping services, a facility particularly useful in the peaks and on summer weekends. On the Alton branch, significant track layout changes took place at Aldershot and Alton. Platform and station building alterations were also carried out at Esher, Walton-on-Thames, Byfleet, Godalming, Rowlands Castle and Fratton. As at Woking and Havant, extensive use was made of prefabricated reinforced concrete components manufactured at Exmouth Junction works for platform extensions and fencing. New ten-wire fences were erected on many stretches of line, and foot crossings incorporating cattle grids were widely provided at the southern end.

Extensive alterations were made to the signalling on the Portsmouth Direct line in readiness for electrification, although projected service density could not justify wholesale conversion to colour lights as on the Brighton line. In the suburban area, the track rearrangements and resignalling between Surbiton and Waterloo, a necessary prerequisite of the Portsmouth scheme, were detailed in Volume 1. Three and four-aspect colour light signals were installed at Woking (controlled from the new power box mentioned above) and on to Guildford. Three-aspect colour lights were also provided at Haslemere, between Havant and Farlington Junction, and between Portsmouth and Southsea and Portsmouth Harbour. To facilitate the operation of a regular-headway service, automatic colour light intermediate signals were installed between Witley and Haslemere (Up only), Liphook and Liss, and Buriton siding and Rowlands Castle, while semaphore intermediate signals replaced Copnor box, between Green Lanes Crossing and Fratton. All new and existing signals were track-circuited. The main sections of new signalling came into use on the following dates in 1937:-

20th June: Portsmouth and Southsea–Portsmouth Harbour

27th June: Woking–Guildford, Havant–Farlington Junction

18th July: Haslemere station area (after the commencement of full electric services on 4th July.)

No fewer than 312 new or rebuilt vehicles were provided for the Portsmouth No.1 electrification, although 28 of these comprised six three-coach suburban units (1579-1584) and five two-coach trailer sets rebuilt from steam stock to cover increased services in the London suburban area, and also possibly summer services on the Alton line (see below). These were covered in detail in Volume 1. For the new combined Waterloo – Windsor/Weybridge via Staines service, eight additional non-corridor 2 NOL units (1883-1890) were provided, again converted from former LSWR steam-hauled vehicles dating from the turn of the century. (Twenty units of this class, 1863-1882, had already been provided for the Windsor line in 1936, but these were funded out of the Motspur Park – Chessington branch budget, again to keep the accountants happy.) For Waterloo – Portsmouth/Alton stopping services, 38 2 BIL units (originally 1911-20/54-71, but renumbered 2011-2048 before entering service) were built. These had side corridors and lavatories in both coaches, and were slightly redesigned compared to the original ten for the Eastbourne electrification. The fast services were worked by a completely new type of four-coach unit, with a gangway provided through the cab ends to enable a passage throughout the train when two or more units were coupled. This was necessary to allow all passengers access to dining facilities, as these were only provided in nineteen of the 48 units built. The standard units were classified 4 COR (numbered 3101-3129) and those with restaurant cars 4 RES (3054-3072).

Maintenance provision for this new stock involved construction of an entirely new depot, including shed, at Fratton, and new carriage sheds at Farnham and Wimbledon. All sheds were of the standard SR design, with brick base, steel girder framework clad in corrugated asbestos sheeting and two rows of glazed panels in the roof. Facilities included hot and cold running water, a vacuum cleaning plant for coach interiors, and a complete drainage system in the floor. The shed at Fratton was only 540ft (eight coaches) long with four roads, whereas Wimbledon and Farnham were 820ft (twelve coaches) with six and five roads respectively. Apart from the shed, Fratton was also provided with an automatic carriage washer and extensive outside berthing sidings. The new shed at Wimbledon, named Wimbledon Park Sidings in working timetables, was on the Up side west of the Durnsford Road overbridge, and further carriage sidings plus a washing plant capable of cleaning two trains simultaneously were also provided. Additionally, the existing workshops nearby (dating from 1915 and adjacent to the generating station) were extended and updated. Further electrified berthing sidings with cleaning stages were laid at Chertsey, Woking, Guildford and at both Portsmouth stations.

The necessary works for the Portsmouth No.1 electrification were carried out notably quickly, the electrification installation in particular taking just twenty months from start to finish. This feat included the construction and equipping of the 26 substations, and the laying of 242 miles of conductor rail. At the height of the works, three complete substations were equipped each month. The equipment for one substation was carried to its location on a special train of eighteen wagons, including a 36-ton breakdown crane and brake van. Following erection of brickwork and concrete switchgear frame, this train usually unloaded the substation equipment on site between 11pm on Sunday night and 4.30am on Monday, the installation then taking the remainder of the week. During the period between December 1935 and November 1936, 188 cable trains were run, employed in laying 309 miles of three-core 33KV cable and 218 miles of pilot cable for the substation remote control system.

The first trial run of an electric train between Hampton Court Junction (the start of the new section) and Woking took place on 1st November 1936 using new 2 BIL unit 1911, while on the Chertsey line certain service trains between Weybridge and Virginia Water, working to the existing steam timetable, were formed of electric stock from 30th November 1936 for staff training. The full electric service between Waterloo and Weybridge via Staines commenced, without ceremony, on 3rd January 1937, while from the same date electric trains started working to existing steam timings on certain services between Waterloo and Guildford/Farnham. Portsmouth and Southsea was first reached by electric stock on 8th March 1937, and the first electric train ran into the Harbour station on the following 11th April. On Sunday 20th May no fewer than twenty twelve-coach electric specials worked between Waterloo and Portsmouth Harbour in connection with the Royal Naval Review, with no interference to the normal steam service even though reconstruction work at Portsmouth Harbour had not been completed. From 29th May certain weekend trains between Waterloo and Portsmouth were worked electrically.

The official opening ceremony, the last attended by Sir Herbert Walker in his capacity as General Manager, Southern Railway, before retirement, took place on Thursday 1st July 1937. The inauguration special, carrying the usual complement of Southern Railway Board members and officers, contractors' officials and journalists, ran from Waterloo to Portsmouth and Southsea in 91 minutes, there to be met by the Lord Mayor of Portsmouth. Following a reception, the Mayor and Corporation laid on a magnificent luncheon in the Guildhall, recorded by the late Charles Klapper as being 'almost in the style of a Victorian railway opening'[6]. The return special, given all the usual fast train stops (plus Surbiton to set down a Director), was booked in 99 minutes. This proved to be a particularly fine run, the motorman being egged on by Raworth, concerned that the 4 COR/RES stock, with less installed horsepower than the earlier Brighton and Eastbourne six-car units, should prove powerful enough for the hilly Direct line. In the event, 78mph, 3mph faster than the official maximum speed, was attained descending Witley bank, while the ride through the inner suburbs on this occasion could only be described as 'exciting'. Full public electric services to the new timetable commenced on Sunday 4th July.

The new timetables introduced with electrification showed an increase in annual train mileage of no less than 88% (4,188,168 electric miles per annum replaced 2,235,464 steam

---

6   Klapper, C.F.: *Sir Herbert Walker's Southern Railway*, p218

A Royal Fleet Review took place at Spithead on Thursday 20th May 1937 to commemorate the Coronation of King George VI, and in connection with this the Southern ran twenty electric specials between Waterloo and Portsmouth Harbour, six weeks before the official commencement of electric services and without interference to the existing steam timetable. On what was then a rare foray away from the Brighton main line, 6 CIT 3042 leads one of these specials, passing the new Byfleet rectifier substation. As this was the best electric stock the SR had, it was presumably conveying 'the great and the good'. *Alex Dasi-Sutton Collection*

miles pa). In the Down direction the basic off-peak service comprised one fast and two stopping trains per hour. The fast services departed from Waterloo at xx.50, calling at Guildford, Haslemere and Portsmouth and Southsea, arriving at Portsmouth Harbour 95 minutes later. From the 8.50am departure onwards, they included restaurant facilities. These fast trains were formed of 4 COR and 4 RES units to make eight or twelve-coach sets depending on the time of day and expected traffic; the normal eight-coach formation was COR+RES, and when twelve-coach trains operated the RES was generally at the centre. Stopping services left Waterloo at xx.27 and xx.57, calling at Surbiton and then all stations to Portsmouth and Southsea, with a portion calling at stations to Alton being detached at Woking. These trains were generally formed of 2 BIL stock (NOLs did occasionally appear to the discomfort of weak-bladdered passengers), and it was quite usual at less busy periods for the Portsmouth and Alton portions to consist of only one two-coach unit each. The service was arranged so that in the Down direction, the xx.27 stopper was overtaken by the xx.50 fast at Guildford to provide connections. Up services were arranged similarly, with the fasts departing from Portsmouth Harbour at xx.20 from 9.20am onwards, and the stoppers from Portsmouth and Southsea at xx.30 and xx.00. In the morning rush-hour the Up expresses consisted of five semi-fasts, calling additionally at Havant, Petersfield and Woking, while in the evening (and Saturday lunchtimes) there were three additional Down semi-fasts making the same stops. There were also additional trains on the Alton line, some of which started or terminated at Farnham. A number of these were diagrammed for corridor stock, with the kitchens of the 4 RES units closed; for example, the 5.47pm from Waterloo was formed COR+RES+COR, with only the front unit continuing from Farnham to Alton. As elsewhere, for the regular traveller on the newly electrified lines, whether Haslemere businessman or Liphook housewife on a shopping trip to Guildford, this new timetable created a revolution in travel possibilities.

At weekends in the summer the advantages of electric traction became particularly apparent. To cater for the heavy holiday traffic to Hayling Island and the Isle of Wight on summer Saturdays, there were four fast workings in each direction between Waterloo and Portsmouth Harbour. In the Down direction, one ran non-stop from Waterloo to Portsmouth and Southsea, one called only at Havant (with a connection to Hayling Island), a third stopped at Guildford and Portsmouth and Southsea, and the fourth made the normal

weekday fast train calls. The Up service was similar, except that the non-stop service did not even call at Portsmouth and Southsea. The twice-hourly all-stations services catering for local traffic had to be fitted in between all these, the loops at Haslemere and Havant proving necessary to achieve this. In both directions, one of these trains was passed at Guildford by two expresses, of which one did not call there. The Sunday service was generally less intensive, but had a minimum of two fast trains each direction per hour, plus special excursions organised by the SR and the National Sunday League.

During the summer timetable periods of 1937, 1938 and 1939, the off-peak and weekend Alton service was actually worked as a self-contained shuttle from Woking. This avoided time-consuming attachment and detachment movements at Woking at a time when heavy holiday traffic to the west meant that up to twenty trains per hour were booked through the station on one line. The Up shuttles actually ran on empty via Byfleet Junction to Chertsey for reversal purposes, again to reduce platform occupation at Woking. In the Working Timetable these services were given the letter headcode O, implying that suburban units were used, and it has been suggested that units 1579-1584, financed as part of the Portsmouth No.1 scheme as mentioned above, were partly intended to provide the necessary stock for this. No known eyewitness accounts exist of suburban stock actually appearing on the Alton line at this time, and it is likely that 2 NOL units, of which there was a surplus on the Western section, were used instead.

On the face of it, the provision of nineteen 4 RES units was far too many for a service which utilised only five of them off-peak and involved kitchen cars running 'cold' on the Alton line in the rush hours. However, the intensive summer Saturday service detailed above required at least fourteen trains. Including a RES in every one of them meant that, no matter if the stock for a working diagram was in the wrong place, a restaurant car would still be available for the advertised journey.

A minor casualty of the Portsmouth No.1 electrification was the direct route between Wanborough and Farnham, by-passing Aldershot. The sparse steam service on this little-used line was withdrawn on the same date as electric services commenced, 4th July 1937, and its halts at Ash Green and Tongham closed. Passengers travelling between Guildford and stations on the Alton branch were now required to change at Aldershot. From Ash Junction the line remained open for freight trains, mainly those serving Aldershot Gas Works.

Portrait of Herbert Jones, LSWR and SR Chief Electrical Engineer since 1912, who retired in 1937.

Portrait of Alfred Raworth, promoted to Chief Electrical Engineer in 1937 and prime mover of the SR main line electrification schemes of the 1930s. Known among his fellow staff as an entertaining raconteur, he explained his crooked jaw as being the result of a cricket accident while still a schoolboy.

PERSONNEL CHANGES

This is a convenient stage to record the retirement of a number of important officers of the Southern Railway Company responsible for that company's electrification policy. These retirements all took place shortly before or after completion of the Portsmouth No.1 scheme in July 1937.

General Manager Sir Herbert Walker, who had served with the London and South Western and then Southern Railway companies, retired on 14th October 1937 at the age of 69. It was Sir Herbert's far-sighted vision and commercial acumen which had been most responsible for the successful development of the Southern Electric as it had become, and on his retirement plans for further electrification extensions were already well advanced. He was subsequently elected to the Board, and continued to serve the Southern Railway Company until it ceased to exist on nationalisation at the end of 1947. He died on 29th September 1949. In May 1952, a memorial plaque was erected in his honour next to the Victory Arch at Waterloo by his protegé John Elliot, then Chairman of the Railway Executive. It remains there today.

Other retirements of key personnel which took place at this time were as follows. Traffic Manager Edwin Cox, who had been responsible for the regular interval timetables which went hand-in-hand with electrification, retired in

October 1936 after no fewer than 53 years of railway service. Richard Maunsell, Chief Mechanical Engineer of the Southern Railway since 1923 and of the SECR before that, was, like Walker, 69 by this time and in ill health, and he retired on 31st October 1937. Chief Electrical Engineer Herbert Jones, at the forefront of electric railway technology since the opening of the City and South London tube in 1890 and Electrical Engineer successively of the LSWR and Southern, retired in 1938. Jones' successor was Alfred Raworth, who immediately amalgamated the previously separate electrical maintenance and new works departments.

Walker's successor as General Manager of the Southern Railway was Gilbert S. Szlumper CBE. Born in 1884, Szlumper entered the Engineer's Department of the LSWR in 1901, rising through the ranks to become in 1913 Resident Engineer responsible for the trackwork of the LSWR suburban electrification, and for the construction of the associated Hampton Court flyover. In 1914 he was appointed Assistant to the General Manager, and in 1920 Docks and Marine Manager. He continued in this capacity under the Southern Railway until he became Assistant General Manager in 1925. Szlumper had been Walker's 'right-hand man' since 1914, and continued to oversee the completion of the remaining electrification schemes planned by his mentor until the outbreak of war in 1939.

Eustace J. Missenden succeeded to the position of Traffic Manager, having been promoted from third-in-command in the same department under his predecessors Cox and Bushrod. Prior to this, Missenden had been Docks and Marine Manager and London East Divisional Operating Superintendent.

Maunsell's replacement as Chief Mechanical Engineer was the individualistic Oliver Vaughan Snell Bulleid, about whose steam locomotive designs arguably more has been written than on any other railway subject. Born at Invercargill, New Zealand, in September 1882, Bulleid commenced his railway career in January 1901 as a premium apprentice at the Doncaster Works of the Great Northern Railway, under CME H.A. Ivatt, whose youngest daughter he later married. An enquiring mind and a penchant for trying out new ideas soon had him noticed, and he quickly rose to the position of assistant to Wintour, the Works Manager at Doncaster. After a time working abroad in France, Belgium and Italy between 1908 and early 1912, Bulleid returned to the Great Northern as Personal Assistant to Nigel Gresley, who had just succeeded Ivatt as CME. A distinguished record of war service was followed by a return to Doncaster and then on to King's Cross in 1923 when, following the Grouping, Gresley became CME of the London and North Eastern Railway and took Bulleid with him. As Gresley's assistant, Bulleid was involved in the design and development of many of the most celebrated LNER steam locomotive designs such as the A1, A3 and A4 Pacifics and the P2 2-8-2s. He was even more heavily concerned with carriage stock design, significantly introducing an all-electric kitchen car on the GNR as early as 1921 and being largely responsible for the luxurious *Coronation* and *Silver Jubilee* streamlined sets with their Allom-designed *art-deco* style interiors.

Actively head-hunted by Walker just before his own retirement, Bulleid was taken on as someone likely to inject some modernity into Southern steam locomotive design, a subject somewhat neglected due to the ongoing electrification programme, and also, with his wide carriage and wagon experience, well-able to supervise the design of mechanical parts and bodywork for electric units. With the competent Lionel Lynes remaining as assistant to the new CME, little changed to start with, Bulleid's first essays in electric stock design, the 1938 'Bognor buffets' for the Mid-Sussex line and the 1939 2 HALs for the Medway scheme, both being largely modifications of existing Maunsell designs. However, the austere and uncomfortable interiors of the HAL units were a world away from the LNER streamliners! As far as electric stock was concerned, Bulleid also collaborated with Raworth in the design of a successful main-line electric locomotive able to cross gaps in the live rail without stalling, and designed the experimental double-decker units of 1949. However, his most enduring contribution to the lot of the travelling public was the all-steel 'six-a-side' suburban coach with welded body construction. This type of vehicle, in 4 SUB and EPB units, formed the major part of the SR electric suburban fleet for more than twenty years, the last of which was not withdrawn until 1995.

THE MID-SUSSEX ROUTE (PORTSMOUTH NO.2)

The electrification of the Mid-Sussex line and associated connections was the second scheme to be financed under the 1935 arrangement with the Treasury. Known as the Portsmouth No.2 scheme because it involved the conversion of a second main line from London to Portsmouth, it comprised the route from Dorking to Horsham and onwards through Arundel to the coastal junction at Ford, the connecting line from Three Bridges to Horsham, and the coastal route from West Worthing to Havant including the Littlehampton and Bognor Regis branches. (As with Farnham – Alton, the Three Bridges – Horsham section was not included in the original 1935 proposals submitted to the government, and permission for its inclusion had to be obtained from the Minister of Transport.) The newly-converted lines made end-on connections with existing electrified routes at Dorking (1925 suburban extension), Three Bridges and West Worthing (1932/33 Brighton scheme) and Havant (1937 Portsmouth No.1 scheme). At a projected cost of £2.75 million, route miles to be converted were 75 and track miles, 165. Much of the route to be electrified traversed arable farmland in Surrey and West Sussex, and concern was raised in Parliament by farmers regarding livestock straying on to the live rail; special attention therefore had to be paid to providing adequate fencing and cattle-grids at crossings, of which there were nearly 200. Following authorisation by the SR Board at their meeting in July 1936, work commenced in mid-1937 as soon as the teams responsible were available following the completion of the Direct line electrification, and was mainly under the direction of the same SR officers. Thus Raworth remained responsible for electrical design and installation and Ellson for civil engineering aspects. However, the rolling stock was now the responsibility of Bulleid, but with Lynes remaining as assistant in charge of coach design, the existing designs of Maunsell were continued with the exception of the buffet cars for the express services.

Incidentally, two other coastal branches, those from Chichester to Selsey and from Havant to Hayling Island, were also looked at briefly at this time with a view to electrification but, unsurprisingly, both were dismissed in short order as unsuitable. The independent West Sussex Railway (formerly the Hundred of Manhood and Selsey Tramway) was offered to the SR but rejected as being moribund and far too lightly laid, while the Hayling branch suffered from a weak bridge across Langstone Creek which would have required extensive rebuilding to be suitable for electric stock. There was also a limit to the number of coastal branches which could sensibly receive a through service from London, and the best to be expected would be an electric (rather than steam) shuttle, little recompense for the expense of electrification.

The power supply arrangements and electrical installations again followed previous practice entirely, and were designed to link in with the Brighton/Worthing and Portsmouth Direct line supplies. Power at 33KV ac was supplied from the Central Electricity Board at four points, three of which already existed: these were Wymering CEB (via Havant substation), Fishersgate CEB (via West Worthing substation) and Three Bridges CEB substation. The new supply was via a CEB substation at Leatherhead. The use of four feeder points meant that alternative high-tension supplies were available to all substations under virtually any emergency condition. Twenty-one new rectifier substations and 19 TP huts were installed, all remotely supervised from the existing control room at Havant which had been designed from the outset to accommodate them. The new substations were located at Leatherhead, Dorking, Blackbrook, Ockley and Kingsfold on the line via Dorking; at Ifield and Roffey Road on the line via Three Bridges; at Horsham, Marlands, Billingshurst, Codmore Hill, Thorndell, South Stoke, and Arundel Junction on the Mid-Sussex proper; at Bognor, and at Angmering, Ford, Barnham, Drayton, Fishbourne and Nutbourne on the coastal line from West Worthing to Havant. As before, several were named after their locality rather than the nearest station. All were of standard design but their external finish varied depending on location, the majority being faced in bare concrete, a few in concrete painted light green to harmonise with their rural surroundings, and a small number left plain brick. Due to the marshy nature of land around the river Arun, South Stoke substation (between Amberley and Arundel) had to be supported on 50ft reinforced concrete piles sunk into the ground to keep it above flood-level. Barnham, Ford and Horsham substations were equipped with additional 33KV feeder cables, while at Dorking provision was made for extension to feed the Guildford – Redhill line (which crossed here) should it be electrified in the future. (At the time of writing, this has still to happen.) Lineside cabling and conductor rails were also exactly as previously, but much of the former had to be carried in ground-level concrete troughing due to the large number of level crossings.

THE NEW BUFFET CARS

FOR THE ELECTRIC TRAINS BETWEEN

LONDON AND BOGNOR REGIS

ELECTRIC TRAINS ARE ALSO NOW IN SERVICE

BETWEEN LONDON & LITTLEHAMPTON
AND WEST WORTHING & HAVANT

SOUTHERN ELECTRIC

From LONDON to	SERVICES No. of trains Weekdays	Average time of Journey h. m.	FARES Cheap "Holiday Return" Tickets s. d.	From BRIGHTON to	SERVICES No. of trains Weekdays	Average time of Journey h. m.	FARES Cheap "Holiday Return" Tickets s. d.
LITTLEHAMPTON ...	42	1 40	**11/–**	BOGNOR REGIS ...	51	54	**5/–**
BOGNOR REGIS ...	19	1 45	**11/10**	FORD	31	36	**5/–**
CHICHESTER	17	1 43	**11/7**	CHICHESTER ...	38	49	**5/3**
HAVANT	14	1 41	**11/7**	LITTLEHAMPTON ...	38	43	**5/–**
HORSHAM	68	1 10	**6/6**	PORTSMOUTH ...	35	1 18	**8/3**

SOUTHERN ELECTRIC

Ad. 4667 50 20 38

Printed by
McCorquodale & Co. Ltd., London

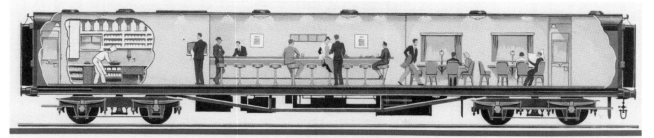

NEW AND GREATLY IMPROVED ROLLING STOCK

Modern electric stock, specially built for the service, is being used. This comprises 292 new vehicles, which have all been built in the Southern Railway's own workshops at Eastleigh and Lancing.

The new stock has vestibule connection at both ends. End-to-end communication throughout the train is thus provided.

BUFFET CARS

The Buffet cars for this service are of an entirely new type. There is a Buffet counter where drinks, both hot and cold, sandwiches and light refreshments will be served. By the counter are pedestal seats and at the side of the coach, leaning rests.

There are also tables of a new design so arranged to give a maximum of room and comfort. Service to each individual passenger will be particularly easy. Grills, light refreshment, fruit, teas, etc., will be served.

The cars are all air-conditioned.

ORDINARY COACHES

The compartments have been decorated in a distinctive form. In the First Class compartments, four decorative schemes have been used, including Indian silver greywood, African mahogany and American black walnut. African mahogany and Nigerian walnut have been used in the Third Class compartments.

M.M. Airstream ventilators have been fitted in the new stock. These ventilators provide a continuous supply of fresh air from outside, without causing draughts.

SEATING CAPACITY

The new rolling stock comprises 39 four-coach motor units, of which 13 are provided with a Buffet Car.

The total seating capacity of the new stock is 15,274 seats.

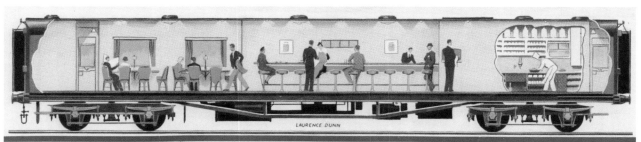

LAURENCE DUNN

SIX PLAQUES IN BRASS
designed by
R. KRUGER GRAY

A NEW FORM
OF DECORATION
IN THE BUFFET CARS

Chicken and Asparagus,
Bread Sauce (corn)
In the border, eggs & toast

Beef and Yorkshire Pudding
In border, horse radish and oxtail soup

Vegetables (cabbage, carrots, potatoes)
In border, radishes

Pork and Apple Sauce
In border, sausages and beans

Fish (hake, cod, sole)
In border, shrimps, cockles, mussels

Lamb Cutlets and
Mint Sauce
In border, sheep's hearts

The new rectifier substations at Leatherhead and Dorking replaced rotary converter equipment provided for the 1925 Western section suburban electrification to Guildford and Dorking. With the Southern's usual mind for economy, the two original 1,250KW converters from Dorking were reused at Hampton Court Junction and Epsom respectively, an increase in capacity being required at both these points to cope with additional electric suburban services. The converter from Leatherhead was utilised in a substation at Tolworth on the new Chessington branch then under construction.

Incidental civil engineering works for the Portsmouth No.2 electrification were numerous. Only one station, Horsham, was entirely reconstructed, but alterations such as platform lengthening and track rearrangement were necessary at virtually all others. At stations where twelve-coach expresses were to call, that is Sutton, Dorking, Horsham, Pulborough, Arundel, Littlehampton, Barnham, Bognor Regis and Chichester, platforms were extended to 820ft. Elsewhere 260ft, enough for four coaches, was deemed sufficient. Starting from the northern end of the extension, the Down bay at Dorking North was extended to form a Down loop and the layout altered to be similar to Haslemere, while extension of the platforms southwards required the rebuilding of an underbridge. At Three Bridges platforms 3, 4, and 5, used by Horsham line trains, were extended northwards. Intermediate stations between Three Bridges/Dorking and

Horsham were little altered other than the raising of platforms and minor track rearrangements. A reversing siding was provided at Holmwood, where one suburban service per hour was to terminate, and at Crawley the goods yard was extended. Reconstruction at Horsham involved the provision of 820ft Up and Down island platforms, each serving a through road and a loop, and entirely new buildings, similar in style to those at Woking and Havant. The main street frontage was on the London side, but a small passimeter booking hall was also provided on the Down side. Access from both to the platforms was via a covered steel footbridge.

On the section between West Worthing and Arundel Junction, a new station had been constructed at Durrington-on-Sea, where a new road crossed the line between West Worthing and Goring-by-Sea. Of characteristic SR concrete construction, work had commenced late in 1936 under the direction of site engineer Henry Greenly, better known as designer of the miniature steam locomotives of the Romney, Hythe & Dymchurch Railway in Kent. The new station came into operation on 4th July 1937 and, although served by steam trains for the first year of its existence, had conductor rails laid through it from its opening date.

At the southern end of the Mid-Sussex proper, the Up bay at Arundel was abolished and the goods yard rearranged, the local electric shuttle to Littlehampton starting and terminating in the Down bay. Platform lengthening took place at

Between Epsom and Dorking North, Mid-Sussex expresses routed via Sutton utilised electrification infrastructure installed for the 1925 Western section suburban scheme. New 4 COR 3144, complete with side destination boards, leads a 4 BUF passing Mickleham Crossing (between Leatherhead and Boxhill) with a Victoria – Portsmouth Harbour/Bognor Regis service in the summer of 1938. The tunnel in the background carries the line under the North Downs. *O.J. Morris*

the country end, and it was necessary to provide lengthy retaining walls in the cutting here to accommodate them. The terminus at Littlehampton was provided with an additional eight-car platform, the existing island was lengthened to 820ft, and the old station buildings demolished and replaced by a 'temporary' wooden structure (which actually lasted until 1990). The opening bridge over the river Arun at Ford, dating from 1862 and strengthened in 1898, was replaced by new steel fixed spans over the weekend of 23rd-25th April 1938, the normal railway service being replaced by buses. At Barnham, junction for the Bognor Regis branch, the track layout was rearranged to facilitate the dividing and combining of trains, while platform extension at the Brighton end involved bridging them over a culvert. At Chichester a new Down bay was provided at the Portsmouth end. It had been intended to replace the station buildings here also, but in the event this was not completed until early in 1961. The closely-spaced halts between Chichester and Havant were elevated to the status of stations, as they were to be staffed (generally by one man carrying out ticket issuing and collection as well as other station duties) when the new electric services commenced. The platforms were lengthened to 260ft using lightweight concrete sections or timber, and small booking huts, of wood or corrugated iron, provided.

Regarding signalling, the levels and distribution of traffic on the Mid-Sussex lines differed from those on the Brighton and Portsmouth Direct routes, and in most cases it was only necessary to modernise and rearrange the existing signalling for the new electric services. In all cases the signalling was track-circuited throughout, with a total of 150 new circuits being provided, and 57 existing circuits being changed over from dc to ac. At only three places, Dorking, Horsham and Havant, were colour light signals installed on an extensive scale, but in 23 other locations intermediate two-aspect colour lights, showing green and yellow indications only, were provided to split long block sections and encourage regular headways. This was particularly necessary on the steeply-graded section between Dorking and Warnham where, even

with electric traction, slower running could occur to lengthen headways unless additional block sections were created. Fourteen level crossings were provided with block-repeating indicators and bells and four, previously-hand worked, were fitted with mechanical opening and closing gear. New signal boxes, to the Southern's distinctive 'glasshouse' design in brick, were built at Dorking North, Horsham, Arundel and Bognor Regis.

At both Dorking and Horsham, colour-light signals were provided throughout the station area, with position-light junction indicators for diverging routes. At Dorking most of the pointwork was rod-operated mechanically from the signal box, only outlying points having motors, but at Horsham the majority of the points were power-operated. In both cases mechanical locking frames were used in the signal boxes, and shunt signals were operated by wire. The new 66-lever frame at Bognor Regis controlled the rearranged semaphore signalling and pointwork there entirely mechanically.

Rolling stock provision for the Portsmouth No.2 electrification was similar to that provided for the Direct line, and all 292 vehicles were built new at Eastleigh and Lancing. For stopping services, 68 more 2 BILs (numbered 2049-2116) were constructed, identical to the earlier units and from the start common-user with them. For fast services, 27 further 4 COR units (3130-3156) and thirteen buffet units, classified 4 BUF (3073-3085) were supplied. The BUFs were similar to the CORs but, instead of the RES arrangement of two cars with catering facilities, they included a buffet car of advanced interior design, one of the first indications that Bulleid was now in charge of rolling stock policy. The Mid-Sussex and Portsmouth Direct CORs were interworked from the start, but the BUFs worked exclusively on Central section trains. As with the pantry cars in the 6 PAN units, catering in the new buffet cars was in the hands of the Pullman Car Company, and the bill-of-fare was similar to that provided in the Brighton line Pullmans.

Maintenance and berthing facilities for all this new stock were spread over the entire length of the route, starting at

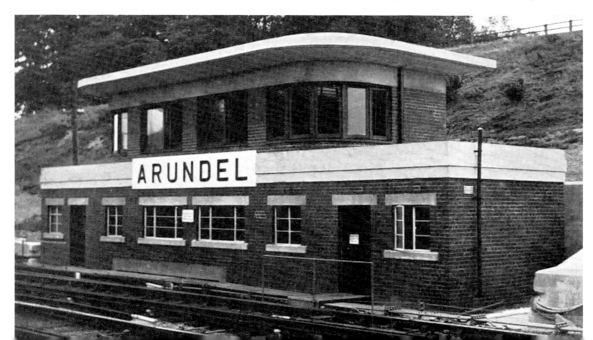

Arundel new signal box, one of four built for the Mid-Sussex electrification scheme in the SR's characteristic 'glasshouse' style, when new in 1938.

the London end where additional carriage sidings were laid at New Cross Gate and a new running shed provided at Streatham Hill. This had accommodation for four twelve-coach and four eight-coach trains, and an automatic carriage washer was also installed. A further new three-road carriage shed was located at Littlehampton. Both these sheds were of entirely standard SR design used elsewhere, and had the same facilities. New electrified berthing sidings were laid in at Horsham, Littlehampton and Bognor Regis, while existing sidings were provided with conductor rails at Ford and Barnham. Where used for carriage cleaning, such as Bognor Regis, they were provided with narrow platforms and flood-lighting. A middle siding was placed between the Up and Down lines opposite the existing shed to the west of West Worthing station for reversing the local trains to/from Brighton.

Work had progressed sufficiently for the first trial trains to run over the newly-electrified lines in May 1938, and in the following month electric stock was used on a number of specials between London Bridge and Bognor Regis. The new rolling stock was phased into service on the Portsmouth Direct and Brighton lines as it was delivered, most of the 4 BUF units running as three-car units prior to the delivery of their buffet cars, these being the last vehicles to be supplied. The official opening took place on 30th June 1938, with the usual civic receptions which had become a feature of SR electrification inaugurations. Regular electric services on the sections newly converted commenced on 2nd July 1938.

Organisation of the new timetable for the varied services resulting from the Mid-Sussex electrification proved difficult, particularly as it was necessary to dovetail them into existing electric timetables on the Brighton and Portsmouth lines. As was normal with the SR's coastal electrifications, the service was improved mainly by acceleration and an increase in the number of through trains, only local services benefiting from a dramatic increase in frequency. In a normal weekday slack hour, there were basically four groups of services. As may be deduced from what follows, they represented a pinnacle of the timetablers' art, and between them were almost endless connectional possibilities. The normal weekday off-peak service is quoted, there being alterations early in the morning and during late evening.

(A) *Brighton Main Line*: The xx.25 Victoria – West Worthing services via Hove were extended to Littlehampton, calling at Durrington, Goring and Angmering. These trains continued to be formed 6 PUL+6 PAN, with the pantry car unit often detached at Hove or Worthing Central and only the PUL running forward to Littlehampton. The corresponding Up service left Littlehampton at xx.09.

(B) *Mid-Sussex via Horsham*: The main express service ran from Victoria at xx.18, most running to Horsham via Sutton and Dorking, but a few via East Croydon and Three Bridges, in either case calling at the stops mentioned. Beyond Horsham calls were made at Pulborough, Arundel and Barnham, where the train divided. The front portion ran to Portsmouth Harbour calling at Chichester, Havant, Fratton and Portsmouth and Southsea, and the rear portion terminated at Bognor Regis. These trains were formed of 4 COR

and 4 BUF stock, the buffet car unit generally running to Bognor. Up services departed from Portsmouth Harbour at xx.23 and from Bognor at xx.55. A twice-hourly stopping service ran from Three Bridges to Littlehampton, calling at all stations and halts, at xx.17 and xx.47, the latter continuing to Bognor. Corresponding Up services started from Bognor at xx.10 and Littlehampton at xx.59. Additionally, an hourly shuttle operated between Arundel and Bognor Regis via Littlehampton, starting from the Down bay at Arundel and giving cross-platform interchange in the Down direction with the fasts with which they connected. All these services were worked by 2 BIL units, although 2 NOLs also regularly appeared.

(C) *Brighton – Portsmouth*: A new semi-fast service left Brighton at xx.47, calling only at Hove, Shoreham, Worthing Central, Barnham, Chichester, Havant, Fratton and Portsmouth and Southsea. The corresponding return workings left Portsmouth at xx.53. Stopping trains on the same route left Brighton at xx.17 and Portsmouth at xx.10, calling at all stations and halts except Durrington and Bedhampton. At the eastern end of the route, the existing xx.50 Brighton – West Worthing stopping trains were extended to Littlehampton and Bognor Regis, while at the western end an hourly shuttle ran between Chichester and Portsmouth and Southsea. All these services were worked by 2 BIL and 2 NOL stock.

(D) *Suburban Service Extension to Horsham*: One train each hour from Waterloo to Dorking North via Wimbledon and one train from London Bridge to Dorking North via Mitcham Junction were extended to Horsham, calling at all stations. Additionally, one other Waterloo train was extended as far as Holmwood.

Rush-hour services involved a number of trains on the Littlehampton and Mid-Sussex lines running in and out of London Bridge. Substitution of steam by electric trains on lines via Horsham also enabled improvements to other services using the northern section of the Brighton main line in the peaks, both main line and outer suburban. Some services divided: for example the 7.05pm Victoria – Brighton detached a portion for Horsham at Horley, while the 5.45pm from London Bridge ran fast to Haywards Heath where it split into Littlehampton and Ore portions. On summer Saturdays additional expresses between Victoria and Bognor Regis, running via East Croydon, Horsham and Littlehampton, were provided. In the Down direction these left Victoria hourly from 8.48am until 3.48pm, and in the Up direction departures from Bognor were from 10.22am until 5.22pm. Another odd service was the late-evening 'theatre special' which ran only on the second Wednesday of each month, departing from Victoria at 11.55pm and running via Horsham to Littlehampton, Bognor and Chichester.

READING AND GUILDFORD VIA ASCOT

The next electrification to be completed using Government loans resulting from the 1935 arrangement with the Treasury was that of the Reading line. Approved at the SR board meeting of October 1937, this was the smallest scheme financed by this agreement, covering just 43 route miles at

An electric test train (possibly the very first) stands in Platform 4 at Guildford in November 1936. It is led by 2 BIL unit 1917, which would be renumbered 2017 prior to entering passenger service. *Box Collection (NRM/SSPL)*

Ascot station, as rebuilt in traditional style for the 1939 Reading line electrification, on 19th May 1969. Little has changed in thirty years, the platforms retaining their original green 'bullseye' nameboards. 2 BIL 2040 and 2 HAL 2616 arrive with the 13.58 from Waterloo, ready to divide into Reading (front) and Guildford via Aldershot (rear) portions. *Southern Images / John H. Bird*

an estimated cost of just under £1 million. Apart from the extension of the 1937 Chertsey line scheme from Virginia Water to Reading, conductor rails were also laid on the lines from Ascot to Ash Vale, Guildford to Aldershot, and from Pirbright Junction along the Southampton main line to the little-used Sturt Lane spur around to Frimley Junction, giving a total track mileage of 88. The section between Ash Vale Junction and Frimley Junction was unusual for an electrified route in being single track.

The work involved was unremarkable and followed previous practice almost entirely. The only innovation on the electrical side was in the 33KV power distribution cables, three single-core un-armoured lead-covered cables being used instead of the three-core armoured cabling previously utilised. These supplied ten railway substations from a new CEB substation at Reading and from the existing installation at Byfleet Junction. The substations were all of standard design and were located at Reading, Winnersh, Wokingham, Bracknell, Ascot and Knowle Hill on the Virginia Water – Reading section, and at Bagshot, Camberley, Sturt Lane and Wanborough on the Ascot – Ash Vale and Aldershot – Guildford sections. There were problems in erecting Ascot substation due to the unstable nature of the surrounding ground, and it proved necessary to sink concrete pile foundations. The substations were all supervised from Woking Control Room, provision for this and further extensions having been made in 1937.

The main incidental works involved the rearrangement of the track layout and station rebuilding at Ascot, where a new spur was built from the country end of the Reading line platforms to the Aldershot line, effectively moving the junction of the two routes from the London end to the country end. This rearrangement facilitated the dividing and combining of London trains into Reading and Guildford portions. Although the lines through them were electrified, the former Aldershot line platforms became little-used other than for berthing race-specials; and because of this these lines soon became known as the 'race spur'. (Their last recorded use was by an excursion from Portsmouth on 20th June 1973, and they were abandoned soon afterwards except for a short section used as a siding.) All lines through the station were completely resignalled with upper-quadrant semaphores, controlled from a new brick-built 'glasshouse' cabin situated at the west end in the fork between the Reading and Guildford routes. Possibly to suit their quasi-rural location and in deference to the affluent horse-owning fraternity, station buildings and canopies were rebuilt in a traditional style, with surprisingly little use of concrete. Elsewhere, works were of a minor nature and mainly involved lengthening platforms to the standard suburban 520ft with concrete sections, and replacing boarded crossings which still existed at minor stations (such as Wanborough) with concrete footbridges. A new goods yard was provided at Virginia Water and it was necessary to rebuild a bridge near Reading to allow collector-shoe clearance.

A further and final batch of 36 units of the successful 2 BIL class (2117-2152) was provided to work the Reading line services, but from the start no operating distinction was made between them and earlier units for the Portsmouth and Alton lines. They were maintained at existing depots at Durnsford Road and Farnham. The rolling stock requirement was based on the operation of six-coach trains in the peaks. (It is worth mentioning that a number of the less comfortable 2 HAL units also worked on this line from 1940, enabling trains to be lengthened to eight coaches to cope with the heavy wartime movement of military personnel.)

Following trial running from the end of October 1938 and the usual formal inauguration involving civic dignitaries of the main towns concerned on 30th December, full public electric services commenced on the newly-electrified sections on 1st January 1939. The new timetable was based on half-hourly departures from/to Waterloo, running fast to Staines and then all stations to Ascot where the train split into Reading and Guildford portions. Single two-car units were often used between Ascot and Guildford/Reading, requiring only a four-coach train from Waterloo. The usual additional trains operated in the peaks, giving a twenty-minute interval service. A peculiar rush-hour working was the 5.37pm (1.37pm on Saturdays) Waterloo – Woking service, which ran via Richmond, Ascot, Camberley and around the Sturt Lane spur to Brookwood and Woking.

Unusually, not long after electric services on the Reading line commenced it appears that a problem arose with the power supply system, as it proved necessary to reduce peak-hour services out of Waterloo from six to four coaches from 24th February. This resulted in severe overcrowding until rectified sometime the following April.

MAIDSTONE AND GILLINGHAM

The electrification to Maidstone and Gillingham, often referred to as the Medway scheme, was the last to be carried out under the 1935 financial arrangements with the Treasury, and the last by the Southern Railway Company. Completion was actually moved forward a year after it was decided to defer electrification of the Hastings line via Battle (see below). Approved by the Board on 14th October 1937 at an estimated cost of just under £1.5 million, the scheme covered 53 route miles and 117 track miles. Included in the scheme were the routes from Gravesend Central to Maidstone West, Swanley Junction to Gillingham, Otford Junction to Maidstone East and the connection from Strood to Rochester Bridge Junction. The only significant incursion of the conductor rail outside the suburban area over former SECR lines in Kent prior to nationalisation, it differed from previous main-line schemes in that only intermediate and stopping services were handed over to electric traction – fast services between London and Chatham or Maidstone East continued to be worked by steam trains en route to or from East Kent and Thanet.

Power for the lines was taken at 33KV three-phase ac from the Central Electricity Board substation at Northfleet, already supplying the substations for the 1935 Sevenoaks electrification by means of a power cable along the Gravesend West branch and thence along the main line to Swanley. Two new substations, at Tweed Hill and Fawkham, were added to this latter section. Completely new 33KV feeder cable routes ran along the lineside from Northfleet to Gillingham, and

New Hythe, on the Strood – Maidstone West line, being reconstructed from a halt into a station using standard components in the spring of 1939, ready for the commencement of electric services that July. In a scene repeated many times throughout the newly-electrified network, passenger services continued to operate through this chaos.

also formed a loop from Fawkham to Strood (there connecting with the Northfleet – Gillingham feeder), Maidstone and back to Greenhill substation (near Otford on the 1935 electrification) via Borough Green. This radial feeder arrangement enabled most of the fifteen substations to be fed from either end in the event of a fault. Apart from the two already mentioned, these were located at Denton, Higham, Strood, Gillingham, Halling, New Hythe, Maidstone, Ditton, Addington, Borough Green, Noah's Ark, Meopham and Lower Bush. As at South Stoke and Ascot, due to the unstable ground conditions it was necessary to construct Denton, Higham and Strood substations on concrete pile foundations. Maidstone substation supplied current to both routes. As with previous schemes, midway between most pairs of substations was a track parallelling hut, designed to reduce voltage drop between substations and to facilitate the speedy isolation of a substation in the event of a fault. All substations on the Maidstone and Gillingham lines were controlled from the existing control room at Swanley, provided for the 1935 Sevenoaks scheme. This was greatly enlarged for its increased role by adding forty new control panels to the existing fourteen, and now resembled Woking in size. It was necessary to replace the main SR electricity feeder station at Swanley, at which high-tension current was taken from the grid, due to a reconstruction of the passenger station for the new electric services described below. A new one was therefore built on the site of the demolished up Otford line platform of the old Junction station, adjacent to the control room, the change-over being carried out without interruption to normal services.

The fifteen new substations had a combined output of 37,500KW. Of these, Tweed Hill and Fawkham, being located on an already-extant cable route, were built to the existing pattern used on the Reading line and previously. However the remaining thirteen, all of the same size, were to a new and much-improved design. Externally, they were smaller and plain rectangular in plan, the standard installation having dimensions of only 40ft by 8ft. This was made possible by

utilising a recooler of revised design, small enough to be located behind the rectifier in the main building, rather than in an annexe as previously. A return was made to an unfaced brick external finish as used for the Brighton installations, the concrete facing used elsewhere having proved difficult to keep clean. The main transformer and switchgear continued to be located outside on a reinforced concrete frame, the former located next to the wall adjacent to the rectifier. The main technical advance was that high tension circuit breakers of a new smaller, simpler and safer design were utilised for the first time. Known as 'oil minimum contraction' circuit breakers, they used air and a non-flammable insulating material rather than oil to maintain the dielectric once the circuit had been broken, a small quantity of oil only being retained to quench the arc and ensure adequate dielectric strength the moment the circuit was broken. Apart from smaller size, an associated advantage was the decreased risk of fire due to the reduction in the amount of oil required.

The main track, signalling and civil engineering work required took place at the two main nodal points of the routes being electrified, Swanley and Strood. At Swanley, the existing Junction station was located east of the bifurcation of the Chatham and Otford lines, with separate platforms for each, and so was wholly unsuitable for the planned electric timetable in which Maidstone East and Gillingham portions of London trains would be divided or combined here. It was therefore necessary to provide an entirely new station west of the junction, and to make space for it the cutting here had to be widened considerably. The new station, named simply Swanley, had Up and Down island platforms 820ft long, enough for twelve-coach trains. The revised track layout included Up and Down loops accessible to and from either route and was designed to minimise conflicting movements so, for example, a train in the Down loop for the Chatham line could pull away at the same time as a Sevenoaks or Maidstone train on the Down main. A new 'glasshouse' signalbox was located at the eastern end of the Up platform between the Up main and Up loop tracks and had an eighty-lever mechanical locking frame. It replaced existing cabins at Swanley yard and Swanley Junction. Colour light signals were installed in the station area and the signalling layout was designed to give the fullest information possible to the driver or motorman. To quote *The Railway Gazette* supplement: 'For example, if a train is standing at the Down main platform a following train for the Chatham line, routed via the Down loop, is advised of a clear road through the station area by the appropriate one of three splitting distant signals; this practice of providing splitting distants for all diverging routes is in effect equal to using a long-range route indicator.' The new station, together with its attendant signal arrangements, was opened to traffic on 16th April 1939, ten weeks prior to the start of full electric services.

The track layout was designed with a short distance between the eastern platform ends and the actual junction to allow space for a bridge carrying the projected Swanley by-pass trunk road. For this reason, only temporary access facilities were initially provided, the existing path to the electrical control room on the Up side being widened and extended to form an approach road to the new station. (In the event the A20 Swanley by-pass road was not built at the time, and when eventually completed in 1966 was located west of the platform ends.) Passing a temporary wooden entrance hall, this gave access to a glazed and roofed steel overbridge, incorporating booking office, ticket barriers and bookstall, with stairs and electric luggage lifts down to the platforms. A further public footbridge, across the platforms but without access to them, was connected to existing surrounding roads and from it a path ran along the south side of the station cutting to the Up-side end of the main footbridge. Platform buildings included 395ft glazed steel canopies to the standard SR design and brick staff facilities and waiting rooms, the latter including a buffet on the Down side.

At Strood, the station platforms were lengthened to 600ft, being extended northwards around the curve towards Strood tunnel using prefabricated concrete sections. The platform canopies were extended to 260ft, a new concrete footbridge between the platforms erected, and (a grim reminder of the times) the existing subway closed and converted into an air-raid shelter for railway staff. It was planned to construct a new station building on the Up side, but this was not done and the existing rambling wooden SER building had to suffice until 1973 (when it was replaced by a CLASP structure). The track layout in the station area was substantially altered, particularly at the southern end, to give access to the Up main platform to trains from the Maidstone West branch (previously they could only run through the loop). The new arrangements also enabled trains on this route to reach berthing sidings located on the Up side of the Maidstone West branch south of the station without fouling the loop from Rochester, and allowed trains from the Chatham direction to reverse onto the Maidstone line without having to run beyond the station platforms. Two new signal boxes, both of 'glass-house' pattern with mechanical frames, were erected at Strood Tunnel (forty levers) on the Up side near the tunnel portal, and at Strood Junction (seventy levers) inside the triangle of lines to the south of the station. As with the

substation here, it was necessary to build Strood Junction box on piled foundations due to the unstable subsoil conditions. Strood station area was resignalled with upper-quadrant semaphores, with these and the associated pointwork being electrically powered only where necessary due to their distance from the signal box. Banner repeater signals were installed at several locations here due to the sharp S-bend of the route between the tunnel mouth and Rochester Bridge Junction, where the existing signal cabin was closed.

All three stations at Maidstone were altered for the electric services. On the branch from Strood, Maidstone Barracks was given new concrete platforms and wooden buildings of standard pattern. Five eight-car length berthing sidings (one Up and four Down) were also provided here. As with other berthing sidings laid for this electrification, these were given lighting and cleaning stages, the latter being concrete planks mounted on posts of the type used elsewhere to carry the high-tension lineside supply cables. Track alterations took place at Maidstone West, where a centre road between the platform lines was provided, long enough to berth an eight-coach train, and the turntable abolished. The Down platform was raised to standard height. At Maidstone East, terminus of London trains via Swanley, a new bay platform facing London was built on the Down side, and both bays electrified. Here too, a centre track between the platform lines was available to berth a train, this time restricted to four coaches. The bays and a new Up berthing siding could also only accommodate four coaches, these restrictions being due to a girder bridge carrying the line over the Medway immediately north of the station and a tunnel immediately south.

Elsewhere, alterations for the new electric services were not extensive. Starting from the London end, platform 1 at Holborn Viaduct was electrified and extended to eight-car length (520ft), a difficult matter in such a congested space and imposing severe restrictions on operation of the station when eight-coach trains were in use. At Cannon Street two additional platform tracks (6 and 7) were equipped with conductor rails, and there were minor signalling alterations at Charing Cross, Waterloo (Eastern) and London Bridge. In order to cope with the 9ft wide 2 HAL stock which was to work the services, it was necessary to increase clearances by setting back various retaining walls and parapets on the routes from Borough Market Junction to Gravesend Central via Bexleyheath, on the North Kent line via Deptford and Woolwich, and on the Blackheath – Charlton spur connecting the two. (The works mentioned also paved the way for working wide-bodied suburban stock over these lines from 1945.) The platforms at Gravesend Central were lengthened at the west end and many additional refuges provided in Fort Pitt, Chatham and Gillingham tunnels. Between Otford and Maidstone East new prefabricated reinforced concrete footbridges replaced foot crossings at Kemsing, Wrotham and Barming. A metal footbridge was provided at Fawkham. On the Strood – Maidstone West route new goods loops and refuge sidings were provided at Snodland and Cuxton to deal with increasing cement traffic, while the wooden halt at New Hythe was converted into a station in anticipation of housing and industrial development. This work involved lengthening the wooden platforms to 540ft and erecting brick platform buildings with 100ft canopies and a steel-plate footbridge, all of similar design to those used elsewhere on the Southern Electric system. A new brick signalbox and manually-operated level crossing gates were also provided here. The rebuilding work was necessarily carried out without interference to traffic, but a contemporary photograph shows that conditions were fairly chaotic for passengers.

A completely new station on a green field site was erected between Swanley and Eynsford on the route to Maidstone and Sevenoaks, just south of Swanley tunnel. Named Lullingstone and completed in April 1939, it was built to serve a projected 5,500-acre housing development, part of the cost being contributed by the developers, Kemp Town Brewery. An airport was also planned, which would have been railway-connected by a short branch. Intended to be served by the hourly Victoria – Maidstone East service, its name appeared in the summer 1939 timetable, but no trains were shown as calling and a footnote indicated that the date of opening would be announced. Development in the area was held up by the outbreak of war, and post-1945 green belt legislation ensured that the surrounding land remained untouched by builders. Lullingstone continued to be shown in timetables, still with no trains calling, until June 1954. The station itself, of standard SR side-platform design and not dissimilar to Bishopstone but without the ornate entrance building, was dismantled early the following year and its canopy framework later reused at Canterbury East in connection with the 1959 Kent Coast (phase 1) electrification scheme. Parts of the platforms remain in 2010, still surrounded by fields.

As with earlier electrifications, signalling alterations, other than those mentioned, were also minimal, as it was felt that the new timetable did not justify wholesale conversion to colour lights. However, any signalling alterations had to be planned with eventual electrification of the Kent Coast routes in mind. In order to achieve consistent performance and even headways with steam and electric services on the heavily-graded route between Swanley and Rochester via the Sole Street bank, intermediate two-aspect colour light signals, automatically controlled by track circuit, were installed. All the newly electrified lines were track circuited as part of the conversion scheme, 210 new track circuits being provided. Where they had already been installed, it was necessary to convert them from dc to ac. Provision of track-circuiting was one of the major incidental expenses of this electrification, costing about £64,000.

New rolling stock was provided in the form of 76 two-coach units classified 2 HAL, each formed of a compartment motor third brake and a side corridor driving trailer composite with a lavatory. Designed under the new Bulleid regime and built at Eastleigh and Lancing, these units were considerably less comfortable than the BIL units provided for stopping services on earlier main line electrifications. To service this rolling stock a new depot was provided on the Up side at Gillingham east of the station. It comprised an 820ft asbestos-clad four-track inspection shed of usual SR design, three electrified berthing sidings with cleaning stages, and a carriage washer, arranged so that a twelve-coach train could be washed either on entering or leaving the depot. Three other sidings were electrified in the Gillingham station area, and two at Chatham.

Works had advanced sufficiently to enable trial running over the newly-electrified sections to commence in May 1939. The official inauguration took place on 30th June, when a special formed of 2 HAL stock conveyed SR Board members and senior officers from Charing Cross to Maidstone West, Chatham and Gillingham to meet the mayors of the towns served. Full electric services between London and Maidstone/Gillingham commenced on 2nd July.

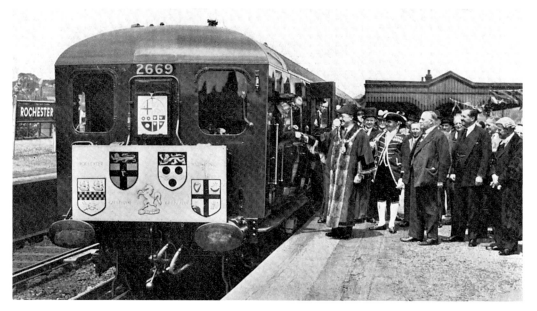

The Cathedral City of Rochester officially joined the SR electrified network on 30th June 1939. The motorman in charge of the inaugural special, led by new 2 HAL unit 2669, shakes hands with the Mayor for the official photograph, while other civic dignitaries and company oficials look on. It is unlikely that the lovingly-prepared headboards, a feature of all SR electrification specials in the 1930s, survived the war.

As usual, the new timetable was a considerable advance on the previous steam service, particularly for passengers using intermediate stations, the basic off-peak service pattern being based on hourly departures and arrivals to/from London on each route. Off-peak, a service left Charing Cross for Gillingham via Woolwich at xx.42, calling at principal stations and detaching a portion for Maidstone West at Strood. It was followed by a Cannon Street – Gillingham stopping service, departing at xx.55 and formed of suburban stock. At Strood, this connected with a 2 HAL unit which formed a shuttle to Maidstone West. The difference in journey times between fast and slow trains led to there being an even-interval, half-hourly service between Strood and Maidstone West. From Victoria, a train formed of HAL stock left at xx.18, calling only at Bromley South and then Swanley, where it divided. One portion called at all stations to Gillingham and the other at Otford then all stations to Maidstone East. As mentioned elsewhere, there were faster, steam-hauled services between London, Chatham, Gillingham and the Kent coast. On both routes, Up trains were arranged on similar lines and there were additional services at holiday times and in the peaks, some of the latter running to/from Holborn Viaduct. For services dividing or combining at Strood or Swanley, the headcode for the front portion was shown between London and the dividing or combining station.

UNFULFILLED SCHEMES

One important main line initially listed for electrification as part of the 1935 agreement with the Treasury was the Eastern section route from Sevenoaks to Hastings via Tonbridge, Tunbridge Wells and Battle, originally planned for completion in 1939 before Maidstone and Gillingham. The 1935 Sevenoaks outer-suburban scheme (see Volume 1) involved the installation of a 33KV feeder cable from the CEB feeder station at Tunbridge Wells along the lineside to Sevenoaks, and there can be little doubt that this was provided with future electrification of the Hastings line in mind. One major difficulty was that standard 9ft wide Restriction 4 main line electric units could not work south of Tonbridge due to loading gauge restrictions resulting from tunnels of sub-standard dimensions, and beyond Tunbridge Wells only special 8ft wide Restriction 0 rolling stock could be used. Although Walker was keen to see the Hastings line electrification implemented, the requirement for a special and separate fleet of units prejudiced some against it, particularly Raworth who was already concerned with the proliferation of main line EMU types and was working towards greater standardisation. The alternatives of widening or singling the tunnels to permit standard-width stock were not considered feasible at this time.

These unusual conditions resulted in the initial electrification report taking longer than normal to prepare, and it was not until 29th April 1937 that Walker submitted a scheme to the SR Board for consideration. It covered electrification of Sevenoaks – Hastings and the Crowhurst – Bexhill West branch, together with construction of a fleet of new Restriction 0 express EMUs of both two and four-coach formation. Unusually, a decision was deferred, one of the stated objections of the Board being that it would divert custom away from the already-electrified route via Eastbourne. A second attempt to 'crack the Hastings nut' was made on 14th October when a revised and slightly cheaper scheme was put forward at one of the last Board meetings Sir Herbert attended as General Manager. Savings were to be made by converting existing steam stock (the 98 8ft³⁄₄in wide flat-sided Maunsell corridor coaches built between 1929 and 1934), and by operating a slightly less ambitious timetable. A decision was once more postponed until December, after which the question of electrifying the Hastings line went into limbo. At the 1938 SR AGM the Chairman stated, 'With regard to our project for giving Hastings and Bexhill a second electric route, by the electrification of the line from Sevenoaks to Hastings via Tunbridge Wells, we have decided after most careful consideration not to proceed with this scheme at the present time.' The idea did not go away however, but during a site inspection at Swanley early in 1939, Raworth stated that he would not agree to narrow-bodied electric units being built for the Hastings line as he did not want the problems of trying to keep two fleets of EMU segregated. This approach must have done more than anything else – up to then – to defer electrification of the line.

Furthermore, it seems probable that, had not the perceived threat of war not caused further schemes to be suppressed, outer-suburban electrification beyond Sevenoaks to Tonbridge and Tunbridge Wells, for which the power supply infrastructure already existed, would have followed on from the Maidstone and Gillingham scheme in 1939. It is very possible that the sixteen additional 2 HAL units 2677-2692, ordered in November 1938 with no particular use specified, were intended for this. Electrification to Tunbridge Wells would have cunningly strengthened the case for extension to Hastings, probably using existing coaches hauled by Bulleid/ Raworth CC electric locomotives (see Chapter 6), which had been designed with Restriction 0-width bodies having that line in mind. By this time the Maunsell steam stock would be in need of replacement or refurbishment, and turning over the northern part of the line to EMU operation would have released a float of vehicles for upgrading.

By the end of 1938 the threat of war and the likely work resulting from it, together with the internal disagreements over the future of the Hastings line, effectively put paid to any other future plans regarding electrification. However, it seems that the Southern did have other minor fill-in schemes apart from Tunbridge Wells in mind, although never recorded in official Board minutes. These might have included the relatively short Grain and Westerham branches and just possibly completion of the new line from Chessington to Leatherhead. Equally likely over the next ten years were Christ's Hospital – Steyning – Shoreham and South Croydon – East Grinstead – Horsted Keynes, providing two diversionary routes between London and Brighton. The electrification of South Croydon – East Grinstead – Tunbridge Wells/Horsted Keynes was, indeed, given preliminary approval by the SR Board, but serious doubts and questions were raised, mostly of a financial nature.

As it was, outbreak of war in September 1939 put an end

to spreading of the SRs electrified network for the time being, and the teams so carefully built up through the previous expansionist decade were dispersed to other essential duties. No further electrification was to take place for another twenty years, by which time the lines concerned were part of the Southern Region of the nationalised British Railways.

SUMMARY OF THE RESULTS AND EFFECTS OF MAIN LINE ELECTRIFICATION

Although electrification of the Brighton main line was an obvious follow-on from the recently-completed suburban schemes, it was not necessarily clear at its gestation in 1929 that commercial success was inevitable. Without the financial impetus provided by a government tax break (the abolition of Railway Passenger Duty; see page 12), it is possible that Sir Herbert Walker would not have been able to advance his far-sighted plans past the SR directors. As it was, the clear commercial and economic advantages which quickly became apparent following completion of the Brighton scheme encouraged investment in further long-distance electrification although, here again, much new capital was to be borrowed from the Treasury under another government financial measure. Between 1930 and 1939, a total of just under 1,000 miles of main-line trackage were electrified at a total cost of £12.5 million, of which just under £8 million was obtained under government schemes and the remainder from various company funds (Capital, Reserve, Rolling Stock Renewals, etc). All this took place when Britain as a whole was in the throes of a recession although, as mentioned at the start of this chapter, particular economic factors meant that the south-east was largely insulated from its worst effects. Due in no small part to its significant investment in electrification, by 1939 the Southern Railway was, in many respects, the most modern of the 'big four' main line companies.

As we have seen, the Southern Railway did not go in for unnecessary wholesale reconstruction and modernisation on electrification, and this resulted in schemes which were relatively cheap in terms of capital expenditure. Such an approach was inevitable given the somewhat parsimonious attitude of the SR Board to new investment, encouraging Walker to concentrate on features which would increase passenger appreciation and numbers, leading to the required rise in revenue. Thus the important advantages for the passenger in the change-over to electric traction were more frequent, reliable services at easily-memorised regular intervals, decreased average journey times, and improved cleanliness outside and in. If these improvements were possible with existing infrastructure such as signalling, stations, etc, then these were not changed. Certainly, the re-use of existing coach bodies for 'new' electric trains, as in the 2 NOLs, fitted this philosophy perfectly!

A downside of this approach was that, although main line electric trains were seen as relatively modern, the solid and reliable image put across by the Southern Electric was uninspiring, even dull, and in the years following became yet more so. With Walker's energies directed mainly towards providing a frequent, reliable and attractive service at minimum cost to the shareholders, outward attention to design, particularly with regard to buildings and rolling stock, often appeared timid or half-hearted by comparison. In this respect it is interesting to consider the modernisation and electrification of the Paris Montparnasse – Le Mans line in France, completed in 1937 and covering a comparable distance to SR schemes of the period. Stations such as Versailles Chantiers and Chartres, rebuilt with concrete buildings in the *moderne* or *art deco* style, displayed a confidence mostly lacking from Robb-Scott's comparable efforts for the SR at Woking and Havant. Likewise, features such as streamlined Budd stainless-steel bodywork, sliding doors and articulation between vehicles of the sprightly class Z3700 units built for this scheme seem in retrospect very modern and exciting in comparison to the 'Nelsons' on the Portsmouth lines and other even more mundane stock provided by Messrs Maunsell and Bulleid.

Furthermore, the Southern's planners did not always get it right, and it is difficult in retrospect to see how certain investment decisions were accepted by the cautious SR Board. In particular, over-optimistic traffic forecasts, or merely developments which could not be foreseen in the mid-1930s (particularly World War Two and subsequent nationalisation), resulted in funds being squandered on some undeniably lost causes. In rural Sussex and Kent and on the south coast, speculative housing developments of the type commonplace in the suburban area did not always take off as anticipated and thus expensive new stations at Cooden Beach and Bishopstone could not attract the hoped-for passenger numbers. The Haywards Heath – Horsted Keynes branch too could never hope to gain sufficient custom in isolation to justify the cost of electrification, and its worth as part of a through diversionary route via Oxted was never to be realised. Similarly, hopes for Lullingstone and its airport (actually located in an area which would now be defined as London outer suburbia) were completely dashed by the War and the green-belt legislation which followed.

CHAPTER 2: WARTIME AND PRELUDE TO NATIONALISATION 1937-47

With the rise of Hitler's fascist Germany and of similar dictatorships elsewhere in Europe through the 1930s, the international political situation became increasingly tense and unstable. By 1937 it had become clear that another European conflict was likely, and this threat resulted in all major UK organisations and institutions, from central Government downwards, beginning the necessary preparations to place Britain on a war footing. As major transport undertakings, the four main line railway companies were involved in these preparations from an early stage. An immediate effect was the curtailment for the time being of other investment, including further electrification. The Munich Crisis of 1938 gave further impetus to precautionary activities which had been in hand since 1937 when the Air Raid Precautions Act became law. Work prior to September 1939 largely concentrated on putting ARP measures into place, and on developing contingency plans for the mass movement of troops and civilians, both able-bodied and wounded.

By mid-1939 an ARP scheme had been devised for every station, and air raid shelters provided. A Chief Warden and Deputy Warden were appointed from staff at each station and other staff members also underwent training to deal with firefighting, first aid, decontamination (following a gas attack) and demolition of bombed structures. A two-coach, steam-hauled ARP instruction train was placed in service in July 1939 and was put on public display at Waterloo. Strategic buildings such as signal boxes, depots and electrical control rooms were protected, as appropriate, with steel window shutters, blast walls and other devices to minimise the risk of damage from air raids. A trial 'blackout' took place in the London area on the night of 11th-12th August, although the railways were largely exempted to avoid disrupting traffic. From 28th August military guards were posted at various stations and bridges in London, and photographs of those at Blackfriars and Charing Cross were published in several newspapers. By 1st September blackout precautions at all stations were completed, although many installations were makeshift and better arrangements were made during the following months. A programme of fitting longer hoods to colour light signals, to obscure the beam from above, had started in 1938. The shorter hoods were never put back as it was found that the longer ones improved signal visibility during daylight hours. One intractable problem was preventing electric trains arcing, as the flashing between conductor rail and pick-up shoes became even more prominent when no lights were showing. Airmen claimed that it was easy to follow the passage of an electric train at night, particularly during frosty weather.

On 30th August the order was given for the civilian ambulance trains to be made ready for service, to be used to move the injured from bombed areas if local hospitals could not cope with the situation. The SR had three of these twelve-coach trains, converted at Eastleigh and Lancing from bogie luggage vans and other miscellaneous vehicles and finished in standard green livery. Comprising nine stretcher vans, a staff mess van and two staff/brake vehicles, each train had the capacity to carry about 300 injured. Military ambulance trains were also provided and there was an important ambulance train depot at Micheldever sidings. One of the civilian trains was inspected by HRH Queen Elizabeth at Victoria on 13th October.

On the day Britain declared war on Germany, Sunday 3rd September 1939, the Southern Railway was as prepared for the forthcoming conflict as any British organisation, and had already been working on a war footing for several days. In fact, so far as the railways were concerned, the war had effectively started on 1st September. Not only did the blackout come into effect and civilian evacuation commence that day, but the Minister of Transport took control of the railways (and London Transport road services) as empowered under the provisions of the 1939 Emergency Powers (Defence) Act. A Railway Executive Committee (REC) was established to act for the Minister and direct operations, but technical and operating staff continued to run the railway from day to day as previously. On 25th September the SR General Manager, Gilbert Szlumper, took overall charge of the REC as Director General of Transport and Movements, War Office, and as a result Traffic Manager Eustace Missenden assumed the GM's duties in addition to his existing ones, and also represented the SR on the REC. Staff from the SR offices at Waterloo and London Bridge were dispersed to various safer locations on the system and headquarters were established at the Deepdene Hotel, Dorking. A dispatch rider service, equipped with sixteen motorcycles, a van for the movement of bulky items, and fourteen assorted motor cars (loaned by members of staff, probably unaware of the likely duration of the war!), was established on 2nd September to link the various offices.

From 1st to 4th September children of school age and younger, as well as various other vulnerable groups, were evacuated from districts considered most likely to be subjected to air raids, including the London County Council area, Croydon, and Portsmouth/Gosport in SR electrified territory. The majority of evacuees first assembled at main line stations, including 12,700 children and others at Waterloo and 9,100 at Clapham Junction, all delivered without incident by special trams. London hospital patients were also sent via Clapham Junction, while children from the Southern Railwaymen's Home at Woking were likewise evacuated and the premises requisitioned for use as a civilian hospital. With many being taken to Wessex and the West Country, the majority of special trains conveying evacuees were steam-hauled rather than electric. However, some did go by electric train to various Sussex towns, though London buses took others directly to their final destinations, given the short distances involved. The whole operation went remarkably smoothly and without significant disruption to normal traffic. Success was at least partly due to only half the expected number of evacuees coming forward; plans had been made on the basis that there would be three million evacuees from English stations but in fact there were only about 1.2 million, of whom approximately half originated from London. There were later evacuations in 1940 after bombing had actually started, but none had a particularly high take-up rate.

Major troop movements commenced on 2nd September and, again, most involved steam trains. Special trains were run in most cases, but some army units travelled in reserved accommodation on ordinary trains and a number of unfortunates were merely advised to travel to a particular station (usually Reading) and then proceed by the first convenient train to their destination. The SR was particularly concerned with the embarkation of the British Expeditionary Force for France, which lasted for several months. Special trains were also run for personnel from Croydon Aerodrome, from Waddon to Southampton terminus and to Bristol. Four troop trains were booked to be electrically worked on 3rd September, including 4x2 NOL from Waterloo to Aldershot, 4x2 BIL from Waterloo to Brookwood, 3+2+3 suburban from Waterloo to Windsor and from Victoria to Coulsdon North. In all cases the stock concerned was diagrammed to take up normal passenger duties afterwards.

Train services were not altered for the first week of war, apart from local arrangements in connection with the movement of troops and evacuees, though cheap day return and excursion tickets were withdrawn from sale. (They became available again from 9th October.) Then, from 11th September, the timetable was drastically reduced and catering services withdrawn. Main line trains were slower and made extra stops. On weekdays, through trains from London to the coast were reduced to 41 to Brighton, seven to Eastbourne and Hastings, five to Worthing, five to Bognor Regis and twelve to Portsmouth divided between the Mid-Sussex and Direct routes. Suburban services were not much slower than before, but were cut in frequency by between 50 and 70%. After a week with remaining suburban trains crammed to bursting (the Epsom to Wimbledon line was particularly bad) and carriage sidings filled with idle stock, but no bombing raids, it was realised that such drastic measures were unjustified, particularly so far as electric services were concerned. Electric stock was of limited use for troop movements and could not be used to haul goods trains. Normal services were restored from 18th September except for some trains to Portsmouth and off-peak non-stop services between London and Brighton. This latter change resulted in corridor PUL and PAN stock being allocated to xx.28 Victoria to Brighton and corresponding Up semi-fast services, a welcome improvement over the LAV units used in peace-time.

Further service reductions were necessary from 16th October, although these were no means as severe as previously. There was a 5% reduction in rush hour services and a 20% reduction in other services. 46 trains now ran daily from London to Brighton, compared with 100 in October 1938, although the average journey time was increased by only two minutes. The exceptionally frequent pre-war service gave much more scope for cuts than services on other lines such as the Portsmouth Direct, where the reduction in the number of trains was much less. There were now forty trains daily each way between Waterloo and Portsmouth via Guildford instead of the 45 of the previous year, but extra stops increased the average journey time by twenty minutes. On the Eastbourne line there were no through London services between the morning and evening peaks and passengers had to travel via Brighton. The situation improved slightly from 20th November when extra trains to the coast were provided in the late afternoon for the benefit of people wishing to be out of London before dark and the onset of blackout. A through train from Victoria to Eastbourne at 12.45pm was introduced and suburban services augmented in the peaks. That Christmas, 200 additional trains were laid on by the SR between 20th and 24th December, all running during daylight hours only.

Cuts in steam-hauled passenger services throughout the country at this time were much more severe, as locomotives were re-assigned to military trains. In consequence, the fastest passenger train in the country in October 1939 was the 7.05am Bognor Regis to Victoria, no less. This service, worked by 4 COR and BUF units, covered the nineteen miles from Three Bridges to East Croydon in 21 minutes, giving an average speed of 54.3mph.

The blackout regulations which came into force on 1st September 1939 were designed to prevent any lights on the ground being visible from the air by enemy bomber crews during the hours of darkness. This was most difficult to implement on moving trains and the modifications necessary to rolling stock are detailed in the following section. However it is worth mentioning here that large numbers of blue bulbs in compartments were pilfered by members of the public attempting to effect their own domestic blackout arrangements at the railway's expense. No doubt they soon found that bulbs designed to work at 70V dc were useless when connected to the domestic mains supply.

There were no air raids until 1940, but warnings were quite frequent. In the event of an air raid warning trains initially stopped where they were, but later in the war it was decided, after considerable debate, that there was no point in this and thereafter trains continued at reduced speed, calling at the first available station to set down any passengers wishing to take shelter. Notices appeared in compartments instructing passengers not to leave the train when it stopped during the alert; to pull the blinds down (if not down already) to give a measure of protection against flying glass; and, if room was available, to lie down on the floor. There was little

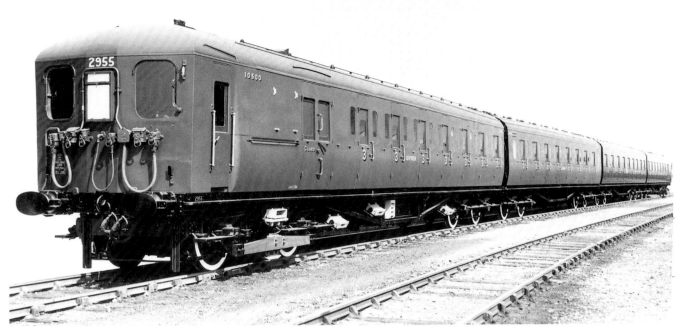

enthusiasm for, or compliance with, the last instruction. After bombing raids started in earnest, it is reported that passengers in services between London and the Sussex coast, brought to a halt by air raid warnings, often had a grandstand view of the dogfights taking place overhead; that is if the train windows had not been replaced by boarding. Air raid alerts in the early morning led to problems concerning the issue of cheap Workmen's Tickets normally issued at this time so, following complaints, the rules were altered so that such tickets would remain on sale for twenty minutes after the 'all clear', a period later extended to half an hour.

In the early part of the war rolling stock production was able to continue at Eastleigh, Lancing and Ashford works, although activity was much curtailed. As far as electric stock was concerned, four orders which had been authorised prior to September 1939 were proceeded with. These included the sixteen additional 2 HAL units 2677-2692 and two 4 LAV units 2954-2955, outshopped November 1939–January 1940 and February/May 1940 respectively. The first of Bulleid's new high-capacity four-coach suburban units, 4101, appeared towards the end of 1941, as did the first Co-Co 'booster' electric locomotive, CC1. Shortages of essential materials and the diversion of labour and resources to special war work then brought such work to a halt, although war damage repairs and overhauls to existing stock continued as far as possible. Similarly, two small signalling projects commenced prior to September 1939 on the Windsor line were completed in the first year of the war. On 21st January 1940 four-aspect colour light signalling was brought into use between North Sheen and St Margarets, worked from a new 'glasshouse'-style signal box at Richmond, while Clapham Junction to Point Pleasant Junction was similarly resignalled from 26th May,

controlled from a new power frame installed in Clapham Junction 'E' box. These schemes allowed three existing signalboxes to be abolished with consequent manpower savings, and no doubt benefited the war effort by facilitating the passage of freight trains serving Feltham marshalling yard.

1940 started calmly enough, with a further slight relaxation of wartime cuts with the introduction of revised 'Emergency Passenger Services' from 1st January. Improvements included the restoration of Pullman, buffet or restaurant facilities to a number of Central section coastal and Portsmouth line services, and the reinstatement of some additional evening peak trains from Waterloo to the Alton line. Much disruption was caused by severe weather at the end of January, but worse was soon to come. In May, the German armies invaded and overran France and the Low Countries, necessitating the forced evacuation of British and Allied forces from the beaches of Dunkirk. The majority of special trains returning evacuated troops from the coast to their bases were steam-worked, and between 27th May and 4th June the line through Redhill and round to Reigate (part of the important Tonbridge – Guildford link which connected the Kent channel ports with the Aldershot and Reading area military bases) was closed to electric services. Passengers for these points had to change onto special buses at Coulsdon North or Earlswood.

Above Bulleid 4 LAV unit 2955 was one of a pair turned out from Eastleigh in 1940 before wartime conditions caused the cessation of new rolling stock construction. Note the partial blanking-over of compartment windows to comply with blackout regulations. *SR Official*

The burnt-out remains of Portsmouth Harbour station following a direct hit during the raid of 10th-11th January 1941. In this view the remains of some of the thirteen vehicles destroyed may be seen. *SR Official*

Now able to operate freely from airfields in occupied territory, Luftwaffe 'reconnaissances in force' on south east England started immediately following the fall of France and gradually increased as the summer wore on, concentrating firstly on ports and shipping along the coast. An early raid in the Portsmouth area at midday on 12th August badly damaged the Harbour station and destroyed three electric units (BILs 2102/2131 and three coaches of COR 3137), but the damage was quickly patched up. Attention then turned to airfields and aircraft factories, and it was just such a raid which caused the first serious 'incident' involving loss of life in the suburban area. During the late afternoon of 16th August bombers, probably aiming at Weybridge, damaged Hampton Wick station and two trains near it, killing ten passengers. Coach 8378 of unit 1476 was damaged beyond

repair. These early attacks were a precursor of the main 'blitz' which took place between mid-September 1940 and May 1941, when air raids virtually nightly devastated London's infrastructure and inflicted serious damage to other British towns and cities. These raids affected the SR suburban area extensively, and also other strategic military targets on the electrified network including the Aldershot and Portsmouth areas. There were innumerable instances of bombs causing destruction, damage and disruption to the railway, and it is only intended to give accounts of a small representative selection here, together with some more general details.[7]

---

7   Specific details of some of the more serious incidents have been recorded by Moody, Faulkner and others – see Bibliography.

Clearing up at Victoria (Central), the morning after the air raid of 9th-10th October 1940. This view shows part of damaged 5 BEL unit 3052, with *Audrey* nearest the camera. *Railway and Canal Historical Society / Spence Collection*

As expected, the most serious and disruptive damage in the blitz occurred around the London termini and their immediate approaches. During the first night of air raids on Central London, Saturday/Sunday 7th-8th September 1940, a high-explosive bomb holed the viaduct at Juxon Street, Lambeth, between Vauxhall and Waterloo, blocking all lines and perforce closing Waterloo station. It was partially reopened from 19th September and all tracks were in use again by 1st October, although in the meantime repairs had been hindered by further raids. The effects of the 'Great Fire Raid' of 29th-30th December closed Waterloo once more for a time, and on the same night the offices at London Bridge were burnt out and the Central side of the station seriously damaged. Fires were started in buildings and on platforms at Charing Cross, and also in coaches berthed there, during another particularly serious attack which took place during the evening of 17th April 1941. This was the most severe raid on the capital up to that date, killing 1,179 people. That same night Blackfriars Junction signal cabin (miraculously, the only large power box destroyed during the blitz) was burnt out, and three nights later the adjacent bridge over Southwark Street was wrecked. With military help a stop-gap replacement bridge was ready in fifteen days, and a perma-

nent structure by October 1942. A temporary brick signal cabin, equipped with a small power frame, was built at ground level, but many non-essential signals were not reconnected for the time being, one effect of which was to close the Blackfriars terminal bays. The colour light signals on the main line were wired to show only 'stop' and 'caution' aspects at this time. The final raid of the blitz, on the night of 10th-11th May 1941, put the whole SR telephone system out of action and for a short period closed all of London's termini. Further serious destruction was caused at Waterloo, Cannon Street, Holborn Viaduct and Elephant & Castle, damage at the latter two stations being so bad that they could not be reopened until 1st June and 1st September respectively. At Elephant a temporary platform, serving the Up Main line only, replaced burnt-out Up Local and central island platforms.

Charing Cross, the morning after the evening air raid of 17th April 1941, when mopping-up was commencing following fires started by incendiary bombs. Suburban unit 1612 in the centre was a complete write-off, as was the body of the front coach of unit 1722 next to it, but the pair of HALs on the right appear relatively unscathed.
SR Official

Outside central London, probably the most destructive incident in the suburban area during the blitz occurred at Wimbledon on the night of 15th-16th October 1940, when a high-explosive bomb hit the vital Durnsford Road power station. This demolished a chimney and damaged the boiler house to the extent that its generating capacity was halved. The following morning no traction current was available anywhere in the area inwards from Egham, Esher and Epsom, and only a skeleton steam service was possible. However, using the 20,000KW still available from the undamaged equipment plus an additional 6,000KW via an emergency high-tension line from Deptford power station, it proved possible to restore limited supplies by the afternoon of 16th October, although electric trains were limited to 30mph with no heating, and some peak hour services were cancelled. Repairs were not completed and normal supplies restored until December 1941, the ugly replacement 100ft steel chimney being better able to withstand future hits. (This was in its turn replaced by a taller steel chimney in 1949, a brick one to match the original proving impracticable.)

On the south coast, the Portsmouth naval base was the target of several air raids. Apart from the raid of 12th August 1940, already mentioned, Portsmouth Harbour station was attacked on 5th December and then again on the night of 10th-11th January 1941. On this latter occasion the station received a direct hit and a gap was blown in the approach viaduct, while fires were started on the platforms which could not be extinguished as water pipes had been severed. Thirteen electric vehicles (of 4 RES 3060 and 4 CORs 3117, 3119 and 3132) were destroyed, including one which fell from the decking into the mud below, and several others were stranded. With platform structures burnt out and the signalbox badly damaged, the station was closed completely until 24th February, when it was possible to reopen platform 1 to special traffic only. Rebuilding of the other platforms and signalbox to enable it to reopen fully had to wait until 1946. Other raids badly damaged Portsmouth & Southsea station.

During an early air raid in the blitz, on 14th October 1940, Selhurst depot cleaning shed was hit, resulting in the mess seen here. Despite the apparent mayhem, only eight vehicles were actually written off on this occasion. *SR Official*

Once the effects of bombing raids could be predicted following experience early on in the blitz, contingency plans were formulated and put into effect to divert services in the likely event of one or more of the London termini being out of action. For example, during the many occasions that Waterloo was closed, electric services were turned round at Clapham Junction, but if the damage was further out, Earlsfield (using emergency crossovers), Wimbledon, Surbiton or even Woking could be used instead. The damage caused by the various bomb types varied considerably, but in many instances viaducts or bridges were breached, or lines blocked due to bomb craters. Railway engineering staff, sometimes with Army assistance, soon became adept at effecting temporary repairs, and few blockages remained for long, although resultant speed restrictions in many cases persisted for some years after the war until more permanent repairs could be carried out. A frequent cause of serious delay was the unexploded bomb, either delayed action or, more often than not, simply a 'dud'. Furthermore, many reports of unexploded bombs proved on investigation to be false alarms, often after traffic had been stopped for several hours. Such devices were dealt with by hard-pressed Army bomb disposal teams, although the so-called 'land mines' were supposed to be the Navy's responsibility. Later, volunteer railwaymen were trained to confirm the evidence of unexploded bombs and to carry out the preliminary stages of making them safe for trains to pass. A set of rules was quickly developed, and it was often possible to get traffic moving again if the suspected device could be screened with loaded coal wagons or sandbags.

Before the war, doubts had been expressed regarding the ability of an electric railway to work during air-raids, but these were soon shown to be utterly unfounded. Indeed, events proved that electric trains could operate if it were possible for trains to run at all. Electric motor coaches had a relatively low axle loading, so could use weakened or temporarily repaired bridges impassable to steam locomotives. Also, electric trains needed only a single crossover to reverse, a major advantage in view of the numerous ad hoc workings required. A further advantage was undoubtedly the simple and robust nature of the low-voltage dc third-rail system, and it is doubtful whether an overhead system would have coped as well. In most cases it proved possible to restore the live rail virtually as soon as damaged track had been repaired.

The effects of wartime mobilisation and the blitz resulted in marked demographic changes in the electrified area. By March 1942 over 9,000 male employees of the SR had been released to join the Armed Forces, and 8,000 women had been recruited to replace them. Most were employed on station duties, but some were trained as guards on electric trains. (As an aside, one result of this was the withdrawal of the large route/destination boards from the sides of suburban trains, ostensibly because they were considered too unwieldy for female staff to handle in high winds!) With the destruction of one third of buildings in the City of London by the end of intensive bombing raids in May 1941, many businesses moved to offices in the West End, resulting in an increased number of passengers using Victoria and Charing Cross in

the peaks rather than the City termini. However some firms and government offices had moved away from the London area entirely, thus easing the rush-hour load generally and allowing some of the oldest suburban trailer set coaches to be withdrawn, as explained in Volume 1. With air raids virtually every night, evening social and entertainment activities declined. Furthermore, as the nights lengthened during the anxious autumn of 1940, many London offices were closing early in order that workers could get home before the air-raid sirens started. This led to the evening rush hour being in full swing by 4.00pm, and the SR adapted its timetables accordingly. With much reduced traffic in the evenings, some services in the middle- and outer-suburban areas were reduced to infrequent connecting shuttles.

Holiday traffic quickly dwindled to nothing, and special workings such as those serving race meetings, which had been such an important feature of the system before the war, also disappeared entirely. Conversely, forces traffic was heavy. It is recalled that Sunday afternoon trains from Waterloo to the Reading line, serving the important military bases in the Aldershot area, were packed solid by Richmond with servicemen returning from weekend leave. It finally proved necessary to withdraw catering facilities from main line electric services from 22nd May 1942, while from the following 5th October cheap day tickets were withdrawn once more by order of the Minister of War Transport, in an attempt to damp down non-essential travel by civilians.

By this time, a more significant development in the wartime spread of egalitarianism had already occurred. Again by order of the Transport Minister, all suburban services which ran entirely within the London Transport area had become third class only from 6th October 1941. With its extensive network, this revolutionary change affected the SR more than any other railway operating in this area, whose relevant outer limits were specified as Windsor, Weybridge (via Staines), Shepperton, Hampton Court, Guildford (via Cobham), Horsham (via Dorking North), Epsom Downs, Caterham and Tattenham Corner, Coulsdon North, Sanderstead, Addiscombe, Hayes, Bromley North, Sevenoaks via Orpington and via Swanley, and Gravesend Central. With a less frequent service and the blackout, it was considered that maximum seating should be used in every train. It was also becoming increasingly difficult to ensure that first class ticket holders were able to travel in accommodation for which they had paid. (Some futile attempts at making first class compartments more easily identifiable in blackout conditions were mentioned in Volume 1.) An explanatory letter was sent from the General Manager to each first class season ticket holder, most of whom accepted the change patriotically and with few complaints. When the change was made, 'third class only' services were specially indicated at stations and, for a short time, on the trains themselves.

From July 1941 the Luftwaffe bombers were diverted to the Russian front and air-raids ceased for the time being, permitting a certain amount of mopping-up and other repair work to commence. However, 'hit and run' raids over southern England and the coast became a constant menace from January 1943, although few reached the suburbs and London

Above Seemingly well-filled with troops, 1925 SECR-bodied suburban unit 1434 departs from Waterloo bound for Windsor via Richmond on 12th December 1942. Visible wartime modifications include steel plating behind both windscreens except at the centre on the motorman's side, orange gas detector paint on the lower half of the offside windscreen, partial plating-over of the cab droplights and a white square just above the solebar in front of the cab door. *R. N. Coombes Collection*

The remains of London Road Viaduct, Brighton, after being hit by a bomb dropped by a fortunate Luftwaffe 'hit and run' raider on 24th May 1943. Rubble from the two spans demolished in the blast litters the surrounding ground. *Spence Collection, Railway and Canal Historical Society*

Damage at Lordship Lane station following a direct hit from a V1 'doodlebug' flying bomb on 1st August 1944. At this time the Crystal Palace (High Level) branch was temporarily closed as a wartime measure. *SR Official*

generally remained relatively free from attack for a further year. On 24th May 1943, for example, a lucky enemy raider attacking Brighton managed to hit London Road viaduct with a 'hopping bomb', bringing down two spans. Temporary repairs allowing limited traffic to pass once more were completed in fifteen days, and permanent restoration took just four months. While the route was blocked, additional trains ran between Haywards Heath and Lewes, connecting there with Seaford, Eastbourne and Hastings services. From 2nd April 1944 the whole of the south coast became a closed area for visitors as preparations for the invasion of France began, and a number of main line services were suspended.

That summer, London and the southern suburbs were once more in the line of fire as V1 'doodlebug' flying bombs were launched from across the channel, the first falling on SR property on 15th June at various locations in South London. During this campaign Tulse Hill signalbox was wrecked on 29th July and bridges at Charing Cross (18th June), Peckham Rye (12th July) and Merstham (early September) destroyed or seriously damaged. At Peckham Rye, a new temporary bridge of rolled steel girders on army trestles had to be erected to carry the Catford loop over the South London line east of the station, while it took six months to repair Hungerford Bridge entirely after a 100ft section had been demolished. Norwood Yard was a target on 23rd June, a particularly destructive day on which Charlton, Hither Green and West Croydon stations were also hit. Flying bombs hit the District Line terminal bays at Wimbledon on 16th June and the eastern side buildings at Victoria on 25th June, while other stations damaged included Forest Hill (24th June), Shortlands (1st July), Raynes Park (17th July), Lordship Lane (4th August) and Falconwood (31st August). The last was particularly unlucky to be hit on the final day of such attacks.

After a short lull, the V1s were followed by the V2 rockets, the first to affect the SR falling adjacent to Hampton Court Junction on 2nd November 1944. Among other damage, the colour light signalling in the area was put out of action, but repairs were completed two days later. On the morning of 5th November a V2 caused the bridge over Southwark Park Road at South Bermondsey to collapse, totally blocking the South London and Tulse Hill lines. A temporary replacement supported by army scaffolding, similar to that provided at Peckham Rye, enabled trains to pass again by the afternoon of 14th November; in the meantime, services between London Bridge and Dorking North/Effingham Junction were diverted in and out of Holborn Viaduct. Peckham Rye carriage sheds were hit on 6th January 1945, resulting in serious damage to the building and destruction of several EMU coaches. SR stations hit by V2s included Petts Wood and Eltham Well Hall (both 14th November 1944), New Cross Gate (25th November) and Chatham (9th March 1945). By this time, rocket attacks were petering out and ceased with the capture of their bases by Allied forces.

Inevitably there were a number of station and line closures in the electrified area during World War Two, but perhaps surprisingly three halts and a new spur line were opened as well. In the former category Shoreham Airport Halt closed from 15th July 1940, while the summer-only Bishopstone Beach Halt, close to Newhaven, closed from 1st January 1942. Through trains from Blackfriars to the sparsely-used Crystal Palace (High Level) branch were withdrawn from 6th January 1941, being replaced by a shuttle from Nunhead running hourly off-peak and every twenty minutes in rush hours. Further wartime economies resulted in the branch service being withdrawn entirely after traffic on 21st May 1944, a body-blow from which it never fully recovered. The

Left Longcross Halt, built in 1940 to provide railway access to the Army training camps at Chobham Common, was located between Virginia Water and Sunningdale on the Reading line. Its basic construction, mainly utilising standard SR concrete components, is clear in this view dating from 1971. The shelter on the Up platform easily surpassed anything on the Wimbledon – Sutton line for crudity, but there was a war on! *Stations UK*

three new halts were all of austere, largely prefabricated, concrete construction, and intended for personnel working in military or munitions establishments. The first was at Longcross, located between Virginia Water and Sunningdale on the Reading line and adjacent to the Chobham Common army camp. Available to military staff only from an unknown date in 1940, it was later opened to the general public from 21st September 1942. This was followed by Hilsea, situated just west of Portcreek Junction on the Portsmouth line, which came into use to serve a munitions factory on 2nd November 1941. Lastly, Halliford, located between Sunbury and Shepperton and serving an aircraft components factory, opened on 1st May 1944. Renamed Upper Halliford from 22nd May, only a Down platform was initially provided as the branch at this point was worked as a single line with electric train staff, the former Up line being used as a siding. An Up platform and footbridge were later provided in May 1946 when double-track working was restored after the war. The new line constructed was a spur from Crayford to the North Kent line avoiding Dartford, coming into service on 11th October 1942. This enabled trains from the Sidcup line to return to London without reversal.

Looking beyond the end of the war, in May 1944 Raworth produced a detailed and far-sighted Report suggesting third-rail electrification to Basingstoke and Southampton. While intermediate stopping services could be operated by electric units, through services to the West Country via Salisbury and to Bournemouth and beyond would have been electrically-hauled from Waterloo, changing to steam traction at Basingstoke and Southampton Central respectively. For these trains, it was intended to build a production fleet of Co-Co 'booster' locomotives, the prototype of which had by then proved very successful on test. An integral part of these

proposals was the complete elimination of steam from Waterloo, enabling office accommodation to be built on a raft over the platforms in the manner of the Grand Central terminus in New York. It was suggested that the rental income from the office space created ('air rights') would easily finance the entire scheme. (This proposal was, of course, many years ahead of its time: electrification was only completed to Southampton in 1967 as part of the Bournemouth scheme, while Victoria was the first SR London terminus to be topped by office accommodation, but not until 1984.)

With the end of the European war in sight, blackout regulations were eased from September 1944, when improved station lighting was permitted. Blackout restrictions were removed entirely from 25th April 1945, two weeks before the German surrender on 8th May, and from 16th June main line services to the coast were increased slightly. After years of shortages, the blackout and other restrictions, the British public was only too ready to resume peace-time travel habits, as witnessed by the huge crowds thronging the concourse at Victoria on the first day of the 1945 summer holiday, Saturday 28th July. G.T. Moody records that on that day 21 trains left for coastal destinations between 9.18am and noon, of which two were formed of suburban stock, and all were loaded to capacity[8]. The War finally ended with the Japanese surrender, announced over the radio at midnight on 14th August. Much confusion reigned the following morning when most workers set off for their offices, unaware that it and the day after had been designated public holidays. Once more the SR ran a number of extra trains to the south coast to cater for public demand.

8   Moody, G.T.: *Southern Electric 1909-1979*, Ian Allan Ltd, ISBN 0 7110 0924 4, 1979. p101

51

With Pullman composite *Rita* removed for wartime storage, 6 PUL 3002 was running as 5 COR when photographed on the four-track section between Copyhold Junction and Haywards Heath forming a Victoria – Brighton semi-fast service on 31st July 1942. Both cab windscreens have been sheeted over except for an oblong aperture on the motorman's side, and orange gas detector paint applied to the nearside windscreen where it is not swept by the wiper. *SR Official*

WARTIME EFFECTS ON ROLLING STOCK

When blackout regulations were first introduced in September 1939, electric trains at first ran in the night hours with no lights at all. The necessary alterations to compartment lighting and blinds were quickly put into effect, however, and suburban units with these modifications were in service by mid-November 1939, operating initially on Crystal Palace (High Level) branch services. The general alterations described here eventually applied to all electric stock, but there were obviously many variations as much of the work was done on an ad hoc basis.

Compartment lighting was changed to comprise one 25 watt pearl bulb and one under-run blue lamp, both in black-painted shades. To make the roll-down sunblinds effective for blackout use, quarterlights and droplights were given an opaque border about 2½in wide. Initially black paint, black paper or fabric (green outside, brown inside) were tried, but the standard finish soon adopted was green paint on the inside of the glass only. It was required that the blinds should always be secured down during blackout conditions. In main line coaches, the toilet windows were generally boarded over except for a glazed slit at the top, while the external glass Airstream wind deflectors of the Eastbourne and Portsmouth express stock were removed and the sliding window sections sometimes replaced by plain glass or hardboard. Later in the war, a shortage of glass made it necessary to replace broken windows with hardboard or plywood, painted green, and many suburban units in particular ended up with most quarterlights and droplights replaced in this way. A few main line motor coaches had their large saloon windows replaced by boarding with a small rectangular glazed area at the centre.

To protect train crews from bomb blast, cab and van windows were also altered. The motorman's lookout was equipped with upper and lower steel protecting panels behind the glass, leaving a narrow horizontal slit through which to observe the line ahead. The offside lookout was replaced by steel panelling, often with a small square, diamond or oval-shaped glazed aperture at the centre. Cab droplights were painted over or replaced by sheet steel covered with hardboard as blast protection, while those on the van doors were treated similarly but with a narrow glazed slit at the top. On most electric stock, orange-coloured gas detector paint was applied to half the offside lookout, but on express units it covered the upper portion of the motorman's windscreen not swept by the windscreen wiper. With the reduction in ambient light levels after dark, a 3in square of white paint was applied to the cab sides at solebar level to indicate the position of the cab door and step, and at the outer ends of trailer sets. Headcode panels were initially illuminated with blue lamps, but soon reverted to white. As explained above, unavoidable arcing often made the progress of electric trains all too visible to German bomber pilots, anyway.

The abolition of first class from the suburbs from 6th October 1941 left the entire fleet of three-coach motor units, plus the London area two-coach SL, WIM and NOL units, with redundant first class accommodation. Downgrading these seats to third initially consisted merely of painting out the '1' indications on the doors, removal of rugs and, where possible, securing up of folding intermediate armrests. On overhaul, many compartments were fully reupholstered to third class standards even though the abolition of first class was only intended to be temporary at this stage.

In 1944 it became necessary to protect coach windows from the effects of blast in the wake of the V1 flying bomb attacks on the south east. It was considered that suburban stock was most at risk, so self-adhesive netting in one of two mesh sizes was applied to quarterlights. Door droplights were at first covered with scrim (linen), but its use was discontinued after a short time. The first unit was dealt with in August and by the end of the war about ninety motor units (including a few NOLs) and thirty trailer sets had been done. The netting was quickly removed once the war ended.

With the end of the war in sight, blackout restrictions were relaxed, and from 23rd September 1944 improved lighting, consisting of two 25 watt pearl bulbs, was permitted. The use of blinds at night was officially still required, but in practice this could not be enforced as on many units they were broken or missing. Normal lighting, consisting of two 60 watt bulbs and open reflectors, was gradually restored to units from 21st November, and, as mentioned previously, on 25th April 1945 lighting restrictions were removed entirely. From this time a start was made on scraping off the 2½in paint border from around the windows.

PRELUDE TO NATIONALISATION 1945-47

Many of the difficulties facing the SR and other main-line railway companies in the immediate aftermath of the Second World War mirrored those suffered by the pre-Grouping companies in 1918 (see Volume 1), only on a considerably larger scale. Incalculable damage had been sustained to both infrastructure and rolling stock as a direct result of enemy activity and this, together with inevitable arrears in maintenance, meant that much was in a depressingly run-down and dilapidated condition by 1945. Once more there were serious shortages both of manpower, as many staff were still serving in the forces, and of necessary raw materials, whose supply remained under Government control. These circumstances meant that the rebuilding of the railway, while carried out with energy and enthusiasm, would be a slow process.

Other changes outside the railways' control also ensured that there could never be a return to pre-war conditions. In particular, The Town and Country Planning Act of 1947 effectively put an end to the uncontrolled suburban housing developments which had been fuelled by newly-electrified train services in the two decades prior to 1939. As already mentioned, destruction of City offices caused many businesses to relocate to the West End, increasing peak-hour usage of Victoria, Waterloo and Charing Cross at the expense of the City termini. A move to shorter working hours compressed the peaks into shorter timespans, particularly in the morning, leading to increased overcrowding at these times.

The Labour Government which swept into power following the 1945 General Election was committed to a policy of nationalising public utilities and transport undertakings, including the railways. Nationalisation involved the state take-over of previously private-enterprise companies and bringing them under the direct control of the appropriate Government Ministry. A White Paper outlining the proposed changes was published in 1946, and the Bill which followed it subsequently passed into law as the Transport Act, 1947, on 6th August that year. This legislated for the setting up of a British Transport Commission (BTC) to which all railways were transferred from midnight on 1st January 1948. A separate Railway Executive (RE) was set up with personnel directly appointed by the Minister of Transport, not the BTC, giving it a measure of independence in its relations with the BTC. The first Chairman of the RE, initially convened in October 1947 to oversee a smooth handover and put in place the necessary new management structures, was Sir Eustace Missenden, GM of the SR.

There were a number of senior management changes in the 1945-47 period. Chief Electrical Engineer Alfred Raworth, main architect of SR electrification policy through the 1920s and 1930s, retired in April 1945. The new CEE was Mr C.M. Cock, an Australian who had been involved in electrification of the Melbourne suburban network and later worked in India before coming to the SR. With Missenden's appointment to the Chair of the RE in October 1947, John Elliot became Acting GM of the SR at that time, overseeing the final months of its existence. It is convenient to mention here that Cock was also appointed to the RE, becoming Chief

Immediate post-war re-equipment of the Southern Railway included construction of a number of new steel-bodied 4 SUB units for suburban services. 4127, placed into service in 1946 and seen here outside Eastleigh Works, was one of ten experimentally given some centre-gangway saloon accommodation rather than the previously universal closed compartments. *Lens of Sutton*

Electrical Engineer, and in 1948 he was succeeded in what was now the Southern Region of British Railways by S.B. Warder, who was also placed in charge of mechanical engineering on the retirement of Bulleid the following year.

Returning to the start of 1945, with the end of the war in sight infrastructure repair and renewal could start, and a programme of track renewal was commenced. A new brick 52-lever signal box at Tulse Hill came into service on 1st July, replacing that wrecked by a flying bomb the previous year. Work commenced on the installation of new four-aspect colour light signals in the Blackfriars area, and the construction of a new Blackfriars signal cabin (replacing that lost in the blitz) in March 1946. The new signalling was brought into use on Sunday 11th August, enabling the terminal bays to be reinstated. The replacement Blackfriars box also controlled new Up starters at Elephant and Castle whose own

signalbox (another war loss) was not replaced. At Portsmouth Harbour two more platforms (making three in total) were reinstated from 1st June 1946, and colour light signalling came into use here on the same date, controlled from a new 'glasshouse' cabin. At this time Portsmouth Harbour was served only by services to/from Waterloo, others terminating at Portsmouth and Southsea, but Brighton services and Sunday trains via the Mid-Sussex ran through from the following 1st August. At the March 1947 AGM, the Chairman announced that up to that date a total of 65 stations had been renovated, while over thirty acres of glass had been replaced in the roofs of the London termini and elsewhere. An important scheme to replace the remaining manual semaphore signalling at the London end of the Brighton line with colour lights was authorised by the Board at the end of 1946, but no work on this was actually carried out until 1949.

Construction of electric rolling stock had recommenced at Eastleigh in November 1944, with completion of wide-bodied high-capacity suburban vehicles started in 1939-40 taking first priority. Work continued through the following years in spite of severe manpower and materials shortages so, by December 1947, 35 completely new four-coach SUB units and 171 additional trailers had been turned out, the latter being used to strengthen pre-war suburban units to four coaches. (See Volume 1 for complete details of the suburban stock renewal plans and eventual execution in the 1939-51 period.) Replacement of main-line stock written off in the war was also put in hand at this time. Twenty-four new corridor vehicles, including eleven COR-type motor coaches and one buffet car, were built at Eastleigh and Lancing in 1946-47 to bring the Portsmouth and Eastbourne express stock fleets back to full strength, although the three dining cars destroyed were not replaced like for like. The construction of seven more 2 HAL units to top up the depleted semi-fast fleet was also well in hand, although none entered service until 1948.

Attempts to improve the condition of existing electric rolling stock in the latter part of 1945 were hampered by a serious spate of vandalism, a phenomenon virtually unknown before 1939. Compartment windows were smashed or their replacement boarding attacked, cushions were slashed, droplight leather straps stolen or cut, lamps removed, and obscenities scrawled on, or carved into, the woodwork. This damage was attributed (by the late G.T. Moody in his notes) to 'demob-happy' troops and possibly to workmen moved in for bomb damage repairs, but no doubt disaffected youth was also responsible for much of it.

Restoration of train services and facilities could also only take place gradually, and the process was by no means completed by January 1948. On the coastal and other mainline routes, many services were reinstated from 1st October 1945, such that between 9.00am and noon the timetable on all three sections had virtually returned to pre-war frequency. Services reintroduced included hourly Waterloo – Portsmouth expresses and a number of Victoria – Brighton non-stops. Half-hourly trains once again served the Waterloo – Alton line and the Victoria to Maidstone East/Gillingham service reverted to hourly. Regarding catering facilities, as a first stage, pantry, restaurant and buffet cars were reintroduced on a limited number of electric services covering the Brighton, Portsmouth Direct and Mid-Sussex lines from Monday 7th January 1946, although not all buffet cars were as yet reformed into the 4 BUF units working on the latter route. Pullman cars officially returned to the Brighton line from the following 4th May, although some had been in use a few days earlier. Again, it was some time before all the cars had been reinstated into the 6 PUL units and trains working to the pre-war *Brighton Belle* timings were initially formed of 5 BEL units 3051 or 3053 coupled to a PUL or COR. With the return of unit 3052 from its makers Metropolitan-Cammell following repairs, it was finally possible to reinstate the complete *Brighton Belle* from 6th October 1947, one or two 5 BEL units forming the 11.00am, 3.00 and 7.00pm Victoria – Brighton and the corresponding 1.25, 5.25 and 9.25pm Brighton – Victoria non-stop services.

In the suburban area, 1st October 1945 saw most routes regain a half-hourly service between the peaks, but three trains each hour served the Kingston 'roundabout' route from Waterloo. The Crystal Palace High Level branch was reopened from 4th March 1946 with a half-hourly shuttle from Nunhead, increased to a twenty-minute frequency in peak hours. Rush-hour services between Holborn Viaduct/Blackfriars and Dartford via Nunhead, together with additional trains from Holborn Viaduct to Bickley, were restored from 12th August, following completion of replacement signalling in the Blackfriars/Elephant and Castle area. There were more additions to the suburban timetable from 7th October, when rush-hour services were restored to the Victoria – Crystal Palace – Beckenham Junction and Victoria – Tulse Hill – London Bridge routes, and Crystal Palace (High Level) branch trains began to run through to/from Blackfriars in the peaks once more. These latter trains were initially formed of six (rather than eight) coaches, but it soon became apparent that passenger losses due to the wartime closure had depressed loadings to the extent that three or four cars were more than adequate at any time of day. Overall, taking both suburban and main line services into account, 84% of the August 1939 timetable had been restored by October 1946, with virtually the full service in the peaks.

Race meetings at courses served by the SR also restarted in 1946. The Easter Saturday meeting at Hurst Park, attended by an estimated 100,000 people, was served by a ten-minute interval service between Waterloo and Hampton Court. Derby Day at Epsom on 5th June was served by no fewer than sixty trains from London between 9.00am and noon, with 34 running to Tattenham Corner from Charing Cross, Cannon Street or London Bridge, and the remainder to Epsom Downs from Victoria.

That same year the SR could once more begin to consider further modernisation of its network and, following the visit of a delegation to the USA, a plan to convert all lines east of Portsmouth to electric or diesel-electric traction was approved by the Board in November 1946. Lines to be electrified in this scheme included –

(1) Gillingham–Faversham–Ramsgate and Faversham–Dover;
(2) Sevenoaks–Tonbridge–Ashford–Dover–Deal–Ramsgate;
(3) Maidstone East–Ashford–Canterbury West–Ramsgate and Maidstone West–Paddock Wood;
(4) Tonbridge–West St Leonards/Bexhill West;
(5) Christ's Hospital–Steyning–Shoreham by Sea; and
(6) South Croydon–Oxted–East Grinstead–Horsted Keynes.

Thus all important main lines to the Kent Coast and some secondary routes in Kent would be dealt with, as well as eastern and western diversionary routes between London and Brighton. Sixty new substations would be required, most to be supervised from a new control room at Canterbury. Estimated to cost about £15 million, it was hoped to commence work in the summer of 1947 if labour and material were available, with completion of the whole scheme by 1955. While it was intended that about 70% of Eastern section trains would be worked by electric multiple units, a sizable fleet of electric locomotives, of the Bulleid Co-Co 'booster' type (see Chapter 6), would be required to work Continental boat trains and principal freight services. An important, and revolutionary, element of the plans was the complete elimination of steam locomotives by the use of diesel-electric traction, seen to be so successful in North America, on non-electrified lines and for local freight and shunting. A small fleet of 350hp shunters and two prototype 1Co-Co1 main-line locomotives, all equipped with English Electric diesel engines and traction motors, were ordered at this time.

January and February 1947 saw the whole of Britain gripped by some of the worst winter conditions in living memory, with heavy snowfalls and continuous freezing conditions causing serious difficulties for the railways and associated industries such as shipping and coal mining. On the SR's electrified lines, problems with iced-up conductor rails were partially alleviated by running special de-icing coaches which spread warm oil on the rail surface at night (see Chapter 6). A worse difficulty was disruption to coal production and distribution. By the start of February the SR had only one week's supply in hand for all purposes and, in order to conserve stocks, substantial train service cuts on the suburban lines took place successively on 5th, 11th and 15th

of that month. On the morning of 4th March a severe gale turned into a blizzard which then froze, virtually paralysing Southern electric services over a wide area that afternoon. Four days later a thaw started which soon turned into heavy rain, causing a number of severe earthslips and rock falls which blocked several routes, including the Quarry line at Merstham. It took some time to clear the debris, much of which was difficult to handle due to its sticky liquid consistency, and it was not until the end of the month that normal working could be resumed. Continuing coal shortages meant that it was some months before the full timetable could be restored.

It was unfortunate that no fewer than four serious collisions involving electric stock blighted the 1945-47 period, all involving loss of coaches which could be ill-afforded at the time, quite apart from death or serious injury caused. The first occurred at Caterham in the morning rush hour of 26th June 1945, when a train leaving the station against signals collided with another entering. The colliding motor coaches from units 1667 and 1774 were both damaged; 8188 of 1667 was cut up, but 9809 of 1774 was repaired and transferred to 1688; a 4 SUB, 4253, was formed up from the remaining intact vehicles.

The remains of 4 LAV motor third brake 10511 from unit 2926 following the South Croydon collision of 24th October 1947 when, as rear coach of the 7.33am Haywards Heath to Victoria, it was run into by suburban unit 1770 forming a following train. *SR Official*

The three other accidents all occurred in the final three months of the SR's existence, two on the same date, and all involved the death of passengers. On the morning of 24th October 1947, in dense fog, the 8.04am Tattenham Corner to London Bridge service ran into the back of the 7.33 Haywards Heath to London Bridge on the Up Main between Purley Oaks and South Croydon. In the ensuing carnage 32 persons were killed, including the motorman of the 8.04, and another 58 injured. The rear coach of the 7.33 (4 LAV 2926) and the front unit of the 8.04 (suburban unit 1770) were all written-off, and some vehicles had to be cut up on site. There was considerable damage to trackwork and debris was strewn across a wide area, but the breakdown gang nevertheless had the local lines cleared by 4.00 the same afternoon, and all lines were in use again by 10.30 the following morning. In the ensuing enquiry it was discovered that the 8.04 had been wrongly admitted into the same block as the 7.33 through irregular use of the emergency release key by the inexperienced porter/signalman at Purley Oaks. Among the Inspecting Officer's comments was that the accident would not have occurred if colour light signals had been installed. As mentioned above, a scheme to resignal this part of the Brighton main line had already been put in motion.

Two weeks later on 6th November, another day characterised by impenetrable fog, the 4.45pm Holmwood to Waterloo, composed of 4 SUB units 4406+4485, ran into the side of the packed 5.16 Waterloo to Chessington South, formed of 4222+4228, as the latter was crossing on to the Chessington branch at Motspur Park Junction. Four passengers were killed and twelve injured. It was ascertained at the ensuing enquiry the duty fogman was failing to observe fog signalling rules correctly; indeed the motorman of the 4.45 was not aware of the other train until he collided with it. Finally that same evening, in conditions of nil visibility, the steam-hauled 4.15pm Ramsgate to Victoria overran protecting signals at Herne Hill and collided with the 6.58 Holborn Viaduct – Wimbledon – West Croydon, formed of 4 SUBs 4250 and 4318, which was crossing over on to the Tulse Hill line at the time. One person was killed and sixteen injured. A trailer in the leading electric unit, 4250, bore the brunt of the collision and was fit only to be demolished on site, and the other three vehicles of this unit were also unfit for repair. The primary cause of this accident was found to be poor observation of signals by the crew of the steam train.

On the day the railways were nationalised, 1st January 1948, brand-new 'all-steel' 4 SUB 4365 displays its ownership as it departs from Holborn Viaduct with a Sevenoaks service. *Getty Images*

CHAPTER 3: DEVELOPMENTS FROM 1948

The intention of this chapter is to provide a succinct overview of the most important developments in the SR electrified area during the British Railways era from January 1948 until the end of September 1983, when the period covered by this book ends. A 'blow by blow' account of events from year to year has not been attempted; instead, major works, changes and other developments over the entire period are categorised and each category dealt with as a group. This era has been covered in greater detail by other authors to whom readers are referred, particularly Michael R. Bonavia, Geoffrey Freeman Allen and G.T. Moody (see Bibliography); inevitably, the choice of subjects discussed here will be subjective to a certain degree.

ORGANISATION, FINANCE AND POLITICS

It is logical to start with an overview of the many organisational and managerial changes which took place in the 1948-83 period, particularly as they affected the administration of lines within the SR electrified network, as this provides a framework for other developments described in greater detail in later sections. As we shall see, the main features of this period were the lack of a consistent or coherent policy regarding the role and financing of Britain's railways as successive Labour and Conservative administrations came and left government, and the gradual slide into deficit as the pre-war system gradually came to terms with post-war conditions, particularly the rise in road transport competition.

Among the manifesto pledges of the Labour Government elected in 1945 was a commitment to nationalise Britain's transport undertakings, of which the four main-line railway companies were easily the largest. The railways were by this time no strangers to direct state influence, exerted through a Railway Executive Committee during and after both World Wars. As explained in the previous chapter, the new Government's plans were published in 1946 and the Transport Bill which followed subsequently passed into law as the Transport Act of 6th August 1947. Under the terms of the Act the four companies, including the Southern Railway, ceased to exist from midnight on 1st January 1948, becoming vested in a new body known as the British Transport Commission (BTC) set up under the Act and answerable directly to the Minister of Transport. Reporting to the BTC were five larger public bodies termed 'Executives', each responsible for one of the different transport modes or other associated activities brought under the BTC umbrella. The Railway Executive (RE) was chaired by Sir Eustace Missenden (former GM of the SR), and included R.A. Riddles and C.M. Cock (the latter also from the SR) as members responsible for mechanical and electrical engineering respectively.

The newly nationalised railway traded under the name 'British Railways' and for organisational purposes was divided into Regions approximating to the areas covered by the pre-1948 concerns; hence the SR became Southern Region with a total route mileage of 2,550. Regional organisation at first saw relatively little change, the existing SR Western, Central and Eastern sections (themselves a throwback to the pre-Grouping era) persisting. Regarding investment, some schemes instigated before 1948 were allowed to continue or be put in hand, including construction of new suburban rolling stock, resignalling of the Central section main lines in the London area and renewal of power supply infrastructure on the suburban lines. However, the grandiose 1946 plans for further electrification and replacement of steam by diesel-electric traction were left 'on hold' for the time being.

The 1948 organisational and managerial structures had little time to bed down before the first significant upheavals followed the October 1951 General Election when a Conservative administration, ideologically opposed to nationalisation and particularly to the Railway Executive, was returned to Government. A new Transport Act passed in May 1953 legislated for the abolition of the RE and gave far greater autonomy to the Regions. The BTC was greatly enlarged to enable it to carry out the overall policy-making and management functions of the RE. Control of the Regions was entrusted to 'Area Boards' and the chief officer of each Region gained authority as a Chief Regional Manager. One result of this was the greater emphasis placed on 'Southern' rather than 'British Railways', in publicity, for example. The Act also led to the reorganisation of management structures, devolving day-to-day operation to three divisions each under the overall direction of a Line (Traffic) Manager, although this took time to implement. These divisions were roughly equivalent in area to the former SR sections. The South Eastern division was set up in October 1958 followed by the Central and South Western divisions in October 1962.

It was becoming clear as the 1950s progressed that BR faced an increasingly bleak financial future, with the loss of much traffic to competing road transport, aided by the 1953 Act's return of the road haulage industry to private hands. A sixteen-day ASLEF strike in 1955 forced many railway customers to switch to the roads, many never to return. Concern was also expressed regarding the operation of unremunerative passenger services and this period saw the first closure of an electrified SR line, the moribund ex-LCDR Nunhead–Crystal Palace (High Level) branch, in September 1954.

The BTC's original answer to this worsening financial situation was a Report which was to become known as the

The dilapidated state of the timber platforms at Honor Oak is very evident as 4 SUB 4365 calls with the 4.17pm Blackfriars to Crystal Palace High Level on 27th August 1954, just three weeks before permanent closure of the branch from Nunhead.
J. H. Aston

'Modernisation Plan', published in January 1955 and shortly afterward ratified by the Government with surprisingly little dissent. This effectively allowed an increase in the investment finance made available to BR over a number of years, originally estimated at £1,200 million in the period up to 1970, enabling many desirable modernisation schemes to take place in an effort to increase efficiency and reduce costs. An important aspect of the plan was the total elimination of steam traction. It has been suggested that the Modernisation Plan largely passed the SR by because it was already relatively modern in comparison with other parts of the BR network, at least in terms of electrification. Extensions of the SR third-rail were initially confined to the Kent Coast lines (Bournemouth and the Isle of Wight were added later), but a number of station rebuildings and resignalling schemes were also included. Some lines not earmarked for electrification on the SR were instead equipped with new diesel-electric units which had many features in common with the latest electric stock, while significant fleets of electric and diesel-electric locomotives were introduced to displace steam from freight, parcels and other miscellaneous traffic.

Unfortunately, the launch of the Modernisation Plan did not halt the slide towards deficit, and the BR Annual Accounts for 1956 showed a net loss for the first time. Despite some notable financial successes as parts of the plan came to fruition, including (on the SR) phase I of the Kent Coast electrification, losses mounted steadily over the following years while estimated costs for the complete plan rose by £300 million. The situation came to a head in 1960 when the mounting deficit plus a substantial staff pay award plunged

the BTC into a financial crisis. In order to try to find a way forward two Committees, one of MPs and the other an invited group of industrialists known as the Stedeford group, were set up. Their reports criticised accounting procedures and other aspects of the BTC organisation, questioned the need to operate unprofitable 'social' services (such as the many lightly-used branch lines), and suggested the importation of managers from outside industry to give BR the necessary keener commercial edge. Proposals contained in these reports, particularly that of the Stedeford group, formed the basis of the September 1962 Transport Act in which the BTC was abolished and replaced by the British Railways Board (BRB). Earlier, in May 1961, Dr Richard Beeching (previously Technical Director of ICI and a prominent member of the Stedeford group) had been appointed chairman of the BTC with a specific remit to reduce the railways' deficit.

Before 1961 had ended, Beeching had put in hand a comprehensive traffic survey of the BR network in order to identify loss-making lines and facilities, and this work continued through 1962. In the meantime a spending moratorium was placed on schemes not yet started. An early change under the new regime was a rationalisation of BR workshop facilities, a programme in which the SR fared badly, with both Lancing and Eastleigh carriage works being closed. Under the terms of the 1962 Act, control of BR passed from the BTC to the BRB on 1st January 1963, with Beeching as Chairman. That same month the conclusions of two years of traffic surveys were published in a document officially titled *The Reshaping of Britain's Railways* but widely (and notoriously) termed the 'Beeching Report'.

The motorman has just handed the single-line train staff to the signalman/porter at Ardingly as 2 BIL 2063 calls with the 4.16pm Horsted Keynes – Seaford service on 9th September 1962. At this time the Down line as far as Ardingly was being used to store redundant rolling stock, the Up line being worked in both directions as a single track. *J. H. Aston*

While containing a number of positive items, the Report also made clear that a significant proportion of the existing network was unremunerative and would need to close for BR to become financially viable once more. Among other loss-making activities targeted were wagon-load freight and its associated yards at local stations, and the provision of intensive services at holiday times. The 1962 Act set up statutory procedures for proposed line closures and service withdrawals, involving the Central Transport Users' Consultative Committee (CTUCC) who could recommend closure or retention based on evidence submitted at a Public Enquiry, but it was the Transport Minister who made the final decision.

The Southern Electric network was largely spared in the Beeching Report as, with the odd exception, only routes with significant traffic potential had been electrified in the first place. Relevant lines originally marked for closure included Haywards Heath to Horsted Keynes and Woodside to Sanderstead (both among the few electrified on questionable economic grounds) but, as will be seen, only the first was closed at this time, the other being successfully given a stay of execution for a further twenty years. Non-electrified secondary routes in Kent, Sussex and Hampshire fared less well, closures removing the two most convenient remaining London to Brighton diversionary routes (Christ's Hospital – Shoreham in the west and Uckfield to Lewes in the east). Among other changes, local freight services were gradually withdrawn through the 1960s, redundant yards at local stations making excellent commuter car parks when tarmacked over. Some local or main-line stopping services were eventually thinned out or withdrawn but in most cases these changes were not implemented until the Region-wide timetable revision of July 1967. Most additional bank holiday trains were dropped abruptly from August 1963, and other extra summer electric services to the coast gradually faded away through the decade.

With a manifesto commitment to halt further 'major' railway closures, the Labour Government which came into power in October 1964 quickly found that the parlous state of BRB finances left them with little choice but to continue with the reshaping plan in the short term. Nevertheless it was inevitable that a Labour Transport Minister would have serious policy disagreements with Beeching (although not, apparently, over railway issues), who returned to ICI in May 1965. Following the reports of further committees and no fewer than three White Papers, a new Transport Act passed into law in 1968. Its main features included writing off the BRB's historical debt and a separation of commercial from 'social' train services, the latter being individually grant-aided as long as the Minister required them to continue. As a result of this new framework, line and station closures came to a virtual halt. On the freight side BR was released from its obligations as 'common carrier', a change which accelerated the closure of station goods yards, eventually affecting even the largest, such as East Croydon. On a positive note, two further electrification schemes on the SR, to Bournemouth and on the Isle of Wight, were authorised and completed during this period; both are described below. Finance was also made available for the wholesale replacement of the pre-war main line electric stock, a process which took place between 1964 and 1972.

From 1st January 1965 a major change of image took place. British Railways became 'British Rail' with a new 'double arrow' symbol, a new typeface and new colours used on rolling stock, stations, staff uniforms, signs and publicity. The new rolling stock liveries (described elsewhere) and station signs did not start to appear until 1966, (July on rolling stock) and it took a further fifteen years for the old green station name-boards, some of which dated from Southern Railway days, to disappear entirely from the Southern Region.

The 1970s opened with the return to power of a Tory administration, committed to reducing the accelerating inflation which had beset the UK in the final years of the previous decade. The railway was once again an obvious target for cuts and, although early threats to make London commuter services financially self-sufficient by huge fare rises were not carried out, major economies were forced on BR. A £10 million reduction in Government subsidy resulted in fare increases of between 9 and 25% in the London and South East area from 28th March 1971, easily the largest rise since nationalisation. Although fixed asset renewal was allowed to continue on the SR, including resignalling, track remodelling and station rebuilding in the Feltham and London Bridge areas, a significant reduction in available investment finance effectively postponed SR suburban rolling stock renewal until the end of the decade. This period was also characterised by persistent serious industrial unrest, with strikes and other action by the railway trades unions causing much disruption. At the same time an attempt to change BR management structures, known as 'Field Reorganisation', failed largely due to opposition from the white-collar TSSA union.

The 1974 General Election was won by Labour, and that same year a further Transport Act passed into law, the main change of which was the replacement of grant-aid for individual lines and services by a cover-all Public Services Obligation (PSO) grant, fixed each year by the Treasury. This allowed reprieve of the lightly-used Wimbledon to West Croydon line, which had been due for closure. The economic recession which followed the 1973 oil crisis made further cuts necessary, leading to successive service reductions, particularly on Sundays, from April and October 1976. These cuts allowed the rolling stock fleet to be reduced by around 1,000 vehicles so, as described in Volume 1, many of the oldest 4 SUB units were taken out of service without any replacement stock being provided. By 1979 further resignalling schemes covering the Victoria area and Brighton main lines had been authorised, the first new production series suburban stock since 1963 (the class 508 units) was at last entering service, and a start had been made on refurbishing Kent Coast express stock (the 4 CEPs) for a further twenty years' service.

1979 heralded the return of a Conservative administration, led by a Prime Minister with a professed preference for road transport, so depressingly tight control of spending on railway investment continued over the following years as expected, while Treasury funding for new roads appeared almost unlimited. Government dissatisfaction with the BRB's operation of train services in the south east led to its referral to the Monopolies and Mergers Commission in 1980. The MMC's report concluded that the railway was in general not working against the public interest, but was actually performing remarkably well given the complexity of the network, the age of much of its equipment and a lack of consistent or sufficient long term funding. It was suggested that a new set of objectives for the railway be formulated by the BRB, and this duly appeared as a 'Passenger's Charter'. However, the improvements suggested would have costed an unthinkable £1,000 million over ten years to implement, so

no more was heard of it. The following year the BRB Chairman drew attention to the need for major expenditure across the network as years of insufficient investment began to take their toll and even Modernisation Plan equipment was reaching the end of its useful life. The railways' cause was not helped by a series of industrial disputes in 1982, culminating in a virtual shutdown of the entire BR network for two weeks in July over the issue of what became known as 'flexible rostering'. 1983 saw publication of the 'Serpell Report', yet another saga in the ongoing but futile effort to make the railway profitable by suggesting a severe pruning of the network. Unsurprisingly, its conclusions were seen as too much of a political 'hot potato', and it was therefore quietly forgotten.

On the Southern Region, the year 1983 saw the delayed but inevitable closure of the Woodside to Sanderstead line in May, while continuing progress on Brighton line modernisation saw the closure of the Coulsdon North suburban terminus in September. Finally, despite delays to the start of crew training caused by yet another industrial dispute, the gradual introduction of the second tranche of new inner suburban stock, in the form of class 455 units, at last permitted withdrawal of the remaining 4 SUBs that September.

MODERNISATION IN THE SUBURBAN AREA 1950-58

Two important projects carried out in the suburban area during the 1950s were complete renewal of the power supply system, and the lengthening of platforms on former SER lines of the Eastern section to allow the operation of ten-coach trains. Known respectively as the 'Change of Frequency Scheme' and the 'Ten Car Scheme' and completed at a total cost of £12.5 million, these two projects, concurrent with renewal of the rolling stock fleet, represented a level of re-equipment and improvement equivalent to the original SR electrifications.

Existing power supply equipment installed for the LSWR and SR dc suburban electrification schemes carried out in the 1914-30 period was clearly obsolete by 1945, and a survey carried out then showed that much of it was in need of renewal. The existing system also had several disadvantages when compared with later installations. The electricity generated was of non-standard voltage and frequency, the manned rotary converter substations were expensive to operate, and the radial cable network which fanned out from the power stations at Durnsford Road and Deptford to the substations was vulnerable to damage. Finally, a total system capacity of about 170 megawatts (MW) was considered insufficient given expanding traffic, particularly in the outer suburbs, and projected extensions to the electrified network. An initial scheme to update power supply arrangements on the Central and Eastern section suburban routes was drawn up and submitted for approval to the SR Board in May 1947, but the uncertainties of impending nationalisation prevented implementation at the time. In general, it was planned to use the same arrangements as for the 1932-39 main line schemes, with power purchased directly from the Grid and supplying remotely-controlled rectifier substations.

In 1950 a revised scheme, now covering all three sections of the Southern Region suburban network, was authorised by the BTC. At a projected cost of £11.5 million, the plans as finally agreed involved complete re-equipment of arguably the most complex electrified suburban network in the world. Possibly because no new lines were being electrified, however, this massive investment in the railway largely escaped press and public notice. Supply to about 900 track miles was to be entirely renewed, using a total of 71 new rectifier substations remotely supervised from three new control rooms and fed from the National Grid at five points via a 'ring-main' feeder cable network. The new scheme differed in detail from the earlier plans. Deptford power station would be retained and re-equipped but the railway-owned installation at Durnsford Road, which supplied the Western section network, was to be closed. Total capacity of the renewed system, on which work began in 1952 and was completed by 1958, was almost trebled, to 480MW. The very large volume of equipment required represented a significant order for the UK electrical supply industry, manufacturers involved including Bertram Thomas, BTH, EE, Hackbridge & Hewittic, GEC and Pirelli.

A major constraint in planning the work was the need to keep the system running while the old apparatus was taken out of commission and the replacement equipment installed. That the project was a success was due partly to meticulous planning but also to the excellent relationship established between the various railway departments and the large range of contractors involved. (To complicate matters further, work went on while the entire output from Deptford was lost for some months in 1953 due to flooding, and this caused many additional problems in keeping the existing system operational.)

The existing (formerly LESC) power station at Deptford was given new generating equipment to supply electricity at 66KV, 50Hz, to four new feeder stations located at Lewisham, South Bermondsey, Brockley and Nunhead, where it was transformed down to the standard 33KV for supply to the substations. The four other new feeder stations, located at Northfleet, Wimbledon, Croydon and Leatherhead, were all supplied directly from the National Grid at the required 33KV. All but one had two feeder cables for onward distribution of electricity to substations via ring cable networks. The exception was Wimbledon, which had five to supply all substations in the Western section suburban area.

The 71 substations, all of which had entirely new equipment, were of three types. 45 were in new flat-roofed brick buildings known to electrical staff as 'bungalows'. Of the remainder, 24 were located in existing pre-war 'cathedral' substation buildings and two in railway arches. There were also seventy track-parallelling (TP) huts, situated between pairs of substations to reduce voltage drop and to provide additional circuit breakers for isolation purposes. All substations were of similar layout, developed from the pattern used in the 1939 Medway electrification scheme. Rectifiers and high tension switchgear were located internally, with the transformer and low-voltage dc circuit breakers outside. The mercury-arc rectifiers and their associated transformers were supplied as complete units by their manufacturers, who differed for each of the three sections. The 29 Western Section substations were equipped with Hackbridge & Hewittic rectifiers of the traditional glass-bulb type, while the 23 Central section and nineteen Eastern section substations had pumpless steel tank rectifiers supplied by English Electric and GEC respectively. The number of rectifiers in each substation varied from one to five depending on the expected load.

The new rectifier substations and TP huts were remotely supervised from three new control rooms located at Raynes Park, Selhurst and Lewisham, controlling 28, 26 and seventeen substations respectively. They were low brick buildings of similar design, containing a 27ft x 8ft mimic diagram showing track layouts and cable runs with indicator lamps and keys to initiate operations mounted in their correct relative geographical positions. The remote-control system was supplied by GEC, and was based on the then-standard GPO-type electro-mechanical exchange equipment. Each discrete control 'system' could control up to four substations and/or TP huts, and was so arranged that no two adjacent substations were controlled by the same system. As with previous practice, the remote-control pilot cables were routed in the same lineside troughing or conduit as the high-tension ring-mains. It was arranged that certain vital inner-area substations could be operated from an alternative control room in an emergency. Raynes Park control room came into use on 2nd October 1954, followed by Lewisham on 18th April 1955 and Selhurst on 21st August the same year.

The basic method of carrying out the work was that supplies were disconnected on a substation by substation basis, such that when one substation was out of commission those adjacent to it remained in service. As the scheme progressed the situation arose that one of the adjacent substations was a new unstaffed installation eventually to be supervised from a control room not yet opened, but this problem was overcome by installing temporary remote-control equipment enabling the new site to be supervised from an existing manned substation. A different complication in the inner area was that the system could not run at all with a major substation out of use. In this case, substation equipment was changed over in a phased sequence such that the first rotary converter and its associated high-tension switchgear was replaced by new equipment whilst the remaining sets remained in use, followed by the second set and so on. This method could not be adopted for the dc track circuit breakers where it was necessary to replace the switchboard as a whole, and in these cases a temporary switchboard was employed, housed in a prefabricated building located adjacent to the substation being dealt with. At Lewisham it was necessary to construct a new HT switch room adjacent to the substation, as it was otherwise impossible to install new equipment until the old switchgear had been taken out of service.

On completion of the scheme, the main benefit to operating staff was the improved train performance available, due both to the raising of nominal voltage from 600 to 660 and to a substantial increase in capacity. One motorman described the effect of the new substation at Ashford (Middlesex) as being 'like the kick of a horse'. From a passenger's point of view the effect was less dramatic, the main benefit being an improvement in train lighting. From the outset the system was designed to operate at 750V, as on the post-war main line schemes, but was not changed over until the last of the 4 SUB units was withdrawn in September 1983. Installation of new equipment also did away with the familiar high-pitched whine of rotary converters at Clapham Junction and elsewhere. Finally, the opportunity was taken to rationalise lighting arrangements on many suburban stations. The mixture of gas and electric illumination (the latter in many cases supplied directly from the traction supply or by a non-standard low frequency system from Durnsford Road) was gradually superseded by standard electric lighting using current taken from the grid at the normal 240V 50Hz. After being made redundant in 1958, the former Durnsford Road power station was finally demolished in the first months of 1965. Its site then lay undeveloped until 1973-74, when the new East Wimbledon maintenance depot was built, as related later in this chapter.

Post-1945 capacity problems in the peaks, particularly on Eastern section (former SER) inner suburban routes out to Dartford, have been mentioned elsewhere. As it was quickly found that the ingenious double-decker prototypes of 1949 did not offer a practical solution to overcrowding, there was no alternative but to lengthen trains. A scheme to cover alterations to allow the operation of ten-coach trains was therefore authorised by the BTC in 1952, at an estimated cost of just under £1 million (not including additional rolling stock required). The scheme covered routes from Charing Cross, Blackfriars and Cannon Street to Dartford, Gravesend and Gillingham, to Bromley North, Orpington and Sevenoaks and the Mid-Kent line to Hayes, Addiscombe and Sanderstead. Additionally, ten-coach trains would be introduced on the Central section London Bridge–Caterham/Tattenham Corner line, though few alterations were required for this. Train formations were to consist of two 4 EPBs and a 2 EPB, the latter ordered specifically for this scheme, giving a total seating capacity of 958, an increase of 186 seats when compared with a similar eight-coach train of centre-gangway SUB or EPB stock. To enable this to take effect, most 4 EPB units were drafted to the Eastern section, displacing SUBs elsewhere.

Significant works were required particularly in and around the London termini, where cramped conditions had already taxed the ingenuity of the SR civil engineers 25 years earlier. Signalling and track alterations were carried out first on the approaches to platforms 1-3 at Charing Cross, at Metropolitan Junction and at Blackfriars, while abolition of the number 5 Up loop at London Bridge was necessary to allow the lengthening of platform 4. Elsewhere, platforms were extended where necessary, generally using prefabricated concrete sections, and some signals resited. Five additional berthing sidings were laid in at Slade Green depot.[9] On the Central

section, it was only necessary to extend the southern end of Platforms 5 and 6 at Purley, as all Down trains split there into separate Caterham and Tattenham Corner portions.

Progress with these works enabled ten-car trains to commence operation on Monday 14th June 1954, covering certain rush-hour services between Charing Cross and Barnehurst/Dartford via Bexleyheath, and a few trips on the Orpington and Bromley North lines. On the first day of operation G.T. Moody recorded that the 5.04pm Bexleyheath line service to Dartford was formed of 4 EPB 5044 + 2 EPB 5703 + 4 EPB 5043; on leaving Charing Cross the front unit had seats to spare but the rear six coaches were full and standing. The number of services worked by ten-coach trains was gradually increased as the necessary new 2 EPB EMUs were turned out from Eastleigh. A year later ten-coach trains commenced operation on the Sidcup (Dartford loop) line, and also on Central section Caterham and Tattenham Corner services. On 11th June 1956 they were introduced on North Kent line services between Charing Cross and Dartford via Greenwich and via Blackheath, and on the Mid-Kent lines, and a few days later were extended through to Gravesend and Gillingham.

Alterations at Cannon Street, the most complex part of the scheme, commenced in November 1955 but it was not until March 1957 that work on platforms 1-5 had been completed, allowing ten-coach trains to serve the City terminus for the first time. Apart from extensive changes to the track layout in the station throat, it was necessary to extend the platforms into the former concourse area here to gain the required length. A month later disaster struck when an overnight fire caused by an electrical fault all but destroyed the existing 143-lever Cannon Street signal cabin, putting all signalling and pointwork out of action. The least damaged part of the cabin was hastily reconstructed using a 47-lever frame 'borrowed' from the London Midland Region (LMR), and most EMU services into Cannon Street had been restored by early May. The complete ten-coach service, covering all the lines mentioned in the opening paragraph, was in operation by mid-June. (To complete the story, a new permanent signal cabin, equipped with the rest of the lever-frame from the LMR, was completed by the middle of December 1957. Building reconstruction at Cannon Street included erection of a low overall roof and demolition of the gaunt and glassless iron frame of the previous roof, for so long a distinctive City landmark, in 1958.)

ELECTRIFICATION SCHEMES

Three further electrification schemes on the SR network were completed in the 1948-83 period; in chronological order of completion these were the two phases of the Kent Coast scheme (1959 and 1961-62), the remaining stump of railway on the Isle of Wight, and Bournemouth (both 1967). In each case the major works carried out are described, followed by a brief outline of the service pattern following electrification and finally any major changes taking place in the years up to 1983.

It will be recalled that the 1939 Medway electrification scheme to Maidstone and Gillingham was planned with

---

9 Slades Green / Slade Green: The final 's' disappeared from 'Slades' on station name-boards in 1953, but local usage of the name Slade Green had always existed, so the name used by the SER and SR up to this time had been incorrect.

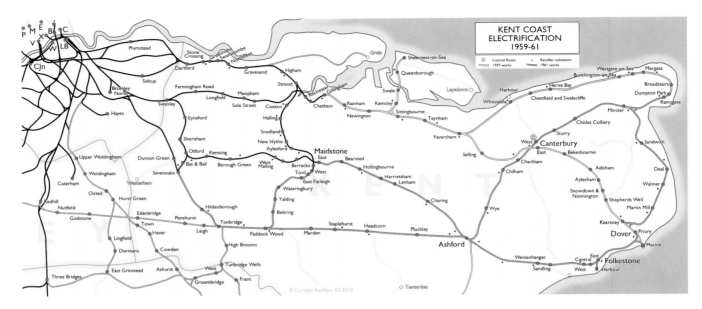

future extensions in mind, and that the Kent Coast routes were included in the SR's stillborn 1946 electrification proposals. Following nationalisation, the 1952 BTC Annual Report indicated that approval had been given in principle to electrify the two main lines through Kent, together with the Tonbridge – Hastings route but, again, no physical progress took place. Three years later the Modernisation Plan placed the Kent Coast lines as a priority for electrification and approval for work to begin on a £45 million scheme covering 310 track miles was eventually given in February 1956.

As finally authorised, the Kent Coast electrification project was divided into two stages, termed phase I and phase II. Phase I was effectively an extension of the 1939 Medway electrification and covered the former LCDR lines from Gillingham to Ramsgate via Faversham, from Faversham to Dover Marine, the Sheerness branch and the Stewarts Lane area, a total of 178 track miles. Phase II included the SER main line from Sevenoaks to Ramsgate via Tonbridge, Ashford and Dover, the Folkestone Harbour branch, Ashford – Minster and associated connections to the Deal – Ramsgate line, Maidstone East to Ashford, and Paddock Wood to Maidstone West. On both the latter routes, end-on connections were made with the 1939 electrifications. Phase II was also originally to have included the Ashford – Ore (Hastings) link, but this was subsequently cancelled. One major change from the 1932-39 schemes was the complete abolition of steam throughout the electrified area, with diesel traction being introduced for freight and on non-electrified lines. These included the Tonbridge to Hastings line, whose sub-standard loading gauge (Chapter 1 refers) once more caused its conversion to be put off indefinitely.

Physical work on phase I commenced in 1957, following the granting of the parliamentary powers required for some of the scheme's major civil engineering works. In most respects electrification fixed equipment followed the standards laid down by the SR for the 1932-33 Brighton and subsequent schemes, but nominal conductor rail voltage was increased to 750. Five new feeder stations supplied current from the National Grid to a network of lineside cables serving 23 unmanned substations, normally about 3½ miles apart. The cables were oil-filled and ran in concrete troughing (with the remote-control pilot cables) generally located at ground level. Most substations had a single mercury-arc rectifier, with a capacity of 2,500KW, but Broadstairs, Dover and Queenborough had two. All were supervised from a new control room at Canterbury, as were the TP huts, located roughly midway between each sub-station pair.

Between Shortlands and Bickley the four tracks were re-arranged by use rather than direction, eliminating conflicting movements over the junction with the Catford loop. Extensive realignment of the junctions and spurs in the Chislehurst area, where the former SER and LCDR main lines crossed and connected, allowed speed limits to be raised from 30/35 to 50mph. Quadrupling took place between Bickley Junction and Swanley, involving the use of concrete retaining walls to avoid disturbing adjacent residential property, a new viaduct across the Cray valley and the necessary reconstruction of St Mary Cray station with two island platforms. New Up and Down loops were installed between Rainham and Newington, requiring new platforms at the latter.

Platform extensions to allow twelve-coach trains to call were needed at most stations on the main lines, and in all 35 were altered or renovated in some way. At Chatham, hemmed in between two tunnels, the Up and Down loops had to be abolished to provide sufficient space for the extensions. Canterbury East's overall roof was replaced by platform awnings using steelwork recovered from the never-opened station at Lullingstone (Chapter 1 refers), whilst at Dover Marine platforms were extended by 114ft at the landward end. An extensive new EMU depot was added to the existing carriage sheds at Ramsgate, and an electric locomotive shed erected at Stewarts Lane.

Canterbury East station, rebuilt for Kent Coast phase I, on 2nd July 1959. The original LCDR overall roof has been dismantled and replaced with canopies whose framework was recovered from the 1939 Lullingstone station (between Swanley and Eynsford), completed but never opened and later removed. 4 CEP unit 7146, in original condition with whistles, calls during its lengthy meander across Kent forming the 12.36pm Sheerness to Dover Priory stopping service.
J. H. Aston

On the Sheerness branch doubling took place from the triangular junction layout west of Sittingbourne as far as Swale. The existing combined road–rail lifting bridge over The Swale (the channel separating the Isle of Sheppey from the mainland) was replaced by an impressive new reinforced concrete structure with a 120ft lifting span on a new alignment, financed jointly by the BTC, Kent County Council and the local paper mills. A new single-platformed halt named Swale, of standard SR prefabricated concrete sections, was bleakly situated at the mainland end of the bridge.[10] Opening for business on 20th April 1960, it replaced a halt of the same name on the closed alignment. The single Sheerness branch substation was normally supplied from Sittingbourne feeder station, Queenborough only being switched on in the event of damage to the submarine HT cables across The Swale.

In all, 95 route miles were resignalled, comprising the entire distance from Factory Junction to Ramsgate, via both Penge and the Catford loop from Brixton to Shortlands. The new colour-light signalling was spaced for a minimum three-

10 Swale Halt: The full title of the new halt, as displayed on the running-in boards, was: SWALE HALT ALIGHT HERE FOR RIDHAM DOCK. There was no actual community at Swale.

A ubiquitous feature of Southern electrification schemes, both pre and post-war, were the prefabricated concrete platform extensions, fencing and other station furniture supplied from Exmouth Junction concrete works. This view shows the country end of Whitstable station on 4th July 1959, where the platforms have been lengthened to take twelve coaches as part of the Kent Coast phase I scheme. The 10.10am Charing Cross to Ramsgate calls, led by 2 HAP 6046. *J. H. Aston*

minute headway, except between Victoria and Swanley where a 2½-minute spacing was required to accommodate peak-hour suburban traffic. Nine new power-operated signal boxes were built, while existing boxes at Swanley, Gillingham, Margate and Ramsgate were retained and modified to control the new signalling. The entire Sheerness branch was controlled from the new box at Sittingbourne, this being the first use of centralised traffic control on the SR. All new boxes had push-button route setting, dispensing with conventional levers, and were externally of 'glasshouse' style, mostly of brick but with some cladding in pastel shades as also used in contemporary station architecture. Modern ac track-circuiting was installed throughout, including on the Sittingbourne to Sheerness and Faversham to Dover routes which were not otherwise resignalled. The new signalling and track circuiting was brought into use on various dates through the spring of 1959.

Trial running between Gillingham and Ramsgate commenced on 1st June 1959. An official opening ceremony took place on 9th June, and on 15th electric services to the new expanded and accelerated timetable began. The basic weekday off-peak service provided not only a massive increase in train miles and improved journey times, but also maximum

connectional possibilities between any pair of stations included. The centre-piece was an express each hour from Victoria, calling at Bromley South, Chatham and Gillingham where it divided. The front portion ran fast to Whitstable, then Herne Bay then all stations to Ramsgate, while the rear portion stopped at Sittingbourne, Faversham then all stations to Dover Priory. An hourly service also ran from Charing Cross to Ramsgate via Woolwich, Dartford and Gravesend, stopping at all stations beyond Faversham. The existing Victoria – Maidstone East service each hour now included a portion for Sheerness (using the Sittingbourne avoiding spur), dividing at Swanley. A further hourly all-stations service meandered from Sheerness right through to Dover Priory, while an additional Sittingbourne to Sheerness shuttle provided a thirty-minute interval between these points. Corresponding up services followed a similar pattern. There were alterations to these patterns during early mornings/late evenings, and also in the peaks when several business trains ran between Cannon Street and Ramsgate via the Chislehurst junctions. The traditional heavy summer Saturday traffic between London and Kent Coast resorts was catered for by two additional Victoria to Ramsgate services each hour for much of the day.

Work commenced for phase II of the Kent Coast scheme as soon as phase I was in operation. Power supply arrangements involved the use of existing feeder stations at Tunbridge Wells (1935 Sevenoaks scheme), Canterbury, Thanet and Folkestone to supply 32 new substations, all but two of which originally had a single 2,500KW mercury-arc rectifier. Of the exceptions, Folkestone had two standard rectifiers while Hollingbourne was experimentally equipped with solid-state silicon diode equipment of 1,500KW capacity. The development of such semi-conductor rectifiers, which were considerably simpler and more robust, led to their use for the following Bournemouth and Isle of Wight electrifications and, later, to the gradual phasing out of the now obsolescent mercury-arc type. Cabling and remote control arrangements followed standard practice entirely, all the new substations and TP huts being supervised from a new control room located at Paddock Wood.

A smaller number of civil engineering works were required for phase II, the majority of alterations taking place at the eastern end, principally in the Ashford and Folkestone areas. At Ashford station the existing eastern end bay platforms were extended to provide two additional through platform lines, the two platform faces therefore becoming islands with the existing non-platformed through tracks between them. Tracks through all platforms were signalled for reversible operation, in particular to enable Up trains from the Canterbury West line toward London via Maidstone East to call at the Down platform and thus avoid crossing the through lines twice. A new covered footbridge and platform buildings, in a somewhat austere style, were provided, although the latter were not completed until 1966. In the Folkestone area the existing Up platform loop at Shorncliffe (later renamed Folkestone West) was extended westwards to form an additional Up line as far as Cheriton, giving two through lines and two loops between these points. Four tracks were also extended eastwards to Folkestone Central station, which was consequently entirely rebuilt with two island platforms. Existing platform loops were also extended at Headcorn, and on the Maidstone East line new loops were laid south of Otford (Up only), at Borough Green (Down only), and at Lenham.

In the suburban area, Grove Park was rebuilt with a new and entirely separate bay platform for the Bromley North branch, thus keeping the branch shuttle totally clear of the main lines. In all, 43 stations were renovated, and at several of these prefabricated concrete platform extensions and footbridges were added. At Charing Cross, there was insufficient space to lengthen any platform to the necessary 800ft for twelve-coach expresses, but platforms 5 and 6 were extended to approximately 740ft, leaving only one coach length off the end.

Apart from existing maintenance facilities already provided at Stewarts Lane and Ramsgate, an entirely new depot, equipped for heavy overhaul of all SR multiple unit stock, was erected on a green field site at Chart Leacon. This was located on the Up side of the main Tonbridge line about one mile west of Ashford station, and connected to it by a second Up line.

Resignalling of the routes involved in phase II covered only the main boat train routes from inside the suburban area at Parks Bridge Junction (Lewisham) to Dover via Tonbridge and Ashford and between Swanley Junction and Ashford via Maidstone East. Six new power boxes, all of the post war 'glasshouse' style with push-button route setting, were provided to control major junction points, but elsewhere along this section automatic signals were used to regulate traffic along the lengthy straight stretches such as Tonbridge – Ashford. The new signals were mainly three-aspect colour lights, but four-aspect were installed from Parks Bridge Junction to Sevenoaks and in the Tonbridge, Ashford and Folkestone areas. To maintain required headways it was necessary to install intermediate signals inside the long tunnels at Elmstead Woods (fast lines only), Polhill and Sevenoaks. The new signalboxes replaced 41 mechanical boxes, of which 33 were abolished completely and the rest retained for occasional or emergency use. Most of the new boxes controlled a considerable area; Tonbridge, for example, covered the main line from Sevenoaks to beyond Paddock Wood, the Maidstone West line from Paddock Wood almost to Yalding, and the non-electrified Hastings Line from Tonbridge as far as Tunbridge Wells (Grove Junction). Having a lighter traffic density, all other sections outside the areas of the new boxes retained semaphore signals manually controlled from existing boxes, albeit equipped with modern ac track circuiting. The revised signalling was phased into use on various dates between 4th February and 29th April 1962, starting with Parks Bridge Junction to Chislehurst Junction and finishing with the Ashford area.

Work had progressed sufficiently to enable steam trains to be replaced by electric units running to existing timings on the Dover Priory – Minster – Ramsgate route from 2nd January 1961, followed by through trains between Charing Cross/Cannon Street and Dover/Ramsgate via Tonbridge and Ashford from 18th June. From this date the all-Pullman *Golden Arrow* Victoria – Dover boat train service was electrically hauled, as were several other through services formed of existing steam stock. Electric trains beyond Maidstone East, also to the existing timetable, began running on 9th October. Finally, the new timetable, with increased and accelerated services worked entirely by new electric stock, commenced on Monday 18th June 1962, after which steam was banished entirely from the South Eastern division.

On the Charing Cross – Tonbridge – Ashford main line there were two services each hour, one running fast from Waterloo East to Ashford where it divided into Ramsgate via Canterbury West and Ramsgate via Dover Priory and Deal portions. The second, leaving Charing Cross ten minutes later, was a semi-fast to Margate via Dover and Minster, detaching a portion at Tonbridge which called at all stations to Ashford. This latter service connected at Paddock Wood with an hourly shuttle to Maidstone West. Two trains each hour also served the route from Victoria to Ashford via Swanley and Maidstone East, one of which was an extension of the existing Maidstone East portion detached at Swanley from the Victoria to Sheerness service, running to Ashford and calling at all stations beyond Maidstone. The second was

a semi-fast to Margate via Ashford and Canterbury West. In the peaks, a number of Tonbridge line services ran to/from Cannon Street. Corresponding Up services followed the same pattern.

Three minor stations were closed on the electrified Kent Coast lines in succeeding years; these were Folkestone East (from 6th September 1965), Grove Ferry (from 3rd January 1966) and Chislet Colliery (from 4th October 1971). The original timetables and service patterns were first significantly altered in the Region-wide timetable revision of July 1967 (see pages 74/75), and there were further changes in subsequent years, particularly on the Chatham lines in 1973. Of the SE division's two most exotic services, the *Golden Arrow* boat train ceased to be all-Pullman from 14th July 1965, when the second class cars were replaced by ordinary coaches. The service finally ended on 30th September 1972, by which time the three or four remaining first class Pullmans had been reliveried in the same unsympathetic variation of BR blue/grey as the *Brighton Belle*. With its dedicated *Wagon Lits* cars also reaching the end of their useful lives and with no will to replace them in the face of declining patronage, the *Night Ferry* through sleeping-car service to Paris and Brussels lasted only a little longer, running for the final time on 31st October 1980. The terminus at Dover Marine was renamed Dover Western Docks from May 1979. Finally, the gradual removal from freight sidings of 750V overhead power lines, never much used and completely redundant following withdrawal of the pantograph-equipped class 71 locomotives in 1976, took place through the 1970s. By mid-1979 they were

intact only at Sittingbourne, Faversham and Shepherdswell, but all had been dismantled by the following year.

Although the Isle of Wight featured prominently as a summer holiday destination served by SR electric services to Portsmouth Harbour on the mainland, at the start of the 1960s its own railway system continued to be steam-worked with increasingly geriatric rolling stock of Victorian and Edwardian vintage. Already, closures due to mounting losses had seen a halving in mileage of the IoW system from just over 55 in 1952 to 25½ four years later, the two routes remaining after this date connecting Ryde with Ventnor and Cowes respectively, diverging at Smallbrook Junction. Beeching's 1963 reshaping plan envisaged closure of both, leaving only a 1¼-mile stub connecting Ryde Pier Head with St Johns Road whence buses would connect to take passengers to their final holiday destinations. At the June 1964 public enquiry into the proposed closures it was contested that buses would have insufficient capacity during the summer holiday period, particularly bearing in mind the narrow and inadequate island road system. These protests had partial success, and in the summer of 1965 the Minister of Transport announced that the 8½-mile Ryde Pier Head – Shanklin section, which carried the bulk of the summer holiday traffic, was to remain open, with the unexpected proviso that it be modernised. Consequently, the Smallbrook Junction – Cowes and Shanklin – Ventnor lines saw their last passenger trains on 21st February and 18th April 1966 respectively.

The major difficulty standing in the way of modernisation

on the Island concerned the loading gauge through the twin-bore Ryde Tunnel between St Johns Road and Esplanade stations, whose restricted height (11in lower than standard) precluded use of modern coaches. The solution had been to use elderly wooden-bodied vehicles of SECR or LBSCR origin with lower roofs, many of which had been transferred from the mainland prior to 1939. The expensive options of altering more recent coaches, building entirely new stock or enlarging the Ryde tunnels had never been justifiable, even before the tighter financial regime of the Beeching era, and the only possible alternative was to find some available second-hand vehicles which would fit. London Transport came to the rescue by making available otherwise obsolescent pre-1938 'Standard' tube stock. This made electrification viable and incidentally ensured that railways on the IoW would continue to operate as a rolling museum. The acquisition, conversion and operation of these tube cars, the only electric stock ever purchased second-hand by the SR, is covered in Chapter 7.

Following the official pronouncement that the Ryde – Shanklin section would remain open and be modernised, the SR decided in October to electrify the line using 46 (later reduced to 43) former LT tube cars, a decision ratified by the BRB the following month. Although dieselisation had earlier been considered it was not expected that the tube cars would last long, and installing conductor rails would enable them to be easily replaced within ten years as and when more modern

LT stock became available. In the event this proved to be an over-optimistic assumption, and their envisaged length of life on the island was to be greatly exceeded.

As finally planned and executed, the Isle of Wight electrification scheme cost a very reasonable £500,000. Electrical installation once more followed standard SR practice, with current purchased from the South Eastern Electricity Board at the usual 33KV 50Hz and supplied to three rectifier substations via a feeder station located at Ryde St Johns Road. The electrical control room was originally also at St Johns Road, but was later closed and supervision passed to Havant control room, connected to the island by telephone link. The substations supplied current to the conductor rails at a nominal 630V dc, slightly different from standard in order to suit the characteristics of the former tube stock. Track layouts and signalling were simplified, but nonetheless manual signal-boxes and semaphore signals were retained at Ryde Pier Head, St Johns Road (formerly at Waterloo Junction and transferred to the island in 1926 following electrification of the SE suburban lines), Brading, Sandown and Shanklin. Shanklin was only manned when the maximum summer Saturday service was in operation. Track was double from Ryde Pier Head as far south as Smallbrook Junction, between Brading and Sandown, and through the platforms at Shanklin; elsewhere it was single.

Newly outshopped Isle of Wight 3 TIS unit 037 stands in the sidings at Fratton depot on 26th August 1966, probably following a test run up the Portsmouth direct line. The leading motor coach is S19, built by the Union Construction Company at Feltham in 1928 and recognisable as a UCC car by its bulged lower body sides. In the event, 037 never ran in service on the Island, its vehicles being reformed into other units following the decision to reduce the rolling stock requirement from 46 to 43 vehicles
E. W. J. Crawforth

The main incidental works concerned extensive alterations at Ryde Pier Head, commenced in 1964, where the number of platform roads was reduced to two, with three platform faces. At other stations platform heights had to be altered to match the lower door openings of the tube cars, mainly done by increasing the depth of ballast to raise the tracks. However, at Ryde Esplanade, originally left unaltered, it was necessary to lower the wooden platform at the insistence of the Transport Minister. The tracks inside the twin single-bores of Ryde tunnel were renewed and raised to improve drainage and alleviate flooding problems, but this also reduced clearances still further and ensured that nothing other than tube stock could work through them again. The engine shed, located on the west side of St Johns Road station, was demolished following the end of steam, but the former carriage works on the east side were retained, modernised and re-equipped to become the electric stock depot.

Most electrification work on the island, including the laying of conductor rails and building of substations, was carried out during 1966 while the remaining steam service continued in operation. From 17th September this was cut back to start from Ryde Esplanade to allow work on Ryde Pier to carry on uninterrupted, and was withdrawn completely after traffic on 31st December to enable final modernisation and electrification works to proceed. Traction current was switched on for the first time in early March 1967 and trials with the first units to arrive continued through the following weeks.

Electric services on the Isle of Wight commenced on Monday 20th March, in time for the Easter holiday traffic, although by that date not all of the electric rolling stock had reached the island. The initial timetable was hourly during the winter, using a single four coach 4 VEC unit, and every thirty minutes in the summer, using seven-coach 4 VEC + 3 TIS formations. The three-coach unit was invariably coupled at the Shanklin end so its driving trailer (lacking collector shoes) was at the centre of the train. On summer Saturdays, a maximum twelve-minute interval service using six seven-car trains was operated, requiring all units in traffic and leaving only a single motor car spare. This frequency required use of the loop and signalbox at Shanklin, with arriving trains running into the Down platform and then shunting to the Up platform using a remaining stub of the Ventnor line south of the station. At other times the Down platform served for all trains, signalled from Sandown. The Saturday service was reduced slightly to quarter-hourly from the summer of 1969, releasing a unit for use on a new shuttle between Ryde Pier Head and Esplanade to replace the petrol trams on the pier tramway which had been closed in January 1969. This shuttle originally had to run empty coaching stock to St Johns Road for reversal.

By 1973, the scissors crossovers at the seaward end of Ryde Pier were in need of replacement and the signalbox was becoming structurally dangerous. The crossovers were abolished in October 1973, single-line working along the former northbound track being instituted instead. The following May a new crossover was installed south of Ryde Esplanade, and the whole area resignalled with colour lights controlled from St Johns Road signalbox. Following these alterations Ryde to Shanklin through trains regained the Down line south of Esplanade platform, while the pier shuttle was effectively stranded on its own independent track (on the east side) for its day's duty, and operated untimetabled 'as required'. In 1978 the loop at Shanklin was finally removed and the platform extended slightly at the Sandown end, enabling an underbridge south of the station to be removed. In 1982 the minimum service interval on summer Saturdays was increased to twenty minutes, reflecting the decreased quantity of available rolling stock following accidents or simply old age.

A further SR electrification scheme suggested in the 1955 Modernisation Plan, but of lower priority than Kent Coast, covered the Western section main line from Waterloo to Weymouth, Basingstoke – Salisbury and Southampton Docks, together with the Clapham Junction – Staines – Byfleet Junction loop. The possibility of utilising the 25KV 50Hz ac overhead system was considered, having been recently adopted as the future standard for railway electrification in Britain, but early studies unsurprisingly indicated that installation of the necessary overhead catenary in the congested Clapham Junction to Waterloo area would be extremely complicated. Similar difficulties applied to an alternative 1,500V dc system using a protected third rail and side-contact pick-up, also briefly considered, while the further possibility of building dual-voltage rolling stock to work off both 25KV ac overhead and dc third rail was not technically feasible at the time. With financial restrictions on railway modernisation imposed by the Government in 1957 in the light of worsening losses, the proposed Bournemouth electrification was put on hold for the time being.

The planning of a suitable scheme using the SR standard 750V dc system went ahead, however, and by 1962 this had been pared down to include just Brookwood (the existing limit of electrification) to Bournemouth, plus the Lymington Pier branch. To enable continued operation of through trains to Weymouth it was intended to operate express services on the push-pull principle. As explained in Chapter 5 (page 153), successful high-speed push-pull experiments were carried out with electric stock during this period, following which Ministry of Transport (MoT) approval was given for passenger trains to be propelled at up to 90mph. With an urgent need to replace steam on the route at the earliest opportunity, authority for a cut-price £15 million scheme to go ahead was eventually given in September 1964. As authorised, the Bournemouth electrification covered 79 route miles, and included Pirbright Junction (Brookwood) to Branksome and the branches from Brockenhurst to Lymington Pier and from Branksome into Bournemouth maintenance depot. In total, 236 single track miles, together with ten miles of sidings, were given conductor rails. In comparison with the Kent Coast scheme major incidental works were few, and further economies were extracted by using existing coaches, suitably converted, to provide much of the electric rolling stock required.

Power supply arrangements included some noteworthy innovations to reduce costs and improve performance. The

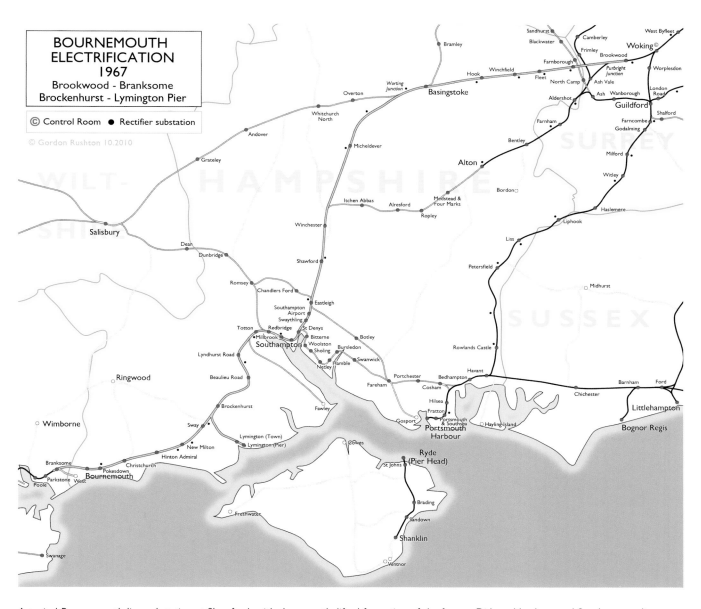

BOURNEMOUTH ELECTRIFICATION 1967
Brookwood - Branksome
Brockenhurst - Lymington Pier

© Control Room ● Rectifier substation

© Gordon Rushton 10.2010

West Byfleet
Sandhurst
Camberley
Blackwater
Woking ©
Frimley
Brookwood
Bramley
Brookwood
Farnborough
Purbright Junction
Worplesdon
Hook
Winchfield
North Camp
Ash Vale
Worting Junction
Fleet
Wanborough
London Road
Overton
Basingstoke
Aldershot
Ash
Guildford
Whitchurch North
Farncombe
Andover
Micheldever
Farnham
Godalming
Shalford
Bentley
Grateley
Milford
Alton
SURREY
Witley
Itchen Abbas
Medstead & Four Marks
Bordon○
Alresford
Ropley
Haslemere
Winchester
Liphook
Salisbury
Liss
Shawford
Petersfield
Midhurst
Dean
Dunbridge
Romsey
SUSSEX
Chandlers Ford
Eastleigh
Southampton Airport
Swaythling
Rowlands Castle
Totton
Redbridge
St Denys
Botley
Millbrook
Bitterne
Southampton
Woolston
Bursledon
Sholing
Havant
Barnham
Ford
Lyndhurst Road
Netley
Hamble
Swanwick
Bedhampton
Chichester
Ringwood
Beaulieu Road
Fareham
Cosham
Portchester
Hilsea
Brockenhurst
Fawley
Portsmouth & Southsea
Bognor Regis
Wimborne
Sway
Gosport
Fratton
Littlehampton
New Milton
Lymington (Town)
Portsmouth Harbour
Hayling Island
Hinton Admiral
Lymington (Pier)
Cowes
Branksome
Christchurch
Ryde (Pier Head)
Pokesdown
St Johns
Parkstone
West
Bournemouth
Poole
Brading
Swanage
Freshwater
Sandown
Shanklin
Ventnor

A typical Bournemouth line substation at Shawford, with the recently lifted formation of the former Didcot, Newbury and Southampton line towards Winchester in the foreground. A southbound crew training trip formed of JB electro-diesel E6012 propelling a pair of 4 TC units (both without their trailer firsts) passes on 18th March 1967. *Southern Images / John H. Bird*

existing 33KV cable network was extended from Sturt Lane Junction (east of Farnborough Main) to Branksome, supplied with electricity from the National Grid via three feeder stations located at Basingstoke, Southampton and Bournemouth. An additional feed was provided from the existing Reading line installation via Sturt Lane substation. Nineteen new substations and twenty TP huts were installed, supervised remotely from a new control room located at Eastleigh. Additional supervisory equipment was also installed in the existing 1937 Woking control room. The substations were housed in uncompromisingly box-like prefabricated structures containing semi-conductor rectifiers as first used at Hollingbourne. On the four-track section from Sturt Lane as far as Worting Junction, five substations were provided, conventionally spaced at 3½-mile intervals. These made use of equipment ordered but not used for the aborted Ashford – Ore scheme. Below Worting Junction economies were achieved by spacing the substations more widely, up to 4⅔ miles apart. This was made possible by siting remote sensors, known as Track Current Relays, midway between each substation/TP hut pair. These were designed to detect any abnormal electrical condition and send a signal via the pilot cable to operate circuit breakers in their adjacent substation and TP hut and thus isolate the section. Substations and TP huts in the New Forest area were painted green to blend in with their surroundings, rather than the drab battleship grey used elsewhere. Conductor rails were fed with electricity from the substations at the standard 750V dc.

The whole main route from Brookwood to Branksome was reballasted and relaid with continuous welded rail on concrete sleepers, but otherwise track alterations and other incidental works were not extensive. Disused central island platforms were removed from stations between Brookwood and Basingstoke, while utilitarian new CLASP buildings, pre-fabricated from concrete sections, were provided at Fleet. Elsewhere, platforms were extended to twelve-coach length at nine stations to be served by express and semi-fast services. New 90mph turnouts were installed between the fast lines and the Bournemouth route at Worting Junction, while the existing side platforms and loops were abolished at Micheldever, the central island platform on the through lines being reinstated instead. At Shawford, the existing goods loop was relaid to passenger standards and given a new prefabricated concrete platform, backing onto (but staggered in relation to) the existing Down platform. The two centre roads through Bournemouth Central were removed. The east-to-south spur at Branksome was taken up, but the west curve was retained to provide access into the new Bournemouth depot, built on the site of the approach to the closed Bournemouth West station and taking in an existing carriage shed. A new 280ft x 40ft four-road maintenance shed of traditional SR design was built adjacent to this, and berthing sidings in the area were rearranged. At Eastleigh new berthing and servicing sidings were provided to accommodate four twelve-coach electric trains, while the existing diesel unit shed was enlarged to house 32 coaches on eight tracks. A further four twelve-coach berthing sidings were provided at Basingstoke.

A former 6 PAN motor coach from unit 3031, hauled by electro-diesel E6043, performs conductor rail clearance tests for the Bournemouth electrification near Millbrook on 6th January 1967. *Southern Images / John H. Bird*

The new station building at Fleet, provided in 1967 for the Bournemouth electrification. One of the first to be constucted to the CLASP design using prefabricated conecte, wood and glass components mounted on a steel framework, its utilitarian and uninviting style is all too apparent. *BR Southern Region Official*

Southampton Central station at the low point of its reconstruction on 15th March 1967. The former main building with its distinctive clock tower has been demolished, but its replacement office block is not yet beyond its foundations. Push-pull fitted diesel-electric locomotive D6520 propels a 4 TC out of platform 1 with a Waterloo-bound working. *Southern Images / John H. Bird*

The lines from Woking to St Denys and from Totton to Branksome were resignalled, except the Brockenhurst and Christchurch station areas. The Southampton area also retained its semaphore signalling for the time being, including the impressive gantries at St Denys and Southampton. The new signalling comprised multiple-aspect colour lights, mostly three-aspect, with continuous track circuiting, and was controlled from new centralised power signal boxes at Basingstoke and Eastleigh, together with extension panels in the existing 1937 Woking box. The additions at Woking were commissioned in June 1966 and controlled the line as far west as a point beyond Pirbright Junction. Basingstoke and Eastleigh power boxes came into use from November 1966, the former controlling from Farnborough to Worting Junction (inclusive), and the latter from that point to Swaythling. The two new boxes were of the cheap prefabricated CLASP pattern. The existing manual box at Winchester Junction, where the line 'over the Alps' to Alton diverged, was retained, treated as a ground frame and locked/unlocked from Eastleigh. (The non-electrified Alton – Winchester line, then worked by DEMUs, was eventually closed in 1973, removing a previously useful diversionary route which had proved its worth during the Bournemouth electrification.)

Rolling stock deliveries commenced in August 1966, while current was switched on in stages between December 1966 and May 1967. By this time the run-down of steam and diversions due to electrification works had caused the existing service to become hopelessly unreliable, but problems were ameliorated by the introduction of the first of the new stock, initially diesel-hauled. It was originally intended to launch the new electric service in June 1967, but late delivery of some rolling stock caused this to be postponed until the following month, after which time steam was entirely banished from the SR. The new electric timetable finally commenced on 10th July 1967 as part of a major region-wide revision of services. Due to ongoing technical problems with the new trains, however, the service did not settle down to fully reliable operation until well into the following year.

A test formation passes Mount Pleasant crossing, between St Denys and Southampton on the newly energised Bournemouth line, on 21st January 1967. The leading unit is 4 EPB 5129, unusually running as a three-coach unit with only one trailer. *Southern Images / John H. Bird*

4 REP high-powered tractor unit 3009 leads a 4 TC trailer unit out of the reversing sidings into Bournemouth Central with a Waterloo semi-fast service in February 1968. The structures of the redundant steam shed, now bereft of track, are in the background. Both units are in their original semi-matt blue finish, which was very quickly found to weather rapidly. *Southern Images / John H. Bird*

The new timetable was based around a two-hourly express, calling only at Southampton between Waterloo and Bournemouth (reached in 100 minutes), thence all stations to Weymouth. An hourly Waterloo semi-fast service calling at principal stations to Bournemouth was extended westwards every other hour, thus giving the necessary sixty-minute interval on the Bournemouth to Weymouth section. These services were all worked by the special push-pull REP and TC multiple-unit stock described in Chapter 7, with diesel propulsion west of Bournemouth. Intermediate stations were served by an hourly Waterloo to Bournemouth stopping train which detached an Alton portion at Brookwood, and by an hourly Waterloo to Basingstoke service which divided a Portsmouth portion at Woking. A number of peak-hour services, as well as boat trains serving the docks at Southampton and Weymouth, were locomotive-hauled. Certain summer-dated trains included a through portion (generally a single TC unit and a locomotive) to Swanage, but these ceased in October 1970 and the non-electrified Wareham – Swanage branch itself was closed in January 1972. There were also through services on summer Saturdays between Waterloo and Lymington Pier, communicating with the ferry across the Solent to Yarmouth (IoW). Increasing patronage led to the adoption of an hourly frequency for the Waterloo – Weymouth fast service in 1974, requiring the building or conversion of additional rolling stock, while timetable re-

organisation caused the loss of the Alton/Portsmouth parts of the stopping services.

Remaining pockets of semaphore signalling on the Bournemouth line were progressively converted to colour-light in the years after 1967. The Christchurch – Pokesdown section was changed over in December 1972, Northam Junction – St Denys (Up lines only) in April 1975 and Totton – Redbridge in April 1977, all controlled from existing signal-boxes. A third line on the Down side was laid from Brockenhurst station to the Lymington branch, coming into operation in October 1979, enabling the junction and its signalbox to be abolished and the branch shuttle kept entirely clear of the main line. Work started on resignalling the Southampton station area at the start of 1979 and, so far as the main line was concerned, was completed in November 1981 when Southampton and Millbrook boxes were abolished. The new signals were controlled from Eastleigh, which now supervised the route from Worting Junction as far west as Brockenhurst. As part of this scheme the ninety degree bend at Northam Junction was realigned to raise the speed limit of the Bournemouth main line at this point from 15mph to 25mph.

In 1983 the Bournemouth line continued to be one of the region's most profitable routes, and plans for rolling stock replacement and extension of the third rail to Weymouth were under consideration.

SOUTHERN ELECTRIC CLOSURES

Because it is mostly the case that only routes with relatively high existing traffic levels or with the likelihood of substantial growth were ever considered for electrification, the number of complete lines on the Southern Electric system to lose their passenger service is small. Three routes were closed in the 1954-83 period, each under widely different circumstances, although all three had in common a lack of traffic potential. These were the Nunhead – Crystal Palace branch in 1954, the Haywards Heath – Horsted Keynes line in 1963 and Elmers End – Sanderstead twenty years later.

The former LCDR branch from Nunhead to Crystal Palace (the terminus later distinguished as 'High Level' by the SR) led a chequered career. Following a period of closure during World War One in order to release men for the armed forces, it was afterwards reopened and then included in the first stage of the Eastern section suburban electrification scheme, completed in July 1925. Through the following fifteen years passenger numbers did not increase to the same extent as on surrounding lines, and much potential traffic was lost when the Crystal Palace itself burnt down spectacularly in 1936. Temporarily closed once more as a wartime economy measure from 22nd May 1944, it was reopened yet again from 4th March 1946 but regained little traffic in the years following. Post-war, the basic service was half-hourly between Blackfriars and Crystal Palace High Level, a single four-coach SUB unit (displaying headcode P or 57) proving more than sufficient for the handful of passengers using it. Neglect and wartime damage had left branch stations at Lordship Lane, Honor Oak, Upper Sydenham and Crystal Palace in an advanced state of decay, particularly the derelict and rat-infested hulk of the terminus building, where extensive areas were roped-off as unsafe and ferns grew luxuriantly through the platform timbers.

Closure proposals were inevitable in the circumstances, particularly as the immediate area was also served by the London Bridge to Norwood Junction route and the former LBSCR station at Crystal Palace, both much busier and offering a wider range of destinations. The final electric trains operated on 18th September 1954, although a steam railtour visited the line the following day. Conductor rails and feeder cables were taken away almost immediately, but track recovery and demolition did not take place until 1956-57, after which the parts of the route were variously redeveloped or retained as a woodland walk. By 1972 prefabricated huts had been erected on the terminus site, to be replaced by permanent housing in 1986. An odd survival is the tiled subway under Crystal Palace Parade, decorated by continental craftsmen in the style of a Byzantine crypt, which used to provide access for first class ticket holders directly from the station into the Palace. Now listed, it is opened to interested visitors on a few days each year.

The derelict and rat-infested Crystal Palace High Level station on 18th September 1954, the last day of train services on the branch from Nunhead. The netting under the roof at the far end was intended to catch falling glass, and ferns may be seen thriving underneath the arches along the centre platform. *Alan A. Jackson*

Most of the passengers joining or alighting from 2 HAL 2674 at Horsted Keynes on 15th September 1963 are clearly railway enthusiasts, using the electric service from Haywards Heath to visit the preserved Bluebell Railway. The branch was to close six weeks later, one of the first casualties of the Beeching Report. *John H. Meredith*

Richard Beeching's infamous report *The Reshaping of Britain's Railways*, referred to earlier, largely ignored electrified SR routes for the reasons given. Only two electrified sections, Haywards Heath – Horsted Keynes and Elmers End – Sanderstead, were originally proposed for closure and of these only the first was actually closed at the time.

Originally forming part of the LBSCR's extensive network of secondary lines serving East Sussex, most of which were also closed under Beeching or before, possible explanations as to why the entirely rural branch from Haywards Heath to Horsted Keynes was electrified in the first place in 1935 have been discussed in Chapter 1. Had post-war Southern Railway plans for further electrification come to fruition it would have formed part of a diversionary route for the Brighton line via Oxted, but in the event it retained its peaceful existence through the 1950s. Mostly served by a single 2 NOL, BIL or HAL unit shuttling hourly between Horsted Keynes and Seaford (headcode 37), there were by this time few passengers other than ramblers and school pupils at Ardingly College, served by the one intermediate station on the branch. In 1958 the route was effectively singled between Horsted Keynes and Ardingly, the former Down line being used firstly

to stockpile newly-built 4 CEP and BEP stock for the Kent Coast electrification, and then from 1959 to store withdrawn steam stock (displaced by electrification) and goods wagons prior to scrapping. Some additional weekend traffic was gained when the Horsted Keynes – Sheffield Park line was reopened as the preserved Bluebell Railway in 1960. The first rolling stock for the Bluebell all arrived over the Haywards Heath line, while a few steam railtours also visited via this route over the next three years.

The last day of passenger services between Haywards Heath and Horsted Keynes was 27th October 1963, when several of the branch trains were worked by an express 6 PAN unit. Part of the branch from Copyhold Junction was subsequently retained as a single track to serve a roadstone terminal established in the former Ardingly station yard, and this remained in operation in 2010. Sheriff Mill Viaduct, which carried the line over the River Ouse between Ardingly and Horsted Keynes, was demolished shortly after closure. More recently the Bluebell Railway, considerably expanded in its operations since 1960, purchased the trackbed in 1996, so it is possible that the remainder of the route might eventually see trains once more.

Exactly why the Elmers End – Sanderstead suburban line was ever electrified in 1935 after having been moribund since 1916 is also open to question, and once again possible reasons have already been suggested elsewhere (see Volume 1). With minimal patronage below Elmers End, the lavish half-hourly through service to London via the Mid-Kent line was severely curtailed during World War Two, when weekend trains were withdrawn entirely after the Saturday lunchtime peak. Post war, traffic did not pick up and from 26th November 1949 through trains to/from London were withdrawn completely outside rush hours, the service at other times consisting of a single SUB unit shuttling between Elmers End and Sanderstead every half hour, the end-to-end journey taking twelve minutes. In spite of this, money was spent extending platforms at all the stations with concrete sections as part of the 'ten car scheme' in 1955, by which time most services comprised a single 2 EPB unit, running virtually empty for much of the day. Further economies took place in November 1959 when trains were withdrawn on weekday lunchtimes and evenings, Saturday afternoons and all day Sunday.

As mentioned, Elmers End – Sanderstead was the second SR electrified line slated for closure in the 1963 Beeching Report. However, despite still declining traffic, the proposals were successfully resisted and the line was reprieved, subject to further review in three years. This 1966 reassessment led only to a further pruning of the service in 1967, when it was reduced to run during Monday to Friday peak hours only. In 1976 the last through London (Cannon Street) trains were withdrawn, by which time the virtually disused intermediate halts at Bingham Road and Coombe Road had been given even more restricted opening hours and several shuttles were terminating short at Selsdon. By now many trains were running devoid of passengers, and a further attempt by BR in 1981 to close the line unsurprisingly proved successful. The first closure in the south east for some years, in its last weeks the line probably saw more passengers than ever before. The last day of service was Friday 13th May 1983, when the two final trains had to be considerably strengthened to cope with demand, being formed of eight (EPBs 5222 + 5251) and six coaches (5720 + 5209) respectively. Following closure, the line was lifted other than a spur off the South Croydon – Sanderstead line to serve an oil depot at Selsdon, served irregularly until about 1990. [11]

11 Although strictly outside our terms of reference, it is worth noting here that the very short section from South Croydon to Selsdon was given conductor rails in 1985, enabling electric suburban trains from London to terminate at Sanderstead once more, albeit via East Croydon. This was followed by complete electrification of the Oxted line to East Grinstead in October 1986. By 2000, the formerly derelict trackbed between Woodside and Coombe Road had been resurrected as part of the Croydon *Tramlink* scheme, which saw light-rail vehicles pass along it en route to and from Beckenham Junction, Elmers End and New Addington.

The number of stations closed on the Southern Electric network in the 1948-1983 period is also very small, totalling just six on the pre-1948 system, and of these only two were not replaced by adjacent or nearby facilities. Of the two closed without an alternative being provided, the run down and little used St Leonards West Marina, situated west of Bopeep Junction on the Eastbourne – Hastings line, had its sparse service withdrawn from 10th July 1967. The site of the station forecourt is now a garage. East Brixton, on the South London line viaduct between Clapham and Denmark Hill, was closed from 5th January 1976. Its wooden platforms and buildings were by then in a dangerous state, and it was deemed uneconomic to replace them given the low level of usage. There is now little evidence that a station ever existed on the site, and trains between Victoria and London Bridge pass one of the most populous areas of inner London without stopping.

The first station to be relocated in the post-war period was the original Gatwick Airport, closed from 28th May 1958 and replaced by the rebuilt racecourse station, itself renamed Gatwick Airport on the same date. This was located slightly nearer Horley and adjacent to the new airport terminal building. Much original structure of the 1935 station, including the main building and parts of the side platforms, survived until 1998. Rationalisation in the Reading area resulted in the separate SR terminus at Reading Southern, onetime end of the peculiar SER incursion into Berkshire, being closed from 6th September 1965, together with the

short stretch of line leading to it. From this date all services from the Wokingham direction, which off-peak included two electric trains each hour from Waterloo plus an hourly diesel unit serving Guildford, Redhill and Tonbridge, were diverted into Reading General, where the existing spur from the SR line was equipped with conductor rails and a new electrified bay platform provided at the east end. For some years the former Reading Southern station building was retained as a garage, but the site has now been redeveloped. The original Crawley station was replaced by a new station, including an office development, on a site adjacent but nearer Three Bridges from 28th July 1968. Here too the original platforms, virtually continuous with their replacements, still exist. Finally, the spacious suburban terminus and attendant berthing sidings at Coulsdon North, situated on a short spur off the Brighton main line south of Purley, were closed as part of a resignalling and rationalisation scheme covering the Croydon area, having had only a Monday to Friday peak service for some years. The final trains ran during the evening rush-hour of Friday 30th September 1983, but were replaced the following Monday by additional services serving the adjacent Smitham on the Tattenham Corner branch. Following demolition the station site and its surroundings were earmarked for the A23 road widening scheme, but in the meantime became a shrubby wilderness with untidy and unplanned light industrial development sprouting where the carriage sidings once were.

Facing page The last rites draw near for another of the Southern Railway's more questionable investments of the 1930s. On Friday 6th May 1983, a week before final closure, 2 EPB 5725 runs into a vandalised and deserted Bingham Road station with the 16.30 Elmers End to Sanderstead shuttle. It is quite likely that the train was carrying more crew members than fare paying passengers. By this time SR suburban stock was being outshopped in blue/grey livery, as seen here. *John Scrace*

Left The commodious former LBSCR suburban terminus at Coulsdon North on 30th January 1982. 4 SUB 4733 has just terminated with a train from London at the end of the morning peak and departs empty for the carriage sidings where it will remain until the start of the evening rush hour. Twenty months later the station would be closed and the last of the SUBs withdrawn from service. *Alex Dasi-Sutton*

Similarly, only a few electrified lengths of line lacking stations were taken out of use in this period. Of these, three had originally been included in the Reading line scheme which commenced operation from 1st January 1939 and were closed within a year of each other. Virginia Water west curve (directly connecting Longcross and Chertsey) and Staines High Street curve (Egham – Sunnymeads) were two short spurs taken out of service from 27th July 1964 and 22nd March 1965 respectively, but neither had ever had a regular timetabled service since electrification, being used solely for ECS and specials, the latter including wartime troop trains between Portsmouth and Windsor. The spur between Sturt Lane Junction and Frimley Junction, used at one time by an infrequent and roundabout timetabled service between Waterloo and Woking via Ascot (mentioned in Chapter 1), was closed from 7th September 1964, but it is doubtful whether redundant conductor rails on the slow lines between Pirbright Junction and Sturt Lane Junction were ever removed, as this section was soon to be incorporated in the Bournemouth electrification scheme. Finally, the Eastbourne avoiding chord between Polegate and Stone Cross was closed from 6th January 1969. Electrified in 1935 this had been used, mainly during business and holiday peak periods, by trains between London and Hastings via Lewes, not calling at Eastbourne. For some years afterwards it was retained, de-electrified and connected only at the eastern end for training permanent way staff and testing track machines, but was lifted in 1984.

DEVELOPMENTS IN AND AROUND THE LONDON TERMINI

Much of the reconstruction work carried out on the Southern Region in the 1948-83 period involved its London termini and their approaches. All had suffered during World War Two to a greater or lesser extent, but it was some years before finance became available for necessary modernisation and rebuilding. This section covers the work carried out on these stations and others in the inner area (to a distance of roughly ten miles out), and also major signalling and track layout changes on their approaches, many of which took place in conjunction with redevelopment of the stations. Only Waterloo, arguably the most modern of the SR's London termini, remained relatively untouched, other than construction of a large new ticket office which opened on 6th December 1970.

The first important resignalling scheme actually carried out under the auspices of the Southern Region following nationalisation covered the Central section main lines in the London area. Routes covered were those from Bricklayers Arms Junction (south of London Bridge) and Battersea Park to East Croydon and Coulsdon North, and also between Tulse Hill and the Streatham Junctions complex. Although this scheme was actually planned in the immediate post-war years, work did not commence until 1949 on replacing the existing Sykes 'lock-and-block' mechanical signalling on these routes. The new signals were all four-aspect automatic or semi-automatic colour lights, spaced to allow a 2½-minute headway. Many were mounted on distinctive curved re-inforced-concrete brackets, characteristic of this scheme. Eleven new signal boxes, equipped with miniature lever

frames, replaced 32 manual boxes, although a small number of the latter were retained for occasional access to goods sidings, etc. With the exception of Clapham Junction 'B', built to a squarer pattern, all were in the pre-war SR 'glass-house' style in brick with radiused corners and flat roofs.

The new signalling was brought into service in five separate stages, I-V, between 1950 and 1955. Stage I covered the Bricklayers Arms Junction – Norwood Junction section, including three new signal boxes, and came into operation on 8th October 1950. The Streatham Junction – Selhurst section, on which some existing pre-war colour light signals were also replaced, formed Stage II and was operational from 5th October 1952, followed by Stage III, which included Battersea Park – Streatham Common and Tulse Hill – Streatham South Junction plus the Streatham North Junction – Streatham South Junction spurs a week later. On these sections a further three new boxes were provided. Streatham Junction box was perched high on the embankment adjacent to the South Junction, and also controlled access to the extensive Eardley carriage sidings. Stage IV covered the complex junctions in the Selhurst – Norwood Junction – Windmill Bridge Junction triangle, controlled from two new boxes, and came into use on 21st March 1954. Finally, resignalling of the Windmill Bridge Junction – East Croydon – Coulsdon North lines, Stage V, was completed on 8th May 1955, with three new boxes. This final stage connected with the existing 1932 signalling to Brighton, so at long last trains between Victoria or London Bridge and Brighton were signalled by colour lights throughout. As will be seen, the 1950-55 installations were destined to have a relatively short life.

Cannon Street was the first SR London terminus on which rebuilding started in the post-nationalisation period although, for various external reasons, work was to drag on for more than a decade. The track rearragements and platform extensions carried out in 1957 for the 'ten car scheme' were only part of a £1.25 million plan for reconstruction. The iron skeleton of the overall roof, left weakened and without glazing after the blitz, was dismantled in 1958 and the original frontage hotel (by then offices known as *Southern House*), condemned. Ambitious plans for complete redevelopment were rejected by the City Corporation, but two featureless office blocks around the station were completed in 1962-65. A new rubber-floored upper concourse at platform level, sheltering under a concrete raft, was ready in 1964, and in the same year rebuilding of a bridge under the platforms to allow road-widening saw crude umbrella canopies erected on the platform ends. The surviving outer walls were demolished and replaced by glass screens, leaving only a short section on either side, each with its distinctive turret facing the Thames. It was not until 1973 that work was finally completed with a new lower concourse and frontage in connection with the widening of Cannon Street itself and reconstruction of the Underground station beneath. Shortly afterwards the tracks into Cannon Street station were once more rearranged and resignalled in connection with 'Operation London Bridge' mentioned later, while between 1977 and 1983 extensive (and expensive) repairs were carried out to the river bridge carrying its approaches.

Taking next the former LCDR City termini, reconstruction commenced at Holborn Viaduct in 1963, when the bomb-damaged and derelict remains of the original frontage were demolished and replaced by a 250ft wide ten-storey office block, again in the characterless style of its time, incorporating railway facilities on the ground and first floors. Subsequently, the dilapidated wooden train shed was replaced by umbrella canopies on Platforms 1, 4 and 5, the only ones served by passenger trains, in the spring of 1967. The disused former parcels platforms 2 and 3 were removed in 1973 and the three passenger platforms, now renumbered 1-3, extended slightly at the concourse end and given new barriers. Rebuilding of the almost adjacent Blackfriars, also still carrying souvenirs of the blitz, followed in 1971-79. A new office building, incorporating the station booking hall and concourse accessed by escalators from street-level, was completed by 1977 as part of the complete redevelopment of the surrounding site, while the platforms and overall roof were reconstructed.

During the same period, considerable track and infrastructure rationalisation took place in the area, including closure and removal of the Metropolitan City Widened Lines connection and of the single remaining track over the original 1864 Thames bridge in 1971. Demolition of the former Ludgate Hill island platform (closed in 1929 and never served by electric trains) followed early in 1973. A year later, running lines between Blackfriars and Holborn Viaduct had been reduced to two. At the same time, control of remaining signalling was concentrated on Blackfriars signalbox, enabling Holborn Viaduct box to close. Resignalling as part of the Victoria Area Resignalling Scheme (see page 83) followed, culminating in transfer of control to the new Victoria Signalling Centre from February 1982.

At the start of the 1970s London Bridge also continued to display evidence of wartime damage, while signalling equipment installed for the suburban electrification schemes had reached the end of its useful life, and the track layout through the station constituted a bottleneck detrimental to the smooth operation of services in the peaks. Work commenced in 1972 on a £23.5 million scheme to reconstruct the station and to modernise track layouts and signalling in the area. Dubbed 'Operation London Bridge', it was to be funded partly by rents from a new office block, *Southwark Towers*, erected as part of the rebuilding. The number of platforms was reduced by removal of the former Nos 20-22 on the Central side and the demolition of an island in the 'low-level' part sandwiched between the Central side overall roof and the high-level South Eastern platforms. The latter alteration allowed the installation of an additional Up loop, without platform, for Charing Cross-bound services. Following these changes, platforms 1-6 were through island platforms on the SE side and the remainder up to 16 terminal bays on the Central side, some of which were lengthened. A new totally-enclosed 30ft wide tubular footbridge connected all platforms, opened in December 1974, and a new subway connected the Waterloo end of the SE platforms with the station entrance adjacent to a new booking office. Tenants occupied *Southwark Towers* from November 1975 and the reconstructed station was officially opened by the Bishop of Southwark in December 1978, although not all work was completed until late 1979.

London Bridge (Eastern section) as it was in the early 1950s. A Charing Cross to Gillingham train, headed by 4 SUB 4351 carrying headcode 82 instead of the correct V (with bar) letter code, pulls away from platform 2 while commuters wait at platform 3. *Denis Battams*

The major part of the expenditure, some £18 million, was spent on reorganisation and resignalling of the approach lines. Track alterations east of London Bridge segregated the lines serving Waterloo and Cannon Street, thereby easing the Borough Market Junction bottleneck and abolishing its signalbox. The approaches to Cannon Street were remodelled, involving complete closure for a month from 5th August 1974 for the work to take place. At both New Cross and St John's stations the island platforms on the fast lines were demolished. At St John's a new single-line reversible spur, ascending at 1 in 45, was constructed to connect the fast lines to the Nunhead – Lewisham route (Tanners Hill Junction – Lewisham Vale Junction), coming into use on 3rd April 1976. Through New Cross an additional through line was laid and the platforms altered to provide a Down side platform (with a bay for LT East London Line trains) and an island; these alterations, together with reconstruction of the buildings, were completed by August 1975. A new signal box to control a wide area around London Bridge, of typically austere 1970s external design, was erected on the former approaches to platforms 20-22 at the southern edge of the station site. The

Central panel took over control of signalling as far out as Anerley, East Dulwich and Clapham from 20th July 1975, while the Eastern panel controlled the Mid-Kent line all the way to Hayes from 28th September 1975, to Woolwich Arsenal from 18th January 1976 and to Hither Green two days later. Lines through London Bridge were totally closed over Easter 1976 to allow the new layout at Borough Market Junction to be installed and to bring the rest of the signalling in the area concerned under control of the new box, full commissioning being completed from 20th April. Between New Cross Gate and Anerley, the new signalling superseded the 1950-55 installation.

The South Eastern side of London Bridge station in May 1978. The previous open footbridge has been replaced by an enclosed walkway and circulating area. The tower block viewpoint for this scene was demolished in 2009 and work underway in 2010 would change the vista again.

Victoria station also remained largely unaltered through the 1950s and 60s, although internal rearrangement and/or rebuilding of some passenger facilities took place, and platforms were extended on the Eastern side in connection with the Kent Coast electrification. One sign of the times was the appearance of an air terminal for British United Airways, opened in May 1962 to provide facilities for air travellers patronising the dedicated trains serving Gatwick Airport. This 13,400 square-foot steel-and-glass building was carried on 15ft stilts inside the train-shed across the northern end of Central section Platforms 15-17, accessed by escalators, stairs and a footbridge.

While little changed inside the station itself, however, extensive work was carried out on the approaches to Victoria during the 1960s. Firstly, Grosvenor Bridge was entirely replaced between mid 1963 and late 1967, the original structures being totally life-expired. The bridge was mostly rebuilt one track at a time, enabling the weekday service of approximately 1,000 trains to carry on almost uninterrupted. Following removal of the track and original structures, replacement prefabricated half-arch and decking sections were towed up the Thames and craned into position on previously prepared foundations, after which the track and electrical fixtures were restored. The new Grosvenor Bridge consisted of four 164ft spans, carried ten tracks (one more than previously), and was designed to withstand twice the load of its predecessor. Following this, work to replace the 1867 iron and steel bridges which carried three of the four 'high level' Central division approach lines over the South Western main line between Pouparts Junction and Battersea Park took place between June 1968 and September 1969. Timetable alterations diverted many services to other termini, and Platforms 16 and 17 at Clapham Junction were electrified in September 1968 to enable some peak-hour suburban services to start or terminate there. Severe restrictions on trains using the route were imposed while reconstruction was taking place, including a speed limit of 15mph. A significant proportion of the work was completed during a total block over the weekend of 18th-22nd April 1969 when most trains, including the *Brighton Belle*, were diverted into and out of London Bridge.

Various grandiose plans for total redevelopment of the Victoria station complex were mooted during this period, but nothing got under way until the mid 1970s. A new glass and stainless steel booking office for the whole station, with fourteen windows, was opened on the Central side concourse on 16th May 1976, while the external fabric of the station was cleaned and renovated in 1979-80. By the end of 1979 the concourse area had been considerably increased by moving the barrier line of platforms 10-13 south by 60ft to line up with platform 9. A new 'Gatwick Rail-Air Reception Centre' was built adjacent to platform 13 (from which most Gatwick trains departed) in 1980, and in the same year platforms 16-17 were renumbered 18-19 in anticipation of the addition of two new platforms on the site of the cab road between Platforms 15 and 16. (These did not come into use until 1987.) A 'Sealink Travel and Car Ferry Centre' opened alongside platform 2 in 1980. Part of this subsequently became offices

for the *Venice Simplon Orient Express* operation, whose train of restored Pullmans (including *Audrey* from the erstwhile *Brighton Belle* and several from the *Golden Arrow*) commenced regular operation out of Victoria in 1982. Office development over the station site was finally under way by 1983, commencing with the six-storey *Victoria Plaza* building, erected on a concrete raft over Platforms 14-19 as far as Eccleston Bridge. To provide room for this the 1962 air terminal had to be dismantled, and after completion the raft gave the platforms a distinctly subterranean atmosphere.

Running concurrently with the redevelopment of Victoria station itself was a vast scheme covering modernisation of the lines serving it, publicised as 'Operation Victoria'. This scheme was authorised in 1978 and included the resignalling and remodelling of a total of 112 route miles (270 track miles) at an estimated cost of £35 million. All were to be controlled centrally from Victoria Signalling Centre (referred to as Victoria SC), a forbidding concrete-clad angular structure actually located on the Down side at Falcon Lane, north of Clapham Junction station. The Central division main line was included as far as Norbury, together with routes to Kensington Olympia, Wimbledon via Sutton, Epsom, Epsom Downs, West Croydon and Crystal Palace. South Eastern division lines as far out as Chislehurst Junction, Otford and Longfield were included, and also the Holborn Viaduct to Herne Hill section. Apart from the abolition of a significant number of existing signal boxes, including some built for the previous 1950-55 resignalling (see above), the scheme saw the replacement of remaining pockets of semaphore signalling in the London area of the SR.

Between November 1980 and the end of the period covered (September 1983), the new Victoria SC gradually took over control of the various routes, starting with the Victoria – Battersea Park – Balham section. Significant conversions from semaphores to multiple-aspect colour lights included Wimbledon to Sutton via St Helier and to West Croydon via Mitcham Junction (March 1982) and Sutton to Cheam/Epsom Downs (September 1982). In all cases level crossings at locations such as Eastfields crossing (Streatham) and Dundonald Road (Wimbledon) were supervised from Victoria SC using VDUs. Following destruction of Epsom Downs signal box by fire in November 1981, the branch from Sutton had been worked as a self-contained shuttle on the Down line. It remained single beyond a point between Sutton and Belmont after through trains were reinstated with resignalling ten months later, only one platform remaining at each of the three branch stations.

Other stations in the inner London area were also rebuilt in the 1948-83 period. At Balham, the hazardous arrangement of a narrow wooden platform either side of the Down slow line, (the latter also serving the Up slow) was replaced by a single concrete island platform serving both lines. The seldom-used island between the fast lines was also rebuilt in concrete, both new platforms also coming into use in March 1954, roughly concurrent with resignalling. New buildings and canopies on the slow platform, in the 'Kent Coast' style adopted by the SR at this time, were completed by 1957. The dilapidated condition of Peckham Rye resulted in a thorough rebuilding at platform level in 1960-61, when the Catford loop platforms were reconstructed in concrete and given new buildings, while a new island and its buildings replaced the undulating wooden side platforms on the South London line side. Space for this latter was already extant between the tracks, having formerly been occupied by the Up main and its platform, abolished in 1933. At Queen's Road (Peckham), a substantial new brick and concrete island platform, with ticket office and shelter, replaced the worn-out and vandalised timber side platforms from 22nd September 1974. As at nearby Peckham Rye, it was possible to use the existing wide space between the tracks where a third line had once been.

OTHER MISCELLANEOUS DEVELOPMENTS: SIGNALLING, TRACK, DEPOTS AND STATIONS

Outside the immediate central area, most SR electrified routes in both suburban and main line areas had retained mechanical signalling on electrification and, as related in Volume 1, even the two new lines (Wimbledon – Sutton and the Chessington branch) were given semaphores. From the late 1950s onwards these routes were progressively resignalled with multiple-aspect colour lights. This coincidentally enabled a reduction in the number of signalboxes (some still of pre-Grouping origin), with consequent staff savings. As part of this process, many traditional hand-operated level crossing gates were superseded by motorised lifting barriers, which could in many cases be supervised from a remote location or even controlled entirely automatically by track circuit. On the south coast, economies were extracted by singling the Seaford branch beyond Newhaven Harbour from July 1973, although the terminus remained fully-signalled with two platforms and a berthing siding.

A number of the larger schemes are worth mentioning individually. On the South Western division, the Guildford area out to Effingham Junction, Ash, Shalford and Milford was resignalled in 1965-66, a new signalbox of CLASP pattern (similar to those at Basingstoke and Eastleigh) being provided on the Up side at Guildford and a fringe box at Ash. In 1970 the main line between Surbiton and Woking, up to that time one of the busiest on the whole of BR still regulated by semaphores, was resignalled, involving replacement of the 1937 'glasshouse' signalbox at Surbiton with yet another CLASP structure. A further large scheme undertaken in 1973-74 covered the Windsor Lines, taking in Richmond – Earley, the Hounslow loop, Staines – Windsor, Ascot – Frimley, Twickenham – New Malden and the Shepperton branch. Known as the 'Feltham Area Resignalling Scheme', all routes were re-equipped with two, three or four-aspect (as appropriate) signals, starting with Bracknell – Earley on 4th February 1973. A new centralised electrically-operated signalbox to control the entire area opened at Feltham on 8th September 1974, and the scheme was completed with conversion of New Malden – Richmond and the Shepperton branch from the following 10th November.

On the Central division, the original 1932 colour light signalling installation between Coulsdon and Brighton had reached the end of its useful life by the late 1970s. A scheme to resignal and remodel the Brighton main line and some associated sections, named 'Operation New Look' was therefore also authorised in 1978. Replacement took on a new urgency following a serious accident at Patcham (between Hassocks and Preston Park) that December, when corroded components caused a signal to show no aspect, resulting in a collision between two Down trains which claimed three lives.

The new installation interfaced with the concurrent Victoria scheme at Norbury, and was entirely supervised from a new signalling centre at Three Bridges, a faceless brick fortress erected in 1981 east of the line. New signalling first came into use in March 1982 around Balcombe Tunnel Junction, which was resited half a mile north of its previous location, followed in November by the Earlswood area. Here, the Quarry line was realigned to allow faster speeds and its platforms abolished. The line south to Gatwick was converted in January 1983, followed by Coulsdon North to Redhill (exclusive), initially controlled from a temporary panel in Redhill 'B' box, the following month. As explained in Chapter 1, this latter section had retained semaphores when the Brighton line was electrified in 1932 (although they were not to disappear from the Redhill station area until 1984).

An important aspect of 'Operation New Look' was remodelling of the complex junctions in the triangle bounded by Selhurst, Norwood Junction and Croydon, to reduce conflicting movements and facilitate the introduction of a more frequent Victoria – Gatwick Airport service. The direct Selhurst – Norwood Junction spur was closed in May 1982. Most flat junctions were abolished by reorganising the layout with two new embankments, built using minestone salvaged from Betteshanger Colliery in Kent. The new layout was completed in October 1983.

It is worth noting here that significant lengths of SR electrified route mileage were still controlled by manual semaphores in September 1983, including most of the Mid-Sussex line south from Dorking to Arundel Junction, and the coastal routes and branches from Brighton to Havant in the west and Ore in the east. The odd pocket even remained in the suburban area, including Woodside – Addiscombe. Lines in Kent that were not resignalled as part of their electrification in 1959-62 also retained their semaphores in 1983.

To cover changes to depot facilities next, the antiquated electrical overhaul and repair shops at Peckham Rye and Durnsford Road, originally dating from 1909 and 1915 respectively, were closed for heavy maintenance purposes in 1958, being replaced that year by a new facility at Selhurst. It is thought that Peckham Rye sidings and sheds survived for stock berthing purposes until April 1967 when the site was taken out of use, the buildings being demolished two years later. In 1974 an entirely new inspection shed and berthing sidings complex was opened at East Wimbledon, on roughly the same site as the former LSWR power station, to provide a base for the South Western division's suburban fleet. The redundant LSWR sheds were removed at about this time and replaced by new sidings as part of this facility. In 1979 it became the first SR depot to receive new rolling stock with sliding doors (the class 508 units), and in connection with this it was necessary to modify the tracks inside the sheds to provide side-pits, allowing access to under-body equipment. Similar new inspection sheds were erected at Selhurst Depot on the site of the former Tennison Road sidings (actually nearer to Norwood Junction) in 1982. Elsewhere, the number of berthing and carriage cleaning sidings at outlying stations was gradually reduced. A new four-track berthing facility at Staines, which came into use in April 1974, replaced existing electrified sidings at Hounslow and Chertsey.

Apart from those already described, a number of other major station reconstructions and resitings took place in the 1948-83 period. Those dealt with up to 1962 were generally given new buildings in the BR style of the time as also widely used for the Kent Coast electrification, featuring plain brick elevations, large windows, decorative panels in pastel shades, and flat sloping canopies. Hot-cathode fluorescent lighting, whose covers were printed with the station name, was a novel feature. As in the pre-war era, much use was made of prefabricated cast concrete components for platforms, fencing and footbridges where appropriate.

In the suburban area, the resited station at Twickenham, on which work had started in 1939, was finally opened on 28th March 1954. Its layout, consisting of an island serving Up and Down main lines, a side platform serving an Up loop and two London-facing bays for Rugby football ground traffic, was slightly revised from what had originally been intended (Volume 1 refers). The peak-hour entrance footbridge was retrieved from London's South Bank, having been built there for the Festival of Britain by the Royal Engineers. For the first few years the main station building was a temporary structure.

On the main lines, the former Gatwick Racecourse station on the Brighton line was rebuilt and resignalled in readiness to serve the adjacent Gatwick Airport, which had been designated the second London airport and was therefore greatly enlarged to the north of its 1935 location, taking over the racecourse site. Renamed Gatwick Airport, all platforms were raised in height and resurfaced, and an additional Up loop (Platform 1) was added on the west side. New platform buildings and canopies, together with a substantial covered footbridge leading straight into the airport terminal building, were also added. It opened in its new guise on 28th May 1958 (when, as explained above, the previous 1935 station closed), and from the following 9th June a dedicated half-hourly Airport service to and from Victoria was introduced, attached to or detached from Mid-Sussex line stopping train in the Up local platform (No.2), made reversible. Further development at Gatwick Airport station took place in 1981, when a mezzanine floor was built across the platforms, incorporating a booking office, shops and escalators down to the main London-bound island Platform 1 and 2, opening on 1st June.

Raised platforms with new edging, a covered footbridge with luggage lifts, 'umbrella' platform canopies and hot-cathode fluorescent lighting units incorporating the station name were all features of the second Gatwick Airport station when opened in 1958. The signal box and substation, however, remained from the station's previous incarnation. Looking rather self-conscious with its newly-applied full yellow ends, 4 LAV 2950 departs with the 9.45pm Victoria – Brighton stopping service on an overcast 15th July 1967. *John Scrace*

The rebuilding of Chichester was unfinished business from the 1938 Mid-Sussex electrification, and was commenced in 1957 as part of the Modernisation Plan. Both platforms were lengthened, widened and raised to standard height, a new covered footbridge erected and an imposing new ticket hall provided on the Up side. Work was completed in 1961.

The 1960s were the decade of Beeching and British Rail. Other than on Kent Coast phase II and the Bournemouth line, the financial climate of the time meant that few stations were rebuilt or enlarged. At Crawley, a resited station to serve the New Town was constructed slightly to the east of the previous one, opening on 28th July 1968. Once more the booking hall, situated on the Up side, formed the ground floor of a substantial office block.

Elsewhere, staff were removed (sometimes completely) from many stations in the quest for economies which, together with a lack of maintenance, led to a significant deterioration in their condition. Between 1966 and 1973 the SR proceeded to replace some of the most dilapidated or war-damaged Victorian station buildings by cheap and ugly prefabricated CLASP structures, already used for new signalboxes since 1964. CLASP (Consortium of Local Authorities Special Project) structures were basically steel-framed boxes clad with concrete panels and plate glass, originally designed for school buildings. Stations to receive them included Sunbury (1966), Belmont, Forest Hill, Hampton Wick (all 1968), Ashtead (1969), Belmont (1970), Kidbrooke and Longfield (1971), Sunningdale, West Byfleet, Lower Sydenham (all 1972), Hassocks and Virginia Water (1972-73). They were set off on the platform side by an inadequate canopy supported on squared-off wooden posts, and in most cases platform waiting shelters were also renewed in matching style. Some stations, including Ashtead and Forest Hill, were also given new prefabricated concrete footbridges, of less substantial appearance than the previous ubiquitous SR version. In the case of Hampton Wick, situated on a high embankment site on the opposite bank of the Thames to Kingston, the platforms were also replaced in similar austere style. In succeeding years CLASP structures wore badly and suffered from escalating vandalism, presenting an increasingly unkempt and unwelcoming face to the prospective traveller.

Later station reconstructions carried out through the 1970s and 80s were mostly less brutal. After Maze Hill booking hall was destroyed by fire in 1971 it was replaced by a striking glass-walled 'box' in June 1972, only arguably more appealing than the contemporary CLASP structures. A new feature was the electrically-operated ticket barrier. Liss, Chelsfield and Elmers End were provided with similar cubic structures in 1973, 1977 and 1978 repectively. In 1972 a new brick booking office at Sheerness-on-Sea replaced the previous LCDR wooden building, badly damaged in an accident the previous year. All buildings were replaced at Ash Vale in 1972-74, in a complex operation that involved the temporary shoring-up of the high embankment on which the station was located. An attractive new entrance building in brick was provided on the Up side, but the platform waiting shelters were of the crude pattern developed to go with CLASP structures. The congested station at Dartford was rebuilt with two island platforms (replacing one island and a single-sided platform), a covered footbridge and replacement buildings on the Up side, the new facilities coming into use on 24th August 1974.

A few later reconstructions were funded by office development on or adjacent to the station site. At Camberley, a new single-storey booking office was constructed as an adjunct to a three-storey office and showroom block erected on former railway land in 1976-77. A red-brick office block of some architectural pretension replaced the handsome but derelict Victorian station building at Dorking in August 1982, the ground floor being partly given over to railway use, including a spacious booking hall. A similar £2.75 million office development adjacent to the Up platform at Wallington was completed in September 1983, the ground floor once more incorporating the railway booking office and other facilities.

Incredibly, only one station on an entirely new site was opened on the electrified SR network between 1948 and 1983. This was Moulsecoomb, situated between London Road (Brighton) and Falmer, convenient for local housing and various further education establishments in the area. Construction work commenced at the end of October 1979 and the new station opened its doors to passengers on 12th May 1980, although a formal ceremony (at which the BR Chairman, Sir Peter Parker, officiated) did not take place until 10th June. The partially staggered platforms were connected by a concrete footbridge. Accommodation comprised a simple single-storey brick building including ticket office, staff facilities and waiting room on the Up (Brighton) platform, and a simple shelter on the Down side.

It has been mentioned earlier how successive British governments after 1948 favoured road construction, and during the period under discussion a network of motorways had been put in place across the UK. In the second half of the 1970s, construction of the M25 London orbital motorway was in hand. The proposed route of this road crossed the SR line between Virginia Water and Chertsey at the awkward angle of 28 degrees, necessitating the construction of a skew bridge of unusual construction to carry the railway over it. Known as the Lyne Bridge, this impressive new structure was mainly concrete, and consisted of a decking suspended from two concrete pylons, located on the motorway central reservation, by stressed steel cable stays. Work started in June 1976 when a deviation around the construction site came into use, and the line was reinstated back to its former alignment over the completed new bridge in February 1979. One of the most interesting civil engineering structures built on the SR in the post-nationalisation era, it is doubtless hardly noticed by the streams of traffic passing underneath following opening of the motorway in 1980.

Finally, the 1965 restyling of the nationalised railway as 'British Rail', referred to elsewhere, led to the proliferation of new station signs across the SR network from about mid-1966, together with the loss of green as the long-standing regional colour. A concerted effort to re-sign station frontages, a surprising number of which still proudly proclaimed 'Southern Railway', also took place from about this time. With the new signs went a black and white colour scheme for many buildings, including the cheap and nasty new CLASP structures mentioned above. While the new platform name-boards consisted of the regulation sans-serif lettering in black on a white background in a style common to the whole of BR, the majority were of a design at first unique to the SR. This comprised a board supported by poles at either end, often straddling a lamp-post and sometimes incorporating an advertisement or timetable board underneath. The previous green enamel 'sausage' (or remaining pre-1948 'bullseye') signs mounted on lamp-posts or under canopies, together with their associated larger green running-in boards at platform ends, were gradually superseded, unsurprisingly remaining longest at some of the least important stations. The last two stations to retain genuine Southern Railway bullseyes are thought to be Bingham Road and Plumstead, both replaced in about September 1980, while the last with post-1948 sausage totems were Stone Crossing and Polegate, which lost them towards the end of 1981.

TRAIN SERVICES AND TIMETABLES

The new improved timetables for the Kent Coast and Bournemouth electrification schemes, based firmly on the pre-war Southern Railway model, have been outlined earlier in this chapter. Here, it is only intended to give a basic outline of other major developments in the 1948-83 period.

The first few years of nationalisation saw a continuation of the programme started before 1948 to restore wartime cuts, so that by the middle of the 1950s virtually the entire pre-war service was operating, with only minor differences. The first real changes came from 9th June 1958, when most Saturday morning and lunchtime peak-hour services were withdrawn, reflecting the post-war decline in Saturday office-opening. The few remaining extra mid-day trains on Saturdays were withdrawn from 4th May 1970. From 15th September 1958 early morning, off peak and Sunday services on the suburban lines were thinned out, mostly from a twenty-minute interval to half hourly, in an attempt to effect economies in the face of declining traffic and to fund a staff pay award. Alterations to Maidstone and Gillingham line services came with their integration into phases I and II of the Kent Coast electrification in 1959-62, for which lavish regular-interval timetables were introduced. Over the next few years off-peak suburban services were further pruned, particularly on Sundays, when a significant number of stations was closed.

Into the 1960s peak-hour patronage from the outer suburbs and beyond continued to increase, but declined from many inner London suburban stations. Peak period suburban services were therefore reduced, mainly on the Central and South Western divisions. The Central division in particular lost peak hour traffic from most of its inner suburban stations from the 1950s onwards. By the middle of the decade, four-coach peak hour trains were being run on some services. Taking the period 16.30 to 18.30, departures from London Bridge were reduced from 31 to 21 via New Cross Gate and Forest Hill, from 24 to sixteen via Tulse Hill and from six to four in each direction on the South London line. From Victoria the services via Streatham Hill were reduced from thirteen to eight.

On the South Western division, the Kingston/Richmond loop lost four of its eight trains, the Hampton Court branch lost one, the Epsom line lost three of its fifteen (but in this case trains beyond Epsom were increased from nine to eleven). The only two trains from Waterloo to Virginia Water via Weybridge were withdrawn. The Windsor/Chertsey via Staines service was reduced from eight to six, and Chertsey lost its through service from Waterloo. In contrast, the Reading/Camberley line service increased from six trains to eleven.

On the South Eastern division, the emphasis moved from the ex-LCDR 'Chatham' lines (from 24 down to sixteen) and the Mid-Kent line (nineteen down to eleven) to the Bexleyheath line (up from twelve to sixteen), the Dartford loop (up from fifteen to nineteen) and the Orpington/Sevenoaks line (up from nine to seventeen).

The result of traffic growth overall was greater over-crowding in the peaks, while off-peak and evening usage continued to decline on many lines in the face of increasing car ownership and home entertainment. To take account of these trends, the monumental task of entirely rewriting the Southern Region timetable, much of which had effectively been 'set in stone' since electrification before World War Two, was embarked upon. Apart from the census of commuter trains, plus additional counts undertaken over a complete week in summer and winter, statistical information on travel patterns was gathered from the results of a passenger survey undertaken on 27th May 1964, in which half a million questionnaire forms were distributed and no less than 52% returned. Additionally, consultants were employed to consider future traffic trends (the effects of Crawley New Town and Gatwick Airport, for example). The chief aims of the time-table planners were to provide more seats in the peaks and to more closely match the service to demand at other times. Additionally, as explained earlier, some changes suggested in the Beeching Report, such as withdrawal of the through Sheerness – Dover stopping trains and thinning-out of the Brighton – Ore coastal service, were incorporated.

While it was basically intended to run the new timetables without extra resources, a modest £500,000 was spent on judicious alterations in the London area to facilitate the flow of trains, particularly into London in the morning rush-hour, and to aid disposal of empty stock more smoothly. These included new sidings for off-peak berthing at Blackfriars and Cannon Street, a crossover at Kent House and central reversing siding east of Sidcup, signalling modifications at London Bridge and Cannon Street, and changes in Clapham Yard where two additional sidings were electrified and others were connected directly to the Down Windsor local lines. No new rolling stock was provided, and it was therefore necessary to reduce some lesser used services in order to release stock for extra trains on other lines. As related in Chapter 5, in order to operate the planned summer Kent Coast timetable, remaining 1932/35 vintage Brighton express stock (the ten 6 CORs, previously spare on the Central division) were transferred to the South Eastern, a move unpopular with staff and passengers who had seen the back of similar Maunsell steam stock only a few years previously!

The BR station building at Liss on the Portsmouth Direct line, built in 1973 to a simple 'cubist' architectural style with considerable use of glass. Very much a product of its time, it was arguably only a minor advance on crude CLASP structures. Similar buildings were provided at Maze Hill, Chelsfield and Elmers End. *BR Southern Region Official*

6 COR 3049, one of ten units reformed from the best former Brighton line PUL and PAN vehicles in 1966, leads a twelve-car formation emerging from Penge tunnel with a Stewarts Lane – Ramsgate crew training trip in early March 1967. This was in preparation for their use on certain peak and relief Kent Coast services with the introduction of the completely rewritten SR timetable from 10th July of that year. The roof-board brackets were still in situ at this stage, but were later removed due to clearance problems. *Brian Stephenson*

The new Southern Region timetables finally came into effect on 10th July 1967, concurrent with inauguration of the Bournemouth electrification and abolition of steam from the Region. Excluding the Bournemouth line, it had proved possible to provide a total of fifty additional services, with approximately 28,000 seats, into the London termini in the morning peak. More trains also worked in the evening rush hour, but this was less concentrated, and overcrowding was consequently less of a problem. On the South Eastern division, the mornings saw as many as seven extra main line and 21 additional suburban services, while in the busiest hour no fewer than sixty trains passed through Borough Market Junction. To make this possible, some trains through Platform 7 at London Bridge did not stop. A number of suburban services started from what had previously been intermediate points on routes, such as Bellingham, Catford or Kent House, and extra trains ran to Charing Cross to cater for the continuing movement of offices from the City to the West End. On the Central division, six more main line trains and five additional suburban services arrived in London in the morning peak, including extra stopping services between East Croydon and Victoria. Services to London Bridge were thinned throughout the day to meet decreasing demand, and the little-used London Bridge – Tulse Hill – Victoria service (a relic of *Elevated Electric* days) abandoned. In the evening, the previously non-stop 17.00 London Bridge – Brighton (the erstwhile *City Limited*) had calls inserted at Hassocks and Preston Park. On the South Western division, Waterloo was served by four extra main line and seven more suburban services in the morning peak.

Certain aspects of the 1967 SR timetable were soon found to be over-ambitious and unworkable, particularly on the South Eastern, and the resulting disorganisation led to the usual passenger complaints and vitriolic Press attacks. It quickly proved necessary to excise or retime a few services, a total of 56 changes being made through the summer and a further 34 from October 1967. However, apart from the 1974 introduction of hourly Waterloo – Weymouth expresses and the 1976 economy-led cuts to suburban services, both of which have been mentioned already, the basic outline of the 1967 timetable then remained in place until 1978, other than relatively minor evolutionary alterations. One change worth mentioning was the withdrawal of off-peak suburban services between Dorking and Horsham from 5th May 1969, leading to closure of Holmwood, Ockley and Warnham stations between the rush hours. A second change, not apparent from public timetables, was a further reduction in peak period suburban train lengths on the Central division, from eight coaches to four.

In May 1978, Central division main line services were reorganised to take account of the increasing importance of Croydon and Gatwick Airport as commercial centres. Brighton line services, in particular, were significantly re-arranged. Thus (horror of horrors), a call at East Croydon was inserted into the schedule of the previously non-stop hourly expresses between Victoria and Brighton, while off-peak mid-Sussex services were diverted to serve East Croydon and Gatwick Airport rather than Sutton and Dorking. (A

residual peak-hour service via Dorking was continued until 1984.) In replacement, the hourly suburban services through the day between Victoria and Dorking were extended non-stop to Horsham. This coincidentally often provided the interesting phenomenon of 4 SUB units rattling along at (almost) express speeds along this section.

The final timetable changes to take place in this period were the major cuts to services which took effect from 1st June 1981, with many more weekend and late evening station closures. This was stated to be necessary due to the economic recession and BR's poor financial situation at the time.

East Wimbledon depot, completed in 1974 on the site of the former LSWR Durnsford Road power station. Home base for the South Western division's suburban fleet, members of 4 SUB, 2 EPB, 4 CIG and 4 VEP classes are visible in this view at the time of opening.

CHAPTER 4: FIRST GENERATION SEMI-FAST ROLLING STOCK 1932-71

For semi-fast and local stopping services on the coastal and other longer distance lines electrified by the Southern Railway between 1932 and 1939, a total of 364 electric multiple units were provided. The first to be designed and delivered were the 4 LAV units for the Brighton main line, these also being the first SR electric units of four-coach formation. All other semi-fast units, including the 2 NOL, 2 BIL and 2 HAL types, had two coaches, giving greater flexibility in possible train lengths. Virtually all were built between 1931 and 1940, the only exceptions being seven more 2 HAL units built after 1945 to make good war losses. In addition, five new driving trailers were constructed between 1950 and 1954 (some on reclaimed underframes) to restore numbers following a spate of accidents. With the exception of the 2 NOLs, which made use of rebuilt LSWR steam stock bodies in the same manner as most of the pre-war suburban stock (see Volume 1), all the vehicles for these types were built new. Throughout this period, which included the 1937 retirement of R.E.L. Maunsell and his replacement as SR Chief Mechanical Engineer by O.V.S. Bulleid, L. Lynes remained responsible for detailed carriage design. Below underframe level, and electrically, the various units described here were almost identical in design and equipment to the contemporary suburban stock with which they could work in multiple, although such workings were not commonplace until after 1945.

Suburban electric units and trailer sets had been described in working timetable appendices and other departmental documents simply as '2' or '3', with train formations shown only by the number of carriages – e.g. '8'. The Southern's main line electric stock introduced the concept of combined digit and letter codes for multiple unit types, for example 4 LAV, 5 BEL, 6 CIT etc. These codes had to be suitable for telegraph use and so had a maximum of five characters, including any digits. Complete trains would be described using the letter part of the code preceded by the total number of vehicles in the train. Examples were '6 BIL', '8 LAV', '10 BEL', '12 PUL' etc. A twelve-car Portsmouth express comprising a 4 RES between two 4 CORs would be shown as '12 CRC', and a similiar formation but with a 4 BUF would be '12 CBC'. Suburban stock continued to be described solely by digits, and the often-quoted code '3 SUB' was never used for the three-car formations. They simply remained '3' until the last disappeared in 1949. The term 4 SUB is thought to have been coined about 1942, with the introduction of new suburban unit 4101 and the first augmented units 4131/32, and has been almost universally accepted. In Southern

Region Carriage Working Appendices, however, four-car suburban units with air (not electro-pneumatic) braking were described simply as '4' until the late 1960s and possibly until their final withdrawal. Certainly in their last years they were clearly marked 4 SUB on their cab fronts.

Some general comments on livery changes, common to all the rolling stock described, are mentioned here to avoid repetition later, while the painting processes involved were described in Volume 1. Those units delivered up to the end of 1938, that is the 4 LAVs (except 2954/55), 2 NOLs and 2 BILs, were outshopped in the same livery as the suburban stock. The basic colour was dark olive green, lined-out in black and yellow, with white roofs, black inner coach ends and underframes, brown window frames streaked to resemble wood grain, and gilt lettering and numbering, shaded black. Class was indicated by 1 or 3 on the lower door panels. Coach numbers were located at either end just below the cantrail, while the words SOUTHERN RAILWAY appeared centrally also below the cantrail, except on the gangwayed side of corridor vehicles in the LAVs and BILs, where the high windows made it necessary to position them on the waist panel instead. Unit numbers were hand painted in yellow above the headcode panel on the cab ends, in a larger script than the coach numbers. All but the first ten BILs were delivered with lining restricted to the waist only and on the final Reading line batch (2117-2152), delivered after Maunsell's retirement, this had been simplified to two parallel yellow bands, without division into imitation panels. The first 76 2 HAL units, for the 1939 Medway electrification, were the last to be delivered in dark olive, now unlined, with numbering in the same style and positions as before. However, the company name, now shortened to SOUTHERN, was in a revised block sans-serif style, positioned centrally at waist level on all vehicles. The additional HALs and LAVs delivered in 1940 were outshopped in a lighter shade, and it was not until 1942 that units were being repainted on overhaul in the definitive Bulleid green, later termed 'malachite', with shaded chrome-yellow 'sunshine' lettering throughout.

There were initially few livery alterations following nationalisation in 1948, and the post-war 2 HAL units were delivered in plain malachite green, still with 'sunshine' lettering, but no evidence of ownership other than an S prefix (for Southern Region) to the unit number. Some repainted units did however display BRITISH RAILWAYS in the space between the motorman's and luggage doors of motor coaches. By this time, only first class compartments were distinguished externally.

A similar shade of green to that favoured by Bulleid was then officially adopted by BR Southern Region early in 1949 for all electric passenger stock, but with block lettering and numbering in old gold, edged black. Coach numbers, located just below waist height, were initially positioned at the left-hand end, but this was soon changed to the right. They were both prefixed (from 1949) and suffixed (from 1951, with the introduction of BR standard coaching stock) S to denote the operating Region and company of design or origin respectively. Unit numbers were small yellow transfers, and some units or replacement coaches built after 1948 had them prefixed S (eg S 2069). Apart from the post-war HALs, of the stock described here this only concerned the all-steel driving trailer composites built for 2069, 2100, 2133, 2653 and 2700. The BR 'lion on wheel' emblem appeared about midway along motor coach sides below the windows from early 1950, but was at first omitted from some units. The 2 NOLs were all withdrawn in this livery, and it survived on many other units until well into the 1960s. In the BR era, first class compartments were additionally indicated by dark blue FIRST totem transfers on the fixed windows.

The most numerous of the Southern Railway's fleet of electric stock for main line semi-fast and stopping services were the ubiquitous 2 BIL units, constructed between 1934 and 1938 and eventually numbering 152 examples. By now 26 years old but still looking smart and well cared-for in the later BR green with silver/grey roof and yellow warning panels, 2101 has just negotiated Woking Junction leading the 12.27 Waterloo to Portsmouth and Southsea service on 13th September 1964. Roof mounted air horns have replaced the original cab-front whistle. Many BILs were withdrawn in this livery.
Brian Stephenson

From March 1957, the 1949 green began to be superseded by a slightly darker shade on repaint, and the new round BR coaching stock emblem replaced the earlier design. Yellow or cream stripes at cantrail height to further indicate the position of first class accommodation were gradually added from about 1962. Small yellow warning panels on driving ends, designed to make approaching trains more easily seen by those working on the lineside, were progressively applied from November 1963, the SR being somewhat behind other BR Regions in this respect. On two-coach units (BILs and HALs) the motor coaches were also given an inverted black triangle in the yellow patch, directly underneath the head-code panel. This officially indicated 'No Luggage Van at Other End of Unit', giving station staff extra time to move luggage trolleys along the platform to the van end of the train. The application of full yellow ends with black unit numbers followed from late in 1966. All 4 LAVs, and the majority of 2 BIL and 2 HAL units, were withdrawn in green, and only three LAVs ever received the full yellow ends. A significant number of BILs and HALs received the corporate British Rail blue livery, with white lettering and 'double arrow' symbol, from 1967. This, as well as some final green repaints, was initially applied by airless spray to give a semi-matt 'eggshell' finish, but this was found to weather badly and was soon replaced by brush-painting once again.

Internal decor followed a similar pattern to the suburban stock and specific information is given where known. Greater detail regarding the evolution of SR and BR upholstery materials was given in Volume 1 but, to summarise, the LAVs, NOLs and BILs were mostly given green or blue-based 'jazz' moquettes in third class and floral tapestry in firsts when new, although there were exceptions. More austere patterns were introduced with the Medway HALs in 1939, and most other units were given these or their immediate successors during general overhaul, which took place every seven or eight years (with the exception of the NOLs, which followed the suburban ten-year cycle). BR standard designs were introduced in the early 1950s, while some LAVs, BILs and HALs gained yellow/black (non-smoking) or red/black (smoking) horizontal stripes in second class and a squared pattern in firsts on final major overhaul from about 1965.

Regarding smoking and non-smoking indications, the 1931-32 LAVs and the first ten BILs were built with SMOKING etched in the glass of appropriate quarterlights, smoking being forbidden in the few compartments not so marked. As they made use of existing bodywork, the NOLs also had these initially. The remainder of the BILs were delivered with the green NO SMOKING and red SMOKING transfers introduced at the end of 1934, while the HALs were the first new EMUs to have the white NO SMOKING triangles which first came into use at the end of 1938. These triangle transfers became standard and were gradually applied to all stock as appropriate, replacing the earlier indications. The original etched quarterlights disappeared over time as they were replaced by plain glass following breakages, a process accelerated by wartime damage, but several LAV vehicles still had them well into the 1950s. By this time NO SMOKING triangles in BR red had replaced the SR version.

The electric multiple units dealt with in this chapter are generally very well documented, and thus it is possible to chart the progress of virtually every vehicle, although minor accidents and short-term temporary reformations are sometimes ignored in what follows. Unit formation changes during the lifetime of the classes concerned are listed as Tables in the main body of the text, while initial unit formations as delivered are summarised in Appendix 4 at the end of this Volume.

THE 4 LAV UNITS 1931-69

The 33 original 4 LAV units, initially numbered 1921-1953, were constructed at Eastleigh Carriage Works on Lancing underframes for the Brighton line electrification, opened for service as far as Three Bridges and Reigate in May 1932 and throughout from the first day of 1933. The original order, to HO 569 dated 16th May 1930, was for forty units, but this was reduced by seven in June 1931 when the plan to operate an hourly semi-fast service between London and Worthing was abandoned, probably for economic reasons. All or most of the underframes and associated running gear, comprising eighty motor coach frames and eighty trailer frames, had already been constructed by Lancing when this part of the order was cancelled, and some were used instead for additional three-coach London suburban units 1795-1801. (Other trailer frames from this order could have been used for trailer set coaches with converted LSWR bodywork, but there is no clear evidence for this.)

The 4 LAV units were formed of two seven-compartment driving motor third brakes, a trailer composite with five first and four third class compartments, and a side corridor trailer composite with five firsts and three thirds plus a toilet at each end. It was this latter vehicle which significantly distinguished these units from the standard suburban stock supplied up to that time. The trailers were formed so that the first class sections were adjacent at the centre of the unit. Bodywork design followed the then current Maunsell/Lynes main line style, sometimes described as period 3 (of five, Volume 1 refers), and was to SR Restriction 4. This was 9ft wide over body, greater than either the new 1925 or converted suburban stock.

Construction consisted of galvanised steel panels on a teak framework, with deal planked, canvas covered roofs except at the domed ends above the driving cabs, where steel was used. Details included windows inserted from the inside and secured by external wooden fillets, wood-framed door drop-lights held in position by a sprung bar and released using a small leather tab, and ventilator bonnets at the tops of all doors. Total seating capacity of each unit was originally 70 first and 204 third, of which only thirty first and 24 third had access to a lavatory. All coaches were on standard 62ft underframes and were close-coupled using the same centre-buffer arrangements as the suburban units, with rubbing blocks on both motor coaches, centre buffers both ends of the corridor trailer and one of each on the compartment trailer (with the buffer at the third class end). Motor and trailer bogies were also of the usual suburban pattern with wheelbases of 8ft 9in and 8ft respectively. Overall unit length was 256ft 9in.

When new, the first 4 LAV units for the Brighton line electrification were tested in passenger service on the Guildford New line during the first half of 1932. Here, 1934 (2934 from 1937) is seen departing from Oxshott with a Guildford – Waterloo train. It is carrying appropriate suburban letter headcode H and the side destination board reads: EFFINGHAM JN – COBHAM – OXSHOTT – SURBITON – WATERLOO. *Topical Press*

The motor third brakes were to SR carriage diagram number 2106 and had a tare weight of 41 tons. Numbered 10501-66, they were allocated to units in numerical order, in pairs. Their layout consisted of motorman's compartment, guard's van and seven third class compartments, each seating ten passengers. Although the bodywork of the passenger section bulged out at the waist, the sides of the motorman's and guard's compartments were inset and flattened in the same manner as the van area of Maunsell's widest steam stock. Unlike contemporary hauled coaches, however, guard's duckets were not fitted. Instead, these vehicles were equipped with rearward-facing roof periscopes, as recently fitted to the 1925 suburban stock, and these subsequently became standard on wide-bodied main line electric units. Outer end buffers were of the small oval type with thin shanks then standard on suburban stock. Front end layout too was entirely conventional, with a large motorman's windscreen on the nearside and a smaller framed window on the offside which opened outwards to facilitate the changing of headcode stencils. A ventilator bonnet was originally fitted above the headcode panel, but these were removed and plated over on first overhaul. Electrically, the LAV motor coaches were equipped with the same Metrovick electro-magnetic control equipment and type MV 339 traction motors as contemporary suburban EMUs. As on other semi-fast units similarly equipped, the equipment compartment behind the cab was cooled by three large flat rectangular ventilators mounted on the roof.

The compartment side of diagram 2306 side-corridor lavatory composite 12023 in 4 LAV 2943, seen at Redhill on 12th May 1951. These were the only electric vehicles to have a single ventilator bonnet above the lavatory windows, placing the LAV units in Period 3 of Maunsell/Lynes coach design chronology. Note also the SMOKING indications etched into some quarterlights, standard practice when these units were built.
Denis Cullum

The compartment trailers were to diagram 2305 and numbered 11501-33. They weighed 28 tons and were arranged with all the first class compartments at one end. The third class compartments were the same as those in the motor coaches and the firsts seated four passengers each side. The corridor trailers, to dia. 2306 and numbered 12001-33, tared one ton more. They were also arranged with the first class compartments at one end, and a partition across the corridor divided the two classes of accommodation, making it necessary to provide a lavatory at both ends. These were the first Southern Electric vehicles to be given this facility, which featured both hot and cold running water, the former warmed by electric water heaters working at line voltage. The third class compartments in these coaches seated four each side and the firsts three, both being similar in seating and decor to equivalent compartments in the gangwayed express stock described in the following chapter.

Another new feature they shared was the balanced sliding door pairs giving access to each compartment from the side corridor. On the corridor side there was a door opposite each compartment, but intermediate windows were large and reached to the eaves in characteristic Maunsell/Lynes style. The frosted glass lavatory windows were surrounded by a single ventilator bonnet. Trailers of both types were not all allocated to units in strict numerical order. The reason for this was that the first twenty pairs of trailers were built before the motor coaches and then stored in sidings, but in the case of the remainder all four coaches for each unit were built simultaneously.

Although similar in many respects to the suburban stock, internally the LAVs were much superior. One novel feature was the provision of folding intermediate armrests in the non-corridor third class compartments. Then considered to be the height of chic, they enabled the seat to be divided two-one-two to clearly indicate, for instance, a young lady's association (or not) with the gentleman sitting next to her. They were lacking in the corridor thirds, but all had end armrests under the quarterlights. The first class seating had the usual arrangement of individual seat cushions, intermediate folding armrests, headrest padding at the sides, and rugs. Third class seating was upholstered using moquette in one of two green-based 'jazz' styles or a bold dark pattern on a fawn background, all newly-introduced, while the firsts had the usual Saladin floral tapestry. Heaters working at line voltage were fitted under the seats in all compartments, controlled by the guard. First class compartments were approximately 7ft 2in between partitions and third class, 6ft 3in.

The 33 original 4 LAVs were built in two distinct batches. 1921-1940 were formed up and delivered between July and October 1931 as their motor coaches were completed, and the first began trial running early the following year. They were run-in in public service on the Waterloo to Guildford via Cobham line over the next few months, and it is reported that they also saw use on the Wimbledon to Waterloo via East Putney rush-hour service. As mentioned above, the four vehicles for each of the remaining thirteen units were built simultaneously and these, numbered 1941-1953, were released for traffic between October 1931 and September 1932. The first stage of the Brighton line electrification came into public service on 17th July 1932, when LAVs commenced operation between Victoria or London Bridge and Three Bridges, with a unit detached at Redhill for Reigate. Apart from extension of the Three Bridges portion to Brighton, this basic pattern continued for the stopping services after commencement of the full electric timetable to the coast from 1st January 1933, while the majority of semi-fast services were also diagrammed for LAV units. In other words, even after electrification all but the fastest trains between London and Brighton continued to be formed largely of compartment coaches with no access to toilet facilities. From 1935, 2 BIL and 2 NOL units could also be seen on Brighton line stopping services, sometimes in multiple with the LAVs, but whereas the two-coach types also worked along the south coast, the LAVs rarely strayed from the main line. 1921-1953 were renumbered 2921-2953 in January 1937, as part of a scheme to tidy-up the numbering of main line electric stock.

In fact, the 4 LAV fleet was not quite as strictly confined to the Victoria/London Bridge – Brighton route as has been suggested. In the 1930s some late evening London Bridge – Brighton services were extended to start from Charing Cross for the benefit of theatre-goers, while from July 1935 a few rush-hour trains between the Eastbourne line and London were diagrammed for four or eight-coach LAV formations. During and just after the War and again in the 1960s, a LAV unit worked a daily Brighton to Hastings diagram, while in 1949 it was not uncommon to see one forming the Bognor Regis portion of the 5.12pm London Bridge to Brighton/Bognor. Throughout their lives a unit regularly ran empty to the workshops at Slades Green (Slade Green from 1953) for maintenance. Circa 1934, this was nightly, with the return journey the following morning. In later years the routine was most weeks, generally on a Monday, travelling via the London Bridge low level platforms and the Dartford Loop or Bexleyheath. Being restriction 4, they were barred from the North Kent route via Charlton and Plumstead until mid-1939, when clearances were eased to allow the passage of 9ft wide stock as part of the Medway electrification scheme.

Two additional 4 LAV units, numbered 2954 and 2955, were ordered on 28th November 1938 to HO 1057 and completed in February and May 1940 respectively, being delivered from Eastleigh complete with partially-obscured windows and other alterations to comply with wartime regulations. Although having the same layout and number of seats as the earlier units, they were designed under the Bulleid regime and styling and interior finish were as on the

1939 2 HAL units. Electrically, they were equipped with the later English Electric electro-pneumatic control system, introduced in 1936, and the traction motors were also of EE manufacture. Externally, cab windscreens and compartment quarterlights were flush-fitting and had corners rounded off to a large radius, while the cabs themselves were of welded steel construction. Inside, the ornate detailing of the earlier Maunsell stock had gone, to be replaced largely by 'Rexine'-covered surfaces, and there were no folding armrests in the non-corridor third class compartments. The motor coaches (diagram 2117) were numbered 10497-10500, tared 44 tons and were identical to those in the HALs except that they had only one periscope instead of two. The compartment composites (dia. 2311) were numbered 11534/35 and weighed 29 tons, while the side-corridor composites (dia. 2310) were a ton heavier and numbered 11999 and 12000. 2954 and 2955 were formed up in numerical order and were delivered in plain light green which, as on contemporary HALs 2677-2692, quickly weathered to a delicate shade of mud.

The 4 LAVs had a lucky war, serious damage affecting only one unit, 2947, which was repaired and returned to service in due course. Afterwards, there were occasional formation changes, but these were generally only temporary. Motor coach 10511 of unit 2926 was destroyed in the South Croydon accident of 24th October 1947 (see Chapter 2), and was replaced by 10764 from 2 HAL 2646.

A number of alterations and experiments involving electrical equipment took place during the lifetime of the 4 LAVs. The MV motors in 2921-2953 were replaced by English Electric examples of the same design in the 1950s, and the original gravity collector shoes were replaced by lightweight spring-loaded shoegear in 1957-58. Some years previously, the entire class had been fitted with conductor rail scrapers to deal with occasional winter icing problems and falling autumn leaves, but these became unnecessary with the provision of spring-loaded gear and were removed. An unusual experiment was carried out in the autumn of 1962 when the motor coaches of 2924 were fitted with 8ft 9in driving trailer bogies at their trailing ends in order to test shoe wear. In 1963, units 2926/36/42/43/52 were experimentally equipped with beamless shoegear similar to that fitted to London Transport R stock used on the District Line, but the trials were not pursued.

Internally, there were also a number of changes. The partitions dividing the first and third class sections across the gangway in the corridor trailer were gradually removed on overhaul from 1950 onwards. Declining demand for first class accommodation in the aftermath of the war resulted in successive deratings of the first class compartments in the non-corridor trailer. From May 1951 most units had all firsts in this vehicle temporarily downclassed with paper labels, and 2921 was out-shopped that month without '1' designations on the appropriate doors, although still with first class seating. 2930 and 2949 were then overhauled in July and November 1951 respectively with all five former firsts reupholstered as thirds. This was evidently considered too drastic, as 2946 and 2950 were then outshopped with only the three ex-firsts at the centre downclassed, the two nearest the end

In pristine condition following its biennial revarnishing, Bulleid-type 4 LAV 2954 crosses Ouse Valley Viaduct leading a summer Victoria – Brighton semi-fast service in about 1955. This was one of a pair added to the fleet in 1940 and based on the 2 HAL design. Livery is the first BR green with 'lion on wheel' badge on the motor coach sides. A steel 'six-a-side' 4 SUB has been added to the rear, greatly increasing the capacity for day trippers to the coast. *SR Official*

being retained. This arrangement subsequently became standard, giving a revised seating capacity of 46 first and 234 third. Following these alterations, the LAV compartment trailer composites were given the revised diagram number 2305/AMD. The downclassed compartments had their armrests secured up and were all eventually reupholstered, but they remained more sumptuous and were favoured by cognoscenti until withdrawal.

Externally, the LAV fleet went through the livery varia-

tions of the 1950s and 1960s, all eventually receiving the final BR green before withdrawal. The yellow cantrail stripes adopted at this time clearly showed up the unusual arrangement of first class compartments in the trailers. All were given small yellow warning panels from 1963 onwards and three units, 2921/31/50, received full yellow ends for their last year or so in service. Finally, the entire fleet had their original whistles replaced by roof-mounted 'raspberry' air horns in about 1966.

Hybrid 4 LAV 2926, reformed with a 2 HAL motor coach and Bulleid wooden-roofed 'six-a-side' ten compartment trailer following accidents in 1947 and 1961 respectively, departs from Haywards Heath with the 10.47 Victoria – Brighton on 7th September 1965. Having lost its side-corridor trailer, this LAV was actually bereft of any lavatory facilities. *John Scrace*

Regarding accidents in the post-1948 period, on 19th September 1961 the unfortunate 2926 was involved in the second major collision of its career, this time at Brighton. On this occasion, corridor composite 12001 was the main casualty, and was afterwards condemned. When the rest of the unit was repaired, a spare Bulleid 1945-vintage ten-compartment 'six-a-side' trailer second was inserted, and paradoxically this LAV was therefore now completely bereft of toilet facilities. As part of this rehabilitation, the three downgraded former first class compartments of the compartment trailer 11509 were reinstated. The revised formation of this unit was now MBS (ex HAL) 10764 + TS (ex SUB 4338) 10359 + TC 11509 + MBS 10512, and seating was forty first and 300 second, all in non-corridor compartments. 2926 was further revised in October 1967 when it exchanged a motor coach with 2941 (which was then withdrawn to take part in a CMEE training course in re-railing at Hither Green). 2943 was involved in a collision in November 1966, resulting in the condemnation of motor coach 10545. This was replaced by 10671 from 2 BIL 2105, a side corridor vehicle with a lavatory. Other LAVs involved in minor accidents included 2929 (Reigate, 1957 and Victoria, 1963), 2932 (New Cross Gate, 1967), 2944 (New Cross Gate, 1960) and 2952.

In May 1967, 2932 lost its own motor coaches, which were replaced by a pair of eight-compartment all-steel 4 SUB vehicles, 10939 and 10940, from unit 4377. The unit ran thus reformed until withdrawal in February 1968, following which the motor coaches were returned to 4377.

In 1967 4 LAV 2932 was reformed with the motor coaches from 4 SUB 4377, giving an increase in second class seating capacity of no fewer than 52. It ran in this condition until withdrawal a year later, after which 4377 was reformed and returned to service. 2932 in this condition was rarely photographed, and is seen here calling at Burgess Hill on 22nd October 1967 with the 11.05 (Sunday) London Bridge – Brighton service, diverted via the Quarry line due to engineering work. These motor coaches were experimentally fitted with a ventilator over the nearside cab window when new, and the blanking plate where it was once located is clearly visible. *J. H. Aston*

By the mid 1960s, the LAVs were undoubtedly becoming work-weary and due for retirement, although a saying among railwaymen that their acceleration improved at speeds above 70mph because the woodworm jumped out was definitely an exaggeration. They were more worn out than other pre-war semi-fast electric stock simply because, being almost entirely confined to one route, they covered greater daily mileages. Despite this, their rugged construction and simple electrical equipment actually made them cheaper to maintain than more recent BR types. Externally, many units showed signs of patched-up paintwork. Inside the second class compartments, the dusty but still comfortable seating was upholstered in faded examples of the three standard BR moquette patterns from the 1950s, and in some it was reputedly possible to see the ceiling panelling moving in relation to the bodywork as the train accelerated or braked hard. A few of the last LAVs to receive a general overhaul, including 2923 and 2939 in May 1966, were given the red/black and yellow/black upholstery in seconds and the squared pattern in firsts.

Other than 2941 which had already gone, the majority of 4 LAV units were withdrawn in 1968, and by November only 2923/24/28/39/49/50 remained. These survived in service until February 1969, although not officially withdrawn until 5th April. In all cases, they were replaced by new 4 VEP stock, although 2 BIL, HAL and 4 COR units continued in use on some Brighton line stopping trains for a short period. 2923 achieved distinction by being the last LAV to work on Waterloo to Reading services (almost certainly a unique event) on 17th October 1968.

Following withdrawal, virtually all vehicles were sold to private dealers for scrap, after stripping of electrical and brake equipment for further use had taken place at Selhurst or Polegate. The vehicles were forwarded to the same scrap dealers as those who were dealing with the PUL and PAN express stock, including J. Cashmore Ltd at Newport, Steel Breaking & Dismantling at Chesterfield, A. King & Son Ltd at Wymondham and Armytage Ltd at Sheepbridge. Pending removal to the scrap yards, about a dozen units made a mournful sight stored in carriage sidings at Blackheath for some months in 1968, while others spent time at Ford or Lancing.

2925 and 2943 ended their useful lives in an unusual way. In the summer of 1968 they were towed to Sherborne (on the SR West of England main line) and used in the filming of a remake of *Goodbye Mr Chips*, following which they were taken to Chesterfield for scrapping that October. All 1931-type LAV vehicles had been broken up by August 1969.

The five HAL-type motor coaches, 10764 from 2926 and 10497-10500 from 2954 and 2955, were not scrapped, but retained for departmental use. In 1968/69 they were converted at Stewarts Lane into de-icing coaches, specifically for use on the Bournemouth line, and their subsequent history is related in Chapter 6. The trailers of 2954 and 2955 were stored at Micheldever until 1972 against possible future departmental needs, and then sold for scrap. 11999 and 11534 from 2954 were not actually broken up (by Wards at Kettering) until May 1975.

THE 2 NOL UNITS 1934-59

Following completion of the Brighton line stock, no further main line units appeared until December 1934 when the first of the 2 NOL units were outshopped. It is arguable whether the NOLs should be included with other main line stock, as here, or with the London area suburban units, of which they were basically a two-coach version and with which they could be operated when required. Each was formed of a motor third brake and a driving trailer composite, with no corridors or toilets. This gave rise to the 2 NOL code, indicating a 'two-coach general purpose unit without lavatories'. The only main line electric units to make use of pre-Grouping coaches, their vehicles were formed from bodywork of LSWR origin altered at Lancing or Eastleigh and mounted on standard 62ft Lancing-built suburban underframes. Total length of the 2 NOL units was 129ft 3in and, as built, seats were provided for 135 third and 24 first class passengers.

The 1935 Eastbourne electrification required a sizeable fleet of electric units suitable for working local stopping trains on the Brighton – Hastings line plus the Seaford and Horsted Keynes branches, and also to operate Brighton – West Worthing services, allowing the ex-LSWR three-coach suburban units then in use to return to the London area. Some evidence exists to suggest that further four-coach EMUs had originally been intended, but that early in 1934 Head Office had a change of heart and decided to order two-coach units instead.

The main argument in favour of the shorter formation was that it was more suitable for lightly loaded local and branch services, and corresponded closely to the steam motor trains the new electric units would largely displace. It also gave greater flexibility, as trains could be made up of any even number of vehicles to platform length limits, the only disadvantage being that the additional driving cabs wasted passenger space in longer formations.

The first and largest batch of 2 NOLs consisted of fifty units numbered 1813-1862, all authorised on 23rd March 1934 and outshopped between November 1934 and May 1935. However, although Eastleigh and Lancing treated them as one straight through order for construction purposes, their financing was more complex. The first eleven, 1813-1823, to HO 804, were actually charged to the Sevenoaks electrification account, then current. Although intended for the Brighton to West Worthing local service, because this had already been paid for in 1932-33 it was unlikely that the Board would authorise any further expenditure, making it necessary to charge them to another current project. Assembled entirely at Lancing, they were completed in November and December 1934 and immediately started work between Brighton and West Worthing. This in turn displaced the '1201' class units back to the London area where, by increasing the pool of stock available, they indirectly provided part of the Sevenoaks requirement.

HO 807 covered the remaining 39 units, all assembled at Eastleigh and intended for south coast local services. 32 units, 1824-1855, were funded from the Eastbourne budget and were completed by April 1935. The remaining seven were however charged once more to the Sevenoaks account,

2 NOL 1862, photographed at Eastbourne in 1935 when newly delivered, was the final unit of the second batch of NOLs, supplied for coastal services from Brighton as part of the Eastbourne electrification. Constructed using LSWR wooden bodywork on new underframes, their similarity to contemporary suburban units of the same origin is obvious. Motor Third Brake 9910, to diagram 686, has Metrovick electro-magnetic control gear, as shown by the power cable conduits running up the left hand side of both cab windows. The extensive lining out on the original green livery is also clearly seen in this view. *Lens of Sutton*

probably to keep down the total cost of the Eastbourne scheme. Numbered 1856-1862, they were outshopped in April and May 1935. Additional suburban units 1595-1599, ordered at the same time and justified to the Board as being required to cover traffic increases, actually provided the remaining requirement for Sevenoaks services as explained in Volume 1. By means of this exercise in creative accounting, Eastern section suburban and south coast local services each ended up with one standard type of EMU, so both operating department and SR shareholders were satisfied. Most of 1824-1862 were ready before the Eastbourne electrification was switched on, and were initially put into storage at various locations, including sidings at Crystal Palace (Low Level) and the new and unused engine shed at Norwood Junction, until required for the commencement of electric services on 7th July 1935. From this time they became common-user with the first eleven units on coastal services out of Brighton.

The origin of the next batch of 2 NOLs, 1863-1882, was

not straightforward either. Ordered on 7th June 1935 to HO 874, they were financed out of the budget for the new 'Motspur Park – Leatherhead Extension' project, which materialised in truncated form as the Chessington branch in 1938-39. These units were completed in February and March 1936 (ie more than two years before the first stage of this line, to Tolworth, was completed) and soon afterwards entered service on the Waterloo – Windsor outer-suburban route, displacing standard three-coach suburban units to other duties. Finally, a small batch of eight units was ordered on 8th January 1936 to HO 899, paid for as part of the Portsmouth No.1 scheme, which included Staines to Weybridge. These were the last conversions of former steam stock into main line electric units and differed slightly from their predecessors. From 3rd January 1937 a combined Waterloo to Windsor/Weybridge service was operated using 2 NOLs, dividing or joining at Staines. Eastleigh was once more responsible for the bodywork conversion of all of 1863-1890.

A summary of 2 NOL orders is shown in the table below:

Units	HO No. (Date)	Financed	Purpose	Date Completed
1813-1823	HO 804 (23.3.34)	Sevenoaks	Brighton – West Worthing	11.34-12.34
1824-1855	HO 807 (23.3.34)	Eastbourne	Eastbourne local services	1.35-4.35
1856-1862	HO 807 (23.3.34)	Sevenoaks	Eastbourne local services	4.35-5.35
1863-1882	HO 874 (7.6.35)	Motspur Park – Leatherhead	Waterloo – Windsor	2.36-3.36
1883-1890	HO 899 (8.1.36)	Portsmouth No.1	Staines – Weybridge	c. 7.36

As well as the 62ft underframes, other fittings such as buffers and couplings on the NOLs were of the usual suburban type. Likewise, the 8ft 9in wheelbase 'central'-type motor bogie and 8ft inner trailer bogies were also the same as fitted to the suburban stock, but the cab-end trailer bogie used 8ft 9in frames as on the SL and WIM units 1801-1812 (the only two-coach motor units up to that time) to enable standard-length collector shoe-beams to be fitted. These same bogie types were also used for all other two-coach semi-fast EMUs of the 2 BIL and 2 HAL types.

The motor coaches of 1813-1882 had the standard Metrovick electro-magnetic control system, but those in 1883-1890 differed in being fitted with English Electric electro-pneumatic equipment, identical to that fitted to suburban units 1579-1584, etc. and entirely underframe-mounted. All had type 339 totally-enclosed traction motors, those in the first batch of fifty being by MV, the others by EE. Thus the HO 874 batch 1863-1882 had MV control gear but EE motors. This coincided with the exclusive ten-year contract for the supply of electrical equipment negotiated between English Electric and the SR referred to elsewhere. An interesting oddity of the Metrovick-equipped NOLs (and the first ten 2 BILs) was the differing power cable conduit runs on each cab. The motor coaches followed the standard suburban pattern with two pipes running vertically from the power jumper and receptacle on to the roof, but on the driving trailer the conduit was looped over the headcode box before disappearing underneath, and then emerged on the roof behind the cab. This tidier latter arrangement was then adopted for EE-equipped motor third brakes (except that the power line ran under the floor the length of the coach), and hence the cab fronts of 1883-1890 were the same at both ends.

The 2 NOL motor third brakes were numbered 9861-9910 (units 1813-1862), 8596-8615 (units 1863-1882) and 9781-9788 (units 1883-1890). All but the last eight were to diagram 686, almost identical as built to those in suburban units 1585-1599, with motorman's, guard's and seven and one half third class compartments, the half compartment or coupé being directly behind the brake van with its seats facing backwards. With their underframe-mounted EE control system, 9781-88 in 1883-90 were similar to the motor coaches in suburban units 1579-1584, except that they too had seven and a half rather than eight compartments, and were to diagram 688. At 43 tons, these vehicles were one ton heavier

than the MV-equipped motor coaches. The lack of an equipment cubicle in the cab enabled them to have a slightly larger guard's van than the earlier units. In all cases, bodies were adapted from LSWR 48ft main-line eight-compartment thirds originally constructed between 1895 and 1902 (some had originally been second/third bi-composites), with one end compartment reduced to a coupé and a steel-panelled van and cab grafted on. The NOL motor coaches with the oldest bodywork were 8598 and 9900 in units 1865 and 1852 respectively from June 1894 and already forty years old when reused.

The driving trailer composites were numbered 9940-50/61-99 (in 1813-1862) and 9912-39 (in 1863-1890), and were made up of motorman's, six third and three first class compartments. All were to diagram 796. Those in units 1813-1862 (vehicles 9940 upwards) weighed 29 tons, the remainder being marked as being a ton heavier. The bodies of all but two of these vehicles were assembled from six compartments of a 48ft third of the same type as those used for the motor coaches, and three compartments from a 46ft bogie first of 1895-1900 vintage. Most of these latter vehicles provided material for two NOL driving trailers. Exceptionally, the third class portions of 9912 and 9913 were made up from five-compartment third brakes with an additional compartment added. In all cases a new driving cab was added at the third class end.

Seating in the third class compartments was the standard suburban five-a-side, while the first class compartments seated four each side with end and centre armrests to divide the seats into two groups of two. Distance between partitions was 6ft 11in and 5ft 10in (approximately) in firsts and thirds respectively. With the exception of livery and seat moquette patterns, both internally and externally the units remained pure LSWR, with most characteristic fittings retained. Being narrow-bodied with a width of only 8ft 1in, the guard's van was equipped with side lookout duckets rather than the periscopes fitted to the 4 LAVs. Unlike equivalent suburban motor coaches, however, these were fitted to both sides of the van rather than just the offside. There were minor detail differences in body finish; for example 1863-1882 lacked the narrow skirting boards at the lower edge of the body side panelling.

From the start of electrified services on the Eastbourne line, NOLs worked virtually all trains other than the London expresses, mostly as single units. Indeed, until the start of World War Two, other classes were rarely seen on stopping trains east of Brighton. However, with the completion of the Portsmouth Direct, Mid-Sussex and Reading schemes in the 1937-39 period, any NOL could in theory turn up virtually anywhere in the electrified area, freely interworking with the 2 BILs provided for these lines and often found coupled to them. By 1939, the official Western section allocation for the Windsor lines was 1855-1890 (and probably 1853/54 also), but this was an excess and they strayed regularly on to services between London and Alton, Reading or Portsmouth. By this means the odd Windsor NOL undoubtedly even reached Brighton on occasion. During the currency of the 1937-39 summer timetables, it is likely that Western section NOLs worked the self-contained Woking – Alton shuttle.

Unit 1883 was from the last batch of eight 2 NOLs, financed from the Chessington line budget but intended for Waterloo – Windsor / Weybridge services. They differed from earlier NOLs in having 1936-type English Electric electro-pneumatic control equipment, and so the path of the power cable conduit on the cab front of the motor coach differs from that of Metrovick-equipped 1862 (on page 99). By 1957, when this photograph was taken, remaining NOLs had been displaced to general duties in the suburban area, and 1883 is seen here at New Cross Gate leading a London Bridge 'roundabout' service. *F. W. Ivey*

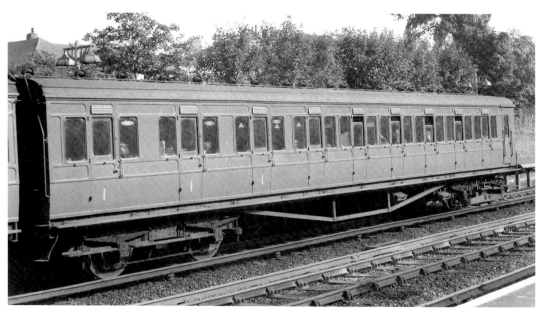

A rear three-quarter side view of NOL driving trailer composite 9978 from coastal unit 1841, in final BR condition with blue FIRST 'hotdogs' and red NO SMOKING triangles on appropriate windows. On this occasion the unit had escaped on to a London service (a not uncommon occurrence) and was photographed at Surbiton on 29th August 1956. *G. M. Kitchenside*

With the outbreak of World War Two, coastal units 1847-1852 were also transferred to London area suburban services, and from 6th October 1941 these and 1853-1890 were downclassed to all-third in line with the remainder of the suburban fleet. In the meantime, the rest of the NOLs entirely disappeared from the south coast in early 1940, being replaced by new 2 HALs. They reappeared in 1941 in general use on Central and Western section main line routes, once more working indiscriminately with 2 BILs, and this continued throughout the war and afterwards. To where they temporarily disappeared in 1940 was never reported and is a matter for conjecture; one suggestion is that they were stockpiled for use on south coast – Aldershot troop trains following the Dunkirk evacuation. Of the NOLs now in the London area, 1847-1850 were generally to be seen on the Nunhead – Crystal Palace (High Level) and Crystal Palace (Low Level) – Beckenham Junction shuttles, both carrying headcode 03. 1851-1890 continued to mainly work Waterloo – Windsor/Weybridge services until September 1943, when they were dispersed to other suburban duties, often working in place of trailer sets.

The use of London area 2 NOLs on suburban services in place of trailer sets seems to have started as early as 1941. In most cases shoe-beams, fuses and traction motors were removed. The probable reason was a wartime shortage of electrical equipment, and later also to cover for the over-enthusiastic withdrawal of 'proper' trailer sets, as mentioned in Volume 1. No data is available before 1944, but from then until 1948 all of 1849-54/56-82/84-90 were recorded as working in this way at various times. In a few cases, including 1857 and 1880, traction equipment was restored and then removed again at a later date. There is a suspicion that NOLs donated motors and other equipment to keep existing three and four-coach suburban units running, and later to get new all-steel 4 SUBs 4355-4377 into service. It also seems likely that the use of NOLs, which had driving cabs, for this purpose eased the transition from three to four-coach units that was then in progress. As the electrical equipment supply situation eased from about the beginning of 1947 the de-motored NOLs were gradually returned to service as motor units after full or intermediate overhaul.

Only two 2 NOLs were withdrawn as a result of war damage, the first being 1828 following bombing at Fratton in June 1941. DTC 9961 was written off, but motor coach 9876 was transferred to suburban unit 1799, an LSWR interloper in an otherwise LBSCR-bodied unit, and ended its days in 4 SUB 4254 which was withdrawn in February 1956. Unit 1855 was involved in a blackout collision at Staines in November 1941, driving trailer 9992 being condemned and motor coach 9903 going to LSWR-based suburban unit 1679, which was later augmented to become 4 SUB 4521 and lasted until about March 1953. In both cases their underframes and bogies were recovered for use in new 4 EPB motor coaches as recounted in Chapter 7.

From 1943, in the midst of the war, a programme was implemented to enlarge the guard's compartment in the 2 NOLs by incorporating the adjacent coupé compartment. The partition between the two was removed, the quarterlights

and droplights boarded over, and the door lettered LUGGAGE. This increased the length of the van from the standard suburban 7ft to nearly 11ft, as on other semi-fast stock, and was presumably to cater for the large quantity of general goods and parcels traffic carried on many of the services they worked. The coastal units 1813-1827 and 1829-1846 were modified between March 1943 and September 1944 (1831 appears to have been the first). 1847-1850 were done in November 1948 as part of their overhaul before returning to the coast. London area units 1851-1854, 1856-1868, 1870-1872, 1874-1877 and 1879-1882 were also altered between 1944 and January 1950, after which no more were done. Vehicles with this modification were given the revised diagram number 684. The EE-equipped units 1883-1890 already had a larger van as all electrical equipment was under-floor, so there was no need to alter these.

Following overhaul and a short period on general suburban duties, most of the previously de-motored NOLs returned to work on the Waterloo – Windsor/Weybridge service in 1948, but first class was restored to 1847-1850 that November and they were reinstated on coastal duties in December. From November 1952, following an accident involving a 2 BIL at Guildford, the 2 NOL fleet was fitted with a safety cut-out device to prevent the brakes being released if there was insufficient air pressure in the system to re-apply them. Until the work was done they were not allowed to work solo, and therefore Western section units 1851-54/56-90 were once more taken off the Windsor line, being replaced by 4 SUBs. Instead, they worked coupled in pairs as SUB substitutes on other lines, until gradually returning to Windsor/Weybridge services during 1953 as they were modified. A few SUB diagrams persisted on the Windsor line after this time, covering for NOLs temporarily seconded to the Wimbledon – West Croydon and South London lines in 1953-54 to supplement the venerable and increasingly unreliable SL and WIM units (which ironically had bodywork less ancient than the NOLs) until there were enough new 2 EPBs to replace them. Throughout this period, the odd NOL could turn up on suburban services anywhere on the SR London network.

1819 collided with a light engine at Eastbourne in January 1951, and 1838 apparently had an accident the same year. Vehicles 9886 and 9946 from these units were condemned, and MThB 9867 and DTC 9975 were reformed as unit 1819. The underframe of 9886 was stored, with other slightly damaged frames, in a siding at Horsted Keynes for some years, after which it was sent to Lancing for reconditioning and then to Eastleigh for use in the 4 EPB programme. A particularly serious collision took place at Barnes in the evening of 2nd December 1955, when the 11.12pm Waterloo – Windsor/Chertsey, formed of units 1853 and 1857, ran into the rear of a stationary freight train as the result of an error by the signalman. Severe arcing due to an incorrectly-functioning substation circuit breaker caused a fierce fire which completely engulfed driving trailer 9990 of the leading unit 1853, resulting in thirteen deaths, while its motor coach 9901 was afterwards fit only to be broken up in Barnes goods yard. 1815 collided with a steam engine at Hastings in May 1957, motor coach 9863 being wrecked and subsequently broken

Diagram 684 motor third brake 9874 of 2 NOL 1826, seen waiting at Brighton at the front of a semi-fast to Victoria in 1948, displays the modification carried out in 1943-44 to incorporate the coupe compartment into the luggage area. The leading quarterlight has been blanked-off and the coupe door marked LUGGAGE. Note also the guard's ducket on the nearside, unique to NOL motor coaches. *Joseph Sietta*

up. It was replaced by 8605 from withdrawn unit 1872. Further unscheduled withdrawals were 1819 and 1833, damaged beyond economic repair in a collision at Lovers Walk (Brighton) in June 1958.

With their wooden bodywork now more than fifty years old, planned withdrawal of the 2 NOL fleet commenced in June and July 1956 when four London area units, 1870, 1871, 1877 and 1878, were taken out of service. This left a total of seventy NOL units, 34 in the London area and 36 on the south coast. At the same time, concern for their deteriorating condition led to the remaining London-area units (1851/52/54/56-69/72-76/79-90) being taken off the Waterloo – Windsor/Weybridge services, a demanding duty involving heavily loaded high-speed running between Clapham Junction and Richmond, for the third and last time. Initially replaced on the Windsor line by new 4 EPBs, they were displaced to other suburban duties for the remainder of their existence. This batch was withdrawn, together with two coastal units 1835/43, between April 1957 and January 1958. The remaining 34 coastal units were scheduled for withdrawal in 1958, but in the event most survived into 1959, by then having largely gravitated to London suburban services to cover for the NOLs withdrawn earlier. On the coast, they were replaced by 2 HAL units (see below), themselves displaced from the Medway lines by main line electrification in Kent. In their final months the early NOLs at last regularly visited Sevenoaks on both Holborn Viaduct and Charing Cross services, and also briefly reappeared on the Wimbledon – West Croydon line. They also continued to work sporadically on coastal services, including the odd London semi-fast, until their last days. The last NOLs to remain in traffic were 1826 and 1830, withdrawn in August 1959 and broken up the following month.

To summarise, year of withdrawal for the bulk of the 2 NOL fleet was as follows:

1957: 1851-52/54/56-64/66-69/72-76/79-89.
1958: 1819/23/33/35/43/65/90.
1959: 1813-18/20-22/24-27/29-32/34/36/37/39-42/44-50.

The fate of the NOLs withdrawn between 1956 and 1959 was the same as that of the wooden-bodied SUBs of similar vintage, their standard 62ft underframes and bogies being recovered for reuse under otherwise new stock. The vehicles were first stripped of electrical equipment at Wimbledon and Strawberry Hill, and were then sent to Newhaven Town sidings, where their bodywork was broken up, mostly by hand. The underframes were then passed on to Lancing Works for reconditioning, including the addition of strengthening members, before going to Eastleigh where new all-steel bodywork was mounted on them. In the case of the four 1956 2 NOL withdrawals 1870/71/77/78, the underframes were used for 4 EPB coaches. The frames of 1835/43/51/52/54/56-69/72-76/79-90, withdrawn April 1957-January 1958, were used for SR-type 2 HAP units 5601-5636, provided for the Kent Coast electrification. Finally, the frames from the remaining 34 units withdrawn in 1958-59 were used under 2 EPBs 5651-5684, the last new units with all-steel bodywork of Bulleid style. These went to the Waterloo-Windsor/Weybridge service, displacing the 4 EPBs which had in turn originally displaced the NOLs four years earlier. Further details of all these types are given in Chapter 7.

It is worth reiterating that the London-area NOLs were taken off the Windsor lines three times in their career: between 1943 and 1948, in 1952-53 while they were fitted with brake compressor failure safety devices and lastly in 1956, a year or so before final withdrawal.

THE 2 BIL UNITS 1935-71

Advance publicity for the 1935 Eastbourne and Hastings electrification scheme published at the time in one journal, possibly using 'inside information', suggested that the new rolling stock was to include five new four-coach units for semi-fast services. However, as with the NOLs, it seems that the planners had second thoughts just before a firm order was placed, and HO 806 dated 23rd March 1934 was actually for ten two-coach units of an entirely new type, classified 2 BIL. As usual for wholly new main line stock, the vehicles were constructed at Eastleigh using underframes and bogies supplied by Lancing. (It has been erroneously suggested elsewhere that the motor coaches were ordered from contractors.) Control and electrical equipment, including type 339 motors, were of the standard suburban type, supplied by Metrovick.

In contrast to the non-corridor NOLs, intended for local and branch workings, the 2 BIL units were designed for longer distance intermediate services, particularly semi-fast London workings. They were therefore given new maximum-width Restriction 4 bodywork with a side corridor and toilet in both vehicles. With the SR's continuing fixation on such facilities, this gave rise to the type designation, meaning 'two coach unit with two (bi-) lavatories, one in each coach'. Formation comprised a motor third brake (diagram 2111) with motorman's cab, guard's and luggage area, seven third class compartments and a lavatory, and a driving trailer composite (dia. 2700) with cab, four third and four first class compartments and a lavatory. In both vehicles all compartments were connected by a side corridor running along the right of the unit (looking backwards from the cab of the MThB). Third class compartments seated four passengers each side and firsts three with folding intermediate armrests, giving a total of 88 third and 24 first class seats in each unit. Overall unit length was quoted as 129ft 6in, oddly slightly longer than the NOLs on supposedly identical underframes.

The prototype 2 BIL was delivered in February 1935 and originally carried the number 1890. The remaining nine appeared a month later and formed what was to become the pre-production batch, initially numbered 1890-1899. 1890 was renumbered 1900 (to make way for the final NOL) in January 1936 and the ten became 2001-2010 in the same order from January 1937. Thus for most of its life the actual prototype was numbered 2010, not 2001 as might be expected.

The driving motor third brakes were numbered 10567-76 and weighed 43 tons, while the driving trailer composites were numbered 12101-10 and tared 31 tons. Bodywork construction was the same as the LAVs, comprising galvanised steel sheeting over a teak framework for the sides and ends and canvas-covered deal boarding on the roofs, excepting the domed ends above the driving cabs, which were steel. The cab end design followed the standard suburban pattern, with a framed outwardly-opening windscreen on the offside, but (with the exception of the motorman's doors) the cab and van sides followed the contour of the rest of the vehicle and were not inset. Thus the cab was full-width which certainly looked better than the slightly starved appearance of the earlier units. The guard's compartment had two roof periscopes, one

for each direction of travel, and two seats so that whichever way the unit was travelling the guard had a forward view. One of the seats was higher than the other, as it was mounted above an electrical equipment box. Being on suburban underframes, there was no gangway between vehicles, coupling being by the standard three-link arrangement with centre buffer, the rubbing block being on the motor coach and the centre buffer on the DTC.

Bodywork and internal design features followed the Maunsell/Lynes period 4 style but differed only in detail from the LAVs, the main alteration being that toilet windows had two ventilator slots above rather than one. Fixed windows were fitted from the inside and were surrounded by thin wooden fillets, those on the corridor side characteristically reaching to the eaves. On each door and also above the headcode panel was a ventilator bonnet. Passenger door droplights were to a revised design, frameless except for a brass bar at the top and locked or released by a lever at the bottom, but motorman's and guard's compartments retained the wood-framed type. Internally, corridor panelling was cream-painted wood whilst in the compartments varnished mahogany or teak prevailed. Access to the corridor was by single sliding door, rather than the balanced pairs in the LAV side-corridor vehicles. On the corridor sides, there were only three passenger doors on the motor coaches and four on the driving trailers. On the latter vehicles there were also three distinctive narrow fixed windows in what would otherwise have been door or droplight positions – these could also be found

An official as-built photograph of diagram 2111 motor third brake 10574 from 2 BIL 1897 (later 2007), one of the ten original units of this class constructed in 1934 for the Eastbourne electrification. Note the full lining-out, not carried by later members of the class. The bodywork of these pre-production BILs was to Maunsell/Lynes period 4 design parameters, indicated by the ventilator bonnets above the door droplights and wooden fillets around the quarterlights. The position of the power cable conduits up the sides of the cab windows shows that they were equipped with pre-1936 Metrovick electro-magnetic control gear. *SR Official*

2 BIL 2010 (built as 1890, then 1900) was the first of the ten original pre-production units of this type, which differed considerably in detail from later examples. The leading vehicle is dia.2700 driving trailer composite 12101, and this view clearly shows the unusual corridor window arrangement. Departing from Hassocks with the 14.45 Victoria – Brighton on 31st May 1968, 2010 carries the second BR green livery in which it was withdrawn less than twelve months later. *John Scrace*

on the trailers of the express 6 PAN units being built at Eastleigh concurrently. First and third class upholstery continued with the floral Saladin and 'jazz' idioms respectively, while compartment dimensions were similar to those in the LAVs, except in the motor coaches where distance between partitions was only 5ft 11in.

Although these first ten 2 BILs featured in SR publicity for the Eastbourne electrification, they did not normally work east of Keymer Junction following their introduction early in 1935. Instead, they were used on London – Brighton/Reigate semi-fast and stopping services in company with LAVs. Several were still spare, and by 1936 four of them were on loan, by weekly turnover, to the Eastern section for a semi-fast Sevenoaks – Cannon Street (am) and return (pm) peak-hour duty, an arrangement which lasted until about February 1939 when the BILs were replaced by brand-new 2 HALs. This particular service was known to staff as the 'Waldron Smithers Train' after the local Member of Parliament who used it from Chelsfield. 2001-2010 only became common user with the remainder of the BIL and coastal NOL fleet when the Portsmouth No.2 scheme was completed in July 1938.

The 2 BIL design evidently proved successful, as three further batches were constructed between 1936 and the end of 1938 to produce a final total of 152 units. Although substantially similar to the original ten and of the same basic appearance, the production units were in fact to a completely redrawn design with, for example, slightly different compartment dimensions, and they were officially one inch shorter. The major innovation was the adoption of the same English Electric electro-pneumatic control equipment as fitted to the final eight 2 NOLs. Many of the components of this system were standard with the Portsmouth 4 COR express stock, but the cab-end jumper cable arrangements were necessarily the same as on earlier suburban and semi-fast stock to enable multiple working with LAV, NOL and early BIL units. This equipment was entirely underframe-mounted and so the cab could be shortened, while the passenger accommodation in the motor coach was reduced by having a coupé with four backward-facing seats in place of the full compartment next to the van. The coupé was unofficially intended for train crews travelling 'on the cushions', and had a shelf opposite the seats on which paperwork could be filled in. While this alteration reduced the number of third class seats to 84, it conversely allowed third class compartment length to be increased to the standard main line 6ft 3in, and also enabled a larger van to be provided for goods and parcels traffic.

In construction and styling details, these units were representative of the final Maunsell/Lynes coach designs, designated period 5. The fixed windows were mounted from the outside in aluminium frames, and the size and spacing of the corridor side windows of the driving trailers altered to do away with the three narrow windows. The frosted glass windows opposite the toilets on the corridor side were omitted, as were the ventilator bonnets on the doors and cab front above the headcode box. As on the last eight NOLs, the position of power cable conduits on the motor coaches was altered so they ran under the floor. Internally, the corridor panelling

was of varnished teak, and use was made of 'Rexine' synthetic leathercloth for much other panel trim. It appears that most production BILs were outshopped with the final green 'jazz' moquette in third class, other than the last 36 (2117-2152) which had one of the blue designs or an uncommon light green 'crazy paving' pattern.

The first 38 2 BIL units to the production design, outshopped between August and December 1936 and numbered ex works 1901-1920 and 1954-1971 (the gap being filled by the 4 LAVs), were ordered for the Portsmouth No.1 electrification. The original requirement had been for only 36 units, ordered to HO 898 dated 8th January 1936, but belated inclusion of the Farnham – Alton line (see Chapter 1) required two more, covered by HO 903 of 27th January. This batch was renumbered 2011-2048 in February 1937 before any went into regular service. 1911 (2021) formed the first electric test train into Woking on 1st November 1936. The next 68 units, 2049-2116, were for the Portsmouth No.2 (Mid-Sussex) electrification, ordered on 6th November 1936 to HO 949 and delivered between June and December 1937. All apart from 2116 (of which more will be said below) were identical to the earlier units. For the Reading line electrification a final batch of 36 2 BILs, 2117-2152, were ordered on the same date but to HO 948. (Intriguingly, the Reading line BILs thus had a lower HO order number than the Mid-Sussex units even though the latter were needed first.) Completed between August and November 1938 after Maunsell's retirement, 2117-2152 incorporated a number of detail differences. These included the provision of a stronger 62ft underframe, with end-loading increased from ninety to 120 tons, achieved by cross-bracing. This followed a (now unrecorded) collision at Woking involving a BIL, in which the frame was badly telescoped. With the revised underframe, large Spencer Moulton self-contained cab-end buffers were fitted, as on the express stock. The bodywork now incorporated wider 'Alpax' aluminium flanges around the fixed windows. These alterations increased the weight of the vehicles concerned by one ton, but otherwise overall dimensions and tare weights were similar to the original ten. The motor third brakes of 2011-2152 were to diagram 2115 and numbered 10577-10718, while the driving trailer composites were to dia. 2701 and numbered 12034-100 and 12111-85.

As mentioned above, 2116, the final unit from the Mid-Sussex batch, differed from the remainder of the HO 949 order. Firstly, it was experimentally fitted with an all-steel roof and, apart from this feature, could be recognised also by individual curved gutters above each door. The experiment was evidently a success and in 1946 the unit was taken into Eastleigh carriage works for a special inspection prior to the construction of the first Bulleid all-steel 4 SUB unit 4111, and was found to be in excellent condition.

By January 1939 the entire 2 BIL fleet, including the ten prototypes, were working semi-fast and stopping services over virtually all the electrified main lines of the Central and Western sections, and the various batches quickly became mixed up. Only eastwards from Brighton and Keymer Junction to Seaford, Eastbourne and Ore were they uncommon until after the start of World War Two.

New 2 BIL 2116, the last of the batch built for the 1938 Mid-Sussex electrification, poses for its official photograph outside Eastleigh Works. This unit was experimentally fitted with a steel roof, and could easily be recognised by individual curved gutters above each door. Note that the waist lining is still divided into 'panels', unlike the express COR and BUF units provided for the same scheme. *SR Official (NRM/SSPL)*

Also posing for its official portrait outside Eastleigh Works when brand new in 1938, 2152 was the final 2 BIL to be completed. Dia.2701 driving trailer composite 12185 is leading. The lining out has been reduced to a pair of yellow lines along the waist, and the 'Alpax' aluminium window frames are wider than on earlier examples. The heavy self-contained Spencer Moulton buffers indicate that a stronger underframe (with end-loading increased from ninety to 120 tons) has been fitted. *SR Official*

Above The comfortable third class compartment interior of Reading line 2 BIL 2137 when new, showing the uncommon light green 'crazy paving' upholstery moquette, which also found its way into some Mid-Sussex COR and BUF units. Looking towards the external door on the non-gangwayed side, this view clearly shows the brass lever used to lock or unlock the droplight. *SR Official*

Right The interior of first class compartment 'D' in driving trailer composite 12061 of 2 BIL 2038, built for the Portsmouth No. 1 electrification. The seats and matching rug display the 'Saladin' pattern, ubiquitous in SR first class compartments until 1939. *SR Official (NRM/SSPL)*

Four units from the 152-strong 2 BIL fleet were written off as a result of war damage. In chronological order these were 2102 and 2131 at Portsmouth Harbour in August 1940, 2014 at Brighton in May 1943 and 2119 at Peckham Rye in December 1944. Of these, it proved possible to salvage the underframe of driving trailer 12037 from 2014, and this was placed into store until 1954 when it was re-used under new all-steel DTC 12855 (see next column). Possibly due to a paint shortage, 2054 was outshopped at the end of the war in battleship grey with white lettering and numbering, being observed in traffic in this state in August 1945.

There was a spate of accidents in the years following, resulting in the destruction of a number of driving trailers. 2056 was damaged in a mishap at Brighton in 1946 and 12079 was written off. 2088 lost 12121 as a result of a fire at Littlehampton in 1950, but although the body was broken up at Eastleigh the frame was reused for steel-bodied replacement DTC 12854, built at the end of 1950. This vehicle, similar to those provided later for units 2069, 2100 and 2133, initially went to 1939-type 2 HAL 2653 in place of 12807, which then went to BIL 2088. Similarly 2056 was reformed with driving trailer composite 12231 from HAL 2646. Although of similar layout to the BIL driving trailers they replaced, these vehicles had their gangways on the opposite side and the seating was considerably less comfortable. 2069 and 2100 were involved in the Ford accident of August 1951, resulting in the writing-off of 12092 and the body of 12133. Driving trailer composite 12166 of unit 2133 was wrecked in an accident at Guildford in November 1952 when the unit, forming the Aldershot line portion of the 8.54pm from Waterloo, suffered a brake air compressor circuit failure, causing it to overrun signals on a downhill gradient and run into a light engine standing outside the station. As recounted below, all three of these units were given new replacement trailers, that for unit 2133 making use of the underframe from coach 12133.

As a result of this latter accident, all BILs (and NOLs, as stated) were fitted with a safety cut-out device and were not allowed to work solo until this had been done. Units so fitted were marked with a white spot on the cab fronts until the entire fleet had been dealt with. The MV 339 motors originally fitted to 2001-2010 were replaced by EE examples in the 1950s. A few units had de-icing scrapers fitted to the shoe-beams of the driving trailers for some time in the same decade, and lightweight spring-loaded collector shoes were fitted in place of the original gravity shoegear in 1958-59.

In order to replace the driving trailers written off in the accidents described above and to restore the number of 2 BIL units, four new DTCs were ordered on 2nd July 1953 to HO 4009 and constructed at Eastleigh in 1954, to basically the same design as those for the seven post-war 2 HALs 2693-2699. To diagram 2705 and numbered 12855-58, in appearance and construction they resembled the post-war 4 SUB stock with all-steel welded bodywork and an upright cab roof end. Internal layout and seating capacity was, nevertheless, identical to the pre-war vehicles with four compartments of each class and a lavatory at the inner end, and the gangway was on the offside. Unlike 2693-2699 they were given false cantrail strips to match the BIL motor coaches, and lacked cab-front handrails and step-plates. DTC 12855 made use of the stored underframe of BIL trailer 12037 from war casualty 2014, and was paired with a post-war all-steel SUB motor coach to form 2 HAL 2700 as described later. 12856 was built on the underframe of accident victim 12133 and went to unit 2133. 12857 and 12858 were entirely new, having the last two SR-design 62ft underframes to be constructed, and were paired with motor coaches 10664 and 10635 to reform units 2100 and 2069 respectively. As all the new driving trailer composites were equipped with heavy self-contained buffers, these were also fitted to motor coaches 10635 and 10664. (10678 of 2133, being from the final batch of BILs, already had them.)

Driving trailer composite 12857 was one of four such dia. 2705 vehicles constructed in 1954 with Bulleid all-steel bodywork as accident replacements. Formed in 2 BIL 2100, it was photographed at Portsmouth Harbour on 15th March 1960. Of almost identical design to the post-war 2 HALs, visible differences include a cantrail-height gutter, to match the BIL motor coach, and a lack of handrails and step-plates on the cab front. To schoolboy enthusiasts of the time, this type of hybrid unit would be known as a '2 BAL'. *Colin Boocock*

Otherwise, units rarely exchanged coaches, but 2008 and 2029 permanently exchanged driving trailers in 1951. A summary of non-standard or hybrid 2 BIL units resulting from these reformations is shown in this table:

Unit	MThB	DTC	Reformed	Notes:
2008	10575	12052	c. August 1951	1936-type 2 BIL DTC
2029	10595	12109	c. August 1951	1935-type 2 BIL DTC
2056	10622	12231	November 1947	1939-type 2 HAL DTC
2069	10635	12858	January 1955	Post-war all-steel DTC
2088	10654	12807	early 1950	1939-type 2 HAL DTC
2100	10664	12857	January 1955	Post-war all-steel DTC
2133	10678	12856	February 1955	Post-war all-steel DTC

The unlucky 2088 in its reformed state only survived until 1st August 1962, when it was involved in another accident, this time a derailment at Barnham. HAL trailer 12807 was overturned and the unit was subsequently written off.

In September 1963, 2006 was the subject of a novel experiment involving de-electrification and lengthening to seven coaches. Dieselisation of the Oxted line had taken place in that year and there was an urgent need for more electrically-heated coaching stock for haulage by BRCW type 3 KA (later class 33) diesel electric locomotives on peak hour services. An unpowered seven-coach set was therefore made up at Eastleigh, utilising the vehicles of 2006 with five spare 'six-a-side' suburban trailers marshalled between. The formation of this trailer set, initially numbered 900, was: Trailer Brake Second (formerly MBS) 10573 + TS 10346 + TS 10349 + TC 11485 + TS 10353 + TS 10351 + TC (formerly DTC) 12107. Overall length was marked as 448ft 10½in. The control and some electrical equipment was disconnected or removed from both BIL vehicles, but the traction motors were initially left in situ. Standard UIC electric heating cables were fitted at the cab ends, to enable supply from the locomotive. TC 11485 was fitted with an underframe-mounted motor generator to supply lighting for the whole set, also fed from the locomotive. The set was painted in the later BR green livery with badges only on the sides of former motor coach 10573. 11485 and 12107 had yellow stripes over the first class compartments at cantrail level and all vehicles were given 'flash plates' on the body ends to cover for the unlikely circumstance of the set being towed under overhead catenary.

Of the intermediate vehicles, the four 103xx series trailers had been built in 1945 for augmenting 1925 suburban units to four coaches and were ten-compartment vehicles seating 120. They were not all-steel, but of identical construction to the first ten Bulleid 4 SUBs with welded steel sides and ends but traditional canvas-covered wooden roofs. 11485, however, was an all-steel nine-compartment vehicle, originally built in 1946 with six longer compartments for the possible return of first class to suburban services, and until 1963 had been formed in one of the first all-steel SUBs, 4115. When altered for use in 900, these compartments were given first class seating, and thus it was the only coach of its type ever fitted out as a composite. It had two second class compartments at one end (marshalled towards the brake end of the set) and one at the other, with the six firsts between. The spacious four-a-side first class seating, with armrests, was upholstered in one of the two original Kent Coast first class patterns, while the second class trim was the maroon 'sprig and octopus' repp. (See Volume 1 for more details.) For their new role, all these vehicles were given replacement fibreglass doors, self-coloured green.

Nine-compartment SUB all-steel trailer 11485 in 7 TC set 701 (renumbered from 900), the only such vehicle ever fitted out as a true composite, in blue livery with appropriate yellow stripe at Selhurst on 10th May 1968. By this time 701 was dumped out of use (although not officially withdrawn) following fire damage to its electrical equipment. *E. W. J. Crawforth*

Trailer set 900, formed from 2 BIL 2006 and five suburban 'six-a-side' trailers, stands berthed at Eridge for its weekend rest in East Sussex after arriving at Tunbridge Wells West with the Friday 5.20pm from Victoria, shortly after its introduction in 1963. (Driving) trailer composite 12107 is nearest. Original waist-level control and lighting jumpers have been removed from the cab end and replaced by a jumper at buffer-beam height for electrical supply from the hauling locomotive, but the redundant headcode panel remains. *Lens of Sutton*

Set 900 entered service on 9th September 1963. Its usual workings were the 7.25am Tunbridge Wells West to London Bridge via East Grinstead and 5.20pm return, both Mondays to Fridays only. Berthing was at New Cross Gate by day and at Eridge overnight and at weekends. From time to time it was also used as a convenient rake of hauled stock for test purposes. In June 1966, as part of a general renumbering scheme for hauled stock, 900 was renumbered 701 and classified 7 TC, although any intention to convert it for true push-pull operation would have been thwarted by a lack of side buffers on the intermediate vehicles. With the closure of the East Grinstead – Ashurst Junction line from 2nd January 1967, it was diverted to run from Crowborough via Eridge, departing at 07.57, with return from London Bridge still at 17.20. Overnight and weekend berthing was then at Crowborough.

701 was taken out of service after traffic on 19th July 1967 and sent for overhaul at Eastleigh, possibly in error. (While out of use, its replacement was an odd rake of coaches just displaced from Waterloo to Basingstoke services by the Bournemouth electrification, comprising a Bulleid brake composite, a BR standard open first and five BR non-corridor seconds, which ran from 21st July until 27th September.) Rail blue livery with full yellow ends was applied, while the headcode boxes were removed from the cab fronts and the apertures sheeted over, significantly altering the appearance of the set. Shortly after its return to traffic on 30th September, a fire damaged the electrical equipment in one of the BIL vehicles and 701 was not used in passenger service beyond October 1967, although not officially withdrawn until May 1969. In the intervening period it was stored in Tennison Road sidings (Norwood Junction), then at Micheldever

The condemned end vehicles of 7 TC 701, together with trailer second 10353, stand in Woking yard on 13th November 1969 following use in a fire brigade training exercise. The headcode panels had been removed and plated over as part of the 1967 overhaul. The former BIL coaches were scrapped shortly afterwards, but the TS saw further use in 4 SUB 4364. *John Scrace*

following withdrawal. The former BIL end vehicles and SUB trailer 10353 were in Woking yard for a fire brigade exercise in November 1969, the BIL coaches being broken up by King's at Wymondham in the following February. All the ex-SUB trailers were however reused, three of the four ten-compartment wooden-roofed vehicles being utilised in additional 4 SUB units 4131 and 4132. Composite 11485 was downgraded once more to second class only, rewired and renumbered for use in 4 EPB 5115.

As with other pre-war unit classes described in this and the following chapter, there was a spate of reformations in the final years of the BILs, and a number of units were withdrawn early as repairing accident damage ceased to be economic. Driving trailer composite 12138 of 2105 was badly damaged in the East Preston level crossing accident in September 1965 and subsequently condemned, following which motor coach 10671 went to 4 LAV 2943, replacing 10545. 2059 was withdrawn in October 1965 following an accident at Durnsford Road depot. Motor coach 10594 of 2028 was damaged by fire at Waterloo in October 1966, and DTC 12051 was transferred to 2 HAL 2626 to replace 12211, lost in a collision the previous month. Conversely, driving trailer 12156 of 2123 was damaged in 1967 and replaced by 12193

from 2 HAL 2608 in February 1968. In 1968 prototype driving trailer 12101 was transferred from 2010 to 2096, while another DTC of the same batch, 12108 from 2007, went to 2055 at about the same time. These swaps were a result of the withdrawal of units 2007/10 and of DTCs 12078 and 12179 that July. 2018 and 2120 were hit by a diesel unit at Portsmouth Harbour in April 1969 and withdrawn, while 2080 suffered the same fate after being damaged in a collision at Balham the following month. Further accident casualties that year included 2122 (in February, location not known) and 2121 at Redhill. By March 1969 motor coach 10594 had been repaired and unit 2028 returned to service with the post-war all-steel driving trailer 12854 from 2 HAL 2653, which had been withdrawn following an accident at Aldershot. The formations of the 'odd' units resulting from the reformations described in this paragraph are listed in the table below:

Unit	MThB	DTC	Reformed	Notes:
2028	10594	12854	by 3.69	Post-war all-steel DTC
2055	10621	12108	late 1968	1935-type 2 BIL DTC
2096	10662	12101	late 1968	1935-type 2 BIL DTC
2123	10689	12193	2.68	1939-type 2 HAL DTC

As mentioned elsewhere, yellow warning panels followed by full yellow ends began to appear from 1963 and 1967 respectively. BILs given full yellow ends while still green had the yellow extended around the cab corners to the front of the motorman's door. A number of units were outshopped in BR blue livery with full yellow ends from December 1967 onwards, and on these the yellow did not extend quite so far. They included 2016/22/24/25/28/32/43/58/62/64/72/75/86/90/98/99 and 2103/11/12/23/33/35/40/49. Many units were still in green with small warning panels when withdrawn. Whistles were replaced by roof-mounted air horns from about 1965, but the BILs were only converted gradually. The last to retain its whistle was 2086, which was already in blue livery when it received its horns in June 1971, just weeks prior to withdrawal.

Mass withdrawal of the 2 BIL fleet began in February 1969 and ended in July 1971, their replacements mainly being either 4 CORs displaced from main line duties or new 4 VEP and 4 CIG units. BILs (and HALs, by this time common user with them) were partly ousted from their duties on the Portsmouth direct and Alton lines from 1967 in connection with the Bournemouth line electrification, and had disappeared entirely from these routes by mid 1969. They were displaced from the Waterloo to Reading line from July 1970, and the last eked out their days on south coast locals from Brighton, where they had worked from their introduction. A '2 BIL Farewell' railtour, organised by the then newly-formed Southern Electric Group, took place on 9th January 1971, initially formed of units 2016, 2112 and 2024. However, a 'hot box' caused 2112 to be failed at Wimbledon about an hour into the tour, and 4 SUB 4693 was substituted. The SUB was later removed at Blackfriars and replaced by 2034 and HAL 2603. The highlight of the tour was an 86mph charge down Sole Street bank, a speed unprecedented for these units. Final runs in regular passenger service took place in the early hours of 31st July 1971, 2034 and HAL 2661 forming the 01.05 Brighton to West Worthing. The last BILs to remain in capital stock and withdrawn on that date were 2016/34/90/98 and 2111/23/35/40. This was not quite the end however, as three of these units, 2111, 2135 and 2140, were resurrected for another Farewell tour on 25th September, starting from Waterloo and ending at Blackfriars. Organised this time by BR (Eastern) Staff Railway Society, this trip broke new ground by running over London Midland routes from Richmond to Broad Street and between Watford Junction and Euston, both recently converted from fourth rail to SR-style third rail.

Years of withdrawal of the bulk of the BIL fleet were as follows:

1969: 2001-05/08/09/12/13/15/18/20/23/30/39-42/44/49/71/73/76/77/79 /80/ 85/89, 2091-94/96/97,2106-09/15/18/20-22/25-29/38/42-44/ 48/49.

1970: 2017/19/21/22/25/26/29/31/35/37/43/45-48/51-55/60/61/63-66/ 68-70/75/82, 2086/87/95, 2100/01/03/04/10/12/14/16/17/23/24/33/34/36/39/41/45/50-52.

1971: 2011/16/24/27/28/32/33-34/36/38/50/56-58/62/67/72/74/78/81/ 83/8 4/90/98/99,2111/13/30/32/ 35/37/40/46/47.

Scrap dealers involved in breaking up the BILs were mainly the same as those who dealt with LAVs, including Armytage's (Sheepbridge), Cashmore's (Newport) and King's (Snailwell), while another involved for the first time was Bird's at Long Marston. Some units were on hand for considerable periods between withdrawal, condemnation and final breaking up, and a few were actually reinstated for a short while. 2118 was stripped of internal fittings following withdrawal and used for Christmas mail traffic on the South Western division in December 1969. A large number of withdrawn BILs (and HALs) were concentrated at Selhurst for removal of reusable equipment during the first half of 1971, while Polegate sidings had been used for similar purposes in 1968-69 and Slade Green in 1970.

Two 2 BIL units escaped the scrap heap at this time. 2037, withdrawn in March 1970, was sent to the BR Research Centre at Derby for experimental use, becoming test unit 024, and was broken up there in about 1975. 2090 was retained for official preservation as part of the National Collection. Originally stored (together with various other NRM stock) in the former Pullman works at Preston Park, Brighton, it remained in operational condition and emerged for a number of open days and exhibitions. In 1985 the unit was taken into Lovers Walk depot (Brighton) for a complete overhaul, including repaint into late BR green livery with full yellow ends. In the following years it was used regularly for open day shuttles and special trains, always working in company with the green 4 SUB 4732 (see Volume 1), retained specifically for this purpose to avoid running a preserved unit with only one motor bogie out on the main line on its own. Some of these tours took 2090 and 4732 over lines which had not been electrified when the BILs were withdrawn, such as to Hastings via Battle in 1986 and to Weymouth in 1989. As the conductor rail voltage on these and other SR lines was now 750 rather than the 660V for which the BILs had been designed, it was necessary to isolate the heating circuits and to fit special 80V light bulbs. Following a 1993 edict banning wooden-framed and screw-coupled coaches working in passenger service over BR track, 2090 was placed into store in the disused and unsupervised carriage shed at West Worthing, where some vandalism inevitably occurred. Fortunately, the BIL was moved in 1996 into safer care at the former St Leonards diesel depot. Subsequently, after high-quality restoration into 'middle-period' BR green in the later shade with carriage roundels on the motor coaches but no yellow cab ends or cantrail stripes, 2090 was put on display at 'Locomotion' (the National Railway Museum at Shildon) in September 2004. While a very long way from the live rail and unlikely ever to run under its own power again, this last BIL is at least safe for posterity.

THE 2 HAL UNITS 1939-71
For the Eastern section electrification extension to Maidstone and Gillingham, completed in May 1939 and often referred to as the Medway scheme, a further 76 two-coach units were constructed at Eastleigh Works on Lancing underframes between the end of 1938 and April 1939. Ordered on 29th April 1938 to HO 1023, they constituted the largest single

With its three-a-side seating, individual back cushions and substantial armrests, the first class accommodation in a 1939 HAL was acceptably comfortable, if not exactly opulent. Upholstery is in jade green uncut moquette with a fawn 'medieval' pattern. *SR Official*

batch of main line semi-fast units ever built by the SR. Each was formed of a seven-compartment motor third brake of similar layout to those in the LAVs, and a side corridor driving trailer composite with four first and four third class compartments plus a lavatory, similar to those in the BILs. Thus only half the accommodation in each unit had access to lavatory facilities, giving rise to the code 2 HAL, which could have meant either 'half a 4 LAV' or 'two coach unit in which only one coach has a lavatory'. A contemporary account stated that this arrangement provided 'the right type of accommodation both for the short distance passenger and the traveller who is going from end to end.'[12] Basic dimensions were the same as those of the BILs, and seating was provided for 24 first and 102 third class passengers, of whom all first class

but only 32 of those travelling third had access to the lavatory. The Medway 2 HAL units were numbered 2601-2676.

An order for a further sixteen units of identical design then followed on 28th November 1938, to HO 1058, with no specific use designated. Numbered 2677-2692, approximate completion dates were November 1939 for 2677-2682 and December 1939 for the remainder. (As described earlier, these final HALs were followed off the Eastleigh production line by two more 4 LAVs, 2954 and 2955, identical in style, equipment and appointments to the 1939 HALs.) Although authorised (according to minutes of the Rolling Stock sub-committee) simply 'to meet additional traffic and maintenance requirements' as mentioned in Chapter 1, it has been suggested that 2677-2692 were actually intended for the projected future electrification from Sevenoaks to Tunbridge Wells, which was not progressed due to the impending war.

---

12 Electric Traction Supplement, *The Railway Gazette*, 30th June, 1939. p72

The brutal interior of a 1939 HAL third class compartment, with hard and fixed bench-type cushions upholstered in the depressing fawn and brown 'Medway' patterned moquette. Other features of note are the scalloped seat tops to indicate the regulation number of places and extensive use of 'Rexine'-covered surfaces, extending even to the luggage rack rail and advertisement/mirror frames. *SR Official*

New 2 HAL 2653, with dia. 2702 driving trailer composite 12807 leading, poses for its official photograph at Eastleigh in 1939. Distinctive features of this stock, including the welded steel cab devoid of guttering, inset cab sides and window corners rounded to a large radius, are readily apparent. Livery is still dark olive green, but lining has now disappeared completely. *SR Official*

The 2 HAL motor third brakes (dia. 2116) were numbered 10719-10810 and the driving trailer composites (dia. 2702) 12186-12231 and 12801-46: all were formed into units in numerical order. Tare weights were 44 tons for the motor coaches and 32 tons for the driving trailers, and overall unit length was 129ft 5in – the same as the final BILs. At underframe level and below, the 2 HAL vehicles also followed almost exactly what had gone before, and end-buffers were of

the heavy self-contained type. Standard electro-pneumatic control equipment and type EE 339 traction motors were supplied by English Electric. One difference from previous two-coach units was the provision from new of a safety cut-out for the air-compressor circuit, preventing the brakes being released if there was insufficient air pressure to apply them again.

The bodywork of these units was of a revised style, the HALs being the first complete units designed under the Bulleid/Lynes collaboration. As such, they formed an evolutionary stage between the Maunsell LAVs and BILs, and the Bulleid suburban stock on which work had already started before the last HALs were built. Basic construction was conventional, with steel body side panels on a teak frame-

work and planked, canvas-covered roofs. The 9ft body width took full advantage of the loading gauge, and it was alleged that the steel body panelling was shaped to provide the maximum room internally. Externally, the corners of all fixed windows were rounded to large radii and the glass was fitted from inside with rubber seals to provide as smooth a surface as possible to aid carriage washing. The cabs were of welded steel construction and, with their flattened motorman's doors, appeared to have been attached to the coach end as an after-thought. Although the offside window still opened outwards in order to facilitate headcode changing, it had only a thin steel frame, giving a rather neater appearance than on earlier stock. The cabs also lacked cantrail guttering and associated downpipes, but there were narrow gutters formed into the frame of each windscreen. Together with the smooth coach sides these changes gave the HALs a rather bare appearance compared with their predecessors, accentuated by their plain dark green livery. On the corridor side of the DTC there was a door opposite each compartment and large intermediate windows which reached higher than the door droplights. For some unexplained reason the corridor on these vehicles was on the opposite (motorman's) side to those of the BILs.

If the external appearance of the HALs was considered plain and spartan, their interiors were more so, with a depressing ambience being likened to a military camp by one author.[13] Gone was the Edwardian woodwork and thick padding of the BILs and earlier stock, to be replaced almost entirely by 'Rexine' covered surfaces and much harder seating; it is thus unsurprising that the 1939 HALs were soon regarded as being amongst the SR's most uncomfortable electric stock. Although the actual arrangement of seats in each compartment was the same as previously, with ten in the non-corridor thirds, eight in the corridor thirds and six in the corridor firsts, their design reflected Bulleid's ideas regarding what constituted acceptable comfort for outer-suburban travellers. In third class the hard narrow seat cushion was fixed and continuous across the compartment, and the backs were scalloped along the top edge, each arc denoting one seat, '. . . thus clearly indicating to the passengers the regulation number of seats provided in the compartment'.[14] End armrests were fitted, but there were no other concessions to comfort. In the first class compartments the backs as well as the seat cushions were separate, being divided by the usual folding intermediate armrests, but they lacked additional padding at head-height and there were no headrests at compartment sides. The tops of the seat backs were again curved, which would later cause difficulties with the attachment of antimacassars (not fitted until BR days).

New moquette patterns, eventually to become common-place in SR electric stock, were introduced with the Medway HALs. The first class seats were upholstered in a dark jade green uncut moquette with a small *fleur-de-lys* pattern in fawn, while the thirds had a pattern of mid-brown moquette with a darker brown 'Renaissance' floral design on them – attractive enough when new, but very depressing when worn or dirty. 'Rexine' synthetic leathercloth was extensively used not only for main panel surfaces, but also for covering small fittings such as picture frames and the supporting rods of luggage racks. Up to the bottoms of the windows, the basic colour was 'nut brown', whilst above, the shade was 'lichen green' in the first class compartments and light stone in the thirds; this included the main partitions, panels around the quarterlights and the ceilings. In the driving trailer compos-ites, the corridor was panelled in wood above the waist, with the ubiquitous brown 'Rexine' below, while the lavatory compartment surfaces were finished in paint or 'Rexine' of a cream shade. Metal fittings were of stainless steel, brass, or painted, and for the first time the emergency communication chains were situated in a recess in the ceiling rather than in an exposed tube.

Following delivery, the Medway 2 HALs were run-in on various Central and Western section suburban and main line services, the latter including Waterloo – Portsmouth /Reading and Victoria – Bognor Regis. They also appeared on special excursions. With the start of electric services to Maidstone and Gillingham on 2nd July 1939, HALs worked between Victoria and Maidstone East/Gillingham, units dividing or attaching at Swanley, and between Charing Cross and Maidstone West/Gillingham, splitting or combining at Strood. They also operated a Strood – Maidstone West shuttle which connected out of a Cannon Street – Gillingham stopping service worked by suburban stock, and in the peaks there were services serving Holborn Viaduct (via Swanley) and Cannon Street (via Dartford), as well as the odd train between Sevenoaks and Cannon Street via Orpington (the 'Waldron Smithers train' referred to in the 2 BIL section). Virtually all services ran from the London termini in eight-coach forma-tions, so after splitting, four coaches ran to each country destination.

Additional units 2677-2692 were virtually identical to the Medway batch, but painted in an experimental shade of light green which quickly weathered to an unattractive khaki. Internally, third class seats were upholstered in an obsolete blue/beige 'jazz' moquette, so Eastleigh was presumably using up roll-ends as wartime economies began to bite. This batch was also equipped ex-shops with regulation blackout fittings, including partially obscured windows. They initially entered service on the south coast, displacing NOLs. By 1941, however, they had transferred to Waterloo – Ascot – Reading/ Guildford services, which had been increased from six to eight coaches, and also to Waterloo – Alton trains, in both cases to help cope with the heavy Aldershot military traffic. Their inferior accommodation when compared to the BILs was of academic interest when most trains were packed anyway. Wartime conditions meant that they soon became commonplace on any electrified main line route, and after 1945 they continued to appear daily on stopping trains between Waterloo and Portsmouth/Alton. However, as with the LAVs and NOLs, their non-corridor accommodation made them less than suitable for journeys of much over an hour.

---

13 Baker, Michael, *The Southern Electric Story*, Silver Link Press, ISBN 0 947971 85 8, 1993. p32

14 Electric Traction Supplement, *The Railway Gazette*, 30th June, 1939. p72

No 2 HAL units were lost as a result of war damage, but seven other two-coach units were. Five were from the main line fleet and included coastal 2 NOL 1828 and BILs 2014, 2102, 2119 and 2131. The remaining two were SL unit 1807 and Windsor NOL 1855 from the suburban fleet. Initial orders for three replacement main line units (HO 3230) and two suburban units (HO 3232) were placed on 5th May 1945, but in the circumstances were held in abeyance. HO 3230 was amended to five units on 28th May 1947, increasing the total order to seven new two-coach units, comprising five main line and two suburban. For convenience (avoiding the design and construction of just two non-standard driving trailer thirds) all seven were eventually built as main-line units of 2 HAL specification, and were turned out from Eastleigh in the latter half of 1948. As before, underframes and bogies came from Lancing.

The new units were numbered 2693-2699 and, although of the same basic layout as the 1939 HALs, were to a revised design having much in common with the new all-steel 4 SUB suburban stock then in production and therefore appeared radically different. Below underframe-level they were entirely standard, but the bodies were made up exclusively from steel sections welded together on jigs, and the sides were curved continuously to give a maximum body width of 9ft 3in. This latter feature enabled six passengers to sit each side in the non-corridor compartments in the motor coaches, giving an increase of fourteen third class seats, while due to welded construction these units saved two tons in weight compared with their predecessors. The slightly bowed cab fronts lacked the traditional domed roof, meeting the sides and roof panels at a right-angle, while the motorman's doors were not inset. There was no cantrail, the sides (and paintwork) curving smoothly into the roof. Another typical late Bulleid feature was the lozenge-shaped window incorporating a ventilator above each door droplight, while the droplights themselves were self-balancing in any position using 'lazy arms' (similar to callipers) inside the door frame. The corners of all windows were rounded, although not to the same extent as in the earlier units. Livery was the then-standard malachite green with 'sunshine' numbering at cantrail height, but being delivered after nationalisation the unit number was prefixed with a small 's'. Due to their all-steel construction, 2693-2699 were quickly dubbed 'tin HALs' by observers. They shared certain detail peculiarities with SUBs 4355-4366, turned out from Eastleigh earlier that year, including step-plates over the buffers and yellow grab handles around both cab look-outs, the latter giving them an 'eyebrowed' appearance. These were necessary in order to change the headcode stencil, as the offside cab window did not open.

The motor coaches (diagram 2127) were numbered 10811-17 and had motorman's, guard's and seven third class compartments. Apart from the necessary two periscopes for the guard, they also differed from a standard SUB compartment motor coach in having one less compartment, and there was therefore a particularly capacious van, 14ft 3in in length, with space for two tons of luggage. The compartments seated six passengers on each side in slightly less austere surroundings than the pre-war units, giving a capacity of 84. The

driving trailer composites (dia. 2705) were numbered 12847-53 and also had the same layout as the earlier examples, except that the side corridor was on the opposite side (as on the BILs) and there was a connecting door from it into the motorman's compartment. The windows on the corridor side were of normal height, and the lavatory window on the opposite side opened at the top. Both these features were borrowed from the Bulleid main line corridor steam stock then in production. There was no change in seating numbers this time, the first class compartments accommodating three-a-side and the third class four: this gave a capacity of 24 first class seats and 32 third. Internally, dark brown 'Rexine' was again used to cover much of the panelling, and the internal side-corridor partition windows had rounded corners and polished metal surrounds. Seating also was similar to the Bulleid locomotive-hauled stock and resembled that in the BILs, with loose seat cushions in the thirds. Upholstery was the then-standard crimson and fawn moquette in the thirds and a dark floral-patterned tapestry in the firsts. While undoubtedly more comfortable internally than the earlier HALs, the riding qualities of 2693-2699 sadly left much to be desired, being quite as bouncy as the Brighton express stock. They entered service on the Eastern section Maidstone and Gillingham services, interworking entirely with earlier class members.

Although fewer, reformations involving the 2 HALs were closely bound-up with the LAVs and BILs mentioned earlier, and some repetition is inevitable to give a coherent story. Unit 2646 was split up early in 1948, motor coach 10764 going to 4 LAV 2926 to replace 10511 destroyed in the South Croydon collision of October 1947, and driving trailer 12231 to 2 BIL 2056, replacing 12079 which had been written off at Brighton in 1946. DTC 12807 from unit 2653 was used to reform 2 BIL 2088 in 1950, and was replaced by new all-steel driving trailer 12854, of exactly the same design as those in the 1948 HALs, at the beginning of 1951. 12854 had been ordered on 2nd November 1949 as part of HO 3618, and made use of the underframe of BIL DTC 12121 from 2088, the body of which had been gutted by fire at Littlehampton in 1950. Following this reformation, the overall length of 2653 was 129ft 6in. Three 1939 HALs were temporarily reformed with BIL driving trailer composites from 1956 onwards. 2601 ran with DTC 12093 from 2070 between June 1956 and August 1957, while 2611 was formed with 12146 from 2113 from about September 1959 until March 1962. 2621 was similarly formed during the same period, but only a photographic record exists and the identity of the BIL vehicle is unclear. Other than these changes, and the withdrawal of 2680 following an accident at Chatham on 5th April 1956, the 2 HAL fleet remained unscathed until the late 1960s.

An eighth unit of the same general design as 2693-2699, numbered 2700, appeared in February 1955, formed of all-steel SUB motor coach 12664 and yet another new driving trailer composite, 12855. This was the last main-line unit to go into service before the general adoption of EP-braked designs. Originally built at Eastleigh in 1950, MThB 12664 was of centre-gangway saloon interior layout with eight bays seating 82, and had originally been formed in the peculiar half all-steel, half LBSCR-bodied unit 4590, from which it was removed in July 1954. DTC 12855 was built in 1954 as part of HO 4009 (dated 2nd July 1953) at the same time and to exactly the same design as the replacement driving trailers 12856-58 for 2 BILs 2069, 2100 and 2133, and made use of the stored underframe from BIL DTC 12037 which had been a war loss. Although almost identical to those in 'tin HALs' 2693-2699, these vehicles had a false cantrail strip and lacked the cab-end grab rails and step-plates. As 12664 originally had only one periscope, 2700 was initially confined to Eastern section services to Maidstone and Gillingham, where solo working of single two-car units was virtually unknown. It was fitted with a second periscope on overhaul in May 1957. Externally, 2700 could easily be distinguished because its driving trailer had the false cantrail strips (intended to match wooden-roofed BIL motor coaches and act as rain-water gutters) lacking on 2693-2699.

In the early 1950s there were a few mixed 2 HAL+4 SUB workings in the rush hours on combined services between Charing Cross or Cannon Street and Maidstone West/ Gillingham, dividing or combining at Strood, the HAL portion being included to give the Maidstone West branch its requisite quota of first class seating as the SUBs were by now third class only. In 1955/56 the first class compartment next to the seconds in the driving trailers of units 2601-76 and 2693-2700 was downclassed, due to a reduced demand for first class accommodation on the Eastern section. Following the introduction of ten-car trains on SE suburban services, certain services out of Cannon Street involving HAL stock were lengthened from eight to ten coaches from 4th March 1957, either by adding another HAL or substituting a HAL with a 4 SUB. These arrangements continued until April 1958 when newer EPB and 2 HAP units took over entirely. At this time the new 90mph HAPs also displaced HALs from the Maidstone and Gillingham lines in preparation for the Ramsgate electrification, resulting in the large-scale transfer of HALs to the South Western and Central section pool. All-steel units 2693-2699 were allocated to the new Gatwick Airport service mentioned below, while the 1939 units and 2700 replaced the coastal 2 NOL units, becoming common-user with the BILs. On transfer, the number of first class seats was restored to 24. A few HALs returned to the Eastern section between June and September 1959, two eight-coach formations running stopping services between London and Ramsgate on a few diagrams for which there were not enough new HAPs.

All-steel 2 HAL 2699, wearing rather grubby later BR green, waits at Reigate with a London train in May 1960. After arrival at Redhill it will attach to the rear of a portion from Brighton (generally a 4 LAV) before continuing northwards. Although by this time the type was specifically allocated to the Victoria – Gatwick Airport service, they did sometimes 'escape' on to other duties, as seen here. Diagram 2127 motor brake second 10817 is leading: its huge van with space for two tons of airline passengers' luggage is readily apparent. *A. J. Wills / © www.southernrailway.net*

A new airport to the north of the original one at Gatwick was opened in May 1958 adjacent to the old racecourse station which was expanded and rebuilt to serve it, replacing the original 1935 station which then closed. Although other Brighton line trains called, the new Gatwick Airport station was specifically served by an extension of the half-hourly Littlehampton – Three Bridges stopping service to Victoria. Between Victoria and Gatwick Airport these trains were strengthened by a 2 HAL unit coupled at the London end and detached at Gatwick ready to be coupled to the next Up service. The budget for this scheme financed the renovation of a number of 1939-type HALs, including 2603/05/21/29/33/44/61/74, which were given improved seating in their second class compartments on overhaul in the 1958-61 period, making them compare less unfavourably with the BILs and LAVs with which they were by then extensively interworking. Although the units concerned would have regularly appeared on the Victoria – Littlehampton trains, they were not generally used for the special airport section, all-steel 2693-2699 being chosen instead. This was due to their huge luggage vans capable of swallowing two tons of suitcases, but the poor riding characteristics and dingy compartments of these units cannot have improved foreign tourists' views of BR. (In fact, much French and Belgian rolling stock at this time still had wooden bench seats, so perhaps the comparison was not so bad.) 2693-2699 were used on the Gatwick Airport service until 1969 when, with the introduction of new 4 VEP stock, they rejoined remaining HALs and BILs, mainly on coastal services but with the odd foray onto other Central or South Western main line duties.

Other than any already mentioned, there were few modifications to the 2 HALs during their lives. As on the LAVs and BILs, new lightweight sprung collector shoes replaced the original gravity shoegear in the late 1950s. From about 1965 onwards the hot water supply in the lavatory was disconnected and the hot tap removed. In April 1962, 2654 was the first Southern Railway-designed unit to be equipped with 'raspberry' air horns (other than experimentally) mounted on the cab roof, replacing the cab front-mounted whistles. The rest were gradually fitted with air horns over the next few years.

As with other classes dealt with in this chapter, the incidence of accidents and other mishaps affecting the HALs showed a sharp increase in the years immediately prior to their withdrawal. 2608 suffered accidental damage at Lovers Walk depot (Brighton) in July 1967 and was disbanded. Undamaged DTC 12193 went to BIL 2123 in February 1968, but motor coach 10726 was withdrawn and converted into de-icing coach DS 70268. This was the first of a batch of six (the others being the HAL-type motor coaches from 4 LAVs 2926 and 2954/55, mentioned earlier) marshalled in pairs as de-icing units 001-003 for the 1967 Bournemouth electrification. These conversions are described fully in Chapter 6. In 1966, unit 2626 was involved in a collision at Vauxhall and trailer 12211 was subsequently cut up, being replaced by BIL DTC 12051 from 2028 in January 1967. 2653, already a hybrid with 'tin HAL'-type driving trailer 12854, was disbanded following a collision at Aldershot in February

1969. Its motor coach was condemned and 12854 was paired with BIL MBS 10594 (repaired following a fire at Waterloo in October 1966) to reinstate unit 2028. Driving trailer 12842 from 2688 was condemned following a derailment at Ascot in February 1968, and was replaced the following month by all-steel DTC 12855 from 2700, which had been disbanded. In this revised hybrid form 2688 only lasted until June 1969 when it too was disbanded, although neither vehicle was scrapped. MBS 10806 went to ad hoc 4 SUB unit 4132 in September 1969, while DTC 12855 went to 2696 in October, replacing 12850 which had been badly damaged in a sideswipe at Balham. Although both vehicles in this unit were still all-steel, it could be identified due to a false cantrail strip on the driving trailer but not on the motor coach. A summary of the few non-standard or hybrid 2 HAL units running in the period 1966-71 is given in the table below:

Unit	MBS	DTC	Reformed	Withdrawn
2626	10744	12051¶	1.1967	10.1969
2688	10806	12855§	3.1968	6.1969
2696	10814	12855§	10.1969	4.1971

¶ 2 BIL DTC ex 2028
§ All-steel DTC ex 2700

Quite a few 2 HAL units were painted blue with full yellow ends between 1967 and 1969, these including 2604/05/07/15/16/21/23/2426-29/32/33/36/40/41/45/47/60/64/65/74-77/83/85-90 and 2693-99.

In common with the BILs, the 2 HAL fleet was withdrawn between 1969 and 1971. The final units remaining in passenger traffic were taken out of service on 31st July 1971 at the same time as the last of the BILs. These were 2610/23/27-29 /61/74/79/95/98 and 2699. As with the LAVs and the BILs, the HALs did a considerable mileage around the SR between various dumping points before being finally dispatched to breaker's yards, which were the same as for the BILs.

The year of withdrawal of the bulk of the 2 HAL units was as follows:

1969: 2606/09/13/17/22/24/26/35/37/39/42/44/51-53/58/59/62/69/70/73/78/88

1970: 2601/04/05/07/11/12/14/18/20/21/25/30/31/34/36/38/40/43/45/47/50 /54/55/57 /2660/63/64/66/71/75/81-83/86/87/89-93

1971: 2602/03/10/15/16/19/23/27-29/32/33/41/48/49/56/61/65/67/68/72/74/ 76/77/79/2684/85/94-99.

A number of 2 HAL motor coaches of both 1939 and all-steel types were involved with the second-generation 4 SUB units (see Volume 1), which were also of Bulleid/Lynes design on 62ft underframes. The first was MBS 10798 from unit 2680, left spare after its driving trailer 12834 was destroyed in the accident at Chatham on 5th April 1956. After gently rusting in Hassocks sidings for four years its body was broken up at Newhaven in July 1960, but the leading end of its underframe was grafted on to to all-steel 4 SUB motor coach 10895 from unit 4355, as part of its repair following collision damage at Herne Hill. The rest were more normal reformations, all occurring towards the end of the HAL fleet's existence. Following the disbanding of 2700 in March 1968, MBSO 12664 (a standard all-steel 4 SUB centre-gangway vehicle apart from its additional periscope) returned to suburban service in unit 4369 in April 1969. The driving trailer of 2644 was damaged and withdrawn in April 1969 and its motor coach 10762 went to SUB 4103 later in that year, replacing 10946 which had been written-off in an accident. The HAL motor coach had exactly the same front end as the SUB vehicle it replaced, so the appearance of the unit was not much altered, but the number of seats was reduced by no fewer than 38. Due to a shortage of suburban units at this time, when HALs 2622 and 2659 were withdrawn their motor brake seconds 10740 and 10777 were formed-up with a pair of spare SUB compartment trailers to produce ad-hoc 4 SUB unit 4131, entering service in May 1969. A similar unit, numbered 4132 and utilising motor coaches 10755 and 10806 from HALs 2637 and 2688 respectively, entered traffic the following September. These two SUBs had a short life, being withdrawn in October 1971. SUB motor coach 10903 was destroyed in a collision at Hampton Court in April 1970, and was replaced in unit 4364 by all-steel HAL motor coach 10811 from just-withdrawn 2693. Similarly, when 11309 from 4625 was destroyed by fire at Selhurst early in 1971, it was replaced by 'tin HAL' MBS 10815 from 2697. These vehicles were

again distinctive in a SUB due to their much larger guard's/luggage van and resultant windowless body side area. 4364 survived until February 1974 and 4625 until the following May, 10811/15 therefore remaining in passenger service for nearly three years after all other HAL vehicles had been withdrawn. A summary list of HAL motor coaches reformed into 4 SUB units between 1969 and 1974, in order of coach numbers, is given in in the table below.

2 HAL MBS	ex unit	Reformed into 4 SUB unit	Date Reformed	Withdrawn
10740¶	2622	4131*	5.1969	10.1971
10755¶	2637	4132*	9.1969	10.1971
10762¶	2644	4103#	2.1969	1.1972
10777¶	2659	4131*	5.1969	10.1971
10806¶	2688	4132*	9.1969	10.1971
10811§	2693	4364	1970	2.1974
10815§	2697	4625	4.1971	5.1974

¶ 1939-type wood-framed HAL MBS

§ 1948-type all-steel 'tin HAL' MBS

* temporary ad-hoc 4 SUB unit using 1939 HAL motor coaches and spare SUB trailers

1941-type 'Sheba' 4 SUB with wooden roof and domed cab ends

Illustrating the condition in which many of the class were withdrawn, 1939-type 2 HAL 2674 leads a mixed eight-coach BIL/HAL formation at Balcombe on 30th May 1968, forming the 13.12 London Bridge to Brighton stopping service. Roof-mounted horns have replaced the whistle, and livery is the later BR green with small warning panel and black triangle to denote that the other end of the unit lacks a van. *John Scrace*

Some of the 1969 HAL withdrawals were stripped of their seats, luggage racks, heaters and advertisement panels, and used for Christmas parcels and mail traffic on the South Western (2606/13/24/42 are recorded) and Central divisions in December 1969. This arrangement was evidently considered successful, as six further units were similarly modified on a more formal basis in late 1970 for the same duties. 2604/05/38/45/89/92 had seats, heaters, luggage racks and commode handles removed and were renumbered 061-066 respectively, although their original coach numbers were retained. They were reclassified 2 PAN, in this case denoting their intended use for 'Parcels And Newspapers', rather than the inclusion of a pantry car. They were apparently originally intended for year-round use, but the scheme was never properly implemented and after service in December 1970 all six were placed in store. 062 was noted out of use at Stewarts Lane the following December, but the rest again emerged for the 1971 Christmas mail traffic before being scrapped early in 1972.

Apart from de-icing units 001-003, four further 1939 HAL motor coaches were modified for departmental use following withdrawal from passenger service. These were 10731/87 (from 2613/69) and 10742/60 (ex 2624/42). They became stores units 022 and 023 respectively, working on regular diagrams carrying CMEE supplies between depots. As with the de-icing units, their full story is related in Chapter 6.

Finally, an interesting survivor was all-steel HAL driving trailer composite 12847. Following withdrawal of 2693 from passenger service in 1970, this vehicle was retained by Selhurst Depot, initially as a 'runner' for moving single SUB-type motor coaches around the sidings there. There it remained, its blue paintwork progressively fading and its windows gradually becoming broken, until hauled off for scrapping by Marple and Gillott in Sheffield as late as April 1983.

As observed in previous illustrations, 'mix-and-not-quite-match' was common on the Southern, starting in the war years and continuing until the end of the first generation main line stock and 4 SUB era. This was possible due to the basic electrical and coupling compatibility of virtually all suburban and main line semi-fast units with Metrovick or EE 1936 control gear. Here, unique hybrid HAL unit 2611, reformed with a BIL driving trailer, waits in the rain at Redhill in about 1960. Both units had suffered collision damage in separate incidents in 1959. This type of reformation would be known as a '2 HIL' by young followers of the SR electric scene!

CHAPTER 5: FIRST GENERATION EXPRESS ROLLING STOCK 1932-72

This chapter covers the detailed history of the express electric multiple unit classes built for the Southern Railway's four main line coastal electrification schemes undertaken between 1932 and 1939. Included are the 6 PUL, 6 CIT and 5 BEL classes for the 1933 electrification to Brighton and Worthing, the 6 PAN class for the 1935 Eastbourne and Hastings scheme, and the 4 COR, 4 RES and 4 BUF classes for the Portsmouth No.1 and No.2 electrifications of 1937 and 1938. (To complicate matters, the 6 PUL/CIT and 5 BEL types were originally classified as 6 COR and 5 PUL respectively until the introduction of the Eastbourne 6 PAN units in 1935, but to avoid confusion they will generally be referred to by their post 1935 designations.) 130 units were provided in all, made up from a total of 603 vehicles, all of which were entirely new. With the exception of the 38 Pullman cars for the Brighton line, they were to SR designs produced by R.E.L. Maunsell and his assistant L. Lynes. The appearance and styling of the electric vehicles closely followed that of contemporary Maunsell/Lynes steam stock, and most were built in the SR's carriage workshops at Eastleigh on underframes and bogies fabricated at Lancing. Only the more specialised vehicles, which included the heavy all-steel motor coaches for the Brighton and Eastbourne line units and the catering cars in the Portsmouth 4 RES units, were ordered from outside contractors, as were the Pullmans. Exceptionally, the buffet cars of the 4 BUF units for the Portsmouth No.2 scheme were designed under the direction of O.V.S. Bulleid following the retirement of Maunsell in 1937 but, at least externally, retained the same general design and styling features.

Although described as 'express' because they were designed for the fastest services on the lines electrified and were of similar standards to the best contemporary SR long-distance steam stock, there were also important technical distinctions between the units described in this chapter and the semi-fast/suburban stock. These included the adoption of a new design of traction motor particularly suited to sustained high-speed running, a more advanced control system which prevented multiple working with other stock, and the provision of through gangways between coaches within each unit.

At an early stage in the planning of the Brighton and Worthing electrification scheme, it had been decided to use multiple unit stock exclusively, and the reasons for this are interesting. As explained in Volume 1, LBSCR plans for high-tension ac electrification of the London – Brighton main line envisaged haulage of existing stock using electric locomo-

tives, and ten years later the same arrangement was briefly considered once more when Walker's dc scheme was first mooted. However, use of third-rail current collection caused difficulties for a locomotive, whose pick-up shoes were concentrated within its own short length. The many flat junctions on the Brighton main line required frequent breaks in the conductor rail, and it would have been very possible for it to become stranded across one of these breaks with no shoes in contact with the rail, a circumstance known as gapping. This presented no problem for an electric multiple unit with pick-ups spread along the two or more coaches of the train and connected to each other through a power line. This was one important reason why EMUs were considered more suitable than locomotives, but they had other significant advantages as well. The power available always matched the number of coaches in the train, for example, and there was the facility to simply divide and combine separate portions at intermediate stations. Finally, despite SR publicity that this was 'Britain's first main line electrification', inside the railway the scheme was effectively treated by Raworth and his team as just another suburban extension and, from this consideration alone, it is doubtful whether anything other than a further fleet of electric units was ever seriously contemplated once detailed planning had started.

At this time in Britain the only railway using electric locomotives with third (and, in this case, fourth) rail current collection on passenger trains was the Metropolitan, which solved the gapping problem by mounting pick-up shoes on the end bogies of each rake of coaches, connected to each other and to the locomotive by a bus line running the length of the train – whether this arrangement was considered for the Brighton line is not known. In collaboration with Bulleid and English Electric, Raworth did in time develop an electric locomotive able to coast across gaps in the third rail by utilising a flywheel 'booster' system but, as fully described in Chapter 6, this was intended primarily for freight and the first did not enter service until 1942.

Before dealing with the individual classes it is again appropriate to consider livery details, which were common to all the units described until their disbanding or withdrawal between 1964 and 1972. Excepting the Pullmans and the 4 BUF buffet cars, all vehicles of the first generation express stock entered service in the standard dark olive green SR coach livery of the period, and there was no significant differentiation between them and the semi-fast stock in this respect. The PUL and PAN coaches had fully-lined sides, both along the waist and between the windows. On the motor coaches the leading corners were lined-out into three panels, but there was no lining on the actual cab ends. Numbering and lettering followed the style of other stock, except that class was indicated by a large block 3 or 1 next to the doors at fascia height on the motor coaches and PAN pantry cars respectively, and by the words FIRST or THIRD below the door droplights on other trailers. The Portsmouth stock was similar, but lining was restricted to waist level on the coach sides only, and on the later Mid-Sussex units (COR 3130 and BUF 3073 upwards) was simplified into two parallel yellow bands, with no separation into imitation panels. A full description of the distinctive umber and cream livery carried by the Pullman cars, which changed in only minor details from 1932 until 1969 (by which time all the PUL composites had been withdrawn and the 5 BEL units repainted), is given in the appropriate section below. The BUF buffet cars were delivered in unlined light green, giving these units when new a somewhat piebald appearance.

From 1939, the liveries applied to suburban, semi-fast and express stock did not differ in any way. An experimental shade of brighter green was tried out in 1938, then in 1942 a definitive unlined and less bright green was adopted, with shaded block 'sunshine' lettering and numbers, and most units received this on general overhaul before 1948. Following nationalisation an identical shade, officially known as malachite green, was adopted by the newly-formed Southern Region, initially with only the BRITISH RAILWAYS lettering on the van sides to denote the change of ownership, but from early 1950 new numbering and lettering in old gold, edged black, appeared, together with the 'lion-on-wheel' emblem on motor coach sides.

From March 1957 this livery was gradually superseded by a darker green with circular carriage stock badge, but some PUL and PAN vehicles did not receive this before withdrawal. Yellow/cream or red cantrail stripes, to denote first class and catering accommodation respectively, were applied from about 1962, but again many earlier units were never so treated. Only the BUF and GRI (converted from RES) catering cars were ever given the red stripe.

With the exception of two of the short-lived 6 COR units (reformed from PUL and PAN stock) and the 5 BELs, no Brighton or Eastbourne units ever received British Rail blue with white 'double arrows' and lettering, but virtually the entire fleet of Portsmouth 4 COR, BUF and GRI units did, starting in 1966. The yellow warning panels applied to cab ends from 1963 were also a rarity on PUL and PAN stock before withdrawal or reformation, although all other pre-war express units received them, including the 5 BELs. The succeeding overall yellow ends were eventually applied to all 4 CORs and their remaining catering derivatives, some while still green. As with the semi-fast stock, a feature of the full yellow ends applied to green-liveried units was that it extended further around the corner of the coach, as far as the front edge of the motorman's doors, and the black unit numbers were sometimes hand-painted. The BELs were unsympathetically repainted into a lined variation of BR blue/grey InterCity livery in 1969, described in detail later.

As in previous chapters, interior descriptions include details of original upholstery patterns where known, although this was poorly documented at the time. Units generally received the post-1939 SR designs on the first or second of their seven or eight-yearly general overhauls, and later the first range of BR patterns. The third class designs from these eras were all described in more detail in Volume 1. Only the 4 COR fleet and catering derivatives, including some former PUL and PAN trailers reformed into it in the 1960s, received the Trojan, plain grey and striped patterns introduced then; again, details are given where known. Window indications of first class, smoking and non-smoking accommodation followed the same changes as the semi-fast stock.

All motor coaches in the express stock fleet had driving cabs and guard's vans, and there were no driving trailers. Significant reformations, resulting in units which were non-standard in some way, are covered by descriptions and tables located in the body of the text.

THE 6 PUL, 6 CIT AND 5 BEL UNITS 1931-64

For the electrification to Brighton and Worthing, it was decided to provide electric multiple units formed of six coaches for the normal express services. Each was to be made up of a pair of driving motor coaches, with all four axles powered, and four intermediate trailers. Three otherwise similar units would be given a greater proportion of first class accommodation, specifically for the *City Limited* business trains between London Bridge and Brighton. There was no question but to continue the long-standing use of Pullman refreshment cars on the route, so each unit would include a composite Pullman trailer. Additionally, three special all-Pullman units would be provided for the popular *Southern Belle* service. Both the kitchen composites for the six-coach units and the motor cars for the *Belle* were new types so far as the Pullman Car Company was concerned, and their design was not without difficulty. Due to the extra weight of their vehicles, the all-Pullman units were to be of only five cars, to give a similar performance to the ordinary six-coach units with the same number of motors. Two units could be coupled in multiple to form a twelve-coach train of ordinary express stock or ten-car *Southern Belle* if traffic levels or the timetable required it.

In designing the express stock, a new traction motor was developed, more suitable than the standard suburban MV 339 design, for prolonged high-speed running at up to 75mph. Designated type 163 and rated at 225hp, the new motor was designed to work safely at speeds of up to 90mph, and those for the 1932 Brighton line units were ordered from British Thomson-Houston (BTH), an unusual choice for the SR. These motors were geared 57:23 to driving wheels of 3ft 7in diameter, and the total nominal horsepower for each unit (eight motors) was 1,800. The control system was also re-designed to work electro-pneumatically, contactor switches for the automatic acceleration equipment opening and closing by the action of compressed air supplied from the brake compressor mounted on the motor coach underframes. Unlike the earlier system used on suburban and semi-fast stock which had electro-magnetic contactors working at line

For a generation, the epitome of the main line Southern Electric to the general public and railway observers alike was the all-Pullman *Brighton Belle*. Passing Wandsworth Common on 15th November 1964, 5 BEL unit 3052, by now 32 years old, leads the 11.00am Down working. Still carrying traditional Pullman umber and cream livery, an elongated version of the Pullman coat of arms (originally designed for the Blue Pullman diesel sets) has replaced the original style on the cab front. *Brian Stephenson*

voltage, this new system operated at 70V dc, supplied from a motor-generator which also charged emergency batteries and provided current for lighting. Although a superior arrangement to that used on the suburban stock, it meant that the two types could not be worked in multiple. Apart from the traction motors, electrical equipment was supplied by Metropolitan-Vickers.

Multiple unit control signals between motor coaches passed along one twelve-core cable, in which three wires were spare. On the cab end, the control jumper to connect this cable to another unit was located below the offside windscreen, with a socket on the nearside. As with the suburban and semi-fast stock, there was a power (bus) line along each unit, but unlike them there was no unit end power jumper.

However, to help prevent gapping, all motor bogies had collector shoes, giving four on each side of a unit. Each motor coach cab end was equipped with a power socket, also underneath the offside windscreen, but this was purely for connection to a hanging cable for movement inside depot buildings where there was no live rail. Intermediate jumpers between vehicles within a unit were also arranged differently from suburban stock, due to the gangway position. The main control and power jumpers were located above the buffers on the compartment and corridor side of the unit (with reference to the trailers) respectively, but the 70V lighting jumper was at roughly cantrail height on the corridor side. With the exception of the lighting cables which ran in external conduit along the roof (or inside the roof of Pullman cars), all other electrical cabling was routed under the floor of each coach.

Experience had already shown that electric multiple unit vehicles tended to ride poorly at speed and so, in a misguided attempt to improve matters, equalising-beam bogies were fitted under all the 1932 Brighton line express stock vehicles, both motor coaches and trailers. These were based on a Nederlandse Spoorwegen (Dutch National Railways) design which SR engineers had visited Holland to look at in 1931, and were therefore known unofficially as 'Dutch' bogies throughout their lives until altered in the 1950s. In this design the equalising beams were straight steel bars of rectangular cross-section, located outside the main bogie frame and connecting the front and rear axle boxes on each side. These bars were attached to the bogie frames through coil springs located inboard of the wheels, an arrangement intended to provide a certain degree of weight transfer or compensation between the two axles on the bogie as they moved vertically to follow undulations in the track. Additionally, pairs of vertically-opposed laminated leaf springs located across the bogie centre provided secondary suspension between the carriage body and the bogie. Motor and trailer bogies were of 9ft and 8ft wheelbase respectively. Unfortunately, on SR track they proved a failure and were soon found to give a poorer ride than the standard suburban types, particularly after some use. As a result, only the motor bogies of the subsequent Eastbourne and Portsmouth express stock were of this type, the well-proven single-bolster suburban design (which had originated on the SECR and was also used for main-line steam stock) then being used for trailer bogies.

Except where noted all express stock vehicles, both motor coaches and trailers, had underframes 62ft 6in long over headstocks, with the bogie pivot centres 44ft 6in apart. Side buffers of the heavy self-contained Spencer-Moulton type with oval heads and rubber springing were fitted at both ends of all vehicles, bringing the total length up to 66ft 2¾in over buffers. A new type of gangway connection was designed for the electric stock, rather than the Pullman type with buckeye coupling by then standard on SR steam stock. The new design was wider but reverted to the use of screw couplings, hence the need for intermediate side buffers, and had a complicated system of clips to hold the flexible gangway connections together and in alignment. It is suggested that its use was due to Lynes being suspicious of using buckeyes on electric units following the fiasco with the MCB couplers fitted to the 1925/26 suburban stock.

Following authorisation of the Brighton electrification scheme, Head Office order 570 was placed with Eastleigh Works on 16th May 1930 for twenty five-coach 'set trains' for fast services, with underframes to be provided by Lancing. A similar order placed on the same date (HO 571) covered three units for the *City Limited* business trains. This suggests an initial intention that all vehicles except the Pullmans would be constructed in SR workshops. Shortly afterwards, it was decided to produce an experimental formation to test the new features prior to series production, and a five-coach unit was ordered from Eastleigh to HO 590 of 17th July 1930, with '. . . car C to be an existing vehicle . . .' At this point, a change of plan resulted in the motor coach orders being diverted to

outside contractors, possibly due to the non-standard all-steel bodywork construction specified. In the event, none of the vehicles included in HO 590 came new from Eastleigh, although two prototype underframes and associated running gear were built for them at Lancing. HO 570 and 571 were amended to twenty and three sets of three coaches respectively, in other words just the three corridor trailers in each six-coach unit.

The pair of prototype motor coaches specified in HO 590 were constructed in the second half of 1931 and delivered in October, one being ordered from Birmingham RCW and the other from Metropolitan CWF (which shortly afterwards became Metropolitan-Cammell Carriage and Wagon Co. Ltd). The BRCW vehicle was numbered 11001 and had distinctive flat body sides continuing downwards to cover the solebars, while the MCWF coach was numbered 11002 and had conventional curved sides and exposed solebars. Otherwise, they were similar in basic design and construction, bodywork being entirely of steel (rather than having timber framework and roof panels which were standard SR practice at the time). Body structure consisted of side, roof and end panels rivetted to a frame built up mainly from channel and angle sections, firmly attached to the underframe. Considered at the time to be more suitable for highly-powered electric motor coaches, this construction method was rigid enough to make additional underframe trussing unnecessary, but conversely helped push the weight up to a solid 57 tons (11001) or 58 tons (11002). This compared with the 41 tons of a LAV MThB. The lack of trussing gave plenty of room to fit most electrical and other ancillary equipment under the body between the motor bogies, with only the current-limit relays for automatic acceleration remaining in the cab. The cab instruments included a speedometer for the first time – this had a bar at 75mph, the maximum speed officially allowed for all pre-war express stock. The guard's van included a single rearward-facing periscope, as on the LAVs.

Externally, 11001 and 11002 were massive but handsome vehicles, based loosely on Maunsell's steam-hauled open thirds 1369-1400 (diagram 2005) of 1930 with a cab and van grafted on to one end. Body length was 63ft 3in over end panels, which were bowed, and overall width over commode handles was 9ft 5in, conforming to SR Restriction 4. Lack of curvature in the profile of 11001 made its actual body marginally narrower than 11002 at waist height. The driving end had a similar layout to the suburban stock, including the domed cab roof, but appeared much neater as there was only one jumper cable, no untidy pipe work or guttering, and no thick frames around the windscreens. The body sides were not inset along the van space, unlike those on the LAVs, although the motorman's door was slightly recessed. A gangway connection was fitted at the non-driving end only. Internal arrangements comprised the usual motorman's and guard's compartments followed by a seven-bay open saloon (divided by a partition into four and three) seating 56 third class passengers with the seats arranged two+two either side of a central gangway. This saloon had no external doors, access being through a sliding door into a vestibule at each end. Each seating bay had a large droplight window, with a

Experimental Brighton express test unit '2001', with BRCW flat-sided motor third brake 11001 leading, stands at Durnsford Road (Wimbledon) when newly delivered on 17th November 1931. The second vehicle consists of a former panelled LSWR saloon brake body, its ends extended with sections to the SR Restriction 4 coach profile, mounted on a new underframe fitted with prototype 'Dutch' equalising-beam bogies. *Charles Brown Collection (RAF Museum)*

balancing arrangement allowing it to be lowered about seven inches, surmounted by a ventilator bonnet. There were also ventilator bonnets above the passenger-door droplights (not found on the production PUL/CIT motor coaches). Although emergency lighting was now available, last vehicle indication continued to be by traditional red oil lamp. SR carriage diagram numbers for these two unique vehicles were 2108 for straight-sided 11001 and 2109 for 11002.

Prototype MThBs 11001 and 11002 were marshalled at either end of an experimental five-coach unit as per HO 590, but all three intermediate trailers were adapted from existing steam stock, probably at Eastleigh. These vehicles have long been an enigma to historians of the Southern Electric, and what follows is pieced together from available evidence. Vehicles B and D incorporated the bodywork of (SR) diagram 129 ex-LSWR saloon lavatory third brakes, 47ft 6in over body, formerly numbered 3087/88 and dating from 1893. These were stripped internally, mounted centrally on the new 62ft 6in Lancing underframes mentioned above, and extended

at either end by about 8ft with a new section of standard SR Restriction 4 profile (like motor coach 11002) to make up the necessary length. The former brake ends were equipped with the new design of gangway connection to couple to the motor coaches, and they were given experimental equalising beam trailer bogies of 8ft wheelbase. Their marked tare weight was 35 tons, but it is likely that they were ballasted to achieve this. Vehicle C (whose identity has, as yet, not been traced) was a standard Restriction 4 Maunsell side-corridor third, formed at the centre of the unit.[15] Through control and power cables were draped loosely along the gangway floors of these

---

[15] It is suggested that this vehicle is likely to have been one of the fifty diagram 2001 'loose' all-thirds from the 783-832 series, built in 1928. At the time of writing the only evidence that has so far come to light is an eyewitness account by the late G.T. Moody, who walked down the unit at London Bridge on 15th September 1932 and described the coach as a 'Southern side-corridor third', with dimensions of 61ft 7in x 9ft 3in and weighing thirty tons.

The other prototype express motor coach, MCWF-built 11002, in ex-works condition and carrying the number of the test unit '2001' as well as its original paint date of 10.10.31. With its curved body profile, this was the vehicle on which the production motor third brakes were based, but detail differences include seven full seating bays and ventilators over the passenger door droplights. *Pendragon Collection*

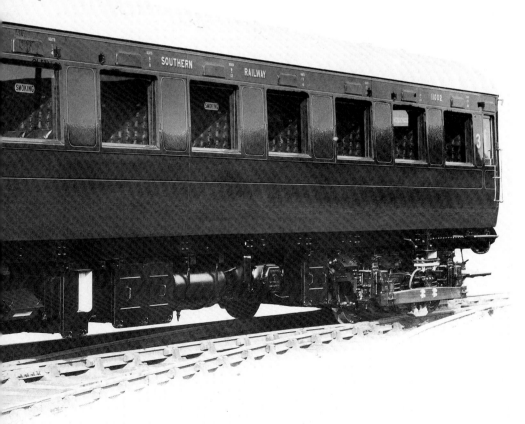

trailers, and vehicle C would have been temporarily equipped with air brakes. It has been suggested that an old Pullman car, similarly altered, was also sometimes included. This formation, given unit number 2001, was in existence by November 1931. It was used in extensive non-passenger trials on the Cobham Line during the first half of 1932, generally at night, and speeds in excess of 75mph were reached. It was also tested on the Brighton line itself when enough sections had been made live. Other tests carried out between St John's and Orpington as early as 1929 involved the use of another redundant Pullman marshalled between two pairs of suburban motor coaches, to evaluate the riding of a Pullman car in a multiple unit formation. The trials were evidently successful, as the units then built for Brighton line fast services had motor coaches similar to the prototypes and included a trailer Pullman car. Experience with 11001 and 11002 led to a number of minor design changes in the production MThBs, including modified bogie springing. Test unit 2001 was disbanded in about November 1932, following which the corridor third was returned to capital stock and the two prototype trailer underframes and their bogies salvaged for further use.

The three types of express EMU, totalling 26 units, built for services to Brighton and Worthing were as follows:

6 PUL units 2001-2020 (6 COR until 1935 and renumbered 3001-3020 at the beginning of 1937). These included two open motor third brakes, a trailer compartment third (TThK), two trailer compartment composites (TCK) and a Pullman composite with kitchen (TPulC), formed MThB + TThK + TCK + TPulC + TCK + MThB. Accommodation was provided for sixty first and 212 third class passengers plus twelve first and sixteen third supplementary-fare seats in the Pullman car. Overall length over buffers was 399ft and width was 9ft 5ft. (Note that 6 PUL 2001 was *not* the experimental unit of 1932, described above.) A composite was marshalled either side of the Pullman car so that both ends of the unit had some first class accommodation for times when the Pullman was closed and locked out of use, thereby preventing through access.

6 CIT units 2041-2043 (also 6 COR until 1935 and renumbered 3041-3043 at the beginning of 1937). These were similar to the 6 PULs, but the three 'normal' intermediate trailers were all-firsts. With their preponderance of first class accommodation, they were specifically for the *City Limited* London Bridge – Brighton business services. They seated 126 first and 108 (or 104 in unit 2043) third class passengers, plus twelve first and sixteen third in the Pullman. Overall length was 386ft and width was 9ft 5in.

5 BEL units 2051-2053 (5 PUL until 1935 and renumbered 3051-3053 at the beginning of 1937). These were the all-Pullman units for the *Southern Belle* service and comprised two motor parlour third brakes, a trailer parlour third (TTh) and two trailer kitchen parlour firsts (TKF), arranged MThB + TTh + TKF + TKF + MThB. They seated forty first and 152 third class passengers, all at a supplementary fare. Overall length was 346ft and width was 9ft 5in.

The production motor third brakes for the PUL and CIT units, numbered 11003-46 and to diagram 2107, were built by the same contractors responsible for the prototypes. Vehicles 11003 to 11024 came from BRCW and the remainder from Metropolitan-Cammell, both sub-lots being completed and placed into capital stock between October and December 1932. Satisfactory testing having been completed, the two prototype motor coaches 11001 and 11002 were also accepted into traffic at this time, being included in *City Limited* units 2041 and 2042 respectively. The others were formed with trailers to make up units as they were delivered, not always in strict numerical order. These vehicles were generally similar to the curved-sided prototype 11002 except that the passenger saloon had only six and one half seating bays, giving a reduced capacity of 52 but a larger brake van. This and other small changes increased the overall tonnage to 59, a weight that was soon found to punish jointed track severely. The cab ends were constructed of armour-plate steel due to concern over the motorman's safety in the event of an accident, there no longer being thirty feet of boiler and smokebox in front of him for protection in the event of a collision. There is a tale (possibly apocryphal) concerning a 6 PUL unit 'running-away' into the running shed at Brighton and smashing into an end wall. While this resulted in the expected large hole in the wall, the cab end of the motor coach escaped with only a few scratches. Passenger doors had no ventilator bonnet above the droplights. Unlike the trailers with which they ran, these motor coaches were not 'handed', so power, control and lighting jumpers and associated sockets were repeated on both sides of the gangway on the inner end.

Internally, the passenger accommodation was divided into two sections of three and a half and three bays respectively. The half-bay was at the van end of the saloon, its four seats facing backwards. The interiors set the pattern for pre-war express stock motor coaches, with plenty of varnished wood and deep hammock-slung 'lift-out' seat cushions. Luggage racks were mounted transversely above the seat backs, and ceilings were finished in white enamel. The upholstery was of moquette in the same bold floral and 'jazz' patterns as used in the LAVs. All but seven of the 29 ceiling lights were under control of passengers, who originally also had bell-push communication with the Pullman Car attendant.

Finishing work on trailer coaches for 6 PUL units taking place at Eastleigh Works in 1932. Bodywork consisted of galvanised steel panels attached to a teak framework, with canvas-covered, deal planked roof. First class seating units, showing three different fabric patterns, are being tested in the foreground by senior staff prior to being fitted into their compartments. Composites 11753 and 11755 would be formed into units 2002 and 2003 respectively, while all-third 10003 also went to 2003. *Charles Brown Collection (RAF Museum)*

Facing page The interior of a 6 PUL motor coach, showing the thickly-cushioned two+two seating either side of a central gangway, luggage racks above the seats and shaded lightbulbs on stalks. *SR Official*

The compartment trailers formed in the Brighton express stock were of entirely conventional construction and of similar appearance to contemporary Maunsell/Lynes steam stock. The steel underframes were first fabricated at Lancing and then sent to Eastleigh for the bodywork to be added. The thirds and composites of the PULs had 62ft 6in underframes and a body length of 63ft 3in, but exceptionally the all-firsts in the 6 CIT units were on standard SR steam stock underframes 58ft over headstocks, 40ft between bogie centres, and had a body length of 59ft. The composites in the 6 PUL units (diagram 2307) were numbered 11751-90, and had five first and three third class compartments seating thirty first and 24 third class passengers. The trailer thirds (dia. 2006) were numbered 10001-20, and seated 68 in eight full compartments and one coupé. The trailer firsts in the 6 CIT units (dia. 2504) were numbered 12251-59 and seated 42 in seven compartments. All these vehicles had lavatories at both ends. The PUL trailers weighed 35 tons but the CIT vehicles, being shorter, were a ton less. Units were formed with all trailer coach side-corridors on the same side, necessary as power, control and lighting cable connections between vehicles were 'handed' as described earlier.

Construction and styling details on all these vehicles corresponded with the Maunsell/Lynes period 4. Fixed windows were inserted from the inside and had thin wooden external fillets. Each compartment had its own external door. On the corridor side, the large windows reached to the eaves, and there were additional intermediate droplights as well as those on doors, which were mostly situated opposite every other compartment. Both door and carriage-side droplights were wood-framed, opened by pulling a small leather tab at the bottom, and were surmounted by a ventilator bonnet. Lavatory windows were frosted, with twin ventilator slots above. Internally, the compartments were similar to those in the corridor trailer of the 4 LAV units, access to the side-corridor being through a pair of sliding doors, balanced so that if one was opened or closed, the other would move equally. Third class compartments seated four a side and were upholstered in similar moquettes to the motor coaches. At least three different upholstery patterns were used in the first class compartments, which seated three each side with end and folding intermediate armrests. All compartments had two passenger-controlled shaded reading lights under each luggage rack.

The 38 Pullman cars supplied for the Brighton electrification were constructed by Metropolitan-Cammell. Of these, 23 were trailer parlour kitchen composites for use as refreshment cars in the 6 PUL and 6 CIT express units otherwise made up of normal SR stock, and were given the type designation A. The remaining fifteen cars made up the three all-Pullman 5 BEL units for the *Southern Belle* service. Six were trailer kitchen parlour firsts (given the Pullman type designation B), three were trailer parlour thirds (type C) and the remaining six were motor parlour third brakes (type D). Bodywork, kitchen and interiors were to the requirements of the Pullman Car Company, but electrical equipment, running gear, couplings, gangway connections, buffers, etc. were to SR specifications identical to those on the PULs. Interestingly, their buffers, although of the standard Spencer Moulton self-contained pattern, had PULLMAN cast on the body. (As related in Volume 1, some of these would eventually find their way onto suburban stock in the 1950s.) With an overall length over buffers of 68ft, these were the longest vehicles to run in SR electric units during the period covered by this book. They were also the heaviest, with the motor third brakes of the BEL units weighing in at 62 tons tare, the kitchen firsts and composites 43 tons and the trailer parlour thirds 39 tons. As mentioned above, for this reason the 5 BEL units were formed of only five cars rather than the six of the PUL and CIT units to give a similar performance with the same installed horsepower.

There is no doubt that these all-electric Pullman cars were considered showcase vehicles by their owning company, the Southern Railway and the electric railway supply industry, and it seems that no expense was spared. Designed under the supervision of W.J. Sedcole, Chief Engineer of the Pullman Car Company, they were of all-steel construction, built on underframes 65ft long over headstocks and with tapered ends. The basic construction methods were similar to the PUL motor coaches, the bodywork being formed of copper-bearing steel panels riveted to a steel framework which was in turn riveted to the underframe. This resulted in a stiff semi-monocoque structure which made external underframe trussing redundant, resulting in more space for equipment including the motor-generators to power the all-electric kitchen equipment. Special attention was paid to producing flush sides, and there were no protruding rivet heads or significant raised mouldings other than a strip along the waist. Sound and temperature insulation were also of above-average standard, the steel floor panels in the passenger saloons being sandwiched between cork sheets, and the sides and roof having two layers of 'insulwood' with a half-inch air space between. In the kitchen and van areas, non-slip flooring consisted of wire mesh embedded in induroleum (a form of linoleum using rubberised flax fibre).

Bodywork was of traditional Pullman style with inset, inwardly opening end doors and oval lavatory windows. The new electric cars differed from contemporary steam-hauled Pullmans in that the body sides tapered inwards slightly from the waist (rather than being exactly vertical), the cantrail was not recessed above the end doors, and windows on the intermediate car ends were oval rather than rectan-

gular. In vehicles with kitchen facilities, the pantry also had an oval window, while the kitchens had a frosted window of lesser depth than those along the rest of the car. Saloon and kitchen windows were equipped with 'wind vane' sliding ventilators supplied by J. Beresford and Co.; these opened from the centre and had small hinged baffles. The driving ends of the BEL motor coaches closely resembled those of the other Brighton express stock, but a narrower body and inwardly tapering cab doors made them arguably less aesthetically pleasing.

Externally, the Pullmans were painted in a distinctive livery which both contrasted with and complemented the lined dark green of the SR-owned vehicles, and served to provide a splash of colour in the middle of the PUL and CIT units. The basic colours were umber and cream, derived from the 1905-10 carriage livery of the LBSCR, with whom the Pullman company in Britain had a very close relationship in

its early years. Umber was used for the lower body sides, a thin strip between the windows and the cantrail, the window frames and car ends including the inset doors, while the panels between the windows were cream. Roofs were white, underframes and bogies black. The umber-painted areas were extensively lined out in red and gold and, betraying the company's American origins, the word PULLMAN appeared in elongated shaded lettering below the cantrail. The Pullman Car Company's coat of arms, comprising a pair of lions holding up a shield with a scrolled ribbon beneath, was located at either end of the lower body side, while at the centre appeared a cartouche containing either the car name in the case of the first class and composite cars, or CAR No. X THIRD CLASS in the case of the motor cars and trailer thirds in the BEL units. Driving ends of the motor cars were lined out and had the coat of arms below the headcode panel.

Pullman composite *May*, formed in 6 PUL (formerly 6 CIT) unit 3041, stands at East Croydon in August 1949. The two-bay third class saloon with sixteen seats is nearest, followed by the toilet and first class coupé, then the eight-seat first class saloon and finally the corridor past the pantry and kitchen. Several features unique to the Southern Electric Pullmans are visible, including the oval end windows, SR electric-type gangway connections and Spencer-Moulton self-contained buffers. The poorly-riding 'Dutch' bogies, with their prominent equalising beam connecting the axleboxes, are also clearly seen. *Joseph Sietta*

In accordance with Pullman Car Company policy all the cars were given a schedule number, and those including first class accommodation were named. Names commonplace among middle and upper-class young ladies of the period, born c.1910-20 and at whom the Pullman service was partly aimed, were chosen. By 1933 most were already somewhat dated, with only about six of the 29 still in popular use for naming babies. The number which appeared on the sides of the third class cars was the final two digits of the schedule number.

The original allocations of the Pullman cars to the units, with the cars' schedule numbers, were as follows:

6 PUL (6 COR until 1935) 2001-2020 (20 units)

Unit	TPulC		Unit	TPulC
2001	275 *Anne*		2011	276 *Naomi*
2002	256 *Rita*		2012	278 *Bertha*
2003	257 *Grace*		2013	258 *Brenda*
2004	260 *Elinor*		2014	259 *Enid*
2005	263 *Ida*		2015	261 *Joyce*
2006	265 *Rose*		2016	262 *Iris*
2007	266 *Violet*		2017	264 *Ruth*
2008	277 *Lorna*		2018	267 *May*
2009	271 *Alice*		2019	268 *Peggy*
2010	274 *Daisy*		2020	269 *Clara*

6 CIT (6 COR until 1935) 2041-2043 (3 units)

Unit	TPulC
2041	272 *Gwladys*
2042	273 *Olive*
2043	270 *Ethel*

5 BEL (5 PUL until 1935) 2051-2053 (3 units)

Unit	MThB Pullman	TTh Pullman	TKF Pullman	TKF Pullman	MThB Pullman
2051	89	86	282 *Doris*	279 *Hazel*	88
2052	91	87	280 *Audrey*	284 *Vera*	90
2053	93	85	283 *Mona*	281 *Gwen*	92

Regarding internal arrangements, the motor parlour third brakes of the 5 BEL units comprised motorman's and guard's compartments, a six-bay saloon seating 48 third class passengers, a lavatory and entrance vestibule. Opposite the lavatory were storage cupboards and the cubicle for the pressure ventilation equipment. There was an access door from the guard's van into the saloon, but no entrance for passengers at this end. The trailer parlour thirds had a seven-bay saloon seating 56, lavatory and entrance vestibule at each end with cupboards opposite the toilets, and ventilation equipment at one end. The trailer kitchen parlour firsts had a short corridor giving access to a lavatory compartment (larger than those in the thirds) and a first class coupé compartment with four seats, followed by two eight-seat saloons. The remainder was occupied by rather cramped pantry/serving and kitchen compartments. Again there was an entrance vestibule at each end of the car. The ventilation equipment compartment was

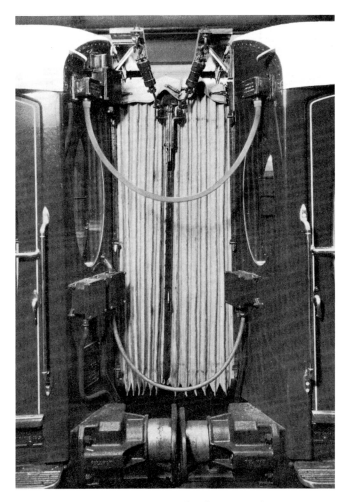

situated between the coupé and saloon, a refrigerator was located in a corner opposite the kitchen, and three other corner cupboards were spaced along the car. The two first class cars in each unit were orientated in opposite directions so that the kitchens were next to adjacent third class cars.

The kitchen composite cars formed in the 6 PUL and 6 CIT units, the only such Pullmans ever built new, had an internal layout starting with a small pantry area on each side of the gangway, one equipped with hot-water urn and the other with sink. This was followed by a two-bay third class section with sixteen seats and then a side corridor giving access to a lavatory and a first class coupé seating four. The remainder of the vehicle followed the layout of the BEL kitchen firsts with two-bay first class saloon seating eight, kitchen and pantry. Between the first class coupé and saloon was situated the ventilation unit, while the refrigerator was opposite the kitchen and three other cupboards were located in odd corners to make full use of the available space.

Traction and control equipment in the 5 BEL motor third brakes was identical to that in the 6 PUL and 6 CIT units, and was the maintenance responsibility of the SR. On the other hand, the all-electric cooking and refrigeration

Facing page An interesting side view showing some features of the gangway and coupling arrangements between two 5 BEL Pullman cars. The gangway concertinas were manufactured from rubberised fabric, lined internally with coarse corduroy. The upper jumper cable connects the 70V lighting circuits between the cars, while the lower one is the power or 'bus' line connecting the current collector shoes at each end of the unit together and hence carrying 660V. Note that the buffers have PULLMAN cast on their sides: following post war swapping on overhaul, some of these would eventually find their way on to lowly suburban units. *SR Official*

Above Clearly displaying modified bogies with conventional leaf-spring primary suspension, Pullman composite *Anne* was also formed in 6 PUL unit 3041 when photographed at Haywards Heath on 26th June 1965. These alterations did not, unfortunately, significantly improve the rough riding of the Brighton express stock. The PUL cars were frequently swapped between units during their last two years in traffic. *Peter Swift*

equipment in the kitchen cars was owned by the Pullman Car Company, and electricity used was strictly metered and charged for. The Brighton line Pullmans broke new ground in being both the first to feature all-electric cooking facilities, and the first electric multiple unit vehicles to feature on-board catering. The kitchen and pantry arrangements were identical in the BEL trailer firsts and the PUL composites, all exposed cooking and preparation surfaces being finished in polished stainless-steel. The kitchen cooking range included a large oven, grill, hot cupboard, four small and two large boiling plates and a four-gallon urn for tea-making, all controlled from a switch panel mounted on the left hand side. Power for these, and the refrigerator, was supplied at 110V dc from a 20KW underframe-mounted motor-generator which was supplied with electricity at line-voltage through the bus line. The supply of hot water for washing in lavatories, kitchen and pantry was provided from tanks fitted with thermostatically-controlled 600V immersion heaters. The additional tea-urn and hot water supply in compartments at the opposite end to the kitchen in the composite cars enabled a Pullman attendant to service adjoining vehicles more easily. Staffing arrangements are detailed in Chapter 1.

Under-seat heating in the passenger saloons, working at line voltage, was similar to that in the SR vehicles, except that it too was regulated by thermostat to provide full, two-thirds, one-third or no heating depending on the ambient temperature. A more interesting feature was the primitive pressure ventilation equipment installed in a small compartment in each car, the locations of which are noted above. Outside air was drawn in through a lower body side aperture into the apparatus, whence an electric fan sucked it through an oil-filter and into a heating chamber, containing thermostatically-regulated 600V heating elements which warmed it if necessary. The warmed air then passed along horizontal ducts located along the car sides about twelve inches above the floor, and through small downward-facing holes into the car interior where it spread upwards from the floor before passing out through roof ducts. A refinement prevented smoky air from a passing steam train (in Balcombe tunnel, for instance) entering the system; if it was detected, a solenoid valve activated by a photo-electric cell closed off the ducts to the saloons and the offending air was returned outside through a roof ventilator. Refined versions of this system, which was supplied by J. Stone & Co, were later installed in the SR Portsmouth and Mid-Sussex catering cars. To show off all this advanced technology, illuminated thermometers outside each lavatory enabled passengers to compare the outside temperature with that inside each car, which no doubt caused interest when they first entered service in the winter of 1933. These thermometers were

mounted in a special frame with a sign stating: 'This car is continuously ventilated with clean fresh air'. Contactor switches for the 660V circuits which powered heating and motor-generator starting were located in two underframe-mounted steel boxes, and all contactors were operated from the 110V circuit so that all electrical equipment was automatically switched off when the motor-generator was shut down.

A detailed description of the interiors of these vehicles, easily the most luxurious ever to run on the Southern Electric system, is made more complicated by the fact that, within certain parameters, all Pullman cars were individually designed internally and no two were exactly alike. Features common to all will be described first, followed by the fine details of representative cars as described in a press release by the Pullman Car Company to the various railway journals of the time; here they are quoted from *The Railway Gazette* supplement commemorating the Brighton line electrification.[16] The first class saloons seated one passenger each side of the aisle in extremely comfortable individual armchairs with upright scalloped backs, while the coupé compartments had two armchairs each side of the table. These armchairs were not fixed to the floor. The third class saloons seated two each side of the central aisles with fixed seats similar to those

---

16 Southern Railway Brighton Electrification, Supplement to *The Railway Gazette*, 30th December 1932. p54

A 5 BEL first class saloon, photographed in June 1939 after its first major overhaul. The original 'jazz'-style upholstery moquette on the armchairs has been replaced by a more traditional design, probably fawn based, together with matching curtains. *SR Official*

in the SR motor coaches, but with small semicircular side headrests but no armrests against the car sides. In both classes various moquette patterns were used in the different cars to complement the panelling. Floor covering in the saloons was diamond-patterned carpet in first class, and patterned rubber of various shades in third. In each seating bay was a table, topped with a traditional Pullman table-lamp with heavy brass base and acetate shade. Small double luggage racks, only large enough for handbags and umbrellas, were located above each window. Ceilings were white, with two rows of lamps, working at 70V from the motor-generator. Those in the first class saloons were hidden by glass diffusers incorporating a coloured pattern, but in third class they had small individual tulip-shaped glass shades, and there were additional lamps at cornice-height between the racks and at saloon ends. Clocks were located above the doors at the ends of the saloons, and push-button operated bells enabled passengers to summon the attendant. Each window had pull-down blinds but it appears that curtains, in fabrics matching the seat coverings, were not fitted until first general overhaul in about 1938. Corridor and vestibule surfaces were varnished mahogany, while the lavatory interiors were finished in *eau de nil* (duck-egg green) with black fixtures and mouldings, and floors of green terrazzo mosaic. The distinctive oval lavatory windows, with stained 'cathedral' glass, have already been mentioned.

The internal panelling in the saloons made use of different timbers, often involving intricate marquetry work. Four different furnishing companies, Morison & Co., H. H. Martyn & Co., Waring & Gillow, and Maple & Co., were involved in designing and producing the interior decor. There was much evidence of *art-deco* styling tendencies, particularly in the third class saloons. Some examples of the decor in individual cars was as follows:

Third Class Car No.85 – decorations by Morison and Co. 'The decoration of this car is of a refined modern tendency in mahogany, pomele and vermilion veneers, with a motif in each panel suggesting a setting sun with the sun rays picked out in boxwood. All the metal-work is finished in satin silver. The rubber flooring is of a modern design in two tones of green, picked out in black. The seat coverings are in velvet moquette in tones of brown and fawn.'

Composite Car Bertha – decorations by H.H. Martyn & Co. 'The general scheme is in three shades of mahogany, with marquetry work introduced in the main panels depicting a Chinese landscape, the principal woods being ash and syca-more. The centres of the panels are of light mahogany with darker shades at outer edges and dark brown mahogany at extreme edges, broken by inlaid lines of weathered sycamore. All metal-work in both first and third-class portions is finished in satin-silver. The carpets in the first-class portion are in tones of green and fawn, whilst in the third-class portions the rubber flooring is carried out in an interesting design in shades of red, green, mottled brown and black. The chairs and seat covers are in moquette in green.'

First Class Car Gwen – decorations by Maple & Co. 'The main panel-work is in figured English walnut with lace wood and laurel lines. Marquetry work is introduced in the prin-

cipal panels and carried out in boxwood, weathered sycamore, and red and white natural pearwood. The metal-work is finished in satin-silver. The carpet is Wilton pile in tones of blue, whilst the chairs are covered in velvet moquette in blue and mauve tints.'

In contrast, composite car *Enid*, formed in 6 PUL 2014 (later 3014), was panelled internally in plain oak, and according to Julian Morel became known as 'the coffin' by the superstitious among Pullman staff.[17] Entirely coinciden-tally 3014 was involved in the accident at Eastbourne in 1958, while *Enid* had been temporarily formed in 3003 when that unit collided with another at London Bridge in 1948. Is there such a thing as an unlucky Pullman car?

The Brighton line express stock led an uneventful life from its introduction until the start of World War Two. Initially, twelve-coach trains were formed of two PUL units, with both Pullman cars staffed, but from 1935, they generally operated with a 6 PAN and gained regular workings to Eastbourne and Ore. The 1938 Mid-Sussex electrification resulted in them reaching Littlehampton with the extension of the Victoria – West Worthing expresses. From the start, the standard of riding of all the Brighton express stock was disappointing, the motor third brakes being particularly bouncy. Worst of all were the 5 BEL motor cars, which quickly developed a characteristic fore-and-aft lurch at speed, much to the embarrassment of the Pullman Car Company and inconvenience of its staff and passengers. Regular third class patrons of the *Southern Belle*, or *Brighton Belle* as it was renamed in 1934, no doubt soon learned to avoid these vehicles. Two 6 PUL units, including 3015, were painted in an experimental shade of light green in 1938. The *City Limited* name was lost from the timetable in 1934, but the services themselves retained their special character until the start of World War Two.

The commencement of the 1939-45 war initially resulted in a 'stop-go' period for Pullman and other catering services on trains. At first withdrawn completely from 11th-17th September 1939, they were then partially reinstated from 18th September until 15th October, although with a severely curtailed menu and no Sunday service. A 'Permanent Emergency Timetable' then came into force, with limited services between London and Brighton or Eastbourne only during weekday mornings and evenings, and until midday on Saturdays. A number of Pullmans were painted in a wartime livery of overall umber brown at this time. There is evidence to suggest that the three 6 CIT units were stored out of service during the early part of the War, possibly due to their reduced seating capacity. Certainly Pullman composites *Gwladys* (from 3041) and *Olive* (3042) were running in other PUL units at this time, while *Ethel* (3043) was noted formed in 6 PAN 3035 in January 1942. Unit 3043 was noted stored in Leatherhead carriage sidings, with the pantry car from 3035 in place of *Ethel*, the following November.

Only one unit was seriously damaged as a result of enemy action, 5 BEL 3052 being hit by a bomb while standing in

---

17 Morel J: *Pullman*, David and Charles, ISBN 0 7153 8382 5, 1983. p143

Victoria's platform 17 during an air raid on the night of 9th-10th October 1940, at the height of the London blitz. Motor coach 90 being badly damaged, the unit was withdrawn from service. 3051 and 3053 soldiered on until all Pullman and buffet services were finally withdrawn completely 'for the duration' from 22nd May 1942.

The Pullman composites were removed from their units and stored, as were the three complete 5 BELs. From mid 1942 until 1946 the PUL and CIT units therefore ran as 5 COR. The electric Pullman cars were stored at various locations around the system, and the records of some observers have survived. By August 1943 for example, eleven composite cars had gathered at Epsom Goods, including *Bertha, Brenda, Daisy, Elinor, Enid, Grace, Gwladys, Ida, Naomi, Olive* and *Rose*. The whole of damaged and tarpaulin-covered 3052 was noted at Crystal Palace (High Level) in January 1944, while by June 1944 composites *Bertha, Brenda, Daisy, Enid, Grace, Gwladys, May, Olive* and *Rose* were in Coulsdon North sidings, some evidently having been moved from Epsom. Other reported storage locations included Leatherhead carriage sidings and a site in Devon, and it is likely that other cars were also moved around from time to time. While in outside storage, some were given an overall coat of workshop grey, red lead or khaki in an attempt to slow down deterioration.

With the exception of the *Brighton Belle*, Pullman services were reinstated on 1st May 1946, although not all Pullman composites had been formed back into their units by this date, and it was not until mid 1947 that the last had been restored. In most cases the Pullman composites returned to their original PUL units. Exceptions to the original allocations are listed below:

Pullman Car	Post-War Allocation	(1932 Allocation)
Olive	3002 (a)	(2042/3042)
Gwladys	3017	(2041/3041)
Ethel	3018	(2043/3043)
May	3041	(2018/3018)
Ruth	3042	(2017/3017)
Rita	3043 (b)	(2002/3002)

(a): *Olive* was also reported formed in 3002 in the early part of the war, prior to the 1942 withdrawal of Pullmans.

(b): Following restoration of Pullmans, 2043 was initially formed with *Anne* from about August 1947 until December 1947, and was then reformed with *Rita* on a permanent basis in December 1947.

In May 1946, 5 BEL 3051 was temporarily made up to six cars by substituting trailer parlour kitchen firsts *Mona* and *Gwen* from 3053 for trailer parlour third 86, and re-entered service in this formation. 3051 and 3053 were then restored to their proper formations in October and November 1946 respectively, but 3052 did not reappear until September 1947 following extensive repairs to war-damaged motor car 90. During this period the units ran to the pre-war *Belle* timings, often paired with a 6 PUL or 4 COR unit. With all three BEL

units now back in service, the *Brighton Belle* was formally reinstated with the start of the winter timetable on 6th October 1947.

With the wartime reduction in demand for first class seating on business trains between London Bridge and the south coast, former *City Limited* units 3041-3043 (by then reinstated and running as 5 COR) had various compartments downclassed to third on an ad hoc basis from 1943. As may be seen from the table below, they were the last to have their Pullmans restored but, from about July 1946 until February 1947, 3041 and 3042 were both made up temporarily to 6 COR with additional trailers 10073 (TThK) and 11859 (TCK) respectively. (These had just been completed at Lancing as war replacements for the Portsmouth 4 COR fleet and, as described later, were awaiting the completion of new motor coaches before being reformed into unit 3119.) By mid 1947 a standard layout for the downclassed compartments in the former CIT units had been agreed, with one trailer becoming all-third and two compartments from each of the other two being downclassed. 12254/59/53 became trailer thirds 10113-15 (with revised diagram number 2016) respectively, with seven third class compartments seating 56. 12255/52/58/57/51/56 became trailer composites 11862-67 (dia. 2319) in order, with thirty first and sixteen third class seats. The appropriate seats were reupholstered, but tare weight remained unchanged at 34 tons. With these alterations completed and with restoration of their Pullmans between April and December 1947, 3041-3043 were reclassified 6 PUL.

Post-war incidents and resulting reformations involving the PUL stock up to 1964 were not numerous. 3003 and 6 PAN 3029 were involved in a collision at London Bridge in January 1948 in which motor coaches 11006 and 11056 were severely damaged. Following repairs, 3003 gained PAN MThB 10056 (ex 3029) in June 1949, while 11006 went to PAN 3026. 3014 was involved in the Eastbourne collision in August 1958, resulting in MBS 11027 and TSK 10004 being written-off. It was subsequently given motor coach 11074 and trailer 10044 from disbanded PAN 3032. 11074 was in turn withdrawn in about January 1959, being replaced by 11075, also from 3032. In a further permanent exchange of Pullman cars in about 1948, 3001 received *Bertha* and *Anne* went to 3012. A number of other units temporarily swapped Pullmans or ran as 5 COR from time to time during this period, purely because the overhaul or revarnishing of the Pullman and normal SR vehicles rarely coincided. For similar reasons a Pullman was occasionally transferred to a 6 PAN unit while the other vehicles of the PUL concerned were being shopped, and conversely 3012 ran as a 6 PAN in 1957. 4 RES unit 3072 ran experimentally with Pullman *Brenda* in place of its 'cafeteria car', although not in passenger service, in November 1956, some years before the 4 PUL rearrangements of 1964. This was apparently in connection with the Brighton express stock bogie rebuilding programme, described later.

A summary of the known long-term reformations involving the PUL stock prior to 1964 is listed in the table at the top of the next column, the numbers of vehicles reformed into these units being shown in bold type. The many reformations from 1964 are dealt with later.

Unit	MThB	TThK	TCK	TPulC	TCK	MThB	Reformed
3001	11043	10017	11783	**278 Bertha**	11784	11044	circa1948
3002	11003	11002	11753	**273 Olive**	11754	11004	5/46
3003	11005	11003	11755	**257 Grace**	11756	**11056***6/49	
3012	11023	10020	11789	**275 Anne**	11790	11024	circa1948
3014	**11074***10044$	11757	259 Enid	11758	11028	8/58	
3017	11033	10009	11767	**272 Gwladys**	11768	11034	5/46
3018	11035	10012	11773	**270 Ethel**	11774	10036	5/46
3041	11041	10113§	11862¶	**267 May**	11863¶	11001	4/47
3042	11002	10114§	11864¶	**264 Ruth**	11865¶	11042	12/47
3043	11015	10115§	11866¶	**256 Rita**	11867¶	11016	12/47

Notes:

* Former 6 PAN motor third brake (with 'Airstream' sliding window ventilators); subsequently replaced by similar 11075 in about January 1959.

$ Former 6 PAN trailer second.

§ Trailer third downclassed from trailer first.

¶ Trailer composite downclassed from trailer first.

In 1947 6 PUL 3016 and 6 PAN 3034 were experimentally fitted with electro-pneumatic brakes. While previous experiments in 1927 using CP ac stock (see Volume 1) had proved unsuccessful, in the intervening years considerable improvements had been made to the design of the EP brake and it had been widely adopted for use on other electrified lines, including London Transport and the LMS Wirral and Southport stocks. With the SR looking to improve performance of its suburban electric units, including shorter braking times and stopping distances, superseding the hitherto-standard Westinghouse air brake with the EP brake seemed a desirable option. There were two reasons why express stock was chosen for the tests, rather than suburban stock for which the system was initially intended. Firstly, the express twelve-core control cable had three spare wires (10, 11 and 12) which could be utilised for brake control, whereas all eight wires in the suburban-type control cable were already utilised. Secondly, the express units were fitted with 70V motor-generators and batteries which could provide the necessary uninterrupted electrical supply to the brake valves.

The new brake equipment was fitted at Lancing Works under the supervision of Westinghouse staff, and initial calibration and testing took place on an electrified siding adjacent to the Works and later on the main line in off-peak periods. The two units concerned were then coupled together in Brighton inspection shed ready for thorough trials which took place on 9th-10th December. On the first day, the carefully pre-arranged programme of tests was concerned with comparing stopping distances and times of the EP and straight air brake – the former proved superior both in shorter stopping distances and absence of surging. On the second day, attempts were made to mishandle the brake and expose it to extreme conditions, but again it performed excellently. As a result of these tests, the SR significantly decided to adopt the electro-pneumatic brake for all future electric

rolling stock, a decision endorsed by the Southern Region of British Railways on nationalisation. 3016 and 3034 retained their experimental brakes for a short period in normal service, during which time they could only work in multiple with each other. They were then removed in mid-1948 and transferred to the two experimental double-decker 4 DD units then under construction (see Chapter 6), the PUL and PAN reverting to standard.

The disappointing riding characteristics of the 'Dutch' equalising-beam bogies fitted to the Brighton express stock have already been noted, and in August 1952 those of PUL 3001 were altered by removing the equalising bars and fitting conventional leaf-springs and swing-links, probably as an experiment. By 1955 passenger complaints concerning rough riding had reached such a pitch that it was agreed to spend £50,000 on modifying the entire PUL and BEL fleet similarly in an attempt to improve matters. HO 4216 of 6th September 1955 authorised the conversion of 92 motor bogies and 138 trailer bogies, covering the SR vehicles of 3001-3020 and 3041-3043, while HO 4217 of the same date dealt with the twelve motor bogies and 64 trailer bogies of 3051-3053 and the Pullman composites. Initially given to Lancing, the job was transferred to Brighton Works, where the actual bogie modifications were carried out. However, the bogie exchanges took place at Peckham Rye, the main mechanical and electrical overhaul shop for Brighton and Eastbourne express stock, and in connection with this twelve standard 12t open goods wagons were modified to transport the bogies between Brighton and Peckham Rye. Work on these bogie alterations commenced in December 1956 and was completed by March 1959. Whether the modifications (see photo on page 135) were a success is open to question; certainly, the riding of the Brighton express stock remained disappointingly rough.

Other post-war changes to the Pullmans were few and mostly cosmetic. In about 1950 use of the term THIRD CLASS on the sides of appropriate cars ceased, CAR No.85, for example, replacing CAR No.85 THIRD CLASS. At some time the third class seating was reupholstered with scalloped backs and small folding centre armrests. There were various changes to the lining-out on the cab-ends of the 5 BEL motor coaches with each successive overhaul, and from about 1960 a splendid elongated version of the Pullman crest, originally designed for the diesel Blue Pullman sets, was applied to the front and side panels of 3051 and 3052, those on the cabs only to be obliterated a few years later by small yellow warning panels. In 1962 cars 256-262 were renumbered in the Pullman schedule as shown below; the new numbers were shown on the car ends:

New Number	Old (pre-1962) Number	Name
294	258	*Brenda*
295	260	*Elinor*
296	259	*Enid*
297	257	*Grace*
298	262	*Iris*
299	261	*Joyce*
300	256	*Rita*

In early BR green livery, 6 PAN 3029 pulls out of London Bridge forming the 9.16am ECS to New Cross Gate, after arriving with the 6.49 from Ore on 15th August 1956. The addition of 'Airstream' ventilators to the earlier PUL design produced arguably the best-proportioned of the Maunsell/Lynes express motor coach types. *J. H. Aston*

THE 6 PAN UNITS 1935-64

For the Eastbourne and Hastings electrification, completed in July 1935, a further seventeen six-coach corridor express units were provided, classified 6 PAN. These were ordered on 23rd March 1934 to HO 805, with the trailers to be built at Eastleigh on Lancing underframes and bogies, and '. . . two motor coaches per unit to be supplied by outside contractors . . .' (It was unusual for outside contract work to be mentioned in a rolling stock HO order.) Although generally very similar to the Brighton line corridor stock built three years previously, they differed in a number of details. The main development was the inclusion of a 'pantry' or buffet car in place of the Pullman, although staffing was still in the hands of Pullman Car Company personnel. The formation and composition of the trailers also differed slightly, concentrating all first class accommodation at the centre of the unit. Between the two motor third brakes were a corridor trailer third, the pantry car (which also had five first class compartments), a corridor trailer first and another corridor third. Overall unit length was 392ft 2in and seats were provided for 72 first and 240 third class passengers. Originally numbered 2021-2037, the class was renumbered to 3021-3027 at the start of 1937, as part of the main line electric stock renumbering scheme which also affected other classes mentioned in this and the preceding chapter.

The 34 all-steel motor coaches, to diagram 2112, were similar in almost every respect to those in the PULs. Metropolitan-Cammell were responsible for 11047-63 and BRCW for 11064-80. They were allocated to units as they arrived from the contractors, being added to capital stock between March and June 1935. Metropolitan-Vickers once more supplied the control system and other electrical equipment, but the type 163 traction motors were this time supplied by English Electric, although identical to those of BTH manufacture in the Brighton stock and interchangeable with them. Following problems with rough riding on the PULs, the design of the equalising beam motor bogies was slightly modified, the improved smoothness (which lasted only a short time) being strikingly demonstrated by Assistant CME Lionel Lynes on a Victoria – Eastbourne press run. Inviting selected journalists into the leading motor coach as the train travelled at speed between Three Bridges and Haywards Heath, Lynes lifted a floor inspection hatch and proceeded to stand on the motor casing. Charles Klapper records that he managed to keep his balance quite satisfactorily and '. . . went back after his party piece looking like the cat that had swiped the cream'.[18]

18 Klapper, C.F. *Sir Herbert Walker's Southern Railway.* Ian Allan Ltd, ISBN 0 7110 0478 1, 1973. p215

The main difference in outward appearance concerned the windows where, instead of the droplights and louvres used on the PULs, fixed window panes were fitted, secured from the outside by flanged aluminium window glazing pans. At the tops of the windows were Mead, McLean and Co. (MM) 'Airstream' sliding glass ventilators, then newly-designed and described in contemporary literature as 'two moveable frames above each large fixed window . . .' with 'a concave glass deflector close to the fixed panel'. These deflectors were actually two flared glass panels, mounted externally. In theory, the forward motion of the coach drew fresh air along the inside face of the deflector, which was tapered outwards at the rear opening. Most air drawn in went straight out again, but some went into the coach and some stale air was sucked out. All this relied on the sliding panels being opened the correct amount, which was doubtless seldom done despite instructions inside the coach.[19] This type of window ventilator was used in all subsequent open motor coaches of SR express stock, and also in various catering vehicles. A further change was that the passenger doors had frameless droplights for the first time. Internally the saloons also resembled those in the PULs with deep cushioned seats, transverse luggage racks and plenty of varnished woodwork in figured mahogany, the panels above the seats having the woodgrain arranged diagonally in a diamond pattern.

Many features were common to all the trailers which, with

the exception of the pantry cars, were externally virtually identical to the same vehicle types in the 6 PUL and 6 CIT units, except that intermediate corridor droplights and ventilators were replaced by distinctive narrow panels of plain glass to eave-height (also found in DTCs of 2 BILs 1890-1899 and Maunsell period 4ii steam stock), and door droplights were of the frameless type as on the motor third brakes. Their number series also continued from the earlier batches and, unlike the motor coaches, they were allocated to their units in tidy groups. Internally, all these vehicles differed from the Brighton stock in that conventional single sliding doors connected the compartments to the side corridor, rather than the balanced double-door arrangement of the earlier units. Below underframe level, one change was that (with two exceptions – see below) standard 8ft wheelbase suburban-type trailer bogies were used in place of the equalising beam variety in an attempt to improve riding. The trailer corridor thirds (diagram 2010) had eight compartments and one coupé with a toilet at each end of the vehicle, were on 62ft 6in underframes and were numbered 10021-54. The seven-compartment trailer firsts (dia. 2506), also with a toilet at each end, were mounted on 58ft steam-length frames and were numbered 12260-76.

The pantry cars, to diagram 2600 and numbered 12501-17, were unusual vehicles, being basically side corridor firsts with a small buffet facility at one end. They were provided because the Pullman Car Company had been in financial difficulties over its Brighton line cars, and it was therefore decided that future catering vehicles in electric units should

19 Electric Railway Traction, Supplement to *The Railway Gazette*, 28th June 1935. p24.

Diagram 2600 trailer pantry first 12509, formed in 6 PAN 3029, at East Croydon on 26th May 1963. This rare view of the corridor side shows the unusual window arrangement, including a pair of 'Airstream' sliding ventilators, fitted to compensate for a lack of intermediate door droplights. By this time the pantry compartments in these vehicles had been permanently closed for a number of years. *Denis Cullum*

be owned by the railway company, although on Central section services staffing and supply continued to be undertaken by Pullman. On 62ft 6in frames and weighing 32 tons, internal layout comprised a refreshment kitchenette with two serving counters (presumably to allow easier service to both ends of the unit), sink and Stone's electrically-heated hot water urn, followed by five first class compartments and a lavatory. The corridor side mainly had the usual Maunsell-style high windows reaching to the eaves, including a pair opposite the pantry, but two were lower and surmounted by Airstream sliding ventilators, necessary because the only external doors were at either end of the passenger section. The compartments also had single large windows with Airstream ventilators rather than the usual external door and quarterlights, this feature making them unique among SR side-corridor vehicles at the time. In contrast to the motor coaches, these windows were conventionally fixed with wooden fillets and the ventilator section was slightly shorter. The purpose of this window arrangement was to allow folding tables to be fitted in the compartments if required, these being stored in a cupboard next to the lavatory. The kitchenette section also had two windows of this type, both frosted on the main panel. The pantry cars were marshalled so that the catering area was at one end of the first class section, adjacent to a trailer third. Originally devoid of identification, by 1936 they had been lettered REFRESHMENT CAR.

Exceptionally, pantry cars 12516 and 12517 were mounted on the two prototype underframes built in 1931 to HO590 and salvaged from test unit 2001, and therefore had 'Dutch' equalising-beam bogies. These were replaced by the standard type in October 1956 and November 1955 respectively.

From the start of regular electric services on the Eastbourne line the Brighton and Worthing stock rosters were modified so that the seventeen new 6 PAN units ran in conjunction with existing 6 PUL stock, inaugurating the 6 PUL+6 PAN formation which was to become standard for expresses from London to Worthing/Littlehampton, Brighton, Eastbourne and Ore for the next thirty years. The pantry cars themselves were not a success however, quickly becoming unpopular with Pullman staff due to their cramped kitchens and limited catering possibilities. It was possible to serve little more than tea and biscuits, and the original plan to operate a corridor service into adjacent coaches, which were again provided with bell-pushes to summon the attendant, proved unworkable in practice, particularly during busy periods. Experimental use of a trolley, made up especially in the Pullman Works at Preston Park, proved equally unsatisfactory. The refreshment service ceased from 27th May 1942 as part of the general wartime withdrawal of catering facilities but, unlike the Pullman cars, the vehicles themselves remained in their units as most of their accommodation was seating anyway. Their kitchens reopened with the restoration of buffets from 7th January 1946, but staffing was soon reduced from two to one and they were eventually given up as a bad job and closed by the early 1950s, after which passengers wanting a drink or snack had to ensure they were travelling in the PUL unit. As mentioned above, some 6 PANs did in fact occasionally operate as 6 PUL, to keep the Pullman

car in service when the rest of the PUL vehicles were being overhauled. 3032 was the usual choice for this treatment before disbanding in 1958, running with *Lorna* in 1951/52, *Naomi* in 1952, *Ethel* and *Olive* in 1957, and possibly others which escaped record.

Only one 6 PAN unit, 3030, suffered serious war damage, trailer third 10039 being destroyed by a landmine at Brighton in May 1943, and it ran as a five-coach unit until a replacement was built new at Lancing in 1946 as part of HO 3078 dated 2nd November 1944. Although identical in internal layout to the original, the replacement 10039 was a diagram 2009 vehicle built to 4 COR drawings and differed in detail, particularly concerning the doors and corridor side window layout. One minor wartime change was that the external glass deflectors of the Airstream ventilators on the motor coaches and pantry cars were taken off. They were gradually reinstated on overhaul from 1945 onwards, only to be removed again, this time permanently, by the late 1950s.

Accident damage in the post war period resulted in motor coach exchanges. 3029 was involved in the London Bridge accident of 1948, and 3026 was damaged at about the same time. Following repairs, 11056 of 3029 went to 6 PUL 3003, 3026 acquired PUL motor coach 11006 from 3003, 3029 received 11066 from 3025, and 11054 from 3026 replaced 11066 in 3025. 3032 suffered minor damage in the collision at Eastbourne on 25th August 1958 and was subsequently disbanded, with motor coach 11074 and trailer second 10044 being formed in 6 PUL 3014 from October 1958. Its remaining coaches were withdrawn, trailer first 12271 and pantry car 12514 being scrapped at Newhaven in February 1961. As related above, MBS 11074 was itself withdrawn in about January 1959 and cut up at Lancing soon afterwards, its place in 3014 being taken by 11075, also from 3032. 3023 was involved in a siding collision with 4 BUF 3079 at New Cross Gate in September 1962, motor coach 11051 being damaged. Four intact vehicles from the unit were then stored in Hassocks sidings (a dumping ground for vehicles awaiting their fate since LBSCR days) until June 1963 when, with MBS 11051 repaired, 3023 was formed up once more and returned to traffic. Oddly, by early 1964 the same four vehicles had returned to Hassocks, only to return to service once again by the following May. 3024 had its sides scraped by derailed 4 LAV 2929 at Victoria in August 1963, but was patched up. As with the PULs, some units did not receive the second BR green before their demise between 1964 and 1966.

A summary of long-term 6 PAN reformations in the 1945-63 period is listed in the table below. Numbers of reformed or new vehicles are shown in bold type.

Unit	MThB	TThK	TPanF	TFK	TThK	MThB	Reformed
3025	11067	10029	12505	12264	10030	**11054**	circa 1949
3026	11053	10031	12506	12265	10032	**11006***	circa 1949
3029	**11066**	10038	12509	12268	10037	11055	circa 1949
3030	11077	**10039**†	12510	12269	10040	11072	circa 1949

*   Former 6 PUL MThB with saloon window droplights and ventilator bonnets.

†   Built in 1946 to 4 COR drawings.

THE 4 COR, 4 RES AND 4 BUF UNITS 1937-64

The Portsmouth Direct main line (Portsmouth No.1) electrification scheme, the first to be carried out by the Southern Railway using finance available under the 1935 arrangement with the Treasury, required a further fleet of electric units specifically for express services. By this time some service experience had been gained with the Brighton and Eastbourne units, and accordingly a number of important design changes were incorporated into the new express stock for the Portsmouth line. These were desirable not only to overcome certain shortcomings of the earlier types but also to effect economies in construction and operation, necessary as the 1930s were becoming increasingly difficult financially for the SR, for reasons outlined in Chapter 1.

Firstly, each unit was of four rather than six-coach formation, being made up of two driving motor coaches and two trailers. This gave greater flexibility in train length, allowing formations of four, eight or twelve coaches to be diagrammed depending on anticipated traffic levels. Secondly, each motor coach had only one powered bogie, equipped with a pair of type 163 traction motors manufactured by English Electric. These differed in detail from the EE and BTH examples fitted to the earlier express stock as they were designed for a higher nominal rating of 250hp, achieved mainly by casting additional ribbing on the motor casings to improve heat dissipation. This was considered necessary in view of the longer non-stop runs on the Portsmouth Direct line, but nevertheless the installed power of a twelve-coach train of Portsmouth express stock was little more than three-quarters that of a PUL+PAN formation (twelve motors instead of sixteen), and this was found to be barely adequate for maintaining schedules given the gradients involved. Thirdly, all vehicles except the restaurant trailers were built at Eastleigh on Lancing underframes, and the motor coach bodywork was of conventional wood-framed construction rather than all-steel.

The major innovation, however, was the provision of through gangways at the driving ends of the motor coaches, enabling an unobstructed passage throughout the train. These were fitted in order that all passengers travelling on a particular service should have access to refreshment facilities, even though only some units had catering vehicles. It was these end corridor connections, together with the resultant offset headcode panel, which gave the Portsmouth units their distinctive 'one-eyed' appearance. This feature, coupled with their Portsmouth associations, quickly led to them being dubbed 'Nelson stock' by staff. They were also widely known as 'Pompey stock' or as 'belly-wobblers', the latter due to the rapid sideways oscillation of the leading gangway connection as a train formed of these units passed at speed.

A total of 48 express units (192 vehicles) was built for the Portsmouth No.1 electrification (Waterloo – Portsmouth via Guildford, and Woking – Alton), completed in July 1937. A further 39 units (156 vehicles) of similar design, but with differing catering facilities, were then constructed for the Portsmouth No.2 scheme (Dorking/Three Bridges to Littlehampton, Bognor Regis and Portsmouth via Horsham), completed the following year. There were three classes of Portsmouth express EMU originally built, as follows:

4 COR 3101-3155. The standard express units for the Portsmouth routes (without catering facilities), each was formed with two open motor third brakes (MThB) flanking a corridor trailer third (TThK) and corridor trailer composite (TCK), giving a total seating capacity of 194 third and thirty first. The first 29 units were for the Portsmouth No.1 scheme and the remaining 26 for the Portsmouth No.2 scheme.

4 RES 3054-3072. These were the nineteen restaurant car units for the Waterloo – Guildford – Portsmouth express services. Motor coaches were the same as those in the CORs, but the trailers were a diner first (TDF) and a kitchen diner third (TKDTh). Total seating was 104 third and thirty first, plus dining seats for 12 first and 36 third.

4 BUF 3073-3085. These were the thirteen buffet car units for the Mid-Sussex line, principally for Victoria – Horsham – Bognor Regis expresses. The motor coaches and trailer composite were the same as those in the CORs, but the other trailer was a buffet car (TBuf) of advanced interior design. Total seating was 128 third and thirty first, plus 26 unclassed seats in the buffet car.

The SR-built vehicles of the Portsmouth No.1 stock, that is complete 4 COR units 3101-3129 and the motor coaches for 4 RES units 3054-3072, were all authorised on the same date, 14th May 1936. Unusually for electric stock, however, the different vehicle types were given separate Head Office order numbers, with HO 924 covering motor third brakes 11081-11176, HO 925 the COR trailer composites 11791-11819 and HO 926 the COR trailer thirds 10055-83. The RES trailers were ordered from outside carriage builders, but it was planned that some completion jobs would be carried out at Eastleigh following delivery from the contractors, although details of what these were are now lost. HO 931 and 932, both dated 9th June 1936, covered this finishing work on diner firsts 12232-50 and kitchen diner thirds 12601-19 respectively. Conversely, the single order HO 950 of 6th November 1936 covered the entire fleet of express stock for the Portsmouth No.2 (Mid-Sussex) electrification, comprising all vehicles of 4 COR 3130-3155 and 4 BUF 3073-3085.

Apart from differences mentioned, the Portsmouth express stock was electrically and mechanically similar to the earlier express EMU types, with which they could work in multiple. Dimensions of all vehicles were of the standard instituted for the 1932 PUL stock, with a body 63ft 6in in length on an underframe 62ft 6in over headstocks and fitted with self-contained buffers at both ends. Motor bogies, located only at the driving ends of the motor coaches, were of the 9ft wheelbase improved equalising beam type (as fitted to the PANs), while trailer bogies were of the standard 8ft suburban type. Jumper cable arrangements on the cab ends of the Portsmouth No.1 batch were also the same initially, with a control jumper and power socket (for connection to a depot shore supply) on the offside under the headcode panel, and only a control jumper receptacle on the nearside. However, the Portsmouth No.2 units were equipped with a 660V power jumper (to connect all pick-up shoes in the train) on the nearside from new, and the Portsmouth No.1 fleet had them added retrospectively to conform, probably in the latter half of 1938.

With the additional weight of all-steel construction now being considered unnecessary, the motor third brakes had conventional bodywork made up of galvanised steel side and end sheeting attached to a teak framework, with canvas-covered roofs of deal planking. Otherwise, they closely resembled the 6 PAN motor coaches, with an identical interior layout seating 52 and with the same large Alpax aluminium-framed windows fitted with MM Airstream sliding ventilators above. In order to redesign the front end to accommodate a gangway connection, it was necessary to abandon the traditional domed roof line above the cab, although the vertical corners were still rounded-off. The headcode panel was moved from the central position to the offside, in place of the left-hand lookout. (Before the design was finalized, there was apparently considerable discussion regarding the exact position of the headcode.) The gangway connection itself consisted of a steel rubbing plate connected to the cab front by the usual concertina of rubberised fabric and suspended from the top. Two sliding plates produced a smooth surface to the front of the gangway connection when closed. Lever-operated clips along the vertical edges of the rubbing plate aligned and located with another gangway connection when two units were coupled. Internally, a door was provided to shut off the motorman's compartment when not in use. These vehicles, to diagram 2114 and numbered 11081-11254, had a tare weight of 47 tons.

The trailer thirds and trailer composites had the same internal layout as equivalent vehicles in the PUL/PAN stock. The thirds (diagram 2009) had eight compartments and a coupé, connected by side corridor to lavatories at both ends. Numbered 10055-10109, they seated 68 and weighed 33 tons. The composites (dia. 2309) had five first and three third class compartments, seating thirty and 24 respectively, again with a side corridor and end lavatories, and with the same tare weight. Those in the CORs were numbered 11791-11845 and those in the BUFs 11846-58. Both these vehicle types had corridor side windows which reached to the eaves, and each compartment had its own external door on the non-corridor side. They were representative of the final period 5 of Maunsell/Lynes carriage design, and had various refinements when compared with the Brighton and Eastbourne units. There were no ventilator bonnets above the door droplights, and all fixed windows had Alpax frames mounted from the outside. Droplights were again of the frameless Beclawat type locked by a lever device at the bottom, and window and door arrangements on the corridor side were altered to eliminate the narrow windows and to reposition the external doors so that they were between (rather than opposite) compartments. In each 4 COR unit, the trailers were marshalled so that the first class compartments were at the centre, adjacent to the trailer third, or to the buffet car in the 4 BUF units. The side-corridors were on the same side on both trailers; as with the Brighton and Eastbourne stock this was obligatory as these vehicles were 'handed', with the lighting jumper cable sockets only on the corridor side.

The interiors of all these vehicle types were also similar to the earlier express stock, but a major innovation was the use of 'Rexine' to cover various panels in place of varnished wood

or white paint. In the third class compartments cream and beige were the predominant colours used, and light blue with light grey in firsts. Seat upholstery was as before, with mainly green or blue-based 'jazz' patterns in the thirds and floral tapestry in the firsts. These (and the 2 BILs) were the last units to be so finished internally when new, as we have already seen that Bulleid had different ideas regarding interior finishing, first expressed in the 2 HALs of 1939. The motor coach interiors were further developed from the PANs, with semicircular headrests at the aisle ends of the seats, more padding on the coach sides and arched tops to the internal doorways.

As explained earlier, basic construction of the trailer vehicles for the RES units was contracted out to independent carriage builders, with Metropolitan-Cammell being responsible for trailer diner firsts 12232-50 and BRCW for trailer kitchen diner thirds 12601-18. The trailer diner firsts were to diagram 2505 and weighed 33 tons. Internally, they consisted of five ordinary first class compartments connected by side corridor with a toilet at either end, and a two-bay dining section at one end with a transverse vestibule adjacent to the gangway connection. The corridor section was identical to that in the composites, with a side door to each compartment and corridor windows that reached to the eaves. The dining saloon, however, had windows similar to the motor coaches, with sliding Airstream ventilators. (These lined-up with the edges of the fixed windows, unlike those on the PAN pantry cars.) Internally, the dining section seated twelve in loose chairs arranged two+one either side of the off-centre aisle, with 'Rexine'-covered tables equipped with small Pullman-style table lamps which were actually fixed to the car sides.

Due to their kitchen equipment the trailer kitchen diner thirds, to diagram 2571, were heavier at 35 tons. Their internal layout comprised a transverse vestibule, a five bay dining saloon seating 36 with a lavatory compartment let-in on the nearside at the vestibule end, and pantry and kitchen compartments, with a side corridor on the nearside. Exterior styling was again similar to the motor coaches, with large windows, but the three opposite the kitchen on the corridor side lacked Airstream ventilators. On the kitchen side, there were four small windows, unevenly spaced. The seating accommodation in the dining saloon once more consisted of fixed 'Rexine'-surfaced tables and loose chairs, this time arranged two+two each side of the aisle. The kitchen equipment was comprehensive, comprising a cooking range with four hot plates, two grills, one steaming and four roasting ovens, refrigerator with wine cooling cabinet, and water boiler. As on the earlier stock, this equipment was all-electric, with the boiler and ovens working directly off 660V and the grills, hot plates and refrigerator supplied from a 200V motor-generator mounted on the underframe. The refrigerator compressor and motor were also underframe-mounted. All working surfaces were of stainless steel with chromium-plated fixtures, and the kitchen was ventilated by two roof-mounted MM 'Monsoon' ventilators.

The 4 RES units were marshalled with the kitchen at the centre, the kitchen end of the TKDTh then being adjacent to the first class dining saloon. Forced-air ventilation equip-

4 RES trailer kitchen diner second (TSRKB) S12604S, formed in unit 3066, at Havant on 27th August 1957. This view shows the kitchen side of the vehicle, with four small windows. Although demand for full restaurant facilities on Waterloo – Portsmouth expresses had declined since the War, trade seems fairly brisk on this occasion. *RCTS Collection*

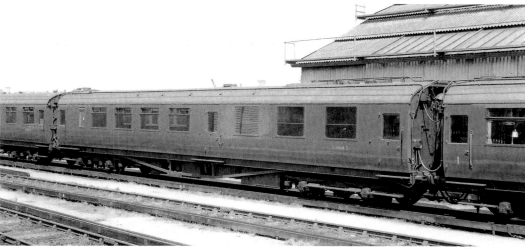

The corridor side of RES trailer kitchen diner second S12616S from unit 3062, parked in Fratton depot on 10th July 1961. The three large windows, without ventilators, indicate the position of the gangway past the kitchen. *RCTS Collection*

ment was used in both first and third class dining areas, with Stone's pressure ventilation units mounted on the underframe supplying air into the saloons through ducts at floor level. The dining tables were hinged to the car sides so they could be folded upwards to aid floor cleaning.

The last vehicles of the Portsmouth express stock off the production line at Eastleigh were the buffet cars for the Portsmouth No.2 (Mid-Sussex) scheme; this was because their internal design was totally revised just as construction was about to begin early in 1938. This coincided with the retirement of Maunsell as chief mechanical engineer and his replacement by O.V.S. Bulleid. What Maunsell had originally intended is not known, but his successor had very advanced ideas regarding coach interior design (as Assistant CME of the LNER in charge of coaches he had been instrumental in commissioning the *Coronation* and *Silver Jubilee* streamliners) and decreed that the 'Bognor buffets' should be redesigned internally.

These vehicles, to diagram 2601, were numbered 12518-30 and weighed 37 tons. As finally built, their interior layout comprised two lavatories and a cross vestibule, a saloon with sixteen seats at tables, a long bar counter with ten stools, and finally a kitchen and pantry area. Externally, they were

rather plain, with large expanses of windowless side around the kitchen and bar area 'so as to ensure greater privacy' to patrons, and only a few large windows, mainly at the saloon end. These windows were fitted with a primitive form of double glazing and did not have opening panels as the coaches were again force-ventilated. A Stone's pressure ventilation unit was fitted to the underframe feeding 'continuous supplies of filtered fresh air' to ducts situated at floor-level under the buffet counter and one of the saloon tables. This time stale air was designed to be removed through four electric extractor fans fitted along the roof, but in case of problems there were opening windows behind the bar, in the corridor opposite the kitchen, and in the kitchen itself, the latter also having additional MM 'Monsoon' ceiling extractors. The catering equipment was again all-electric and generally similar to that in the RES kitchen cars. It consisted of a stove with ovens and hot plates, a refrigerator, a hot water heater, a milk boiler and a coffee machine. The heating elements in the ovens, milk, water and coffee heaters worked at line-voltage, but the grills and hot plates operated at 70V and were supplied via an underframe-mounted motor-generator. The refrigerator differed in being supplied at 660V so that it continued in operation when the low-tension supply was switched off.

New 4 BUF buffet car 12519, formed in unit 3074. It was thought that forced-air ventilation made opening windows in the saloon unnecessary, but these coaches were soon found to be claustrophobic on hot days and sliding ventilators were fitted post-war. The light green livery contrasted with the darker green of the rest of the train. *NRM/SSPL*

The unusual interior of a BUF buffet car as designed by O. V. S. Bulleid, clearly showing the 'scalloped edge' theme adopted. *NRM/SSPL*

The outstanding feature of the electric buffet cars was their interior arrangement and decor, quite unlike anything previously seen on the SR. The edges of the tables and bar were scalloped, each arc accommodating one seat. There was no cornice rail dividing walls and ceiling, but the bar and saloon areas were divided by a number of vertical webs, which continued the scalloped edge feature. The colour scheme was predominantly light stone with dark brown edging, and the walls were decorated with cast plates of 'antique' brass depicting food subjects, although some of these had to be hastily changed on entry into service to avoid offending the religious sensibilities of certain passengers. These plaques did not survive the war, the brass being requisitioned for more pressing purposes. The floor was covered in Royal Wilton carpet of a specially-commissioned pattern in black with old gold diagonal stripes, the stools and curtains had matching fabrics in either bright green or red and gold, and metal fittings were enamelled in complementary shades. The swivelling stools around the saloon tables had low backs and sheet-metal legs incorporating a handbag shelf.

These buffet cars were delivered in a new lighter shade of green, devoid of lining, making them stand out clearly from the standard dark olive green of the rest of the train and drawing attention to the facilities provided. Buffet car 12519 in unit 3074 was named *City of Portsmouth* when new, and carried that place's coat of arms on the sides at fascia height.

The 4 COR units were built in two batches a year apart, with 3101-3129 for the Portsmouth No.1 electrification appearing between February and April 1937 and 3130-3155 for the Portsmouth No.2 scheme being delivered between May and July 1938. The coaches in these units were formed up in strict numerical sequence. The 4 RES units appeared later in the spring of 1937 but, being marshalled as the catering vehicles were ready after arrival from the contractors and completion at Eastleigh, were not all in strict number order. The last RES trailers did not actually enter traffic until July 1937, and in the meantime one pair of RES motor coaches (from 3056) were temporarily formed up with ordinary COR trailers for a publicity photograph near Petersfield prior to the start of electric services. At least one RES (3057) ran in service as a three-coach unit on the opening date of the electrification pending delivery of its TKDTh. The 4 BUF units were delivered between May and July 1938, but it appears that some also ran in service as three-coach units for a short time due to the late delivery of the buffet cars.

When electric services on the Portsmouth Direct line commenced in July 1937, the standard formation for express trains between Waterloo and Portsmouth Harbour was either COR+RES+COR or COR+RES, the twelve-coach formation having a total of ninety first and 492 third class seats, excluding those in the dining cars. The roof boards carried on these services were confusingly lettered WATERLOO – PORTSMOUTH – ISLE OF WIGHT, and staff at the Harbour station soon became adept at turfing out holiday-makers who expected that their train would continue to Sandown, Shanklin or Ventnor. One change from previous practice on main line electric services was that the restaurant cars were manned by SR staff rather than by Pullman. On the Mid-Sussex route however, the steam-hauled expresses had included Pullman cars, and so the buffet cars of the BUF units continued to be staffed by Pullman personnel, and their bill of fare was identical to that on the Brighton line Pullmans. On these services COR+BUF (+COR) ran from Victoria to Barnham, whence the leading unit was detached to run on to Portsmouth while the rear of the train, including buffet, turned sharp left to terminate at Bognor. Central section units also appeared regularly on other main line services to Brighton and Eastbourne, while Western section units were diagrammed for certain rush hour trains between Waterloo and Farnham/Alton, with the catering facilities of the RES units out of use. Only the catering units were religiously kept to their respective sections, and from mid 1938 it seems that any of the 55 CORs could appear on any working diagrammed for the class.

The Portsmouth express stock had been running in service for little more than two years when war in Europe broke out for a second time. As an important naval base, it was inevitable that Portsmouth would suffer more than its fair share from the attentions of German bombers, and thus there were several incidents involving SR electric trains. The worst occurred on the night of 10th-11th January 1941, when the Harbour station was bombed and seriously damaged, totally destroying units 3060, 3117 and 3119 and one MThB from 3132. The remaining three coaches of unit 3132, marooned in platform 4, were not recovered until September 1946; in the meantime they were painted grey and stripped of external brass fittings. (The destroyed vehicles were cut up on site in March 1941.) Several other units received extensive air-raid damage when Fratton depot was hit, while in the London area three vehicles were destroyed when a V1 flying bomb fell at Wimbledon Park on 29th June 1944. In all, 25 vehicles from COR, RES and BUF units were written off as war losses, this total including eleven motor coaches, four trailer thirds, four trailer composites and six catering cars.

Other, less severely damaged, vehicles were repaired and reformed with undamaged coaches as necessary, resulting in a high proportion of 'odd' formations. Further changes had resulted from the withdrawal of buffet and restaurant facilities as from 27th May 1942. The twelve remaining BUF buffet cars were removed from their units and stored, firstly at Epsom Goods and later at the temporarily-closed Crystal Palace (High Level), where most remained until at least August 1945. All the body sides were repainted with the near-malachite shade of green in use by that time (including window glass) and roofs painted grey in about May 1943 in an attempt to slow down deterioration while in outside storage. Restaurant cars, conversely, remained in traffic with their kitchens closed, as most of their space was seating anyway. As with the PANs, a minor wartime modification was the temporary removal of the external glass deflectors from the Airstream window ventilators of 'Nelson' stock. Again, they were replaced from 1945 onwards, only to be discarded permanently by about 1960.

With the end of the war in sight towards the end of 1944 the construction of 26 new express stock vehicles was authorised, to replace those written-off as a result of enemy action and to return the COR/RES/BUF fleet to full strength. However, with an over-provision of catering facilities on Portsmouth Direct line services already clearly apparent, the three restaurant cars destroyed were not replaced like-for-like. Instead, it was planned to make up three additional 4 CORs utilising motor coaches from the three disbanded RES units and new trailers ordered in place of destroyed catering cars. With a single exception, the new coaches were ordered on 9th November 1944. HO 3075 covered eleven motor third brakes, to be built at Eastleigh on Lancing underframes. Eight trailer thirds were covered by HO 3078, of which seven were for the COR fleet and one was for 6 PAN 3030 to replace destroyed 10039 as explained earlier. HO 3079 included five trailer composites and, strangely, a single RES trailer diner first, the only such vehicle to be built in SR workshops. Given that this vehicle was to be formed in a COR anyway, exactly why it was ordered, rather than an additional trailer composite, is unclear. Unusually, it appears that both body-work and frames of all these trailers were to be constructed at Lancing, possibly due to workshop capacity constraints at Eastleigh, which was gearing up for 4 SUB production. The final new vehicle required, replacement buffet car 12518, was ordered on 9th December 1944 to HO 3076, with Eastleigh bodywork on a Lancing underframe.

Catering facilities were reintroduced on 7th January 1946, with the buffet cars reformed into their units. All but one of the new vehicles to replace those lost in the war were outshopped between May and November 1946, although not all units including them had been formed up until the following February. The eleven new motor third brakes were given the numbers of the vehicles they replaced, but of the seven new trailer thirds intended for the Portsmouth stock, four were direct replacements and three (10110-12) were in place of destroyed trailer kitchen diner thirds 12606/15/17. Of the five new trailer composites, four were direct replacements and the other (11859) was in place of TDF 12249. The new trailer diner first, a direct replacement for 12234, never actually ran in a 4 RES unit but was numbered as trailer composite 11860, into which configuration it was eventually rebuilt. The final new vehicle constructed was the replacement buffet car 12518, but this was not formed into 3074 until October 1948 following completion the previous month. As a result of these changes, three 4 RES units (3058/60/63) were abolished and three more 4 CORs were formed, numbered 3156-3158.

The 1946/48 replacement stock was built to the original designs exactly, and within a few years became indistinguishable from the original pre-war coaches. To utilise all available vehicles it was necessary for additional CORs 3157 and 3158 to have a trailer diner first in place of a trailer composite. 3157 was therefore given 1946 replacement vehicle 11860 as mentioned above, while 3158 was given the remaining spare 1937-built TDF, formerly 12232 and now renumbered 11861. From an SR drawing dating from 1945, it appears that it had already been used as a composite during the war, the dining saloon being converted into a third class area. The sixteen seats were arranged three+one with an off-centre aisle, and standard COR saloon inner seat ends with semi-circular headrests were used. In unit 3158, 11861 was formed with the third class saloon area adjacent to the MThB. Unlike 11860 it was never properly rebuilt, and was withdrawn for depart-mental service in 1964. (After spending some time at Micheldever, 11861 went to Brockenhurst where it was eventually broken up in about 1967.)

4 COR 3147 was damaged in a collision at Woking in December 1955, in which the underframe of MThB 11212 was damaged more severely than the body. Subsequently, the body of 11212 was repaired and mounted on a spare under-frame which had come from war victim 11082 of unit 3101, damaged in June 1944 at Wimbledon Park and unused since.

Unique trailer composite 11861, converted during the war from RES trailer diner first 11132 by replacing the dining area with a third class saloon (nearest the camera) having seating arranged three+one either side of an off-centre aisle. From 1946 until 1964 it was formed in 4 COR 3158, made up from spare vehicles following war damage. Seen at Redhill on 5th January 1951, it retained the external glass baffles on its 'Airstream' ventilators at this time. *Denis Cullum*

The BUF buffet cars had pressure ventilation and, as mentioned, were built without opening window panels in the saloon area. In practice this arrangement evidently provided insufficient fresh air, and at some time (probably during overhaul in the 1950s) they were given Beresford Pullman-type sliding ventilators. These were radiused at the top corners and opened at the centre, in contrast to the Airstream type which opened at either end. At the same time the curtain rails were repositioned below the ventilator section.

It has already been mentioned that those restaurant cars written off in the war were not replaced, and as demand for the lavish full meal service on Waterloo to Portsmouth expresses gradually declined through the 1950s, it was suggested that the sixteen remaining trailer diner thirds might be converted into buffets. In February 1954, 12613 in unit 3072 was gutted by fire, and the opportunity was taken to rehabilitate this vehicle as a 'cafeteria car' offering self-service snacks. Authorised by HO 4194 of 29th April 1954, the rebuilding work was carried out at Eastleigh, where similar conversions had been undertaken a few years earlier on pre-war SR, LMS and LNER hauled stock. The saloon was reduced in length by half a bay, but as the toilet was replaced by seating also, it retained its capacity of 36. The kitchen area was replaced by a servery with counter facing the saloon, a kitchen with sink at the rear, a store and a staff toilet. The windows at the kitchen end were modified or repositioned to suit the new internal arrangements, but remained of Maunsell style, and the kitchen and store were given their own external doors. Following these alterations, completed by November 1955, 12613 was given the revised diagram number 2602. While work was in progress, the remainder of 3072 operated as a three-coach unit on Western section suburban services between July 1954 and July 1955, mainly on the Hounslow loop. With its catering car reinstated, 3072 returned to traffic on the Portsmouth Direct line in February 1956, and was reclassified 4 BUF when remaining unrebuilt RES units were disbanded in January 1964.

Late in 1960 the decision was taken to rebuild all sixteen of the RES kitchen diner seconds, with HO 4855 of 10th October authorising the conversion of five into open seconds and the remaining eleven into a new type of buffet known as a griddle car. (The numbers seem to suggest that 'cafeteria car' 12613 was to be included in this scheme, unless an error was made.) Then the latest idea in catering vehicles on BR, the griddle car had a counter with a grill on which hot snacks were cooked by a griddle chef in full view of the customer. In the event, due to high conversion costs and then doubts about the future of catering services, only three griddle car and no open second conversions were ever carried out. (These latter, for which no drawings can be traced, would have resulted in five CORs with all second class accommodation provided in saloons.)

'Cafeteria car' 12613 from unit 3072, in final blue livery with red cantrail stripe, parked at Gatwick on 1st August 1971 following withdrawal. This 'one-off' vehicle, reconstructed from a RES kitchen car following fire damage, was later purchased for use as a transport cafe at Shepherds Bush and survived for a number of years. *J. H. Aston*

The three griddle car conversions involved kitchen diner seconds 12602/05/09 from units 3056/65/68 respectively, and the work was once more carried out at Eastleigh. Transformation involved total gutting and reconstruction of the interior and new body sides with unpainted aluminium-framed BR Mark 1 style windows, somewhat deeper than the original Maunsell type. The new internal layout was virtually identical to the three BR standard Mark 1 griddle cars built new at Eastleigh at the same time, and consisted of a bar area and counter, a separate griddle counter and a saloon with seats at tables. Interior panelling was in shiny mahogany-effect and white laminates, the floor was tiled, and the bar area had low-backed bench seats with scalloped backs. Externally, these handsome coaches were lettered BUFFET and GRIDDLE, and had the red cantrail stripe then recently introduced to denote a catering vehicle. Their revised diagram number following conversion was 2572. The dining area of the trailer firsts which ran with them was also altered so that there were only two tables, each seating two, and eight loose chairs. The three units returned to traffic early in 1962, with 3065 and 3068 being ready for Easter and 3056 shortly afterwards. The modified coaches retained their original numbers, although not formed into their original units (see list below). With a staff of just two (the aforementioned griddle chef and a bar attendant) they offered considerable operational savings over the restaurant cars, and proved popular with most customers, although the 'self-service' arrangements were disliked by some. 3056/65/68 were reclassified 4 GRI and renumbered 3086-3088 in December 1963:

Unit	MBS	TGri	TDF	MBS
3056 (3086)	11143	12605	12245	11144
3065 (3087)	11162	12602	12237	11202
3068 (3088)	11167	12609	12240	11168

Cars 12602/05/09 were in units 3068/65/56 respectively before conversion.

MBS 11095 of unit 3108 was the first SR-designed main line vehicle to be given roller blind headcode arrangements, being experimentally equipped in 1958. The blinds were the large-numeral type until 1961, when 11096 was also fitted with a blind box and both were given small-numeral blinds. About 1960, following experiments with suburban and main line EP-braked electric stock, the battery and motor-generator set provision on COR/RES/BUF motor coaches was halved. Thereafter, one motor coach of each unit was fitted with the motor-generator and the other with the emergency battery. This was followed from about March 1962 by the general provision of roller blind headcode equipment, driver-to-guard 'loudaphones' and bells, and a second heater in the guard's compartment. The COR and RES units were done first, the BUFs not being dealt with until the summer and autumn of 1964. These alterations had been authorised by HO 4620, dated 28th October 1959, which for some reason was delayed in implementation. New motor-generator sets were also fitted at this time.

In September 1962 MBS 11242 and buffet car 12524 from 4 BUF 3079 were written-off in a shunting collision at New Cross Gate sidings and the unit was disbanded. Trailer composite 11852 and motor coach 11241 were held as spares, but did not have long to wait before coming in useful. In February 1963, 3134 ran into 3139 at Drayton Crossing (near Chichester), seriously damaging MBSs 11186 from the former and 11195 of the latter. 11186 was cut up, but 11195 was repaired and reformed into 3134, together with spare TCK 11852 and MBS 11241 from 3079. (Thus 3134 retained only one of its original vehicles, TSK 10088.) Of the two spare undamaged coaches originally from 3134, MBS 11185 was used to reform 3139 and, after a short period in storage, TCK 11824 went to 3158 in 1964 (see below). It is probable that all this mixing occurred simply because coaches from 3079, 3134 and 3139 were all in works together and reforming them this way required the minimum of shunting.

THE LAST YEARS OF THE FIRST GENERATION EXPRESS STOCK 1964-72

The final eight years of service for the Southern Railway express units built for the main line electrifications of the 1930s were extremely complicated, with a large number of reformations and the appearance of some (generally short-lived) new types. To briefly summarise the situation, the first units to be disbanded were the remaining unconverted 4 RES units, some of which had their trailer kitchen diner second replaced by a Pullman composite, still in Pullman livery, from a 6 PUL or trailer second from a 6 PUL or 6 PAN. The remainder of the PUL and PAN units were gradually withdrawn between 1964 and 1966, Pullman car working on normal service trains other than the *Brighton Belle* ceasing from the timetable revision of 18th April 1966, concurrent with the full entry into service of replacement 4 CIG and 4 BIG stock. Following this, RES motor coaches were further reformed with former PUL and PAN trailers to form ten additional 4 COR units. Ten 6 COR units were also made up at this time from the best of the redundant PUL and PAN motor coaches and further trailers, but were of limited use and had only a short life. The Portsmouth 4 BUF and 4 GRI units were withdrawn in 1970-71 as their duties were taken over by further new stock, while the *Brighton Belle* service ended on 30th April 1972 when the three 5 BEL units were finally taken out of traffic. The bulk of the 4 COR fleet remained in service until 1971-72, latterly eking out their days on the Waterloo – Reading line and on south coast locals until the last was withdrawn in September 1972.

In January 1964 the first serious moves were made in the withdrawal of the 6 PUL and 6 PAN units which, although only approximately thirty years old, were life expired and for which replacement stock was by then on order. The first changes were in the catering arrangements on the Portsmouth Direct, Mid-Sussex and Brighton lines. The trailer kitchen diner seconds of the remaining unconverted 4 RES units were withdrawn, without ever having been painted with the red cantrail stripe denoting catering facilities. At the same time most of the 4 BUF and 4 COR units working on the Mid-Sussex route were transferred to the South Western division to join their sisters on the Portsmouth Direct line, being replaced on Victoria to Bognor Regis/Portsmouth Harbour services by spare Kent Coast 4 CEP and 4 BEP stock from the South Eastern division. A few Central division COR and BUF diagrams were retained to cover miscellaneous workings, particularly rush-hour services between the south coast and London Bridge.

Above 4 COR 3142, from the second batch for the Portsmouth No.2 electrification, runs into Fratton leading a twelve-coach Portsmouth Harbour – Waterloo semi-fast service on 23rd August 1969. These had the unit end power jumpers from new. It is wearing the later BR green livery, but has gained a full yellow end with black unit numbers. The original stencil headcode panel was replaced by roller-blinds in 1963. *Southern Images / J. H. Bird*

6 PUL units 3004/14/17/18/20 were disbanded at this time and their Pullman cars marshalled into 4 RES units in place of the kitchen cars, the units concerned being redesignated 4 PUL. 6 PANs 3027/31/33 were also disbanded and their trailer seconds, together with ex-PAN TSK from PUL 3014, were marshalled into other RES units in place of the withdrawn kitchen cars, and these units were reclassified 4 COR(N). These rearrangements allowed redundant restaurant cars and the worst PUL and PAN motor brake seconds to be taken out of service whilst retaining a full complement of Pullman cars and gangway-ended COR-type motor coaches in traffic. They also enabled eight or twelve-coach trains to operate on the Brighton line in which all passengers had access to the Pullman.

The catering service changes on the two Portsmouth routes took effect during the weekend 3rd-6th January 1964 and the 4 PUL and 4 COR(N) reformations were carried out over the following two months. These units took their numbers from the former 4 RES series, but numbers 3058 and 3060-3064 were not used. Revised overall length of the 4 PULs was 264ft 6in (according to 3054) or 267ft 2in (according to 3055), but that of the 4 COR(N)s was unchanged. In both cases the former dining end of the trailer first was arranged to be at the centre of the unit, next to the Pullman or trailer third. In the 4 PUL units the Pullman car was orientated with the kitchen end next to the trailer first. The formations of these units are shown below:

4 PUL Units 3054-3059 (5 Units)

Unit	MBS	TDFK	Pullman	MBS
3054	11140	12248	*Clara*	11177
3055	11141	12246	*Gwladys*	11142
3056	11154(1)	12233	*Ethel*	11153
3057	11146	12247	*Elinor*	11145
3059	11172(2)	12242	*Enid*	11149

(1) Replaced by 11214 in September 1964
(2) Replaced by 11128 in September 1964

4 COR(N) Units 3065-3071 (7 Units)

Unit	MBS	TDFK	TSK	MBS
3065	11155	12235	10034	11156
3066	11164	12238	10033	11163
3067	11166	12239	10046	11165
3068	11160	12236	10045	11159
3069	11170	12241	10042	11169
3070	11229	12250	10041	11171
3071	11174	12243	10044	11173

Of those units rebuilt or reformed from the 4 RES class, the 4 PUL and 4 COR(N) classes were allocated to the Brighton line, working almost exclusively on the hourly services between Victoria and Littlehampton via Hove. The three 4 GRI units 3056/65/68 remained, as 3086/88/87, on the Waterloo – Portsmouth line, as did the 'cafeteria' unit 3072.

HO 5331 of 2nd March 1964 gave authority for the conversion of the motor nose suspension of one 4 COR motor bogie to suit EE 507 traction motors, in universal use on SR post-1951 EMU stock, as an experiment. The work was done in about July 1964, but nothing further came from it.

An interesting reformation took place in June 1964 when two 4 COR units, 3124 and 3148, had one motor coach replaced by a 6 PUL MBS, resulting in two units with a through-gangwayed COR driving cab at one end and non-gangwayed PUL cab at the other. A likely explanation for this peculiar rearrangement is that it released a pair of COR-type motor coaches for the push-pull trials mentioned later. Revised formations were 11127 + 11814 + 10078 + 11034 (3124) and 11208 + 11838 + 10102 + 11036 (3148) with 11034 and 11036 being the PUL motor coaches (from 3017 and 3018 respectively), in both cases marshalled next to the TSK. The two units normally ran together with the PUL coaches at the outer ends to retain a gangway throughout the train, and were mainly used on the 8.45am Haslemere to Waterloo and the 7.17pm Waterloo to Farnham commuter services. It is recorded that their additional horsepower

enabled them to put up some fine performances on these runs. They were also used, with a 4 BUF coupled at the country end, on summer Saturday reliefs between Waterloo and Portsmouth Harbour, although buffet access would have been limited. 3124 and 3148 were returned to their original formations and became interchangeable with the rest of the COR fleet once again in July 1965, the PUL motor coaches then being withdrawn.

During 1964 vehicles from a number of withdrawn first-generation express stock units were involved in trials of experimental push-pull equipment. Motor coaches 11028 (from 3014) and 11075 (3032), with four former PUL TCKs between, were used first on the South Western division between Wimbledon and Farnborough and later on the South Eastern division between Victoria and Dover. Hauled and propelled by a BRCW type 3 KA (D65xx at that time) diesel electric locomotive, all experimental test equipment was situated in the unit to avoid having to modify the locomotive. The traction motors were removed from the motor coaches and experimental control gear fitted. These tests were concerned with the control of the diesel engine from a remote driving trailer cab, and proved successful. The whole of 3027 was also used on the South Eastern, coupled to the unit mentioned above to provide a twelve-coach train, powered by an E5000 HA class electric locomotive. COR motor coaches 11154 and 11172 (earlier formed in 4 PULs 3056/59 respectively) were also used with PAN motor coaches 11057/58 from withdrawn 3031 for tests on the Central division in 1964.

Apart from the testing of experimental equipment, these trials may also have been concerned with an abortive 1963 proposal to use pre-war express stock in diesel powered push-pull formations on the Oxted line, an advantage over most hauled stock at the time being that the vehicles were electrically heated. The intention was to use redundant PUL and PAN vehicles to form eight three-coach 'half-sets', numbered 301-308, each comprising a driving trailer converted from a motor coach and two normal trailers. These 'half-sets' would have been used in pairs to make six-coach formations, hauled or propelled by KA diesel electric locomotives. Although specific coaches were allocated these proposals fell through,

probably due largely to a reluctance to spend limited funds on already life-expired rolling stock. Before long, much more modern electrically-heated BR Mark 1 stock was to become available, anyway.

However, following on from the earlier tests, one experimental six-coach trailer control (6 TC) unit numbered 601 was made up in June 1965 using de-motored COR motor coaches 11154 and 11229 (the latter from 4 COR(N) 3070) and spare PUL/PAN corridor trailers in the formation: driving trailer brake second (DTBS) 11154 + TSK 10014 + TSK 10009 + TCK 11768 + TSK 10041 + DTBS 11229. TSK 10041 had its gangway on the opposite side to the other trailers. The former motor coaches had their motor bogies replaced by standard 8ft SR trailer bogies, with BR speed recording gear attached to the leading axles, giving a revised tare weight of 34 tons. The unit-end brake pipes were moved to the waist-level position and ETH cables fitted to enable the heating to be provided by a locomotive. Standard 27-wire EPB control wires were installed through all the coaches, with a waist-level jumper under the offside of the cab ends. Type 3 KA diesel electric locomotive D6580 was fitted with similar multiple unit control to enable it to operate in full push-pull mode with 601, and this included the ability to start the diesel engine from the leading cab when the locomotive was at the rear of the formation. The unit was used for comprehensive testing of push-pull operation for the forthcoming Bournemouth electrification, and on trial was successfully run at speeds of up to 90mph with the locomotive at the rear. 601 was therefore the operating prototype for the 4 TC units, and D6580 the first of the push-pull fitted KA (later class 33/1) subclass. (Both types are described in greater detail in Chapter 7).

Following these tests, 601 and D6580 were placed in passenger service on rush hour Oxted line services from 17th January 1966, when the pair appeared at London Bridge on the 16.20 to East Grinstead. Their booked diagram, Mondays to Fridays only, included the 06.45 and 09.12 East Grinstead to London Bridge, the 07.55 and 16.20 London Bridge to East Grinstead, and the 17.32 East Grinstead to Victoria and 18.49 return. The pair also initially worked on Saturdays.

Nights and Sundays were spent berthed at East Grinstead and weekdays off-peak at New Cross Gate. In June 1966 the former motor coaches were further modified by the removal of the cab-end gangway connections and plating over of the apertures. From July 1967, 601 saw use on Waterloo–Andover trains, before being relegated by August to the (then unadvertised) Clapham Junction – Kensington Olympia rush hour shuttle, otherwise being parked in Clapham Yard. By this time any of the nineteen push-pull fitted class 33/1 locomotives could be used, but if one was not available a standard class 33 substituted, running-round at each end of the journey. In August 1967 the 6 TC was painted blue with full yellow ends, and survived in service until June 1971, when it was damaged in a collision with a milk tanker at Kensington Olympia and summarily withdrawn. After spending some time in the Micheldever dump, 601 was broken up at Brockenhurst early the following year.

There were various other changes involving the 6 PUL/PAN fleet in addition to all the reformations noted above. The Pullman composites were frequently swapped from unit to unit in an attempt to keep the best in traffic as the SR vehicles in the PUL units (both four and six-coach) were disbanded. Thus when 3016 was withdrawn in about April 1965, *Iris* was transferred to 3006. Following an accident at Brighton in September 1964, *Alice* went from 3009 to 4 PUL 3059, and then moved on again in September 1965 to 6 PUL 3041, replacing *May*. *Lorna* went to 3057 in place of *Elinor* in February 1966, but the whole unit was withdrawn a month later.

Although 6 PAN 3027 was officially withdrawn in August 1964 following completion of push-pull experiments, a further unit with the same number appeared in passenger traffic the following October. Lacking a pantry car, this second '3027' was effectively a 6 COR, and was formed: MBS 11018 + TSK 10010 + TCK 11769 + TCK 11757 + TCK 11758 + MBS 11035. Paradoxically, it will be noted that all the coaches for this scratch unit had actually come from PULs 3009/14/18, the former having been involved in an accident at Brighton. It ran for almost a year before being withdrawn in its turn in about September 1965.

Most of the motor coaches, trailer seconds and composites, as well as other miscellaneous vehicles, left over after the complex reforming exercises were sent to Micheldever sidings as spares, 11774 being derailed on arrival during a blizzard. By March 1964 the coaches listed below were stored here, in the sidings laid out in the chalk pit excavated by the LSWR to provide hardcore for construction work at Southampton Docks:

Trailer Seconds: 10006/12. (2)

Motor Brake Seconds: 11007/08/28/33-36/39/40/59/60/75. (12)

Trailer Composites: 11757/58/61/62/67/73/74/77, 11861*. (9)

Trailer Firsts: 12270/72. (2)

Trailer Pantry Firsts: 12507/11/13. (3)

Trailer Kitchen Diner Seconds: 12603/07/11/12/14/18. (6)

* Former RES trailer diner first, latterly running in unit 3158.

The other withdrawn RES kitchen diner seconds, 12601/04/08/10/16/19, were stored at Strawberry Hill. The whole batch of them was soon sent to Newhaven for cutting up – those from Strawberry Hill about August 1964 and those from Micheldever at the same time or soon afterwards. This was an abortive operation however, as it was overlooked that Newhaven had ceased scrapping coaches in about May 1964. It was therefore necessary to forward them elsewhere, and some were moved around and stored at several locations before finally being broken up. 12618, for example, was moved from Micheldever to Newhaven in August 1964 and to Hassocks the following November. In May 1965 it was sent to Hither Green yard for use as a shed on wheels and was later cut up on site. A number of others met their end at Cohen's scrapyard, Morriston (Swansea) as late as 1966.

Four vehicles from the PUL and PAN fleet were retained for intended use as a departmental test unit. These were PAN motor coaches 11057/58 from unit 3031, and Pullmans *Bertha* and *Ruth*. Following withdrawal in 1964, the motor coaches had been involved with push-pull trials later that year and on testing the Bournemouth electrification conductor rail in 1966-67, but otherwise spent their days languishing in sidings at Coulsdon North, Lancing, Micheldever and Stewarts Lane. The original coach numbers were first prefixed DS, but later they were given departmental numbers DS70258/59. The two Pullmans went to Micheldever on being taken out of service in 1965 (being allocated numbers DS70260/61 respectively), where *Ruth* unfortunately suffered some internal fire damage. The four coaches were actually formed up into a unit allocated the number S15, being observed as such at Coulsdon North sidings in October 1968, but the conversion order was cancelled and the four coaches condemned. Both Pullmans were retained for preservation, but the two PAN motor coaches were sadly broken up, being sent for scrap from Stewarts Lane to King's at Wymondham in about March 1972.

The arrival of the Brighton replacement stock in the form of York-built 4 CIG and 4 BIG units between late 1964 and early 1966 at long last enabled the gradual withdrawal of the remaining 6 PULs and 6 PANs, and the disbanding of the temporary 4 PUL and 4 COR(N) types. With the exception of the *Brighton Belle*, Pullman cars ceased to operate on Central division services from the commencement of the summer 1966 timetable on 18th April, all catering now being in new 4 BIGs, existing 4 BEPs or the remaining 4 BUFs. A farewell tour for the PULs, organised by the Locomotive Club of Great Britain, took place on 24th April. Formed of former 6 CIT unit 3041 incorporating Pullman composite *Anne*, and by this time complete with air horns and small yellow warning panels on its cab ends, the tour ran from Victoria to Ore, Eastbourne and Brighton.

Following withdrawal, remaining Pullman composites, PAN pantry firsts, ex-RES trailer diner firsts and the majority of PUL and PAN motor coaches were sent for disposal, but the twenty best motor coaches from these latter two classes were retained to be formed with redundant corridor trailers into ten 6 COR units, numbered 3041-3050. At about the same time other remaining ex-PUL and PAN trailer seconds and composites were made up with the spare COR-type motor coaches to form a further ten complete 4 COR units, 3159-3168. Condemned vehicles were scrapped by a number of different firms, including G. Cohen at Morriston, Steel Breaking at Chesterfield and A. King Ltd at Wymondham. In particular, King's were responsible for breaking up virtually all the composite Pullmans and PUL/PAN motor coaches withdrawn at this time.

The 6 COR units had the formation motor brake second + trailer second + trailer composite + trailer first + trailer second + motor brake second, and were formed up between November 1965 and April 1966, appearing in the sequence 3044-3050, 3042, 3041 and finally 3043. (3045 and 3046 initially ran for a short period as 5 COR.) All except 3041 (see note below) had an overall length of 399ft, a width of 9ft 5in, and originally seated 72 first and 256 second class passengers. Formations were as shown below:

Unit	MBS	TSK	TCK	TFK	TSK	MBS
3041(1)	11041	10113	11862	12273	10048	11001
3042	11012	10011	11762	12268	10037	11011
3043	11043	10017	11783	12260	10021	11044
3044	11020	10016	11781	12262	10026	11019
3045	11077	10039	11782	12269	10040	11072
3046	11004	10002	11754	12263	10025	11003
3047	11062	10049	11753	12274	10050	11061
3048(2)	11022	10018	11785	12267	10036	11021
3049	11029	10005	11759	12265	10032	11030
3050	11010	10008	11766	12261	10024	11009

(1) Unit 3041: MBS 11001 was one of the two prototypes and therefore had 56 (rather than 52) seats. Trailers 11862 and 10113 were former 58ft 6 CIT TFKs, downclassed to TCK and TThK respectively in 1946. This unit therefore had eighteen fewer second class seats and was about 14ft shorter.

(2) Unit 3048: TSK 10018 and TCK 11785 subsequently replaced by 10035 and 11756 respectively.

All vehicles were repainted into the final BR green, the motor coaches also gaining small yellow warning panels where they did not already have them, driver-to-guard 'loud-aphone' communication and roof-mounted air horns. In a few cases, including the straight-sided prototype motor coach 11001, these changes were done before the PUL unit in which they were working was disbanded. (This vehicle, and three others from 6 PUL 3041, became the major portion of 6 COR 3041.) Very oddly, units 3042 and 3045 were repainted into the early eggshell British Rail blue with full yellow ends and black unit numbers in early 1967, the only units with this style cab to be so treated.

Initially, the 6 CORs were treated as spares on the Central division, spending most of their time berthed in sidings at Ford (four units), Balcombe (two units) and Gatwick Airport, and only appearing in traffic irregularly. In July 1967, however, all were transferred to the South Eastern division for the commencement of the new, completely revised time-table, being used on peak-hour, relief and special workings between Victoria/Cannon Street and the Kent Coast via Chatham. The first class compartments in the composite were downgraded and roof board brackets removed to ensure sufficient clearances under some rather tight bridges on these routes. As related elsewhere, the more intensive schedules introduced from 10th July were soon shown to be over-ambitious and unworkable, and after a few months of general operating difficulties certain trains were excised from the timetable, enabling the 6 CORs to be dispensed with. Most then returned to the Central division and once more were placed in semi-retirement in the sidings they had left six months earlier, performing the odd movement, usually empty stock, until they faded away between 1968 and 1970. 3047-3049 returned to the South Eastern for the occasional Saturday Kent Coast working in the summer of 1968, and two units (including 3042) were noted dumped in Folkestone East sidings that October. The last recorded runs of these units in passenger service on the Central division took place in early November 1968, the final workings being 3041+3046

The unfamiliar sight of 1932 Brighton express stock in British Rail blue with full yellow ends. 6 COR 3042, one of two such units painted in this livery in 1967 and the only one with former PUL motor coaches, stands parked at Folkestone East on 22nd October 1968, by which time it had effectively been withdrawn.
RCTS Collection

Four 6 COR units, including 3046 and 3044, in store at Ford on 24th March 1969. By this date these units too had performed their last runs in revenue-earning service and would shortly be taken away for scrapping. *Southern Images / John H. Bird*

on the 08.03 Hove to London Bridge and 17.24 return on 31st October and 1st November, 3046 and a 4 COR on the 08.22 London Bridge to Littlehampton on 5th November, and finally the same combination on the 08.03 from Hove a day later. Most vehicles from these units were purchased for scrapping by J. Cashmore at Newport, and some were not actually cut up until 1971.

Returning to 1965, the ten additional 4 COR units 3159-3168 were made up using the twenty serviceable motor coaches previously in units 3054/55/57/65-69/71 and PUL/PAN trailer composites and trailer seconds from the spares pool or from 4 COR(N) units. The first two were formed in October 1965 and the remainder between May and July 1966. Their initial formations were as shown in the table below:

Unit	MBSO	TSK	TCK	MBSO	Formed
3159	11159	10045	11773	11160	10/65
3160	11149	10007	11764	11153	10/65
3161	11177	10010	11765	11140	7/66
3162	11142	10053	11789	11149	6/66
3163	11145	10054	11788	11146	6/66
3164	11155	10034	11787	11156	5/66
3165	11163	10033	11775	11164	5/66
3166	11165	10046	11751	11166	5/66
3167	11169	10042	11784	11170	5/66
3168	11173	10044	11776	11174	7/66

The trailers were all given new toilets and were reupholstered with plain grey tapestry in the second class compartments and the black/yellow or black/blue square patterned moquette in the firsts, but were still readily identifiable by their different windows, door ventilator bonnets and (in the former PUL coaches) double sliding compartment doors. Carriage working notices stated that they were 'not to carry roof boards between Purley and Caterham', and that they were banned from the Sheerness branch, between North Kent East Junction and Crayford Creek Junction via Greenwich, between Blackheath and Charlton, Strood and Paddock Wood, Holborn Viaduct and Blackfriars, Elmers End and Hayes and, like all pre-war stock, west of Pirbright Junction following electrification of the Bournemouth line (other than ECS to/from Eastleigh for overhaul). This latter exclusion was not due to clearance problems, but because the heating circuits were designed to work at a line voltage of 660, and could not cope with the increased voltage of the Bournemouth route. While most of these exclusions were irrelevant to normal use, unit 3159 was pressed into service to work an emergency Woking – Basingstoke shuttle on 11th July 1971, following a collision which completely blocked the main line at Surbiton. The heating circuits had to be disconnected but, as it was high summer, this was fortunately not important. Other than this, these units were totally interchangeable with the rest of the COR fleet.

It had originally been intended that Pullman facilities, by then seen as wasteful of space and staff, should be withdrawn

3165 was one of ten additional 4 COR units made up from former RES motor coaches and spare PUL and PAN trailers in 1966. On 29th September 1968 it is seen at Milford, setting back before crossing over to return to Portsmouth, on a day when engineering work blocked the line towards London. At this time 3165 retained green livery, by now rather faded, with the small warning panel introduced in 1963. The trailers were readily identifiable by ventilator bonnets over the door droplights and a lack of raised window frames. *Alec Swain*

entirely from Central division services in April 1966, but it was later decided that the all-Pullman *Brighton Belle* should continue. The official reason given was that, having been out of service during World War Two, the three 5 BEL units were not quite life-expired. (Nostalgia and affection for the train on the part of senior management must have been a contributory factor, too, as a shrinking catering demand had already made them uneconomic.) In March 1964 all three units were fitted with roof-mounted air horns at Lancing Works, and two years later they had gained small yellow warning panels, obscuring the Pullman crest and clashing painfully with the cream part of the livery.

In 1968/69 the three 5 BEL units were fully refurbished at Eastleigh, 3052 being outshopped in December 1968 and 3051 and 3053 the following February and May respectively. Electrically, the only major change was that the original BTH motors were replaced by later EE examples from the COR pool, but the cab controls were also modified to make them similar to those in the CORs, and driver-to-guard 'loudaphones' fitted. Internally, seating was reupholstered in the new British Rail standard patterns adopted for the 1966 Bournemouth line stock, with the first class armchairs covered in charcoal grey check moquette and the second class

seats in blue/green check with plain blue head and armrests. All seats were given white nylon antimacassars embroidered with PULLMAN in blue at the bottom edge, most of those in second class being double-ended and draped across a pair of back-to-back seats. New mustard yellow carpets and light orange curtains were fitted, but the fine polished marquetry remained together with car names and Pullman crests above the internal partitions in the first class cars. Externally, however, there was no mention of original ownership or names, all cars being painted in a modified version of the standard InterCity blue/grey livery with white lining on the blue portion. The words BRIGHTON BELLE appeared in white on the lower body side at the centre of each vehicle, and also in blue across the yellow cab ends. The original Pullman schedule numbers, prefixed and suffixed S, became the BR coach numbers, appearing at each end of the car. For a few months at the end of 1968 and early 1969 it was possible to see the *Brighton Belle* formed of 3052 in blue/grey coupled to 3053 still in umber and cream. 3051 and 3052 originally retained headcode stencil panels following overhaul, but 3053 was given roller blind equipment at Eastleigh before being outshopped, and the other two units were soon modified to conform.

By 29th May 1968, 5 BEL unit 3053 had lost its Pullman crest under a yellow warning panel, but retained its hand-painted unit number above the headcode panel. It is seen waiting at Brighton with the 17.45 *Brighton Belle* service to Victoria. *John Scrace*

The 4 COR, 4 BUF and 4 GRI fleet survived long enough for virtually all to be painted in British Rail corporate blue livery, the only exceptions being vehicles condemned before 1967. A number of early repaintings, starting with 3152 (August 1966) and also including 3078 and 3103/08/10/14/21/24/32/33/36/43/47, were given the original sprayed eggshell finish with small yellow warning panels and white unit numbers, but this was soon replaced by the single-coat brushed gloss finish with full yellow ends and black unit numbers. Several units, including 3142, received the full yellow ends while still green, and the last to remain in green were 3111 and 3123. The full yellow ends did not particularly suit the Nelson stock, as paint quickly wore away from the gangway rubbing plates and sliding doors, exposing the previous colour scheme or even bare metal. This showed less when the overall finish was dark anyway. As on other units originally equipped with whistles, from the mid 1960s the CORs, BUFs and GRIs were fitted with roof mounted air horns. At about the same time, overhauled units were reupholstered with Trojan patterned tapestry in the motor coaches, and all had been done prior to withdrawal. The matching compartment styles were those described above for the refurbished trailers in units 3159-3168. A further alteration at this time concerned the equalising-beam motor bogies, some of which were modified in about 1969 to simplify maintenance and (marginally) improve their riding qualities.

There was a significant number of reformations involving COR and BUF stock between 1964 and 1970, quite apart from the complex changes involving the RES units etc. outlined earlier. Among units involved in collisions during this period (with date and location if known) were 3074 (Brighton, September 1964), 3147 (1964), 3116 (c.1964) 3081 and 3161 (Durnsford Road, late 1968) and 3163 (July 1970). All were eventually returned to service following reformation with vehicles from other units. Particularly notable was 3161, one of the additional units made up in 1965-66 using PUL/PAN trailers, which was reinstated in July 1969 with only one of its original coaches. In its second incarnation 3161 was formed with repaired MBS 11246 from 3081, TSK10003 which had been spare, TCK 11828 from 3138 and MBS 11140, the only coach the unit had previously.

Two further accidents in 1970 resulted in the first permanent withdrawals from the COR and BUF fleets. COR 3127 was condemned in January following a serious side-scrape incident, although motor coach 11133 was reformed into unit 3118 following repair. After use in civil defence exercises for a few months the rest of 3127 was scrapped, although the trailer underframes were reused for rail carriers. 3078 sustained damage after 'running away' inside the confines of Selhurst depot that August and was afterwards withdrawn, although it too donated a motor coach (11249) to another unit (3163) which remained in traffic.

1970 saw a remarkable excursion by a COR unit. On Sunday 8th November, 3135 was hired by the Locomotive Club of Great Britain for a 'North London Electric Train Tour'. Starting from Victoria at 09.31½, it ran via Clapham Junction to Richmond, where locomotive D6532 shunted it into one of the terminal platforms; it then ran to Broad Street, then to Watford Junction, then to Croxley Green and back to Watford Junction, then to Euston. After a forty-minute layover it ran via Kensal Green and Willesden Junction High Level to Richmond, regaining South Western territory unassisted, then to Staines, Windsor (reverse), Staines, Weybridge, Clapham Junction, Longhedge and Victoria with arrival at 17.36. As with the similar BIL tour of 25th September 1971, mentioned earlier, this was possible due to conversion of the London Midland Region dc lines from fourth to third rail.

The next major change resulted from the arrival of further 4 CIG and 4 BIG stock to displace the CORs, BUFs and GRIs from the Portsmouth Direct line and from Central division main line services. Further reorganisation of catering diagrams took place between the autumn of 1970 and May 1971, resulting in the withdrawal of the remaining 4 BUF and 4 GRI units. Of the BUFs, 3078 was withdrawn prematurely in August 1970 as mentioned above. Further examples were withdrawn in October and the last at the beginning of 1971, with the exception of 'cafeteria car' unit 3072 which survived in capital stock until May. Some BUFs ran without their catering equipment from October 1970, including 3075, 3080 and 3085 – in this guise they were treated as being interchangeable with normal CORs. Three BUFs were dumped in a line in a siding opposite Wimbledon flyover well into 1971. Of the GRIs, 3087 was taken out of traffic in September 1970 while its sisters remained in service until April 1971, latterly being utilised on rush hour services between London Bridge and Littlehampton. 3072, 3086 and 3088 were thus the last pre-war catering units to remain in service, albeit with post-war buffet equipment. Following withdrawal, 3086-3088, together with BUFs 3072/77/82/84, were stored in the Down sidings at Gatwick Airport from May until about October 1971. 3087 was not scrapped, but in 1972 became departmental unit 054. Based at Eastleigh, it was finally cut up in 1975. Other vehicles retained were 'cafeteria car' 12613 from 3072, purchased for use as a transport cafe, and buffet 12529 from 3084, reserved for the National Collection but subsequently destroyed by fire.

By the beginning of 1972 the three 5 BEL units were also due for withdrawal, the poor state of their bogies causing particular concern. It was announced that the *Brighton Belle* service would end on Sunday 30th April 1972, the day before the new summer timetable came into effect. The final runs took place in a blaze of publicity, never before or since given to SR electric trains. On the official final day of operation 3052 and 3053 worked the regular 09.45 Brighton – Victoria and 11.00 return. 3051 worked the SEG-organised *Southern Belle* railtour around Sussex departing from Brighton at 12.20 and visiting Horsham, Bognor Regis, Littlehampton, Lewes and Newhaven Harbour before returning to Brighton at 17.00. For this trip, the only 'private enterprise' excursion of the day, the unusual headcode 29 was used. 3052 and 3053 then returned to London with the scheduled 17.45 departure for Victoria, where the two units separated. The rest of the day's scheduled *Brighton Belle* services, 19.00 to Brighton, 20.45 to Victoria and 22.00 to Brighton, were worked by 3053 on its own. Meanwhile, 3051 formed a special 'cheese and

Newly outshopped in lined blue/grey livery with full yellow ends following its final overhaul, 3052 poses for its official photograph at Lancing in 1968. At this stage the unit retained its original stencil headcode panels, but these were later replaced by roller-blind equipment. *BR Southern Region Official*

4 COR 3106 runs into Falmer forming the 09 14 Brighton – Eastbourne service on 27th April 1971. Having themselves just been displaced from main line duties, these units were at this time gradually replacing BILs and HALs on local services along the south coast from Brighton. 3106 displays the final overall blue livery with full yellow ends in which virtually all the 'Nelson's ended their days. Always one of the more attractive and well cared-for stations on the coast, the Brighton-bound platform at Falmer had nonetheless gained one of the crude CLASP-style waiting shelters then much in vogue on BR. *John Scrace*

wine' run from Brighton to Victoria (tickets £7.50 each) arriving at 19.51. It then coupled to 3052 and the pair formed the final £10-a-seat 'Champagne Special' which left London at 22.30 and dawdled its way to the coast. Its arrival at 23.52 was greeted by the Haywards Heath Silver Band playing the inevitable 'Auld Lang Syne' and 'Land of Hope and Glory', and by hordes of well-wishers. To stand on the platform at Victoria or Brighton cost 50p. This was not quite the end, as someone had overlooked the fact that a unit had been booked for a private party the following week and this trip did run.

Following withdrawal, the BEL motor coaches were stripped of reusable electrical equipment for use in CORs, and the vehicles sold. Surprisingly, not one was cut up, all being purchased by various interested parties. There was much discussion at the time, most of it ill-informed, regarding the saving or replacement of the *Belle*, but after 2.7 million miles in passenger service the 1932 cars were definitely life-expired without comprehensive re-engineering, and the building of new stock for such a specialised service was simply uneconomic. There was an alleged attempt by Western Region management to foist one or more of the unreliable and rough-riding diesel Pullman sets on to the SR, possibly for use on the Brighton line, but this was firmly nipped in the bud. The subsequent fate of some of the *Brighton Belle* cars is given at the end of this Chapter.

Withdrawal of the *Belle* left the 4 COR units as the only remaining Southern Railway pre-war express stock. On displacement from their main line duties in 1971, the class was reallocated to the Waterloo – Reading line and to south coast locals, in both cases replacing 2 BIL and 2 HAL units. The fleet remained basically intact until 1971, with only 3127 being permanently withdrawn from service in 1970 following an accident as noted above. In contrast to the BILs and HALs, withdrawal of the bulk of the COR fleet tended to be in waves rather than a few at a time. Nine units were withdrawn in 1971, these being 3110/21/24/34/44/50/61/62/67. The remainder were taken out of service in 1972, the last in October. The final scheduled workings on the Portsmouth Direct line via Haslemere took place on Sunday 31st July 1971, a twelve-coach formation composed of 3110+3144+3118 forming the 10.10 Waterloo – Portsmouth and Southsea and 12.12 return.

CORs were displaced from the Reading line by 4 CIGs as from 2nd January 1972, and the last booked working from Portsmouth took place on the following 5th August when 3145 and 3122 formed the 05.40 to Brighton, although in the event CORs turned up as replacements on VEP diagrams on a number of occasions during the following weeks. The final timetabled COR working to reach the Capital took place on 31st August when 3131+3142 worked the 06.48 Brighton to London Bridge, returning empty. Through September, the ever-diminishing number of units worked from Brighton to Seaford and Eastbourne, the last scheduled passenger service taking place on the fine morning of Saturday 30th September when 3102 worked the 08.35 Haywards Heath to Seaford and 09.50 return to Brighton. At Seaford, the helpful crew shunted the unit out of the station and back in again for the benefit of photographers. That afternoon 3136+3145 worked

a football special from Brighton to Portsmouth and return. The following day, Sunday 1st October, 3102+3143 formed the SEG *Nelson Farewell* special from Waterloo, the units reaching Sheerness, Margate, Dover Marine and Folkestone Harbour in the first part of the day. During the return to London a bone-shaking maximum of 86mph was reached through Headcorn. This was followed by a run down to Portsmouth Harbour via the Direct line and back via the Mid-Sussex. This was still not the end, however, as 3116+3123+3142 formed a BR Staff Association tour on 9th December 1972, this excursion being the final visit of the 1937 express stock to Portsmouth. The three units then returned to Barnham for berthing, this run being the last time a pre-war SR express unit ran under its own power.

Apart from the *Brighton Belle* Pullmans, a number of other first generation express stock vehicles survived into preservation or were obtained for other uses, some having been already mentioned previously. A complete listing includes complete 4 COR 3142 (11161+10096+11825+11201), COR motor coaches 11179 and 11187, PUL trailer composite 11773, Pullman composites *Ruth* and *Bertha*, buffet car 12529 and the 'cafeteria car' 12613. With the sad exception of the two SR-design catering vehicles, the PUL composite and one of the BEL motor coaches, all still exist, although their states of repair vary widely. Apart from this, the underframes and bogies of a number of trailers were converted into car carriers, and in this guise survived well into the 1980s. Finally, a number of seating units were recovered from withdrawn PUL, PAN and COR motor coaches by far-sighted staff of the Bluebell Railway, and these are now fitted in restored SR coaching stock in use on that line, including Maunsell open thirds 1309 and 1336, and Bulleid semi-compartment corridor third brake 4279.

The following paragraphs describe the subsequent history of vehicles from the first generation express stock which survived beyond December 1972, when the last of the 4 COR units turned a wheel under its own power. Comments made in the present tense are at the time of writing, May 2010.

PULLMAN KITCHEN COMPOSITE CAR 278
BERTHA
Originally formed in 6 PUL 3012, *Bertha* was moved to sister unit 3001 when Pullman Cars were restored in 1946, and was withdrawn in 1965. Retained by British Rail for possible departmental use (see above) and finally stored at Micheldever, it was purchased by a private individual and moved to the nascent Ashford Steam Centre. It then transferred to the Nene Valley Railway, Peterborough, in February 1976, (in company with the Southern Electric Group's 4 COR 3142) and later to the Mid Hants Railway, before finally coming to the Bluebell Railway in 1982, following which serious restoration could commence. It was necessary to adapt it for steam-hauled use, so new gangways and steam heating were fitted, the latter having pipes located in place of the original electric heaters. During storage with BR, *Bertha* lost most of her internal fittings, but the interior has now been completely reconstructed and the fine marquetry restored. For the first class section, it was possible to purchase a number of Pullman

armchairs from the Ffestiniog Railway. Repainted in full Pullman livery, *Bertha* returned to service in 1989, both with fellow Bluebell Railway Pullmans on the *Blue Belle* dining specials or as a refreshment coach on other service trains. Following a change of ownership she was moved yet again in 2001, this time to the Swanage Railway. At the time of writing *Bertha* is understood to be undergoing overhaul at Carnforth.

PULLMAN KITCHEN COMPOSITE CAR 264 *RUTH*

Ruth was the other ex-PUL Pullman composite stored for possible departmental use. Together with five locomotive-hauled Pullmans acquired at the same time, this car was purchased by Bulmers Cider Co. of Hereford who had it moved from Micheldever to BR Swindon Works with a view to having it restored to main-line running order. The estimated cost was found to be too high, however, mainly due to internal fire damage sustained whilst in store. Bulmers therefore offered *Ruth* to the 6000 Association (the volunteer support group for ex GWR *King George V*, also owned by Bulmers), who paid the original BR purchase price. It spent a number of years static at the premises of Bulmers at Hereford, used as HQ by 6000 Association Members. Following sale to a private individual, *Ruth* was acquired by Sea Containers Ltd, owners of the VSOE Pullmans, and is presently stored as part of the VSOE reserve fleet. Little of the original interior remains.

PULLMAN KITCHEN FIRST CARS 280 *AUDREY*, 281 *GWEN* AND 284 *VERA*

Following withdrawal, *Audrey* and *Vera* were initially purchased by private individuals. *Audrey*, bought by David Lowther (an Eton schoolmaster), was cosmetically restored into Pullman livery at Steamtown, Carnforth, and took part in the *Rocket 150* celebrations in May 1980. *Vera* was purchased by Euro-MP Amedee Turner and placed on a short length of track surrounded by landscaped flower-beds in the owner's garden at Westleton, Suffolk, where it was used for entertaining at village fêtes and other events. It retained the final BR blue/grey livery, but the roof was repainted in 'proper' white. *Gwen* was purchased by a catering company and became the main dining room of 'The Horseless Carriage' restaurant at Chingford Hatch, Essex, before moving to the Colne Valley Railway in 1981, at first on loan.

Audrey was the first to be purchased by Sea Containers Limited, in connection with the *Venice Simplon Orient Express* project to return to service a complete rake of British Pullman cars. Completely restored and overhauled during 1981 in a workshop specially set-up for this work at Carnforth, it re-entered service with the inaugural run of the VSOE in May 1982. Modifications included the fitting of standard electric train heating, a dynamo to supply lighting, Pullman gangways and buckeye couplings, and LNER-type double bolster bogies. The kitchen was stripped out and new equipment provided to heat liquids such as soup and coffee, as no actual cooking is performed on the VSOE British Pullmans. Both interior and exterior were finished to an immaculate standard, with an appropriate, though not authentic, *jazz-*

style moquette on the armchairs. The original celluloid table-lampshades were replaced by fabric, and the passenger bell-pushes plated over. Since then the car has been in regular service on the train, both on the London Victoria – Folkestone Harbour runs, generally hauled by a class 73 Electro-diesel, and on numerous special excursions.

Vera was also subsequently purchased by Sea Containers in 1985, and was taken by road to Stewarts Lane where it was displayed at the Open Day that year, still in virtually the same condition it had been withdrawn by BR thirteen years previously. Restored in exactly the same manner as *Audrey*, but at Stewarts Lane, *Vera* re-entered passenger service on the VSOE in 1988 and since then has also regularly been in use. In 1989 both vehicles were fitted with BR 'B4' type bogies with coil springing.

In 1988 *Gwen* was also purchased by Sea Containers and moved to Stewarts Lane, but then spent a decade in store as part of the VSOE reserve fleet before being totally restored for main line running in 1999, in the same manner as *Vera*. Since then she has also been a regular member of the VSOE British Pullman train.

Nearly eighty years after their introduction, it remains amazing and delightful to see *Audrey*, *Vera* and *Gwen* still working in the *Venice Simplon Orient Express*, frequently all together in the same train. Apart from their different bogies, they may also be easily identified from the other cars in the train, which have straight sides, by their slightly bulging profile.

PULLMAN KITCHEN FIRST CAR 282 *DORIS*

Doris was purchased on withdrawal by the chairman of City Industrial Ltd, a firm of shopfitters. Following restoration into Pullman livery at BR Derby Works she was installed on a siding next to the company's premises, adjacent to Finsbury Park station from whose platforms she could be seen. Externally unaltered save for the blanking-off of the gangway connections, *Doris* was used as a dining room for company board meetings and entertaining clients. In 2006 *Doris* was sold to the Bluebell Railway and that April moved to Horsted Keynes, still in excellent condition both externally and internally. It is eventually intended it she should be fully restored and altered for steam haulage in the same manner as *Bertha* for use in the *Blue Belle* Pullman dining train.

PULLMAN KITCHEN FIRST CAR 283 *MONA*

This vehicle was purchased by Allied Breweries and was originally intended for the *Eastleigh End* public house at Chertsey. Instead, it moved north to become the restaurant at *The Brighton Belle* (renamed from *The Railway Inn*) at Winsford, Cheshire, where it was adjacent to the West Coast main line. *Mona* stood on a short length of track and was connected to the main building at the lavatory end. The side facing the road was in a reasonable approximation of Pullman livery, but the other side was in cream and very dark brown, totally devoid of lining and lettering. Internally, the lavatory and coupé remained intact, but the main saloon was reseated in a two+one layout, using seats from former second class locomotive-hauled Pullmans. The kitchen area was completely gutted and fitted with tables and loose low-backed chairs. *Mona* was kept in generally very good condition with gleaming brasswork, but unfortunately on the occasion of the author's visit in December 1995 the corridor window opposite the coupé had been broken and was boarded-over. In 2000, *Mona* became part of the VSOE reserve fleet and was moved to Stewarts Lane, where it remains in unrestored condition in 2010.

OTHER FORMER 5 BEL VEHICLES

In 2010, the only former *Brighton Belle* First to remain in use as a static restaurant is Car 279 *Hazel*, located at the Black Bull Inn, Moulton, North Yorkshire. With their slightly cramped two+two seating, the second class cars proved to be of less use either for luxury dining trains or for static restaurant accommodation, and some eventually found homes as normal hauled coaching stock on preserved railways. Parlour car 286 and motor cars 292 and 293 have become part of the VSOE reserve fleet; of these, it was planned to convert the latter into a driving trailer with staff accommodation, avoiding the need for a spare locomotive to haul the train between its home depot at Stewarts Lane and London Victoria, the usual starting and finishing point for VSOE excursions. Although work started in 1999, it appears that this idea has now been shelved. Motor car 289 has been converted into static accommodation at the Little Mill Inn, Rowarth, Derbyshire, while Motor car 291 and parlour car 287 spent some years on the North Norfolk Railway before moving to the Keith and Dufftown Railway. Car 291 has since been acquired by the 5 BEL Trust (more later). Motor car 290 has unfortunately been broken up at Carnforth following a fire.

An extremely ambitious project to resurrect a complete five-car *Brighton Belle* unit for electric operation on the Southern third rail network was started in 2008. As this is written in April 2010, the 5 BEL Trust has taken ownership of motor cars 288/291 and parlour thirds 285/287, and is hoping to acquire Kitchen First *Doris* from the Bluebell Railway. The aim of the Trust is to have a working unit by 2012, and restoration work on the vehicles owned is well under way at a site in Derby. To comply with present main-line operating requirements it is intended that the unit will be fitted with 1963-type control equipment, EE507 motors and buckeye couplings between cars. The author and no doubt all readers of this book await further developments with interest.

4 BUF (EX 4 RES) 'CAFETERIA CAR' 12613 FROM UNIT 3072

Upon withdrawal this unique vehicle was purchased by H&G Car Parks Ltd, who sited it in their lorry park on the former Uxbridge Road goods yard site off Wood Lane (located roughly where the M41 'Westway' crosses the West London line north of Kensington Olympia) for use as a transport cafe. By 1974 it was situated on the only length of track left on the site, the remaining sidings having been lifted. By this time it had been repainted dark navy blue, and a flat-bed trailer from an articulated lorry was parked alongside to provide access and

to serve as a veranda. Internally, some of the original loose seats were still in use, supplemented by a number of kitchen chairs, and the original electric catering equipment had been replaced by new Calor Gas fittings. However mains electricity had been laid on to work the lighting, the original fittings having been replaced by fluorescent tubes. A telephone, mains water and a drain connection had all been provided. In 1974 it was open from Monday to Saturday, its presence being advertised by a somewhat out-of-gauge sign reading TRANSPORT CAFE inserted in the roof board brackets. By the winter of 1978/79 at least one side of the vehicle had been repainted a reddish rust-brown. It was still in use in April 1979 but was demolished soon afterwards, possibly following a fire.

COMPLETE 4 COR UNIT 3142

This unit, one of the three used on the final railtour of 9th December 1972, was chosen for preservation by the Southern Electric Group, an enthusiast organisation formed in 1970 as a result of interest shown in the pre-war SR main line stock then being rapidly withdrawn. It was selected as being the best remaining unit retaining unmodified equalising beam motor bogies. Following its final run in passenger service, it was sent empty to Barnham sidings where, as a result of Christmas mail traffic, a series of derailments on the Brighton line and winter conditions generally, it remained until the end of April 1973. Unfortunately, it was accidentally left 'cut-in' electrically, and a minor fire occurred in composite 11832 as a result of water penetrating one of the jumper cables. Its replacement was 11825 from 3135, originally purchased privately, the final formation of the unit as preserved then being MBSO 11161, TSK 10096, TCK 11825 and MBSO 11201. 3142 was moved to Selhurst on 28th April, hauled by class 73 electro-diesel E6047. At Selhurst, composites were exchanged between 3142 and 3135 and re-usable items such as compressors and loudaphone equipment removed. The COR was finally dispatched to the erstwhile Ashford Steam Centre, its new home, on 26th May, being hauled from Selhurst to Bricklayers Arms by E6036 and on to Ashford via Maidstone East by E6049. Ashford Steam Centre was chosen as the base for the unit as it was still connected to the SR electrified network, but for various reasons it rapidly proved to be a poor choice and it was necessary to search for a new home.

3142 moved to the Nene Valley Railway near Peterborough on 27th–28th February 1976. The NVR was soon to open and was in urgent need of air-braked coaching stock to run with its collection of (largely foreign) air-braked steam locomotives. During the rest of the year considerable progress was made in restoring and maintaining the unit, culminating in its first trip along the line on 29th November, hauled by French Nord Railway 4-6-0 3.628 and ostensibly for brake tests. It was repainted in olive green with an approximation of the original waist-level lining, and formed the rolling stock of the Nene Valley's official opening special on 1st June 1977. It was regularly used in passenger service on the line through that year, and even made its television debut in a (very short) sequence of the serial *Secret Army*. Attention to running gear

was the priority the following winter, following which 3142 featured more prominently in further episodes of the same series filmed in 1978.

The COR continued in use on the Nene Valley Railway for several more years, but as that organisation obtained more stock of its own it was used less and less, and by 1983 it was stored virtually permanently in Wansford Tunnel where the damp conditions caused a marked deterioration in its condition. A new home was therefore required, and it was decided to transfer the unit to the former Pullman Works at Preston Park, at that time recently rented by the nascent Brighton Locomotive Works Association. 3142 moved from Peterborough to Brighton on 4th/5th September 1986, the first leg taking it via March, Cambridge and the Lea Valley line to Temple Mills marshalling yard, hauled by 31 230. The following morning, with 73 128 now in charge, it ran back on to the SR at Clapham Junction via South Tottenham, Gospel Oak, Willesden Junction and Kensington Olympia, followed by a final trundle down the Brighton line to Preston Park via Redhill. Restricted to a maximum speed of 35 mph, the unit ran faultlessly throughout.

Restoration work at Preston Park continued at a steady, if slow, pace, mostly invoing stripping paintwork, fitting replacement bodywork parts where where they had rotted, and repainting. Removal of successive coats eventually revealed the original lined SR olive green. It was very apparent that Maunsell wooden-framed coaches, once assembled, were not designed to be dismantled. A highlight was the refitting of stencil headcode panels to the cab ends to return them to pre-1960s condition. Motor coach 11161 was cosmetically restored to late BR green livery with small yellow warning panel, and appeared on the BBC TV *Byways* programme on 20th April 1990. However for various reasons conditions at Preston Park deteriorated steadily and by 1991 yet another move became imperative.

Fortuitously the former diesel depot at St Leonards, redundant following the electrification of the Tonbridge – Hastings line in 1986, had been taken over by St Leonards Engineering Ltd as a site for the restoration of preserved diesel and electric stock. The SEG was invited to move 3142 to St Leonards and the offer was accepted. The move took place on Saturday 29th June 1991, the vehicles being shunted in the morning so that the Group's CCT, used for storage and unbraked, was marshalled between the two COR trailers. 3142 was hauled along the east 'Coastway' by 56 001 *Whatley* in the early afternoon, with reversals in Brighton station, Eastbourne and at St Leonards depot itself. Restoration work continued at the new site, and three coaches (not including Trailer Second 10096), now all resplendent in dark green, were hauled to Brighton and back by 73 104 to appear at the Lovers Walk Depot open days on 21st–22nd September 1991. In January 1993, 3142 was joined at St Leonards by motor coach 11187 from unit 3135, which had originally been privately purchased and located in a back garden in Hertfordshire. While at St Leonards, appreciable restoration of the external bodywork was carried out on this vehicle.

Increasing commercial contract work by St Leonards Engineering Ltd, including light maintenance of the new class 171 diesel units in use on the Brighton – Hastings – Ashford service, led to the SEG being given notice to move 3142 again in 2004. In February the unit was moved by road to the Woodpax site at Sheffield Park (close to the Bluebell Railway), and in January 2005 motor coach 11201 was placed on display in Horsted Keynes station where it is a major focus of publicity for the SEG. Motor coach 11187 was moved to under-cover accommodation at the London Transport Museum Depot at Acton in December 2005, allowing major restoration work to continue on this vehicle, concentrating particularly on refitting the interior. The remaining three vehicles, MBS 11161, TS 10096 and TC 11825, were transferred to the East Kent Railway at Shepherdswell, where they continue to be stored in the open and with limited access for restoration work to continue.

4 COR MOTOR BRAKE THIRD 11179 FROM UNIT 3131

On withdrawal from BR service, this vehicle was reserved for the National Collection. Externally it has been restored as far as possible to 1937 'as new' condition, including the refitting of a stencil headcode panel, but lacks external deflector plates on the window ventilators. Internally, it remains largely as withdrawn, complete with Trojan upholstery. Although normally on permanent display at the National Railway Museum, York, it has travelled south to appear at Open Days at Woking in 1988 and at East Wimbledon depot the following year.

CHAPTER 6: MISCELLANEOUS ROLLING STOCK

The first part of this chapter deals with two small projects outside the mainstream of Southern electric rolling stock design and not dealt with elsewhere, both somewhat unconventional and both instigated during the regime of O.V.S. Bulleid as Chief Mechanical Engineer (1937-49). These were the three 'booster' electric locomotives, produced as a collaborative venture between the SR and English Electric, and the two 4 DD double-decker suburban units. While the locomotives could be considered successful, by the time that a production series was required (for the 1959-62 Kent Coast electrification scheme) traction technology had moved on, and they remained a small non-standard class of limited use. On the other hand, the double-decker units were an ingenious experiment which failed but, notwithstanding this, they remained in regular passenger service for 22 years. It is therefore perhaps unfair to lump them, as the late Sir John Elliot does in his memoirs, with Bulleid's *Leader* and tavern car eccentricities.[20] The latter part of the chapter gives full details of the considerable number of conversions of former Southern Railway designed electric rolling stock for departmental use, mentioned previously in Chapters 4 and 5 (and in Volume 1 in the case of suburban stock).

THE BULLEID/ENGLISH ELECTRIC CO-CO 'BOOSTER' LOCOMOTIVES

Although multiple unit electric stock was used for passenger services on all the lines electrified by the Southern Railway on the dc third-rail system between 1925 and 1939, freight and parcels trains on the electrified lines continued to be steam-hauled. This was partly to keep a large fleet of modern steam motive power displaced by electrification usefully employed, but also because an electric locomotive able to bridge gaps in the live rail without stalling had yet to be designed. As discussed in Chapter 5, this was one reason why the SR utilised EMU stock on express services to Brighton, although locomotives had been briefly considered. A further concern was the danger to staff posed by conductor rails in freight marshalling yards, particularly during dark hours.

Nevertheless, it was acknowledged that the full benefits of electrification could only be gained when all traffic used this form of propulsion, and with this in mind an order (HO 847) was placed at the end of October 1936 with the SR workshops at Eastleigh for two prototype electric locomotives. This order was very much 'in principle' because, as will be seen, a great

deal of design work had to be carried out before construction could commence. The SR's Electrical Engineer for New Works, A. Raworth, also visited private locomotive builders during October and November to discuss the project.

These discussions ran concurrently with comparative brake tests of steam and electric traction on unfitted goods trains between Norwood and Three Bridges. The steam-hauled test was carried out on Sunday 11th October, and comprised K class 2-6-0 No 2352 hauling a load of 956 tons tare, including brake van. The electrically-hauled test utilised 6 PUL motor coach 11004 (from unit 3002), at 59 tons and with four motors the nearest the SR had to a true main-line electric locomotive, hauling a 540-ton load, and took place on Sunday 8th November. Because this load was nearly five times that which the PUL MThB was designed to haul, and to avoid burning out its resistances, 2352 assisted from the rear, but was taken off at Purley and followed uncoupled because the test train was going so well. In both trials brake tests were made from a speed of 30mph on the downgrades at the southern portal of Quarry tunnel and between Earlswood and Salfords. The braked proportion of both test trains was roughly 10% of the total train weight, and stopping distances were found to be similar.

Although the PUL motor coach performed surprisingly well, two expected problems came to light during its day as a freight locomotive. Firstly, the short distance between collector shoes, only 46ft 6in, was the cause of frequent gapping, resulting in loss of power with consequent bunching and surging of the train. Apart from severe discomfort for the guard, in extreme cases this could result in coupling breakages. Secondly, the standard EMU series-parallel control system, giving only two effective power ranges, proved too inflexible.

Resulting from these tests, there were some proposals for a Bo-Bo mixed traffic type. The basic requirements were for a locomotive capable of hauling loose-coupled freight trains of up to 800 tons at a speed of 35mph on level track, and able to haul 425 ton vacuum-braked passenger trains at up to 75mph. The ability to maintain a drawbar pull over gaps in the live rail was also required, as was the ability to work in and out of freight yards using battery power or by picking-up current from an overhead supply. From the tests with the PUL motor coach, it was concluded that a locomotive weight of about eighty tons would be needed to meet this freight-haulage specification. A good deal of preliminary work was done and a number of outline drawings were produced, particularly by English Electric which was at this time exclusive supplier of electric traction equipment to the SR.

---

20 Elliot, Sir John: *On and Off the Rails*, George Allen & Unwin, ISBN 0 0438 5089 8, 1982. pp38-40

The problems of maintaining drawbar pull over gaps in the live rail and of providing fine-enough control were solved in a very neat way by adopting what quickly became termed 'booster' control. In this system, a generator and motor set were mechanically coupled on the same armature axle, with a heavy flywheel between. The motor, fed with electricity from the 660V supply, turned the generator. The generator could then feed the traction motors to boost the electricity supplied to them from the third rail, the applied voltage being varied to control the speed. This enabled a large number of control positions to be used resulting in very fine power gradation. The flywheel stored kinetic energy which could be used to turn the generator and thus supply the motors for a short period while passing over gaps in the live rail. English Electric designed an electrical system for the proposed Bo-Bo machine incorporating two such 'booster' sets, each feeding the two traction motors on one bogie.

During 1937 and 1938 personnel changes in both Mechanical and Electrical Engineer's departments, detailed in Chapter 1, had a significant effect on the future course of development of the proposed electric locomotive. Maunsell retired in October 1937, being replaced as Chief Mechanical Engineer by Bulleid, while Jones retired early in 1938 and was succeeded as Chief Electrical Engineer by Raworth, who immediately amalgamated the electrical running/maintenance and New Works departments. While the proposed locomotive had up to this point been a purely electrical department initiative, the new CME showed interest in the project from his arrival. Departmental rivalries were therefore put aside and ensuing discussions soon resulted in more ambitious proposals for a 100-ton six-axle Co-Co electric locomotive, which would have greater haulage and stopping ability as well as a wider route availability. It was agreed that mechanical design work would be passed to the CME's drawing office at Waterloo, and instructions to commence schematic design of a Co-Co locomotive were given in 1938. Following some preliminary design studies, the SR Board formally approved the construction of two prototypes later that year. Detailed mechanical design was carried out by W.

P. Bollen at Waterloo, but dissatisfaction with progress made led to his move to Ashford in March 1939 (coincident with the transfer there of HO 847) as temporary Chief Draughtsman to speed up this work and supervise construction.

Design was eventually completed in the summer of 1939, and construction of mechanical parts for both prototypes was at an advanced state at the outbreak of war. It proved possible to complete mechanical construction despite wartime conditions and both locomotives were towed from Ashford to Brighton in the summer of 1940 for the installation of electrical equipment. In the event the deteriorating international situation severely curtailed activity and the first was not ready for testing until the autumn of 1941.

Numbered CC1 in Bulleid's alphanumeric style, which was based on continental practice, the completed locomotive was of all-steel construction and weighed-in at a solid 99 tons. CC1 consisted of a box-like body 54ft long and 8ft 2¼in wide, mounted on a substantial underframe and riding on two six-wheel bogies. The narrow body-width would have enabled these locomotives to work on the Tonbridge – Hastings line, if and when that section was electrified. The cab ends were slightly bowed and, with their domed roofs and radiussed windscreen corners, bore more than a passing resemblance to the 1939 2 HAL units. A standard EMU headcode panel was originally fitted between the cab windows, and there were six lamp irons to take white discs or oil lamps. As no numerical freight train headcodes then existed, six electric marker lights with folding white discs were soon added, the top set being built on to the headcode panel front. No facilities for working in multiple were fitted, but a power jumper socket was located below the offside cab window to allow one of the booster sets to be run-up using the hanging cable land-lines located in Selhurst and Brighton depots. Livery was originally workshop grey with two thin horizontal white lines along the body sides, curving down on the cab fronts to meet at the centre of the bottom edge to form 'whiskers'. A further white line ran along each side of the roof, again meeting at a point on the domed ends. The red buffer beams were inscribed CC1 in yellow.

In completely original condition, the first of the Bulleid / Raworth Co-Co 'booster' electric locomotives, CCI, is seen on test hauling a lengthy freight train at an unknown location (probably at the southern end of the Brighton main line) in 1942. It carries its original lined workshop-grey livery and EMU-style stencil headcode panel.

The 3ft 6in diameter wheels were of the fabricated Bulleid-Firth-Brown pattern and each axle was powered by a 245hp motor of type EE 519A, geared 65/17 with forced ventilation. This gave a nominal total power rating of 1470hp. The bogies did not have normal bolsters, instead being pivoted to the main underframe on segmental bearings. This arrangement was necessary to provide adequate access to the centre traction motor on each bogie. Primary suspension was by flexible fifteen-leaf laminated springs, which transmitted weight from the bogie frames to the axles through secondary coil springs. Each bogie had two short shoebeams on each side, suspended between pairs of axle boxes and each fitted with standard gravity shoegear. There was also originally a sandbox on both sides of each axlebox, but late in the war a compressed air-operated ice scraper was fitted on each leading shoebeam and to provide electrical clearance the sandboxes behind the leading axles at either end were removed.

CC1 was equipped with Westinghouse air brakes of the type fitted to SR electric multiple unit stock, but vacuum equipment was also fitted to brake passenger and fitted freight trains. The vacuum brake valve on the cab desk also controlled the locomotive air brakes by means of a vacuum/air proportional valve. An additional air brake could also be applied to the rim of the motor-generator flywheel in an emergency. Each wheel had two cylinders, each applying a force to one brake block, and as each had its own slack-adjuster there was no rigging other than the linkage between bogies and to the handbrake in each cab. Two motor-driven compressors provided air for the brakes and also to operate the control system and raise the pantograph. Air brakes were a relatively unfamiliar feature on a British locomotive at this time and required considerable fine adjustment to make them work satisfactorily, with long empty unfitted freights causing particular problems.

The 'booster' motor-generator arrangements designed by English Electric for the Bo-Bo design proved suitable for CC1 without any changes and were adopted, each set powering one of the three-axle bogies with the three motors connected in series across the generator end of the machine. Each booster set was force-ventilated by a blower coupled directly to it. An ingenious method of control was obtained by using the generator in what was known as 'buck-boost' mode. The controller had 26 notches. When the locomotive was started, the generator side of the motor/generator took current from the live rail and acted as a motor, applying a back electro-motive force (BEMF) to the traction motor terminals nearly equal but of opposite polarity to that being supplied from the conductor rail, thus cancelling out or 'bucking' the line supply. As the controller was notched-up the generator excitation and hence BEMF was gradually reduced, thus cancelling out less and less of the line supply until at notch sixteen the motors were eventually receiving half of their nominal voltage. From notch seventeen upwards the generator worked as a generator and 'boosted' the line voltage supplied to the traction motors. The last three notches (24-26) were weak-field which enabled additional acceleration for higher speeds on passenger trains. Weak-field was selected by a separate lever and could only be activated once the train had been started and accelerated in full-field. The maximum speed in full-field for freight work was about 35mph, and on passenger trains weak field could be selected at about 40mph. Official top speed on passenger work was the same as that of express EMUs, 75mph, although this was often exceeded in practice.

To operate the locomotive the compressors were first started up, and when the pressure had risen to the 50psi needed to operate the booster control mechanisms, first No.1 and then No.2 motor-generators were started up. After allowing these to run-up to an operating speed of 1,700-2,000 rpm, the deadman's foot pedal was depressed, the desired reverser position chosen and the notches on the controller selected one at a time, at which point CC1 started to move. Drivers were instructed not to notch-up or down when passing over a conductor rail gap.

A retractable pantograph was fitted for current collection from an overhead wire, which it was proposed to erect in freight sidings and yards owing to the dangers of exposed conductor rails in such locations. Due to the high currents involved, the box-type pantograph was fitted with a grooved steel contact strip filled with stiff graphite paste. The centre of the roof was recessed to take the pantograph, which was raised and lowered by air pressure. If a locomotive was parked under the wire and away from the live rail with the para-graph lowered, it was necessary to attain 50psi pressure in the air system to raise it, and a hand pump was therefore included in the equipment compartment for this purpose. Initially only two sidings, at Lovers Walk (Brighton) and Balcombe, were given overhead wires to test the system, both chosen because they presented challenging installation diffi-culties. No further wiring was done due to wartime restrictions, and instead conductor rails were laid in the reception and departure tracks of certain Central section freight yards, initially at Norwood, Three Bridges, Horsham, Lewes and Chichester, and later at New Cross Gate and Polegate, so that CC1 (and later CC2 and 20003) could work trains in and out of these yards.

For passenger work a steam-heating boiler for carriage warming was fitted, electrically heated by 24 elements, each in its own quartz-lined tube. The boiler was under briquette water-treatment and the water level was automatically controlled. The water heater was supervised by the fireman, which was just about all he had to do.

CC1 made its first test runs on a Sunday in the autumn of 1941, with two light-engine return trips from Brighton to Three Bridges. These were followed later by a number of successful runs between Victoria and Brighton pulling four-teen coaches of heavy Maunsell boat train stock, and by some test trips hauling freight stock, both loaded and unloaded. (The earliest known sighting of such a test train was on 3rd December 1941 at South Croydon.) Its first runs in passenger service appear to have been in February 1942, when it worked a daily diagram for two weeks without failure hauling eleven coaches on Waterloo – Portsmouth Harbour fast services in place of the usual COR+RES+COR EMU formation. By 1944 the locomotive was finally helping the war effort by operating regular freight trips between Norwood Yard, Horsham and Chichester to special EL timings, which had to be substituted

CC1 makes an interesting comparison with an ex-LBSCR K class 2-6-0, the type used for comparative freight trials with a 6 PUL motor coach in 1936, at Purley some time during the latter part of World War Two. The livery carried by CC1 at this time is unclear (probably black), but it has certainly lost its lining and a marker light has been mounted on the original stencil headcode panel. *Lens of Sutton*

by a slower contingency steam diagram if CC1 were unavailable. An attempt was made in that year to work to EL timings with one of Bulleid's new Q1 0-6-0 steam locomotives but, even with special arrangements to clean the fires at each end, the timings proved impossible. CC1 was initially based at Durnsford Road, Wimbledon, for maintenance purposes.[21]

21 CC1 and its load of eleven coaches was first observed by the late G.L. Gundry forming the 8.45am Waterloo to Portsmouth passing Wimbledon on 24th February 1942. On 28th February he saw the same train at Raynes Park and noted in his diary: 'Some flashing at shoes, going well.'

One early problem (which had been anticipated) was that, due to the flywheel arrangement, the booster-generator was able to 'feed' a short circuit in the traction supply near the locomotive, such as might occur when a metal object fell between a running rail and the conductor rail. This happened because the circuit breakers protecting the motor/generator were not fast enough, and could result in damaging flashovers in CC1s electrical equipment. It took some time to solve as it required a very high-speed relay to give the necessary protection. A current-sensitive device known as a 'current limiter' eventually provided the answer, but it required some redesigning before proving reliable in a traction environment.

CC2 arrives at Bognor Regis with a short parcels train (one LMS van) when new in 1946. Being delivered after the war, it was finished in lined malachite green with its ownership and means of propulsion proudly displayed above the cab. Differences from CC1 as originally completed include the lack of headcode panels but the addition of connections for multiple unit operation. *R. Stumpf Collection*

When the war situation improved, work was resumed at Brighton on the second prototype, CC2, during 1944. By this time Raworth had retired and the new SR Chief Electrical Engineer was C.M. Cock. Much of the electrical equipment for this had been stored following completion, and Cock took the opportunity to introduce some changes from experience gained with CC1. There were two major alterations: firstly control jumper sockets and air brake pipes were fitted to the cab fronts for possible future multiple-unit operation, and secondly handwheel controllers were used with duplicated positions on either side of the cab for eventual single-manning. The MU connections consisted of two sockets with the brake pipes between them located at waist level between the cab windows. New booster sets with a slightly increased current rating were fitted, the two already delivered being held as spares. CC2 was painted from new in malachite green with

yellow lining at the top and bottom and SOUTHERN in black-edged gilt on the body sides. There was also a narrow board above the cab windows at each end lettered SOUTHERN twice in yellow with a 'flash' between the words. Marker lights with fold-down discs were fitted from the start, the headcode panel being omitted. CC2 emerged from Brighton Works in the autumn of 1945 and, following a short series of tests including a twice-daily return trip down the Brighton line hauling ten empty Pullman cars for a period in early 1946, was released to traffic on further EL-timed freights, including trains from New Cross Gate and Lewes. By this time maintenance responsibility for the two electric locomotives had been switched to Brighton, although any heavy lifting or booster set changes still had to be dealt with at Durnsford Road or at Peckham Rye, both of which had the necessary gear.

On 7th August 1948, 20003 is seen nearing completion at the far end of the Erecting Shop in Eastleigh Locomotive Works on the occasion of an RCTS visit. It carries post-war SR malachite green livery, now lettered 'British Railways', and clearly displays the revised cab end design, based loosely on a post-war 4 SUB and unique to this locomotive. *J. H. Aston*

The construction of a third electric locomotive, to the same general design as CC1 and CC2, was approved by the SR Board in 1945, being justified financially as the replacement for a steam locomotive destroyed by enemy bombing in 1940. At this time further main-line electrification was being actively considered by the Directors, and further alterations were made to the design in anticipation of a larger production order. With Brighton Locomotive Works fully committed to building Bulleid light Pacifics, construction and electrical installation of 'CC3' were undertaken at Eastleigh. Work commenced in 1947 but was not completed until 1948, so this third locomotive was allocated the British Railways number 20003 from the start. By this time, S.B. Warder (who was later to become notable as architect of BR's industrial-frequency ac main-line electrifications) had taken over as Chief Electrical Engineer.

Although the basic arrangements were unchanged, the underframe of 20003 was 1ft 6in longer to enable the cabs to be lengthened by 6in each, cramped driving positions being one criticism of the original design. The cab fronts were altered to superficially resemble the latest flat-fronted Bulleid 4 SUB stock, although the slab sides conspired to give the ends the 'look' of a particularly severe middle-aged lady. The boiler water capacity was increased to 220 gallons, but battery boxes were smaller and additional ventilation was provided for the booster starting resistances. The booster sets were slightly different and not interchangeable with the original type. Modified traction motors, designated EE 519/2B, were provided; these had the armature windings secured by wedges rather than banding, allowing the top speed to be increased to 85mph and the one-hour rating increased to give a nominal maximum 1,530hp, the tractive effort/speed characteristic remaining unaltered. Slight changes to the bogie design included axle box covers secured with four bolts instead of two, and each had only four sand boxes (one at each corner). MU jumper cable sockets were again fitted, in the same position as on 20002, but as the system was different the two could not actually work together. Provision was made for dual driving conditions but only one set of controls was actually fitted in each cab. 20003 was initially outshopped in malachite green livery with BRITISH RAILWAYS in sans-serif type centrally at waist-level on each side, and numbers in the same typeface located inboard of each cab door.

The main advance over the two previous locomotives concerned the control system, giving much-improved driving arrangements for passenger and freight operation. With CC1 and CC2 it had been necessary to start and accelerate in full-field, which meant running through the 26 notches, returning the controller handle to 'zero', selecting 'weak field' then notching up again. On 20003 there were only 23 full-field notches and then three stages of field-weakening, so when hauling passenger trains the driver could use full field to accelerate, then switch directly to weak-field when conditions were suitable for sustained high-speed running. When working goods trains, only full-field notches 0-23 could be used.

With the end of the war, CC1 had been repainted in the same malachite green livery as CC2 in 1945. Following nationalisation in 1948 the SOUTHERN markings were painted out and replaced by BRITISH RAILWAYS in the same style. The two were renumbered 20001 and 20002 under the new BR numbering scheme, but from photographs it seems that, initially, at least 20002 did not carry the new numbers on its sides while still in malachite. Later in 1948 20002 was painted in an experimental livery of mid blue/grey with silver lettering and lining, and was towed to Kensington Addison Road to be displayed there with variously-coloured steam locomotives and other stock in an attempt to find an acceptable corporate image for the newly State-owned railway. In the event, the LMS diesel livery of gloss black with aluminium-coloured bogie sideframes, lettering and a broad horizontal waist-level stripe was chosen, and all three locomotives had been outshopped in this colour scheme by 1950, complete with the first BR 'lion on wheel' badge midway along the body sides.

From their introduction the three Southern 'booster' locomotives had, for obvious reasons, been nicknamed 'Hornbys' by staff. With nationalisation, the SR's ambitious post-war electrification plans were shelved and thus the expected series production never took place. Until the end of 1948, 20001-20003 were used entirely for freight traffic, but at this time concern was being expressed regarding the difficulty of working the steam-hauled Newhaven boat trains amid the intensive electric services on the Brighton main line. With electrification of the short spur into the boat train platform at Newhaven Harbour having taken place in 1947, thoughts naturally turned to using one of the electric locomotives on this run, and the first such working took place on 15th May 1949. 20003 successfully hauled twelve coaches and two vans, totalling 370 tons tare, from Victoria to Newhaven Harbour

in fifteen minutes less than the normal steam timing. From then until their withdrawal, this service was a regular working for one of the original 'boosters', although in the 1960s one of the later Kent Coast E5000 HA locomotives was sometimes used instead. On summer Saturdays in the 1950s the locomotive off the Down Newhaven boat train was used to haul the Birkenhead – Hastings through train, generally composed of ex-LMS stock, between Brighton and Eastbourne before returning light to haul the Up Newhaven. Another regular coastal working from Brighton occurred from 6th January 1964 until October 1965, when 20001-20003 were used on the 10.12am through service to Exeter and Plymouth and its corresponding 10.40am up working, diverted in and out of Fratton to enable a diesel or steam locomotive to take over. The class rarely worked on the South Eastern division, but for a few months from early July 1962 one was used to work the Newcastle – Dover car sleeper from Longhedge Junction and return, again in order to provide steam-heating for the ex-LMS stock utilised on this service.

Other passenger workings included various specials, such as those carrying royalty or foreign dignitaries, and race-day trains, virtually all on the Central section/division. Between 1965 and 1968 they were used to haul the royal train carrying the Queen and her entourage to the Derby at Epsom (Tattenham Corner) on the first Wednesday in June, and for these workings they were turned out immaculately.

In 1956 a new livery was adopted for BR diesel and electric locomotives, consisting of overall bright green with thin horizontal bands of white, red and white along the waist and the second BR locomotive emblem about half-way along the sides. The heavy solebars and window frames were picked-out in light green/grey and bogies were now black. 20003 was the first to be so dealt with, in that year, followed by 20002 in April 1958, the latter having its useless multiple-unit sockets removed at this time. 20001 was repainted later in 1958, and that November the class was reallocated to Stewarts Lane where they were maintained in the new purpose-built electric locomotive shed shared with the E5000 class HA locomotives then being delivered for the Kent Coast electrification. However, their sphere of operation did not change, freight on the Central section centred on Horsham yard remaining their chief activity. At the same time, heavy overhauls were transferred to Eastleigh. All three became class 70 in the first BR numerical classification system of 1965.

The horizontal body side lining and grey solebars were done away with in about 1964 and at the same time all three locomotives had extensive front end modifications, with remaining marker lights, headcode discs and lamp brackets removed, whistles replaced by roof-mounted air horns, and standard roller-blind headcode panels fitted between the cab windows. On 20001 and 20002 these were the older, deeper type, but the shallower version was used on 20003, which also had its multiple unit cables and external supply sockets removed. Various other minor livery variations appeared from this time; for example 20002 and 20003 had green cab roofs and white roof centre in 1964. 20003 gained small yellow warning panels and white cab-window frames prior to working the royal Derby day special in June 1967, while

Resplendent in the black and silver livery then standard for British Railways main line diesel and electric locomotives, 20003 stands at Eastbourne in the company of various BR standard steam locomotives on Friday 1st June 1951. It was forming part of an exhibition of modern traction put on for delegates attending the 1951 International Union of Railways' Conference. Although very smart when newly applied, the rather impractical silver underframe and bogies quickly weathered in service. *Bluebell Railway Museum Archive/J. J. Smith*

In 1965-68 the 'booster' locomotives were used to haul the Royal train from Victoria to Tattenham Corner on Derby Day. On 29th May 1968 it was the turn of 20001, seen here at Tattenham Corner after arrival. It has been turned out in immaculate condition by Stewarts Lane staff, and is in final blue livery with full yellow ends and roller-blind headcode panel. Sadly, this fine machine was withdrawn just six months later. *John Scrace*

20002 gained full yellow ends while retaining green livery. British Rail blue with full yellow ends was confined to 20001, which was outshopped in this livery in July 1967, prior to working a royal train from Waterloo to Winchester.

In the face of declining freight traffic and being a small non-standard class, the three Bulleid Co-Cos were withdrawn early, with many years of life still left in them. 20003 was the first to go, in October 1968, and was sold to Cohens at Kettering where it was scrapped a year later. 20002 followed in December 1968 but 20001 lasted another month, its final duty being a 'Farewell' railtour on 4th January 1969, organised jointly by the Bulleid Pacific Preservation Society and the LCGB. Having plenty of copper in their electrical equipment the scrap value was relatively high, and both locomotives were sold to Cashmores at Newport where they were cut up the following August without any serious preservation attempt having been made.

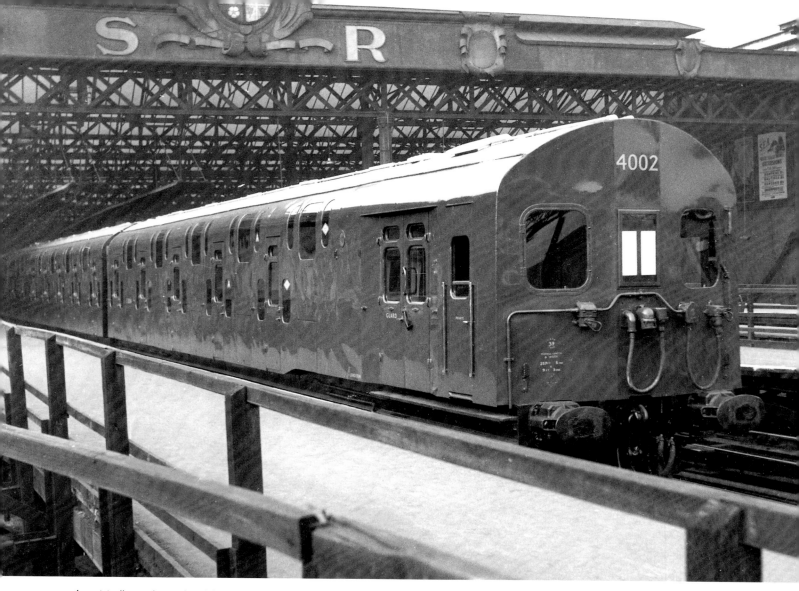

As originally outshopped with large unit numbers and centrally-positioned control jumper, 4 DD 4002 stands at Charing Cross following its official inspection on 1st November 1949. Diamond transfers on the windows indicate that the leading upper / lower deck compartment pair is for LADIES ONLY. *F. W. Ivey*

THE 4 DD DOUBLE-DECKER UNITS

The problem of peak-hour overcrowding after 1945 due to a continuing increase in passengers on the SR's suburban routes, particularly on Eastern section lines out of Charing Cross and Cannon Street to Dartford, has already been mentioned elsewhere in this volume. With its 'six-a-side' seating, the new generation 4 SUB suburban stock did offer a useful increase in seating capacity over previous units, an eight-coach train of the pre-production '4101' type cramming in no fewer than 936 seats compared with approximately 600 in the standard pre-war motor unit + trailer set + motor unit formation. However, even with this increased number of seats, standing was still not eliminated on the busiest services, and was only possible in some discomfort due to the decreased compartment width. So the production post-war version was given slightly wider compartments and most had centre gangways in three vehicles, reducing the overall seating in an eight-coach train to 772, although standing was now much more comfortable. The lines concerned, already equipped with modern four-aspect colour-light signalling on the busiest sections, were running to their full capacity at the height of the peaks, so the number of trains could not be increased. If it was not feasible to increase further the number of seats within the existing eight-coach train length, the only other possible course of action to relieve overcrowding was to lengthen trains. This solution was resisted at the time due to the estimated £10 million capital cost and upheaval involved.

In the quest to provide more seats within the constraints of the eight-coach train length and weight, an electric unit was designed of a type previously unknown on Britain's railway network, a double-decker. The idea originated during discussions between Bulleid and Missenden in 1948, just after nationalisation, and the plan to build an eight-coach prototype was approved by Riddles and his staff as an important and valuable experiment.[22] True double-decked suburban trains with enclosed stairs had been in use in continental Europe for more than ten years, as typified by the SNCF push-pull sets in use in the western Paris suburbs, but it was impossible to fit two full decks into the restricted British loading gauge. Instead, it appears that Bulleid and his designers took inspiration from the internal arrangements of a Rome bus, described in the SR staff magazine dated September 1931. Under the title 'Method of Packing Passengers', it showed a design in which the upper and lower decks were zigzagged with the upper deck passengers sitting above, but reversed to, their lower deck counterparts whose heads were at the same level as fellow travellers' shins! The access to the upper compartments on these vehicles was via external stair rungs, which did not improve their popularity with female travellers. The particular operating advantage of this odd compartment arrangement was that it kept vehicle height to a minimum.

With his interest in the unconventional and different, it seems likely that the Southern's CME took far more interest in the design and construction of the double-decker units than in the more mundane electric stock then in production. Design work actually started as a series of sketches by staff in the Lancing drawing office, and their plans were originally a Southern Region 'official secret' until *Brighton Evening Argus* reporters smelt-out and published the following story in early February 1949:

A full-scale plywood model of a type of carriage that may one day revolutionise railway travel is nearing completion at Lancing Carriage Works.

It follows months of work by draughtsmen who have been experimenting with a design which may help railways to overcome the problem of rolling stock.

The 'two-in-one' carriage is an idea which may take years to fulfil. It is at the infancy stage, according to railway officials, who are loth to talk about it.

In fact the model-making at Lancing appears to be as secret as the latest development of atomic research. No one there will talk of the double-decker carriage.

Top officials say 'Sorry, No statement. Not allowed to say anything', and lesser officials, with furtive, over-the-shoulder glances, say 'We mustn't say anything – but we have seen it and it looks as if the idea is pretty good.'

Despite the secrecy, the model *has* been built, and it looks as though the Railway Executive are greatly interested in the possibilities of 'up and down' railway travel.

The publicity in the *Argus* was remarkably fortuitous as the plywood mock-up was due to be shown to the press and public at Marylebone later that month anyway. Coincidentally, the Head Office Order HO 3529 to build an eight-coach double-decker train had been given to Eastleigh Works on 9th February 1949. Due to a higher than standard loading gauge on the Dartford line, where the experimental units were to work, it proved possible by using smaller wheels and a lower underframe to increase the internal height of the coach bodies from the standard 8ft 2in to 9ft 0¾in, just enough to fit in the alternating 'upper' and 'lower' deck compartments. Other than the use of internal stairways and a normal railway compartment seating plan with facing seats, the arrangement adopted proved very similar to that in the Italian bus mentioned above. And in spite of warnings from the intrepid *Argus* reporter, the real double-decker train took just nine months to emerge from works.

The train was in the SR's standard form for new suburban stock, comprising two four-coach units classified, predictably, 4 DD. Each unit was formed of two identical motor third brakes to diagram 2128 with motorman's and guard's compartments at the outer ends, flanking two similar trailer thirds, classified A and B, to diagrams 2020 and 2021 respectively. Passenger accommodation in the motor coaches comprised five pairs of compartments, while the trailers had six compartment-pairs plus an extra low-level compartment at the centre, with no access to an upper compartment. The end compartments in all coaches were lower ones, but an upper compartment adjoined the guard's van in the motor coaches. The motor coaches seated 120 (including ten tip-up seats in the upper compartments) and the trailers 156 (including twelve tip-up). Built at Eastleigh on underframes and bogies fabricated at Lancing, the two units were numbered 4001 and 4002. Formations were as shown in the table below. Note that the reversed numbering of the trailers in 4002 was probably no more than a quirk of Eastleigh Works.

Unit	Motor Third Brake	Trailer Third	Trailer Third	Motor Third Brake
4001	13001	13501	13502	13002
4002	13003	13504	13503	13004

The coaches were of all-steel construction similar to the post-war SUBs from 4111 upwards, but virtually every dimension and fitting was non-standard to enable the seating arrangement to fit within the loading gauge and to keep down the tare weight. They had flat sides, although the doors to the guard's compartments were inset, and the lower edge of the bodywork was cranked-up from the cab ends to the rear of the brake van, to provide clearance for motorman's and guard's stepboards which were lacking from the passenger doors. Cab windows resembled those on the SUBs, but a roller-blind headcode panel, flush with the cab front, was fitted. On the lower deck, the compartment quarterlights were at a lower level than the door droplights, while upper deck compartments had a large centre window flanked by two much narrower ones, all curved to match the body side contour and sealed due to limited clearances. For the same

22 In the organisation of the nationalised British Railways, Sir Eustace Missenden (a former SR General Manager) was Chairman of the Railway Executive, and Robert Riddles (from the LMSR) was Chief Mechanical Engineer.

'Passengers' (probably models) squeeze into the less-than-comfortable lower deck compartment of a 4 DD unit for a publicity photograph when new. The meagre cushions, limited headroom and lack of space for briefcases and other luggage are the most obvious negative features. Steps to the adjacent upper compartment, whose horizontal cushion is only inches above the heads of these gentlemen, are between the seat ends on the right. *BR Official*

reason there were no commode handles, and the door openings had cast internal step-plates inscribed MIND THE GAP. As well as droplights, the doors had the characteristic Bulleid lozenge-shaped toplight with a ventilator slot at each end. Fixed windows were attached from the inside in aluminium frames. Original livery was early BR malachite green, with large hand-painted unit numbers in the usual position but no evidence of ownership.

Internally, the complex S-shaped partitions were of plywood, and other fittings were aluminium to save weight. For the same reasons, the meagre horsehair-stuffed seat and back cushions were thin and hard with a large gap between them, and there were no headrests on either deck. Upholstery was originally the red-brown leafy pattern also being used in new SUBs at this time. The seating was basically six each side, divided into three+two where the four steps between the upper and lower compartments were located. There were also two folding seats in each upper compartment, located below the window and facing inwards at a slightly lower level – these proved unpopular, with most passengers preferring to

stand rather than to squat among their fellow travellers' feet. The lower deck had no provision for luggage whatsoever, but there were ledges behind the upper deck seat backs, due to space required for door clearance, around which were situated luggage rails. The majority of internal panelling was covered with 'Rexine'. Due to the fixed upper deck windows, it was necessary to provide pressure ventilation, consisting of fans located in the space between each lower deck compartment. These drew in air from inlets beneath the body and this was heated as necessary before being blown through ducts above the seat backs in the upper compartments. The fans had two speed settings and cut-in automatically when the motor-generator control switch was closed. Thus (in theory, at least) the fans were always in operation when the units were in service. The passenger communication valves (the 'emergency cord') were non-standard in that each cord operated its own individual valve, and there were no cords in the upper compartments. Interior lighting was by fluorescent tubes to save space, supplied from inverters mounted underneath each motor coach.

Special bogies were required due to the reduced height from the rails to underframe level. Motor bogies generally conformed to the 'central' suburban design, although dimensions differed, and each had two of the new type EE 507C traction motors. They were located in the usual position at the outer ends of the motor coaches. Trailer bogies were bolsterless, using instead the segmented bearing design originally developed for Bulleid's Co-Co electric locomotives. The underframe was carried directly on the bogie frame, supported on four radial segments lined with a low-friction fabric material. Primary suspension was by means of laminated springs mounted on the axle boxes, while secondary suspension was provided by helical springs. The axle boxes themselves were of fabricated steel rather than the usual cast iron, in order to save weight. The original plan to use standard disc-type wheels, but of only 3ft 2in diameter, went awry when the suppliers did not deliver on time, and so Bulleid decided to risk using fabricated wheels of the Bulleid-Firth-Brown type (as on his Pacifics and the electric locomotives described above), to which the tyres were welded. These had the added advantage of being lighter, but were to prove unsatisfactory in service. He wanted to use hollow axles to further reduce weight and aid welding to the wheels, but in the prevailing economic climate could not find any firm willing to manufacture the small quantity involved.

Control gear was similar to the 1936 equipment in the post-war SUBs, using electro-pneumatic contactors working at 70 volts. However, the power for control and auxiliary circuits was provided by motor-generators, one on each motor coach, and not from the power line by means of a potential divider as on the SUBs. 27-core control cables were used for the first time on the SR, although the allocation of individual lines differed from that adopted for the later EPB and subsequent stock. The unit-end control jumpers and sockets were originally mounted centrally under the headcode panel. As on the SUBs, there was a power jumper, connecting the bus lines, and hence collector shoes, of the two units together when working in multiple. This was located under the motorman's window, with a socket on the opposite side connected by a conduit cranked-up at the centre to clear the control jumper. A further innovation was the use of the Westinghouse electro-pneumatic brake, unusual in that it was not self-lapping. The brake and main reservoir pipes were mounted on the bufferbeam, again unlike the EPBs. The actual brake equipment fitted to the units had formerly experimentally equipped 6 PUL 3016 and 6 PAN 3034 in 1947-48 for trials. (See Chapter 5.) The non-standard braking and control equipment made the 4 DD units a coupling class on their own. Screw couplings were provided at unit ends and the usual centre buffer + three link coupler between intermediate vehicles. (This explains the different diagram numbers for the two trailers: diagram 2020 for 13502/3, with centre buffer at both ends, and diagram 2021 for 13501/4, with one centre buffer and one rubbing block).

A comparison of the principal dimensions and other statistics of the 4 DD stock with the standard 4 SUB then in production is interesting, and is shown in the table at the top of the next column:

Dimensions		4 DD	4 SUB
Overall Length:		257ft 4½in	257ft 4½in
Overall Width:		9ft 3in	9ft 3in
Height:	Rail to Roof:	12ft 9in	12ft 3in
	Rail to Floor:	3ft 8½in	4ft 2½in
Wheel Diameters:			
	Motor Bogie:	3ft 2in	3ft 7in
	Trailer Bogie:	3ft 0in	3ft 6in
Number of Seats (all third class)		552*	386
Tare Weight Per Passenger		0.265 tons	0.347 tons

Note:
* Included in this figure are 44 tip-up seats in the upper compartments

Following tests, an official inspection of the two new units took place at Charing Cross on 1st November 1949, followed by a Press and VIP run to Dartford and back. Those on board included Herbert Morrison (then Lord President of the Council and interested as MP for East Lewisham), Alfred Barnes (Minister of Transport) and Bulleid (by then working for CIE). Everything performed exactly as required and Morrison, naturally enough not knowing who was in charge of what, said to Bulleid: 'This is wonderful. It is just what my electors want. How many can we have by Christmas?'

However, when the 4 DD units entered passenger service the following day, 2nd November, various snags quickly arose. The BFB wheels in particular proved troublesome with cracks appearing, possibly due to strains resulting from the sluggish action of the bogie bearings on curves. The units were withdrawn the next day for modifications and spent most of the following two months in works, only appearing in traffic between 18th-22nd November. They eventually re-entered service again on 6th January 1950, now with wheels of standard construction as originally specified. By this time the early BR 'lion on wheel' badge had been applied to the motor coaches immediately below the windows of the second upper-deck compartment from the guard's van, at a higher level than on other stock, and the hand-painted unit numbers replaced by smaller transfers. After returning to passenger service the upper deck ventilation equipment proved to be the main cause of trouble, and throughout their lives the units spent various periods out of traffic while this underwent unscheduled repairs.

Due to their larger-than-standard dimensions, the 4 DD units had a very restricted route availability. Throughout their working lives they were based at Slade Green and were used between Charing Cross or Cannon Street and Dartford or Gravesend via Bexleyheath only. Special arrangements were made when it was necessary for the units to be worked to Lancing or Eastleigh for overhaul. Initially they operated all day, being uncoupled and working separately between the peaks, and it must have been highly inconvenient if their diagrams became disrupted whilst working apart. They were never used on Sundays.

In service, it soon became clear that the double-decker units were not a success, either with passengers or with the operating department. A particular problem was that loading and unloading at station stops took longer than usual because there was only one door to 24 seats, rather than to ten or twelve as was the case with conventional slam-door suburban stock. Quite why such an obvious design flaw was not spotted during the earliest stages of development is unclear. If double-decked trains had been adopted generally, this would have led to longer station stops, particularly at London Bridge and Waterloo, and thus a less frequent service would result, cancelling out the advantage of greater seating capacity. Furthermore, the upper decks were unpopular with most passengers, who found them hot and claustrophobic due to

A very rare view of 4001 and 4002 forming a service train in completely original condition. The pair is seen passing Stone Crossing Halt with a morning Cannon Street to Gravesend service on either 2nd or during the week of 18th-22nd November 1949. *Ken Nunn Collection (LCGB)*

Left In the second BR green livery, 4001 approaches Cannon Street leading an afternoon service from Gravesend via Bexleyheath on 12th June 1959. By this time the 27-wire control jumper had been moved to the offside from its former central position, although blanking plates clearly reveal its former location. *R. C. Riley*

the lack of opening windows and the unreliable ventilation system. Women felt vulnerable in the upper compartments and the lack of a communication cord exacerbated these fears. These concerns were brought to the fore on 31st January 1950 when a female passenger was attacked and badly injured by two youths while the train was travelling through Blackheath tunnel. (The offenders were subsequently caught and sentenced to seven years each.) The thin hard seats were also a cause of complaint.

In view of the longer station stops, ventilation problems and limited route availability, it was quickly decided that no more double-decker units would be built, and a Press announcement to this effect was made on 6th December 1950. Increased capacity would be achieved instead by the more expensive alternative of lengthening trains from eight to ten coaches. 4001 and 4002, now non-standard and somewhat freakish twins, were then confined to rush-hour services only, and thereafter never again worked apart. They continued to operate Monday to Saturday until 1959 when, due to the decline in Saturday office opening, additional morning and lunchtime rush-hour services on this day were abolished. A typical weekly diagram for the units, dating from 1956, was as follows:

Monday to Saturday mornings

ECS	Slade Green – Dartford
5.24	Dartford – Cannon Street
6.13	Cannon Street – Dartford
7.02	Dartford – Charing Cross
7.52	Charing Cross – Crayford
8.27	Crayford – Cannon Street
9.14SX	Cannon Street – Slade Green
9.12SO	Cannon Street – Dartford
ECS SO	Dartford – Slade Green

Monday to Friday afternoons

ECS	Slade Green – Crayford
2.27	Crayford – Cannon Street
3.16	Cannon Street – Gravesend
4.22	Gravesend – Charing Cross
5.34	Charing Cross – Barnehurst
ECS	Barnehurst – Slade Green

Saturday midday

11.21	Slade Green – Cannon Street
12.16	Cannon Street – Gravesend
1.22	Gravesend – Charing Cross
2.28	Charing Cross – Dartford
ECS	Dartford – Slade Green

After the initial difficulties with wheels and ventilation equipment were resolved, so far as this was possible, 4001 and 4002 underwent no significant modification through the remainder of their 21-year existence. Early on, the control jumpers and sockets were relocated from the centre of the cab ends to the offside, possibly to make them more accessible to staff at platform level. The original mounting holes were plated over, but the power line conduit remained cranked-up over the original jumper position. From photographic evidence, this work had been done by 1954. Following general overhaul in 1958, the units were outshopped in the second, darker, BR green livery with round coaching-stock badge. A little later the original headcode blinds with large numbers were replaced by a new type with smaller numbers, also incorporating two red blanks which indicated 'last vehicle'. As on the later EPB stock, these were lit from behind using a 70V supply delivered from a line-driven motor-generator, backed up by battery, and could therefore replace the tail lamps formerly carried. The 4 DDs had gained small yellow warning panels by the summer of 1963, being among the first SR electric units to be so treated, and these were superseded by full yellow ends with black unit numbers by 1969. Their final overhaul was in the autumn of 1970, when they were painted in blue with the 'double arrow' symbol positioned directly behind the recessed guard's van doors. At the same time they were renumbered 4901 and 4902, their original numbers being used for the prototype PEP stock introduced in 1971.

By this time the 4 DD units were being put to very limited use on less busy trains at the beginnings and ends of the peaks, so that loading times would not be too extended. During their final year in traffic, they worked the following Monday – Friday diagram:

07.36	Slade Green – Charing Cross
08.27	Charing Cross – Slade Green
ECS	Slade Green – Charing Cross
16.27	Charing Cross – Dartford
ECS	Dartford – Charing Cross
18.04	Charing Cross – Dartford
ECS	Dartford – Slade Green

The last day in service for 4901 and 4902 was 1st October 1971, the official reason for withdrawal being that they were due for major overhaul and that the expenditure could not be justified on stock that was put to such limited use. By this time they had run more than 700,000 miles in passenger traffic. After being taken out of service they spent a few weeks in sidings at Plumstead before being moved to Hoo Junction for cutting up by Smeeth Metals Ltd. Motor coaches 13003/04 and trailer 13503 from 4902 were acquired by the proprietor of the Ashford Steam Centre, whence they were moved in March 1972. Regrettably, following the closure of this site trailer 13503 was cut up there in August 1984, but the two motor coaches were sold on. 13003 was acquired by a farmer in Kent, while 13004 went to the Northampton Steam Railway at Pitsford and more recently to the nearby Northamptonshire Ironstone Railway at Hunsbury Hill. Both vehicles remained in very poor condition with little restoration work having been carried out, and their future was, and continues to be, uncertain.

Above SR-type 4 EPB 5029 makes an interesting comparison with 4 DD 4002 at Dartford on a rainy day in February 1969. The slab sides of the double-decker unit, by this time with yellow ends, contrast with the curved profile of the 'standard' all-steel suburban stock. *Southern Images / John H. Bird*

Left The last day of service for the 4DD units was Friday 1st October 1971. On this date the pair pass London Bridge with the 15.42 empties from Slade Green ready to form their penultimate passenger working, the 16.42 Charing Cross to Dartford via Bexleyheath. 4001/2 were renumbered 4901/2 at the time of their final overhaul in the autumn of 1970, when they were also given BR blue livery. *Bryan Rayner*

DEPARTMENTAL CONVERSIONS

Railway operation has always required vehicles for internal (in other words, not revenue earning) purposes such as track maintenance, weed killing and the movement of stores between depots. As far as the electrified lines of the Southern Railway and its predecessors were concerned, the petrol railcars employed for overhead line maintenance on the LBSCR ac system were fully described in Volume 1, while on the dc third rail network goods wagons or otherwise redundant coaches, hauled by steam locomotives, were originally used. Such vehicles were often allocated to a particular railway department, hence the term 'departmental', and numbered in a separate series from capital (revenue earning) stock. Redundant electric vehicles first became available for departmental purposes in the immediate post-World War Two period as a result of the suburban stock renewal programme and, in the years following, the number of withdrawn EMU coaches retained for internal use gradually increased. Some of the uses to which departmental electric stock has been put, such as the spreading of de-icing fluid on conductor rails during the winter, are specific to the third rail system.

This section covers electric stock of LBSCR, LSWR and SR origin converted or used for departmental purposes in the period 1945-83. Where a particular vehicle or unit survived beyond the end of September 1983, the general cut off date for this book, an exception has been made and its subsequent history is related until condemnation.

DE-ICING, WATER-CANNON AND SANDITE COACHES

From the earliest days of electrified railways operating in the open air using exposed top-contact conductor rails, problems were experienced on freezing winter nights when a thin layer of ice could form on the upper surface of the live rail. This ice layer drastically reduced conductivity and caused serious arcing, leading to costly electrical damage including burnt out shoegear. In order to alleviate this problem, a special oil-based de-icing fluid was developed by the SR electrical department just after World War Two. When spread on to the live rail surface, this fluid was designed to melt ice already present and to prevent more from forming. Special coaches or (later) self-propelled electric units, converted from redundant stock, were utilised to spread de-icing fluid, and until 2004 these vehicles and their successors formed the major part of the Southern's departmental fleet.

Above De-icing van DS 353, converted from ex LBSCR 9013 from trailer set 1053, parked at Fratton depot in about 1955. The shoebeams on which the spray nozzles are mounted, the periscopes and the oval lookouts on the ends are all clearly visible. *F. W. Ivey*

The first coaches to be converted for spreading de-icing fluid (otherwise known as 'oil spraying') were ten ex-LBSCR 54ft nine-compartment thirds from withdrawn trailer sets, numbered 351S-356S and 396S-399S. With one exception these had been new in 1910-12 or 1921, and had been converted to electric working for the Western and Eastern sections suburban schemes in 1925, retaining their original underframes and bogies. The odd example was 356S (formerly 9003) which had the body of a 1895-vintage six-wheeler lengthened and mounted on a new bogie underframe in 1910. The origins and dates of conversion of these vehicles, together with known depot allocations and withdrawal dates, are shown in the table.

Departmental No.	Ex Coach No. (ex Set No.)	Date Converted	Depot Allocation(s)	Date Withdrawn
351S	9010 (1065)	12/45	Not known	12/56
352S	9116 (1109)	12/45	Durnsford Rd, then Fratton	5/61
353S	9013 (1053)	11/45	Fratton	6/61
354S	9069 (1053)	11/45	Selhurst	2/61
355S	9060 (1060)	11/45	Selhurst	12/56
356S	9003 (1060)	11/45	Brighton	?1961
396S	8957 (1029)	11/46	Gillingham, then Wimbledon Pk	2/61
397S	8958 (1029)	11/46	Brighton	2/61
398S	9079 (1083)	11/46	Fratton, then Wimbledon Pk	5/61
399S	9089 (1083)	11/46	Gillingham, then Wimbledon Pk, then Fratton	?1962

Note:
On nationalisation, the Southern Railway S (for service stock) number suffix was replaced by a DS prefix. Hence 351S became DS 351, etc.

Internal alterations to these vehicles included the removal of partitions to allow the installation of two steel tanks which carried 750 gallons of the de-icing fluid. As they were not insulated and consequently electrically live when fluid was being spread on the conductor rail, these tanks were a potential hazard to staff. The de-icing fluid was fed by gravity through pipes to spray nozzles attached to shoe-beams on each bogie, a valve being turned on and off by the operator who could observe the position of the conductor rail through downward-facing periscopes mounted in place of the end quarterlight at all four corners. There were also small oval-shaped or rectangular lookouts on the coach ends (almost certainly recovered from the guard's duckets of other withdrawn coaches), although it seems that these and the periscopes were not initially fitted to the 1945 batch (351S-356S). Presumably it was soon found unacceptable for the operator to hang out of an open droplight in the cold for observation purposes. Photographs indicate that the arrangement of external pipework varied considerably between different vehicles, suggesting that these conversions were carried out as 'one-offs', without reference to drawings. All

but the end-compartment doors were sealed, and some vehicles had portions of exterior panelling plated over with steel sheet. Screw couplings plus control and jumper cables were fitted to the end which lacked them, enabling these vehicles to operate singly between pairs of electric units with pre-1951 suburban-type control equipment. They were also given handbrakes. Livery was green originally, although in BR days some were painted 'departmental red' (a brownish shade, not the almost scarlet hue used on non-gangwayed hauled passenger stock). The end cantrail panels were filled in with white paint and the service stock number painted on these, while the lettering CHIEF ELECTRICAL ENGINEER'S DEPT originally appeared centrally at waist height.

These first de-icing trailers were allocated strategically to various electric depots around the SR, and were sent out, generally at night, when the weather forecast predicted freezing conditions. Operating instructions stated that they were to be formed between two pairs of two-coach (2 NOL, BIL, HAL) or two four-coach (4 LAV, SUB) units, with the former arrangement to be used wherever possible, but it was permissible to run them between a single pair of two-coach units in cases of stock shortage. They were not allowed to be coupled to express or 1951/57 EPB-type stock with which they were incompatible. Although occasionally formed in timetabled passenger trains, they mainly operated their own diagrams covering routes prone to icing-up, and some details of these have survived. Gillingham-based vans worked to Swanley, Maidstone East, Otford, Sevenoaks and Knockholt. Those based at Selhurst worked two diagrams, the first to Brighton, Horsted Keynes and Seaford (headcode 70 with bar) and the second to Haywards Heath, Three Bridges, Horsham and Leatherhead (h/c 71 with bar). A Brighton van covered the coastal line from Ore to Bognor Regis via Brighton and Littlehampton (h/c 72 with bar), while the Portsmouth Direct and Mid-Sussex routes as far as Horsham (h/c 08 with bar) were dealt with by a Fratton or Wimbledon-based vehicle outstationed at Woking. A Selhurst-based van was regularly steam hauled on the Tattenham Corner branch, generally by an ex-LBSCR E class tank. The de-icing vans were employed extensively in the appalling winter of January-February 1947, proving their worth in helping to keep lines passable to electric stock.

With two exceptions (noted in the table above) these earliest de-icing trailers survived until 1961 or 1962, being superseded by the motorised units and more modern trailers described later. All were broken up at Newhaven, which had been the main graveyard for wooden bodied SUB stock since 1953.

The first powered de-icing units were two converted from pairs of recently withdrawn LBSCR-bodied SUB motor brakes in 1957, from units 4531 and 4557. HO 4388 of 11th February 1957 (Instruction to Operating Depot) authorised these conversions, which were carried out at Battersea (Longhedge Works). The vehicles used were chosen because they were on lengthened ac underframes not suitable for re-use, and had bodywork similar to the existing de-icing trailers. Coaches 8698 and 8864 from 4531 were renumbered DS 349 and DS 350 respectively and were given the unit

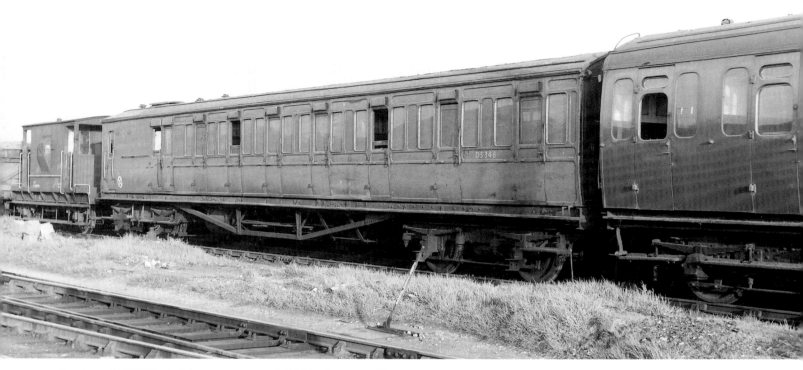

Condemned LBSCR-bodied de-icing motor coach DS 348, from unit S90, stands in the scrap line at Basingstoke together with a redundant wooden-roofed 'six-a-side' augmentation trailer on 18th May 1963, prior to onward dispatch to Newhaven for scrapping. By this time the trailer bogie shoebeams had been removed, but their mountings can still be seen. *R. C. Riley*

number S91, while 8741 and 8899 from 4557 became DS 347 and DS 348 in unit S90. The necessary work evidently did not take long as S91 was outshopped in March 1957 and S90 in April, both carrying the earlier BR malachite green livery but with no external identification other than numbers. Their equipment was generally similar to the trailers, with steel tanks in both coaches, but the oil was only spread from the trailer bogie of each, and periscopes were located on just the offside inner end quarterlights. One vehicle in each unit had to have its inner-end rubbing plate replaced by a centre buffer, and a similar alteration was necessary on other departmental conversions comprising motor coach pairs. Their overall length was shown as 129ft 6ins. The S prefix was dropped from their unit numbers in about 1960.

These little-known units were based at Gillingham for most their short lives, although 90 also spent a period at Fratton. It is thought that they were mainly intended for duties covering Eastern section suburban routes, because by then virtually all electric passenger services were worked by EP-braked stock with which the existing trailer de-icing vans could not operate. They were condemned in November 1961, following which 90 found its way to Strawberry Hill in early 1962 and then to Micheldever on 17th May 1963, where it was photographed with 91 (whose previous movements following withdrawal were not recorded). DS348 was at Basingstoke the following day, probably en route to Newhaven for scrapping, and it seems probable that the other three vehicles followed the same path.

The concept of powered de-icing units having proved satisfactory, ten more were converted using pairs of steel panelled motor coaches from 1925 Eastern section 'long-frame' suburban units, later 4 SUBs in the 4326-4354 series. Originally numbered 92-101, 92 was the prototype (authorised by HO 4653 of 9th July 1959) and appeared in September 1960. Of the rest (to HO 4816 dated 27th June 1960), 93-96 were also outshopped in September and the remainder the following month. Mechanical alterations were carried out at Stewarts Lane and electrical work at Peckham Rye. Individual coach numbers and their origins are shown in the following table:

Unit No	1968 No.	Departmental Coach Nos.	Original Coach Nos.	ex SUB
92	011	DS 70044 / DS 70045	8456 / 8455	4345
93	012	DS 70090 / DS 70091	8446 / 8445	4340
94	013	DS 70092 / DS 70093	8463 / 8464	4349
95	014	DS 70094 / DS 70095	8453 / 8454	4344
96	015	DS 70096 / DS 70097	8433 / 8434	4334
97	016	DS 70098 / DS 70099	8471 / 8472	4353
98	017	DS 70100 / DS 70101	8467 / 8468	4351
99	018	DS 70102 / DS 70103	8422 / 8421	4328
100	019	DS 70104 / DS 70105	8430 / 8465	4332
101	020	DS 70106 / DS 70107	8427 / 8423	4331

Note:

In February 1962, DS 70044 was withdrawn following fire damage, being replaced by DS 70173 converted from 8457 out of 4 SUB 4346.

The conversion work was again minimal in comparison with later de-icing conversions, the coaches all retaining their original Metrovick electro-magnetic control equipment and type 339 traction motors, enabling them to work in multiple with all SUB and pre-1951 semi-fast stock. The interiors were stripped of seats and partitions and most compartment doors were sealed closed, although commode handles were generally left in place. Gangway connections were fitted to the inner ends of each vehicle to allow through access. The downward-facing periscopes were fitted to one of the quarterlights of the third compartment back on both sides, again enabling the operator to detect which side the conductor rail was situated and manually turn the fluid supply on or off accordingly. The actual de-icing equipment was generally similar to that in the earlier vehicles described above, with improvements. Steel tanks located in both coaches supplied de-icing fluid via axle-driven pumps to nozzles mounted on additional shoebeams, also equipped with scrapers, on the inner (trailer) bogies. Heaters warmed the fluid prior to application if necessary to make it flow more easily. Livery was initially the later BR multiple unit green, without badges, lettered De-Icing Unit at the centre of each side. Overall weight of each converted vehicle was 41 tons.

Distributed among the same depots as their predecessors had been, 92-101 generally worked singly, at night, and were rarely coupled to other stock. Initially retaining their original stencil headcode panels, these were replaced by roller-blinds in about 1965, the headcode box standing slightly proud of the cab front. The original whistles were replaced by roof-mounted air horns in 1967, and at roughly the same time the class gained small yellow warning panels. They were renumbered 011-020 respectively in 1968, and in the same year all were renovated and modified to spray a new de-icing fluid formulation. All were now outshopped with full yellow ends, the yellow wrapping around to the front of the cab doors in some cases. BR blue livery also appeared at the end of 1968, with 014 and 016 being the first to be so treated. All were in blue by 1970, some being given white 'double arrow' symbols and others not. As part of its overhaul, Gillingham-based unit 016 had the majority of its external doors sheeted over with steel plate.

Withdrawal took place after the 1978-79 winter season, but many remained on the SR, dumped at sites such as Crystal Palace, Norwood sidings (Tennison Road) and Micheldever for some time. They were sold for scrap to dealers who had dealt with other pre-war stock, including Booths at Rotherham, Armitage at Sheepbridge and the Bird Group. A very decrepit 018, sold to the latter dealer in 1980, was noted buried in undergrowth at the back of Long Marston yard as late as 1982.

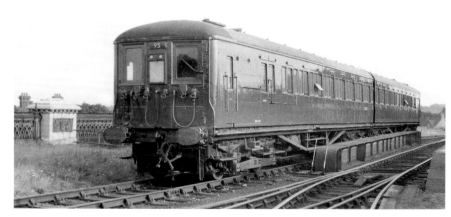

Newly converted de-icing unit 95, formerly the motor coaches of 1925 'long-framed' 4 SUB 4344, stands in Knights Hill sidings (Tulse Hill) on 14th September 1960 in ex-works condition. At this time, stencil headcode panels were retained on these vehicles. *R. C. Riley*

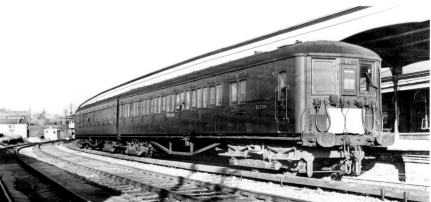

By now fitted with roller-blind headcode equipment and given a small yellow warning panel, 1960 de-icing unit 93 is parked in the Up bay at Pulborough on 4th March 1967, its winter duties almost over. The periscopes on these units were mounted at the centre of each vehicle. *John Scrace*

Four additional non-powered de-icing trailers, initially numbered DS 70050-DS 70051 and DS 70086-DS 70087, were also outshopped in 1959-60, specifically to provide vehicles which could work in multiple with EP-braked stock for the two phases of the Kent Coast electrification. These were modified at Lancing from four of the ten 1946-built SUB augmentation trailers 10391-10400, which were the first truly all-steel SUB vehicles to be constructed. All had previously been formed in 1925-built 4 SUB units numbered from 4300 which were being withdrawn at this time. HO 4617 (dated 19th May 1959) covered the conversion of DS 70050-DS 70051 and HO 4796 (17th June 1960) of DS 70086-DS 70087. The previous identity of each of the vehicles is shown in the following table:

De-icing Trailer	Former Number	Originally in 4 SUB
DS 70050	10392	4345
DS 70051	10399	4351
DS 70086	10397	4304
DS 70087	10400	4349

External modifications included the sealing of all but six doors, only those at the ends and at the centre remaining, although all windows were left intact. To avoid fouling the loading gauge, the side panels at each end were replaced by flat steel plates, slightly inset, on which were located the downward-facing periscopes. Both bogies were fitted with shoebeams, attached to which were nozzles connected to pipes leading from the de-icing fluid tank inside via axle driven pumps. As on the motor units and previous de-icing trailers, the periscopes enabled the operator to identify the position of the third rail and turn on or off the de-icing fluid accordingly, and when in operation the fluid tank was live. To make them compatible with EPB stock, the vehicles were rewired and given waist-level brake and control jumper cables at the ends, 27-wire control cables routed along the roof, and buckeye couplers with Pullman rubbing plates. Tare weight following conversion was 32 tons. The original livery was 'departmental red' with light yellow lettering and black ends, with the legend EE DEICING VAN centrally on each side.

These de-icing coaches were generally operated sandwiched between pairs of EPB or 2 HAP units, but not in passenger trains. They all received overall blue livery in about 1969, and were also given full-length gutters in line with the tops of the door openings, probably at the same time. In about 1970 they were renumbered ADS 70050-ADS 70051 and ADS 70086-ADS 70087. ADS 70086 was withdrawn in 1981 and the remaining three were later renumbered ADB 977362-ADB 977364 respectively, when they were given (as were all SR de-icing vehicles then in service) the class number 930. ADB 977363 was taken out of service and scrapped in 1991 and ADB 977362 two years later, both in blue to the end. ADB 977364 remained in use, based at Ramsgate. Successive repaints saw it appear firstly in Network SouthEast livery and then, in 1997, in the brown, grey and white colours of Railtrack, its new owners following railway privatisation. For the 1998-99 winter season ADB 977364 was transferred to Selhurst and operated in the London area between a pair of departmental 'Hampshire' diesel electric motor coaches as unit 930 301. This formation was still in use until 2005 and until early in 2010 it remained extant, stored at St Leonards, the former de-icing trailer then being towed away for private preservation.

Three further powered de-icing units were provided in 1968-69, particularly for service on the Bournemouth line, on which electrification had been completed in 1967. The raw material for these units were six withdrawn 1939 2 HAL-type motor brake seconds, although only one had actually come directly from a HAL as most were still in passenger service at this time. Four came from the pair of 1940-built 4 LAV units 2954/55, and one from 1932 4 LAV 2926, where it had replaced an original motor coach following the 1947 South Croydon accident. The new de-icing units were numbered 001-003, and the origin of each individual vehicle is as shown in the table.

De-icing Unit No.	Departmental Coach No.	Original Coach No.	ex Unit
001	DS 70268(No.1 vehicle)	10726	2 HAL 2608
	DS 70273(No.2 vehicle)	10500	4 LAV 2955
002	DS 70269(No.1 vehicle)	10764	4 LAV 2926
	DS 70271(No.2 vehicle)	10498	4 LAV 2954
003	DS 70270(No.1 vehicle)	10497	4 LAV 2954
	DS 70272(No.2 vehicle)	10499	4 LAV 2955

The conversion work was carried out at Stewarts Lane, DS 70269 being outshopped first as a prototype in July 1968 with the rest following. DS 70268 ran coupled to green 2 EPB MBS 65364 (from 5750) as unit 001 for the winter of 1968-69 prior to DS 72073 being ready. This was possible as all the de-icing equipment was concentrated in the No.1 coach of each unit.

As it was intended that the new units should be able to multiple with EP-braked stock, the alterations required were considerably more complex than for 92-101. Having simple and sturdy construction with flush body sides, steel cabs and no large windows, the HAL-type motor coaches proved particularly suitable for this type of conversion. Certain items of control equipment were recovered from E5000 HA class electric locomotives which had been converted to electro-diesels, and EE 507D motors replaced the original 339 type. The cab ends were provided with EPB-type jumper cable connections and roller-blind headcode panels, while the inner ends were fitted with gangways. Screw couplings were retained. Most windows and doors were blanked off, those remaining differing on the two vehicles in each unit. Livery was overall blue with full yellow ends. Following conversion, No.1 end vehicles weighed 47 tons, but No.2 end, being virtually empty inside, were originally slightly lighter.

From the driving end, internal layout of the No.1 vehicle started with a cab, followed by separate compartments for the batteries and motor-generator in place of the original van space. These items were necessary for the new control system but there was no room for them on the underframe. The motor-generator was ventilated by prominent grilles on the body sides. A large compartment housed the de-icing fluid tank, still live when spraying was in operation. The rest of the vehicle comprised an operator's compartment with table and cooking facilities, while a small toilet cubicle was installed at the front of the tank compartment. Such home comforts were needed as these units were often out for long periods at

night. There was a small entrance vestibule at the inner end of the coach. The interior of the No.2 vehicle was originally left bare, with a van area partitioned off behind the motorman, enabling these units to substitute if required for a stores unit (see below) to transfer parts between depots.

The system for spreading de-icing fluid was somewhat more sophisticated than in previous conversions, leaving less for the operator to do. The trailer bogie of the No. 1 coach was adapted to spread the fluid, with application nozzles and spreading-shoes attached to a shoebeam; these shoes also automatically detected the position of the conductor rail. The fluid was pumped from the tanks through axle-driven pumps driven via gearing and a dog-clutch which automatically engaged or disengaged depending on the position of the conductor rail as detected by the laying shoes. Additional pick-up shoes were originally mounted on the trailer bogie of the No.2 coach to assist current collection in icy conditions.

Problems with autumn 'leaf fall', in which fallen leaves formed a slimy coating on running-rail surfaces leading to slipping and wheel-flats, became increasingly severe from the early 1970s due to unchecked growth of lineside vegetation, the inheritence of economy drives instituted during the previous decade. To deal with this, in 1970 unit 002 was experimentally fitted with plasma torches on the No.2 vehicle, which played a very hot flame on to the rail surface to burn-off the leaf mulch. As an alternative solution 003 was fitted with water cannon equipment in 1972, again installed in the No.2 vehicle. In this system, pairs of fine nozzles squirted high-pressure water from an 1,800-gallon tank on to the running rails, hopefully dislodging the mulch which was then swept away by fixed wire brushes. As this took place at 10mph it was necessary to haul the unit with a class 73 electro-diesel, as continuous slow-speed running could otherwise have burnt out its resistances. Following successful testing between Shepherdswell and Dover this equipment was also fitted to 001 and 002 in 1973, a year in which sixty units had been taken out of service because of wheel flats caused by leaf slippage.

Unit 002 was written off after it had struck a bridge at Tonbridge in 1978, which resulted in serious damage to one cab. After storage in Tennison Road sidings, Norwood, for two years, it was cut up there in May 1980. A 'new' 002 was then converted from SUB vehicles to replace it (see next page), but 003 swapped identities with it to become 002. Following this, the two remaining HAL-type de-icing units were numbered 001 and 002, with 002 being the former 003.

In 1981 the water cannon equipment was removed from the remaining pair and both were then refitted to spread Sandite, a mixture of fine sand and adhesive, on to the running rails in a further attempt to improve adhesion in autumnal conditions. The sand and adhesive were stored in separate areas and immediately prior to spreading were mixed in a hopper, located at the inner end of the coach. Axle-driven pumps, located internally in a separate compartment, were used to spread the mixture. As water-cannon and then Sandite spreading units, the pair worked over both electrified and non-electrified SR lines, in the latter case hauled by class 33 locomotives.

Appearing rather the worse for wear, 1968 de-icing unit 002 (formerly motor coaches 10764 from 4 LAV 2926 and 10498 from 4 LAV 2954, and later renumbered from 003 in 1981), stands at East Grinstead on 23rd October 1985 whilst on Sandite spreading duties. The unit is being hauled over this (then) non-electrified route by class 33/0 locomotive 33 015, and hence its pick-up shoebeams have temporarily been removed.
Alex Dasi-Sutton

In 1986, 001 and 002 were thoroughly overhauled and given new cab end panelling incorporating smaller EPB-type cab windows equipped with demisters. At the same time they were given a pair of small headlamps under each headcode panel. Both were taken out of service in 1989, as much as anything due to the poor condition of their bodywork, and stored at Eastleigh until being towed away for scrapping by Gwent Demolition at Margam in 1993.

By the late 1970s the 1959/60 de-icing units were due for retirement, and the decision was taken to replace them with ten 'new' two-car units converted from the motor coaches of all-steel 4 SUB units, then being withdrawn in some numbers. Following the accident to the original 002, a further unit of the same type was subsequently converted to replace this. The conversion work was carried out in the repair shop at Selhurst depot over a period of six years. The first to be converted, numbered 004, appeared in 1977 and further units followed this in sequence up to 007. The 'new' 002 was then converted in 1979, followed by 008-013 in sequence, with 013 finally emerging from works in 1982. 002 later swapped numbers with 1967 unit 003, so that the 4 SUB converted units were numbered consecutively from 003. The table (right) gives the numbers of the individual vehicles within each unit, together with their origins.

Unit	No.1 Vehicle	No.2 Vehicle
003	ADB 975594 (ex 12658 of 4604)	ADB 975595 (ex 10994 of 4127)
004	ADB 975586 (ex 10907 of 4361)	ADB 975587 (ex 10908 of 4361)
005	ADB 975588 (ex 10981 of 4121)	ADB 975589 (ex 10982 of 4121)
006	ADB 975590 (ex 10833 of 4380)	ADB 975591 (ex 10834 of 4380)
007	ADB 975592 (ex 10993 of 4127)	ADB 975593 (ex 12659 of 4604)
008	ADB 975596 (ex 10844 of 4385)	ADB 975597 (ex 10987 of 4124)
009	ADB 975598 (ex 10989 of 4125)	ADB 975599 (ex 10990 of 4125)
010	ADB 975600 (ex 10988 of 4124)	ADB 975601 (ex 10843 of 4385)
011	ADB 975602 (ex 10991 of 4126)	ADB 975603 (ex 10992 of 4126)
012	ADB 975604 (ex 10939 of 4377)	ADB 975605 (ex 10940 of 4377)
013	ADB 975896 (ex 11387 of 4664)	ADB 975897 (ex 11388 of 4664)

With the exceptions noted, all the vehicles selected for conversion were of 'semi-saloon' type from the 4121-4130 batch of 4 SUBs, originally constructed in 1946. All had originally been built on new underframes, and were from units withdrawn during the cull of non-standard SUB units in April 1976. They had been stored at Micheldever until towed to Selhurst for conversion.

The modifications to the SUB motor coaches were extensive, and resulted in a complete change in appearance. Electrical and control equipment was altered to conform with that of 1963 EP-braked stock (4 CIG etc), involving the installation of electro-pneumatic brakes, camshaft control gear, new cab controls, 27-wire control cables, and appropriate waist-level control and brake jumper cables at cab ends. As in the 1968 HAL conversions, screw couplings at unit ends were retained and the motor-generator was mounted in the former guard's van of the No.1 vehicle, ventilated by body side louvres, there being insufficient space on the underframe. As all the vehicles concerned originally had EE 339 traction motors, these were changed for reconditioned examples of the standard 507 type. Externally, the cab ends were extensively altered, with the original structure being cut away as far as the van doors and entirely new framing and front panels being fitted. These incorporated EPB-type cab windows with built-in demisters and a standard roller-blind headcode panel, aligned with the bottom of the cab windows. The windows were marginally inboard in comparison to those on Bulleid EPB stock, giving these units a slightly 'cross-eyed' look. Together with the shallower headcode panel, horizontal corner grab-rails and the lack of a buckeye coupling, this made the two types easily distinguishable. Cab doors were replaced by plain panelling and CIG style sliding windows, while most of the body side doors were also panelled over with steel sheet. Livery was rail blue with yellow ends, lettered DE-ICING UNIT centrally in white at waist-level. Internally, new laminate interior panelling and moulded, glass reinforced plastic window frames were fitted. Gangways were fitted to the inner end to permit communication between vehicles in each unit.

Although similar in external appearance, the two vehicles of each unit were fitted out differently. The basic layout was similar to the 1968 units, with the No.1 coach containing the tanks which held the de-icing fluid. For the first time these were insulated with a polythene lining, thereby preventing them being live when spraying was taking place, an undesirable feature of previous de-icing vehicles. The pumps used were axle-driven and operated automatically in the same manner as the earlier units. In most units, the No.2 coach was originally left empty, but extra pick-up shoes were fitted to the unpowered bogie to maximise electrical contact in icy conditions, together with extra conductor-rail scrapers. High-pressure water cannon equipment, identical to that in 001 and 002, was fitted to this vehicle in units 003-005 from new.

005 was experimentally equipped for spreading Sandite in 1980, and subsequently 003, 004 and 006 were adapted in 1981. The rest of these units were subsequently converted, all in a similar manner to 001 and 002. The fleet was classified

930 in 1985 and some units carried the full 9300xx number following overhaul. A few carried unit numbers repeated above each cab window rather than centrally above the headcode. Pairs of marker lights, originally rectangular car accessory fog lamps, were fitted underneath the headcode panel for the autumn 1985 season; these were replaced by permanent sealed beam headlights the following year. With railway privatisation in 1994 ownership of former SR departmental vehicles passed to Railtrack and in the summer of 1996 a programme of refurbishment was commenced at Ashford (Chart Leacon), with 930011 being first to be dealt with. Externally, much of the panelling was replaced, resulting in the disappearance of most side windows. Internally, surfaces were repanelled and strip-lighting installed, while the Sandite gel tanks were repositioned and the delivery pump system renewed. Liveries carried by these units since the mid 1980s reflected the changes in management structure and ownership on the railway, with the once ubiquitous rail blue giving way firstly to red, white and blue Network SouthEast colours and then to the orange, white and grey scheme first adopted by Railtrack. By 2000, they carried a more striking Network Rail livery of dark blue and lime green.

At this period these units, together with slightly more modern cousins converted from EPB stock, continued to be used in autumn for Sandite spreading duties, working to strict diagrams from early October until mid-November. From then on they were used to spread de-icing fluid until early spring, also working to a regular timetable but mostly at night. Divided between EMU depots at Brighton, Fratton, Gillingham, Ramsgate, Selhurst and Wimbledon, the entire fleet remained in service until the start of 2002, although some minor reformations and renumberings had by then been carried out. All were withdrawn between then and 2004, being replaced by newly-built diesel-powered Multi Purpose Vehicles (MPVs), equipped with interchangeable modules for Sandite-spreading and de-icing duties. Although most were scrapped, 930010 survived into preservation and remains extant in 2010.

Above right 004, the first de-icing unit converted from post-war steel SUB motor coaches, stands at Wimbledon Park depot on 7th September 1977, shortly after conversion. Formerly motor brake seconds 10907 and 10908 from unit 4361, this unit differed from later conversions in having prominent horizontal ribbing across the cab front where new panelling has been added. *John Scrace*

Right Ex-2 HAL stores unit 023, in later BR (SR) service stock olive green livery, passes Coulsdon North on 16th July 1983 en route to Lovers Walk depot (Brighton). The large inset sliding doors, clearly visible in this view, were only on one side of the unit. *Alex Dasi-Sutton*

Ex-4 SUB stores unit 024 stands outside Eastleigh Works on 11th May 1973, shortly after conversion, in its original rail blue livery. Unlike the earlier HAL conversions, on this unit the two large inset sliding doors were repeated on both sides of each vehicle. *John Scrace*

STORES UNITS

Until 1970, spare parts and stores were transported between the various rolling stock depots in locomotive hauled vans or trucks. In that year the SR Mechanical and Electrical Engineering Department acquired a pair of two-coach electric units specifically for this purpose, converted from redundant 2 HAL motor coaches at Eastleigh. These units worked weekly diagrams which took them to all the main depots, where special stores sidings were provided for loading and unloading.

Unit 022 was formed from motor coaches 10731 and 10787 from withdrawn HALs 2613 and 2669 respectively, emerging from works following conversion in April 1970. Both vehicles were similar, being virtual mirror images of each other, and modifications were not extensive when compared to the de-icing units with the same origins. Original 1936-type control gear to enable multiple working with SUB stock was retained, as were EE 339 traction motors, but additional waist-level air-brake pipes were fitted to the cab ends to allow haulage (but not multiple working) by EP-braked stock. Roller-blind headcode panels replaced the original stencil equipment. The cabs were otherwise unaltered, but on one side only the van doors were replaced by a large recessed horizontally-sliding door of plain steel sheet, both on the same side of the unit. The original compartment doors were sealed but not panelled over. Internally, the partitions were stripped out and replaced by stowage racks, labelled with the names of the depots the unit was to visit. Livery was standard blue with yellow ends, and the lettering SERVICE UNIT originally appeared centrally on each side. Departmental coach numbers DS 70315 and DS 70316 were allocated. Unit 023, converted the following month using 10742 and 10760 (becoming DS 70317/18) from 2624 and 2642 respectively, was almost identical, but lacked the additional waist-level brake pipes.

A third stores unit, numbered 024, was formed early in 1973, this time utilising motor coaches 10829 and 10830 from all-steel 4 SUB unit 4378 which had just been withdrawn.

The modifications carried out were similar to those for the earlier units, the vehicles retaining 1936 control gear and their original motors, in this case EE 507Cs. The cabs and van areas were unaltered, but the remainder of the interiors were gutted and the original door apertures sealed with plain steel sheet. Two large recessed horizontally sliding doors were set into both sides of each vehicle, and internal racks provided labelled similarly. As on 022, additional air brake pipes were provided at waist level, and the original headcode panel was replaced by a roller-blind unit. New departmental coach numbers were ADB 975250 and ADB 975251 respectively. 024 was originally outshopped in rail blue with yellow ends, and lettered CM & EE DEPARTMENTAL SERVICE UNIT midway along each side. A summary of stores units converted from HAL and SUB units is as follows:

Unit	Departmental No.	Original No.	ex unit	Conversion date
022	DS 70315	10731	2 HAL 2613	4/70
	DS 70316	10787	2 HAL 2669	4/70
023	DS 70317	10742	2 HAL 2624	5/70
	DS 70318	10760	2 HAL 2642	5/70
024	ADB 975250	10829	4 SUB 4378	1973
	ADB 975251	10830	4 SUB 4378	1973

Early in 1982, 023 and 024 were repainted in the new service stock livery of olive green, but 022 remained in blue until withdrawn late in 1983. Following condemnation, 022 was hauled to Andover where it remained parked inside the former goods shed for well over a year before being removed for scrapping by Bird's at Long Marston at the end of 1985. 023 survived in service until February 1984, but it too remained on the SR for a long period, this time dumped at Norwood, until cut up by Booth's at Rotherham in May 1986. 024 survived in use as the last stores unit with 1936 control equipment until December 1984. Further stores units were converted from EPB and HAP stock to replace 022-024, but these are outside the terms of reference of this volume.

INSTRUCTION UNITS

With the significant amount of new equipment being introduced on the SR during the mid 1950s, and particularly with the forthcoming Kent Coast electrification scheme in mind, it was decided to produce a self-propelled instruction unit, to act as a 'mobile classroom' containing teaching facilities and demonstration equipment. The new unit would be used to tour the various depots and provide staff training facilities where none would otherwise exist.

The first instruction unit was numbered S10, and was converted from the three original vehicles of suburban unit 4579. Prior to augmentation with a new 'six-a-side' steel trailer, this unit had been 1782, with bodywork of LSWR origin mounted on lengthened underframes recovered from LBSCR ac electric trailers. It was therefore suitable for departmental use as these frames were not included in the EPB building programme. Upon withdrawal in August 1953, its motor coaches were initially placed into store but trailer 9658 was reformed into unit 4520 until October 1954. Conversion of the three vehicles, which took place at Selhurst, was authorised by HO 4140 dated 30th September 1954. The work evidently took some time, as S10 did not come into use until April 1956.

Externally all vehicles remained virtually unaltered, and the original type 339 motors and electro-magnetic control system were retained. Internally, most of the partitions were stripped out and various items of demonstration equipment mounted. Motor brake vehicle DS 40 (ex 8564) contained the existing motorman's compartment, demonstration power collection, heating and lighting equipment, and a motor-generator/battery set (located above the floor behind the cab on the offside) to allow operation of various items of instructional equipment away from the traction supply. Trailer DS 41 (9658) was fitted out with power control equipment of all three types then in use, while motor coach DS 42 (9817) had a small guard's cubicle with two periscopes at the inner end, followed by instructional brake gear, a lecture and projection room, and motorman's compartment. Gangways were fitted

between vehicles. Original livery was overall malachite green, with the gold lettering C.M.&E.E.'S INSTRUCTION CAR midway along each vehicle at waist height.

S10 was painted blue in about August 1969 with the lettering INSTRUCTION UNIT in white centrally on each coach. It was renumbered 053 in 1971. Rarely seen actually moving, it spent most of its days parked in depot sidings in use for its intended purpose. It was eventually withdrawn in May 1974, mainly due to the poor condition of its underframes, by which time it had long been the only SR unit remaining with pre-Grouping wooden bodywork. This historical significance was evidently ignored and, after being dumped at Selhurst for some time, 053 was quietly broken up and burnt at Ashford in May 1976, although much internal equipment was salvaged.

A new instruction unit, this time with four vehicles, was converted at Selhurst in the first months of 1974 from withdrawn all-steel 4 SUB 4367. It was numbered 055, individual coach numbers being ADB 975319-22. Again, all vehicles were stripped internally, but there were few electrical or mechanical alterations. EE 507C traction motors replaced 339s, but 1936 electro-pneumatic control equipment was retained. However multiple working with similar stock was no longer possible as virtually all the jumper connections and sockets were removed from the cab ends, giving the unit an unusually bare appearance. Only the power jumper receptacle remained, to allow lighting and heating to be powered from a 660V depot shore-line when parked inside a shed. As with other departmental SUB conversions, 055 was equipped with roller blind headcode panels, through gangways were provided between intermediate vehicles, and most doors were sealed shut. Livery was rail blue with yellow ends, and the lettering 'Instruction Unit' appeared midway along each side. Much of the internal furniture and demonstration equipment was recovered from 053 (S10), and included lecture rooms with tiered seating and blackboards in each motor coach, and demonstration control, brake and signalling equipment in the two trailers.

With the withdrawal of the 4 SUB fleet and wholesale resignalling, much of the demonstration equipment in 055 was obsolete by the mid 1980s, and it was officially taken out of service in November 1985. After spending some time dumped in New Cross Gate sidings, it was scrapped by Booth's at Rotherham in August 1987.

The origins and formations of the instruction units are summarised in the table on the right.

Unit	Departmental Coach No.	Converted from	ex SUB unit
S10 (053)	DS 40	MBS 8564	4579 (1782)
	DS 41	TS 9658	4579 (1782)
	DS 42	MBS 9817	4579 (1782)
055	ADB 975319	MBS 10919	4367
	ADB 975320	TS 10171	4367
	ADB 975321	TC 11470	4367
	ADB 975322	MBS 10920	4367

Replacement instruction unit 055, modified from all-steel 4 SUB 4367, stands in New Cross Gate sidings on 29th September 1984, by which time it was effectively out of use. Note that all jumper cables have been removed from the cab front, giving an unusually 'bare' appearance for an SR electric unit. The remaining socket could be used to power the heating, lighting and demonstration equipment on the unit from a 660V shore line when the unit was parked away from a conductor rail.
Alex Dasi-Sutton

TOWING UNITS

Other than those used for de-icing units 90-101 and instruction unit S10, the motor coaches of a number of other pre-war SUBs were retained for a short period following withdrawal. Coupled in pairs, they were mainly used to tow withdrawn wooden-bodied SUB and NOL vehicles from Durnsford Road, where re-usable electrical equipment was removed, to Strawberry Hill, where shoebeams and jumper cables were taken off prior to onward dispatch to Newhaven for scrapping. Motor coaches used for this purpose were officially allocated to Durnsford Road for maintenance. A few also saw use as depot shunters 'for internal use only'. Internal User vehicles were officially not to work outside the depot limits but in practice sometimes did so. Modifications generally consisted solely of replacing the rubbing block of one vehicle with a centre buffer to enable them to be coupled back to back.

The following descriptions are in chronological order of withdrawal from capital stock. Unless otherwise mentioned the vehicles concerned had bodywork of LBSCR origin on lengthened ac underframes. The unit number in brackets after the 4 SUB unit number refers to the original three-coach unit from which the motor coaches originated. Vehicles which were not given numbers in the Internal User series did not officially exist; they were withdrawn from capital stock and written off, but were used by the depot engineers for their own purposes until they were finally beyond repair.

4402 (1775) was the first of Durnsford Road depot's towing units. Its motor brakes 8557 and 9810 were withdrawn from passenger service and used for depot towing from February to June 1953, when they were stripped and taken to Newhaven on 8th June 1953 for their bodies to be cut up. The underframe of 8557 was used for EPB motor brake 14263, and that of 9810 for 14264.

4252 (1761) was withdrawn from passenger service in March 1953 and its motor coaches 8738 and 8896 became a Durnsford Road – Strawberry Hill towing unit from May 1953 until September 1956. They were then taken to Hassocks on 4th October 1956 but their final cut-up date (at Newhaven) is not recorded.

4202 (1209) was withdrawn in March 1954 and its LSWR 'bullet nosed' motor coaches 8013/14 were used as the Peckham Rye depot shunter between March 1954 and January 1955, after which the pair became a Durnsford Road – Strawberry Hill towing unit until July 1956. Also dumped at Hassocks in September 1956, they were subsequently scrapped at Newhaven, their underframes being used for new EPB vehicles: 8013 for trailer 15440 (one of five converted from motor coach underframes) and 8014 for motor brake 14503.

4559 (1767) was withdrawn in October 1954 but it was not until March 1955 that motor coaches 8744 and 9802 entered departmental service as a Durnsford Road – Strawberry Hill towing unit. They were used until September 1955 and again in 1957 (their whereabouts in 1956 are not recorded), and were then broken up at Newhaven some time in 1957.

4564 (1769) was withdrawn in February 1956 and its motor coaches 8746 and 9804 were then used as a Durnsford Road – Strawberry Hill towing unit from about July 1956 until October 1958, following which they were scrapped at Newhaven on 9th November 1958.

4543 (1746) was withdrawn on Saturday 15th September 1956, and its motor coaches employed from the following Tuesday as a Durnsford Road – Strawberry Hill towing unit. 8715 and 8881 were renumbered 081046/47 respectively in the Internal User series. They were taken out of service following a collision at Durnsford Road in May 1959. Both were broken up at Newhaven on 18th May 1959.

4557 (1764) was withdrawn in October 1956 and motor coaches 8741 and 8899 were used temporarily as a Durnsford Road – Strawberry Hill towing unit until about April 1957. They were then sent to Battersea shops for rebuilding in April 1957 as de-icing unit S90 and their subsequent history is detailed above.

The second 4505 (formed with vehicles previously in 4547, 4556 and 4559) was one of those 4 SUBs formed up entirely from LBSCR-bodied and ac-framed coaches in 1956-57. When 4556 was taken out of service in 1956, its motor brakes and LBSCR trailer were taken to Hassocks on 9th August, but almost immediately were returned to Selhurst for a quick varnish and, with a second LBSCR trailer (9461 from 4547), it returned to passenger duties on (mainly) Western section suburban services as the 'second' 4505 (one of the 4501-4518 series that covered for the withdrawn 'Windsor' NOLs) until May 1959. It then went to Newhaven (possibly in error) with 081046/47 of 4543 on 18th May 1959. It was returned to Durnsford Road and, from June 1959, was used to transfer the final batch of 'Coastal' 2 NOL withdrawals that had started in February 1958, and was itself then sent to Newhaven in about May 1960.

The motor coaches of 1925 long-framed SUB 4342 (1515), 8449/50, became a towing unit at Durnsford Road from 17th June 1960 following withdrawal from capital stock. They arrived at Strawberry Hill on 28 June 1960, but for some reason were not driven back to Durnsford Road. They were then taken to Newhaven on about 13th July 1960, probably in error, but were returned to Durnsford Road for further towing duties. Once back at Wimbledon, vehicles 8449 and 8450 were given internal user numbers 081269/70 respectively. Following the end of the last pre-war SUB stock in 1962 they became internal user vehicles there. Unit 4342 was the longest-lived of all the Towing Units, remaining at Durnsford Road where it was used as a shunting unit until withdrawal in December 1969. It was out of use for a further year until scrapping took place in December 1970. It is possible that 4342 owed its long life to retention for possible rebuilding as a de-icing unit, but this was never carried out.

A summary of towing and shunting units converted from pre-1939 suburban motor coaches is shown in the table. The final column shows the dates that particular units were in use for towing withdrawn coaches between Durnsford Road and Strawberry Hill.

Unit	Coach Numbers	Internal User Numbers	In Use as Towing Unit
4202	8013+8014		3/54–7/56
4252	8738+8896		5/53–9/56
4302	8131+8132		2/61–11/61
4342	8449+8450	081269+081070	6/60–2/62
4402	8557+9610		2/53–6/53
4505	8736+8894		6/59–5/60
4543	8715+8881	081046+081047	9/56–5/59
4557	8741+8899		10/56–4/57
4559	8744+9802		3/55–9/55, then 1/57–10/57
4564	8746+9804		c.7/56–10/58

Twenty years later, one pair of motor coaches from a post war all-steel 4 SUB, 11305 and 11306 from 4623, were retained for shunting within the confines of Strawberry Hill depot following their withdrawal in 1982. By this time the depot was used for 'Rolling Stock Development' purposes such as the testing and commissioning of new stock, but it seems that the SUB vehicles saw little use. They were finally scrapped in 1985, at Horwich Works, probably to enable interior fittings to be re-used in the EPB facelifting programme taking place there.

TEST UNITS

A two-coach 'Mobile Test Unit' was made up from withdrawn long-frame 1925 SUB motor coaches 8420 and 8473 (from units 4327 and 4354 respectively) in 1961, to HO 4852 of 30th September 1960. Numbered S15, departmental coach numbers were DS 70057 (8420) and DS 70058 (8473), and early BR malachite green livery was retained. The actual usage to which this unit was put is not known, but it was withdrawn in 1967 and, after being dumped in Coulsdon North sidings and then Micheldever for a number of years, was finally cut-up by Cashmore's at Newport in January 1971. As described in Chapter 5 an order for a further test unit, using 6 PAN motor coaches 11057/58 from 3031 with Pullman composites *Ruth* and *Bertha*, was subsequently cancelled at the end of 1969. The motor coaches were eventually scrapped by King's at Wymondham in March 1972, but both Pullmans survived into preservation.

Three further units retained for test purposes following withdrawal, already mentioned elsewhere, are summarised here for completeness. 2 BIL 2037 was sent to the BR Research Centre at Derby following withdrawal in March 1970, and became test unit 024, with vehicle numbers DS 70321 (motor coach) and DS 70322 (trailer). Following storage since withdrawal in September 1970, former Portsmouth express 4 GRI 3087 became departmental unit 054 in October 1972 but remained on the SR, being based at Eastleigh. New vehicle numbers were ADB 975255 (motor coach), ADB 975257 (trailer), ADB 975258 (trailer, former griddle) and ADB 975259 (motor). The use to which either was put is not known, and both were cut up at their base depots in 1975. Finally, 4 SUB 4748 was fitted with experimental thyristor control equipment at Strawberry Hill following withdrawal in April 1976. It was used for tests before being scrapped later the same year.

OTHER DEPARTMENTAL VEHICLES

Apart from de-icing vehicles 351S-356S and 396S-399S, three other former LBSCR 54ft thirds from trailer sets were retained for departmental purposes following withdrawal. Vehicles 8951/52 from set 1026 became 434S and 435S in January 1947, but their intended purpose and subsequent history is unknown. 590S was reported as converted in September 1947 from 8961 out of set 1031 for the CME Department, and was utilised as a stores van at Lancing Works.

CHAPTER 7:
SOUTHERN ELECTRIC STOCK 1951-83

Prototype 4 EPB S 5001 departs from Waterloo on a demonstration run to Guildford via Cobham, conveying dignitaries from the Ministry of Transport, British Transport Commission and Railway Executive, on 14th January 1951. The roller-blind headcode panel is displaying two white blanks rather than the correct '42' headcode. This view illustrates the original cab-end arrangement, with a power jumper under the nearside windscreen. *Denis Cullum*

This chapter outlines Southern Region electric rolling stock designed and built in the period from the end of 4 SUB production in December 1951 until the last unit of the same class was withdrawn from revenue service in September 1983. The SUBs were the final production EMUs to be designed in the Southern Railway period and, as the terms of reference of this book are to cover in detail just the pre-nationalisation SR electrification schemes and their subsequent history up to 1983, only briefer details of the entirely post-1948 stock are included here. In all instances such stock displaced Southern Railway designed units on routes already electrified in the 1914-39 period or was built

for the post war schemes covering the Kent Coast and Bournemouth lines which were effectively extensions of, or branches off, routes previously converted. Also included are the second-hand tube railway cars purchased from London Transport to provide rolling stock for the 1967 Isle of Wight electrification. Main line locomotive classes introduced during this period are also described: as well as the one straight electric and two electro-diesel types, it has been decided to include the BRCW type 3 diesel electric locomotives, as these were an integral component of the 1959-62 Kent Coast and 1967 Bournemouth electrification and modernisation schemes.

Prior to 1952, SR electric multiple unit classes could be divided by important technical differences into suburban/semi-fast and express types. As explained earlier, the express stock had different motors, control equipment, lighting and jumper-cable arrangements which made it incompatible with other stock, causing inflexibility in operation. This was one of the main reasons why a clean break with previous practice was made in 1951 with the introduction of the EPB system, from which time all new electric units built were equipped with a newly-designed control and braking system common to all types. With the exception of a few miscellaneous vehicles noted in Chapter 4 and the PEP prototypes, all new SR electric stock built between the end of 1951 and 1974 utilised this system. Other benefits of the revised system included much improved brake performance with graduable application and release, and a 27-core control cable providing sufficient spare wires to allow for future developments.

The new braking and control arrangements involved adoption of the self-lapping electro-pneumatic brake in addition to the Westinghouse air brake, a control system in which contacts were actuated by low-voltage from a motor-generator and battery set, and a new arrangement of jumper and brake cables all located at waist height. A further development was the use of automatic Pullman-type buckeye couplings, with their associated sprung rubbing-plates above, to couple units together. These features enabled units to be divided and combined entirely from platform level for the first time. The first units fitted with this equipment were termed 1951 stock. There were later developments to form 1957, 1963 and 1966 stocks, but all units fitted with it could work together in multiple subject to certain restrictions, mainly relating to gear-ratios and current draw. Its versatility even eventually extended to enabling certain SR-based diesel and electric locomotives to work in multiple with EMUs. Classes equipped with this system could not work in multiple with earlier stock and usually (but not always) had the letters EP or P included in their three-letter class codes (eg 4 EPB, 4 CEP, 2 HAP). All units of 1951/57/63 stock were fitted with versions of the English Electric type 507 traction motor, first introduced on 4 SUB 4130 in 1947 and in 1949 adopted as standard by the SR. It was generally rated at a nominal 250hp, at a ratio of one motor per coach.

A brief survey of basic electrical arrangements in the 1951/57/63 stock fleets is worth including at this point. 1951 stock had conventional electro-pneumatic control gear, but a further improvement over earlier stock was the addition of a weak-field controller setting after the 'full parallel' position, suitable for prolonged high-speed running. In 1957 stock the system was modernised so that the contacts were operated by a camshaft activated by oil pressure, and miniature circuit breakers replaced some fuses. Following trials on some 4 EPB units, four-coach units of 1957 stock, which included the 53xx EPBs and the production Kent Coast CEP/BEP fleet, had a motor-generator mounted underneath one motor coach only and a battery set under the other, so the two had to be distinguished as 'No.1 end' and 'No.2 end' vehicles. On earlier four-car units, the second motor-generator set was removed and the resulting spare stock of sets was used to replace life-expired equipment on the 4 COR units. After these were withdrawn, the sets, with traditional Southern economy, were fitted to 2 HAP units. 1957 stock was divided into phase I and phase II types, but electrically there were only minor differences. Other than the adoption of a single central non-driving motor coach with four motors connected in parallel pairs, electrical equipment in the 1963 stock was generally similar, but its design was updated with, for example, diodes replacing various relays. (The 1966 stock was specifically designed for the Bournemouth electrification, and its non-standard electrical arrangements are described later.)

Whether suburban or main line, all SR 'slam-door' electric stock built between the end of 1951 and 1974 had welded steel bodywork assembled on a jig and a separate underframe, a method of construction originated by Bulleid and Lynes in 1946. The BR standard stock, although based on Mark 1 design parameters with different styling and dimensions from the SR-design units, used broadly similar constructional methods. Bodywork of BR standard 1951 and 1957 stocks, constructed at Eastleigh on (mostly) Ashford underframes between 1954 and 1963, went through various detail design changes. As far as non-gangwayed EPB suburban and HAP semi-fast stock were concerned, 1951 stock units could be identified by quarterlights inserted from the inside and without raised external frames, a headcode panel of the same depth as the cab windscreens, and external wiring conduits along the roof. 1957 stock was divided into phase I, which had similar bodywork but without external roof conduits, and phase II, which additionally had thick external window frames and beading around the door openings. Later units built to phase II standards in 1962-63 had revised cab ends with a shallow headcode panel and tapered windscreens. With the express 4 CEP and 4 BEP units, all apart from the six 1951 stock prototypes had bodywork with raised window surrounds, but only the final few units, outshopped in 1963, had later phase II style cab ends with tapered windscreens. Other permutations and differences are mentioned in the body of the text. It is convenient to mention here that units built up to 1961 were originally equipped with whistles mounted adjacent to the motorman's windscreen, but these were gradually replaced by roof-mounted air horns from 1963.

Until 1963, all new SR suburban stock followed the time-honoured arrangement of a single door to each seating-bay or compartment, a layout dating from the earliest days of railways. A clean break with this design was made when the prototype PEP suburban units, with power-operated sliding doors, were delivered in 1972. The PEPs had other advanced features, and could not be worked in multiple with 1951/57/63/66 EP-braked stock. The first production batch of 'new generation' suburban units on the SR, the 43 class 508 units delivered in 1979-80, was somewhat simplified in comparison with the PEP prototypes, but experience quickly showed them to be unsuitable for regional operating conditions. As a result a further new design, class 455, began to be delivered to the SR late in 1982. These reverted to include some features found in 1963 stock, but still could not be coupled to EP-braked units. Delivery of class 455 units continued through 1983 and they ousted not only the last of the 4 SUBs, but also the 508s, three cars of each unit of which were gradually transferred to the Liverpool area third-rail lines.

Regarding liveries, units outshopped prior to March 1957 carried the early Southern Region malachite green (apart from the odd exceptions mentioned below) with the 'lion on wheel' emblem centrally on motor coach sides. Lettering and numbering was in old gold, edged black. Coach numbers were generally just under waist height near the right-hand end of each vehicle, and were prefixed S. On vehicles of basically Southern Railway design on reclaimed 62ft underframes (in 4 EPBs 5001-5053 and 5101-5260, 2 HAPs 5601-5636 and 2 EPBs 5651-5684, plus a few other miscellaneous vehicles) they were also suffixed S. Unit numbers were carried above the headcode panel on non-gangwayed stock and above each windscreen on gangwayed units. On suburban stock these were also sometimes prefixed S if outshopped before about 1956, but this was not universal, even within a particular class, and disappeared with the first revarnish. From early 1957 the darker green began to appear on new and repainted units, together with the revised circular BR badge. Small yellow warning panels were progressively added from 1963, the first units to have them from new being the 1963 stock Brighton replacement 4 CIG and 4 BIG types, which were additionally the last units to be delivered in green. Yellow (sometimes cream) and red cantrail stripes, denoting first class and catering areas respectively, were also introduced from about the same time. Motor coaches of the 2 EPB and 2 HAP classes had an inverted black triangle on the yellow panel which signified 'no van at other end of unit' – vital information for luggage loaders on station platforms – as on remaining pre-war two-coach units.

From mid-1966 new and overhauled stock started to appear in the new British Rail blue livery, initially still with small yellow warning panels. The original colour was a semi-matt shade applied by airless spray. Numbering and lettering, and the new 'double-arrow' symbol, were white, while underframes and bogies were dark brown. The only new stock in this livery were the 4 REP, TC and 4 VEP types for the 1967 Bournemouth electrification, although these had polished aluminium BR symbols. The blue was rapidly found to wear and fade badly, so a more glossy shade applied by brush was soon adopted, together with full yellow ends, on which unit numbers and other lettering were black. The first SR electric units to appear in this new standard livery were the refurbished former LT tube trains for the Isle of Wight. Some units appeared in green with full yellow ends for a time in the 1967-72 period. From 1967, it was decided that express stock should be outshopped in the InterCity livery of blue with a light grey band along the windows, edged white with plastic tape. The later 4 CIGs, BIGs, VEPs, REPs and TCs were new in this livery, by which time all other suitable units were also receiving it. By about 1972, underframes and bogies on repainted vehicles had reverted to black. Through the 1970s overall blue was standard on non-corridor stock, but from 1980 the blue/grey express livery was applied universally, other than on the remaining SUBs which were due for early

withdrawal. The position in September 1983 was that all express and new sliding-door suburban stock was in blue/grey, while non-corridor stock carried a mixture of all-blue and blue/grey liveries.

Liveries carried when new by particular SR electric units (and the Bournemouth line TC trailer units) introduced between December 1951 and September 1983 are listed below. Unless indicated, all green units originally had plain green cab ends. Units outshopped in the sprayed semi-matt blue all originally had small yellow warning panels, while those in overall brush-applied gloss blue or blue/grey (plus experimental 2 PEP 2002 in unpainted aluminium) had full yellow ends from the start. The white carriage numbers on the semi-matt blue finish were smaller than hitherto, but reverted to approximately their former size when the gloss finish was adopted.

Early Malachite Green:	4 EPB 5001-5053, 5101-5260(1), 2 EPB 5701-5778, 4 CEP 7101-7104, 4 BEP 7001-7002.
Later Dark Green:	4 EPB 5301-5370, 2 EPB 5651-5684, 5779, 5800. 2 HAP 5601-5636, 6001-6173, 4 CEP 7105-7211, 4 BEP 7003-7022, MLV 68001-68010, 4 CIG 7301-7336(2), 4 BIG 7031-7048(2).
'Eggshell' Blue:	4 REP 3001-3011, 3 TC 301-303, 4 TC 401-428, 4 VEP 7701-7720.
Gloss Blue:	4 VEP 7721-7807, 3 TIS 031-037, 4 VEC 041-046, 4 PEP 4001-4002.
Unpainted Aluminium:	2 PEP 2001.
Blue/Grey:	4 CIG 7337-7438, 4 BIG 7049-7058, 4 VEP 7808-7894, 4 REP 3012-3015, 4 TC 429-434. Class 508 508001-508043, class 455/8 5801 upwards.

Notes:

(1) 5001/2/6/7 were originally outshopped in a non-standard 'bog grass green' shade, but were repainted into standard malachite on first revarnish c.1954

(2) Small yellow warning panels

Although obviously particular unit classes within the SR EMU fleet were intended for particular types of service, until 1973 members of a particular class were to all intents and purposes 'common user' and so, for example, any 4 CEP could turn up on any Central or South Eastern service diagrammed for the type. In that year depot allocations were introduced as part of the 'Maintrol' initiative to tighten maintenance procedures, and from henceforth units worked diagrams entirely based from their home depot. Depots to which electric units were allocated included East Wimbledon (WDON), Bournemouth (BOMO) and Fratton (FTON) on the South Western division, Selhurst (SHST) and Brighton (BTON) on the Central, and Slade Green (SLGN) and Ramsgate (RMGT) on the South Eastern. Later the depots were given simpler two letter codes, these being WD, BM, FR, SU, BN, SG and (briefly RM, then) RE respectively. Class numbers for the various unit types were introduced at the same time, but did not oust the traditional SR alpha-numeric codes.

Later SR-type 4 EPB 5188, fitted with guttering along the cantrail, emerges from Crystal Palace tunnel and passes the antediluvian 'A' signal box with the 1.10pm Victoria to Blackfriars service via West Croydon, Sutton and Wimbledon, on 5th July 1964. In late BR green livery with small warning panel, this unit retains the larger size of digits in its roller blind headcode panel. *Brian Stephenson*

SUBURBAN AND SEMI-FAST NON-CORRIDOR STOCK BUILT OR INTRODUCED 1951-83

Resulting from successful trials of electro-pneumatic braking on a pair of six-coach Brighton express units in 1947 and then on the double-decker prototypes (see Chapters 5 and 6), the first EMU designed from the start with the new control and braking arrangements came off the Eastleigh production line in December 1951. This was 4 EPB 5001, and was built as part of the same order (HO 3638) as that for the last of the 4 SUBs. In terms of basic design, structure and passenger accommodation 5001 was all but identical to the SUBs, being formed of two eight-bay saloon motor coaches, a ten-bay saloon trailer and a ten-compartment trailer, giving a seating capacity of 386. The three saloon vehicles consisted of new steel bodies on reclaimed underframes and bogies from former SECR-bodied SUBs, and the motor bogies were of 9ft wheelbase 'eastern' type, but equipped with new EE 507D motors. The compartment trailer was a 1946-built augmentation vehicle (formerly in 1925 SUB 4333), rewired and renumbered but otherwise unchanged.

Externally only the cab ends of the motor coaches differed significantly from the SUBs. The windscreens were narrower,

incorporated demisters, and neither opened. On the driving side there was a motorised windscreen wiper, hung from above. The headcode arrangement consisted of a central glass window identical to the windscreens, behind which there was a pair of numerical roller blinds, illuminated from the back. Unfortunately, the combination of an almost-flat SUB-style cab end, smaller windscreens and a flush headcode panel resulted in a rather characterless appearance, unrelieved by the plain green livery. To reduce draughts, the cab had horizontally-sliding windows instead of external side doors, access being via the guard's compartment, in which one of the two external doors on each side opened inwards. The 27-wire MU control jumper cable was located under the offside front cab window and a power jumper on the nearside front, while the pair of brake hoses was necessarily repeated on each side. Although cab ends had the buckeye couplings and rubbing plates already mentioned, coupling of vehicles within unit was by the same centre-buffer and three-link chain arrangement first introduced in 1928. Another electrical difference was that internal lighting worked off the motor-generator at 70V and individual bulbs were connected in parallel rather than series.

Following delivery to Durnsford Road depot and testing, which proved generally successful, 5001 commenced passenger service on the Guildford New line via Cobham in January 1952, carrying numerical headcode 42. It was soon joined by fourteen more units 5002-5015, which completed the original order. Following a hiatus until the spring of 1953 due to a government-induced interruption in the supply of sheet steel to the railway industry, the type was then in continuous production at Eastleigh works until the spring of 1957, the total eventually reaching 213. All new vehicles utilised reclaimed underframes and bogies from pre-war SUB coaches, and units up to 5053 incorporated one ex-SUB compartment augmentation trailer, as in 5001. They gradually superseded remaining pre-war SUBs with wooden bodywork, with about 140 going to the Eastern section. A significant number of Central section services, generally those serving Charing Cross or Holborn Viaduct, also had them for operating convenience. The Western section had the remainder.

The production fleet was divided into two series: 5016-5053 originally had the 9ft wheelbase 'eastern' motor bogies, whereas 5101-5260 had the 8ft 9in 'central' type. Later, more 8ft 9in bogies became available, including some from withdrawn 4 SUB units in the 4326 series and some from the pool of spare bogies, and these were fitted to 5016-5053 and also to 5001-5015, the exchanges being completed by the autumn of 1964. A further variation was that 5138-5260 were built with low-level gutters along the cantrail, whereas others had only high-level strips, as on the SUBs. The cab-end power jumpers were soon found to be superfluous (and indeed the cause of occasional electrical malfunction), so later units from 5176 upwards were outshopped without them and their associated pipework, leaving just a socket to connect to a depot shore-line. Others were modified to this configuration, which coincidentally resulted in a tidier cab end, on first overhaul or before.

Having proved the experimental 4 DD double-decker units an impracticable means of increasing capacity on overcrowded Eastern section suburban lines out of Charing Cross and Cannon street, a plan was drawn-up to increase the length of rush-hour trains on these routes to ten coaches. The civil engineering work necessary for the 'ten-car scheme' is described in Chapter 3, but so far as rolling stock was concerned the plan involved construction of 66 two-coach motor units. A further twelve of the same type were also required to replace the venerable 1909-vintage LBSCR stock on the South London and Wimbledon to West Croydon lines, and to lengthen the Central section's London Bridge to Caterham/Tattenham Corner peak hour trains.

Because all existing underframes to be recovered from pre-war SUB stock were required for 4 EPB construction, the two coach units were entirely new. Classified 2 EPB, each was formed of an eight-bay motor third brake with the saloon divided by partition into two groups of four, and a driving trailer third with five compartments at the inner end, a four-bay saloon and the cab with associated entrance vestibule. This gave a seating capacity of 186. Although superficially similar to the four-coach units, they were structurally different, being based on the BR standard Mark 1 non-

corridor coach design. The sides were less curved, the windows had corners of a sharper radius, and the doors lacked the toplights. In contrast to Bulleid stock, the quarterlight glazing was actually flat glass, and the side panels were slightly recessed to accommodate them. The cab ends had a wide centre panel and narrow side panels, and the roof end overhung slightly. The underframes were 63ft 5in long (longer than the previous SR suburban standard) and were fabricated at Ashford. Both motor and trailer bogies were also to BR designs, although these were not very different from the SR types. The initial unit, 5701, was outshopped with buckeye couplers between vehicles as well as at unit ends, but these increased the overall length too much and were quickly replaced with the standard centre-buffer arrangement with which the rest of the class was fitted from new. As with the 4 EPBs, the first 27 had power line jumper cables on the cab ends but these were soon removed. 79 2 EPBs were outshopped between 1954 and 1958, numbered 5701-5779. 5779 was an additional unit for the Central section. 5756 was experimentally equipped with Girling disc brakes from new until early 1964, and saw little use in passenger service during this period.

Concurrently with the production 2 EPBs, a further fifteen units to a similar basic design were delivered from Eastleigh in 1954-55 for use on the Newcastle – South Shields line, where they replaced refurbished North Eastern Railway electric stock dating from 1920. They differed from the SR units in having express ratio gearing, a larger brake van and hence only seven seating bays in the motor coach, a solitary eight-seat first class compartment in the centre of the driving trailer, and headcode arrangements incorporating a destination blind and five lamps. Their seating was also non-standard, with deep fixed wire-framed cushions rather than the lift-out type. Seats were provided for 164 third class passengers and eight first. The first class compartment was downclassed on abolition of this class on the Tyneside electric services in May 1959. The Newcastle – South Shields line was de-electrified in 1963 and the fifteen units returned south in very poor condition. All were overhauled and modified at Selhurst and Eastleigh before returning to service on the SR, the cab ends being given phase II standard roller-blind headcode panels (less deep than those on other 2 EPBs), and air horns were mounted on the cab roofs. The former first class compartment retained its deeper cushions and double luggage racks. On re-entry into service the 'Tyneside' units, now numbered 5781-5795, were initially common user with the rest of the 2 EPB fleet. From 1972 they were allocated to Selhurst for use on more lightly-loaded trains on the Central division, but two years later all went to Wimbledon, seeing out the remainder of their days on services from Waterloo.

Below One of fifteen 'Tyneside' 2 EPB units built at Eastleigh for the Newcastle – South Shields line, 5785, at its birthplace on 27th June 1964, after its return south but prior to its re-entry into service following refurbishment and cab-end alteration to SR standards. Modifications included replacement of the original destination blind and marker-light arrangement with a standard roller-blind headcode panel to the SR's new shallow pattern first seen on the final 4 EPBs, CEPs and HAPs. *J. H. Aston*

It is convenient to mention here that a further BR standard 2 EPB, 5800, was constructed in 1960 at the same time as the first 53xx 4 EPBs (see below) as an accident replacement. It was not given the number of the unit it replaced as it differed in having 1957-type equipment, and consequently its battery equipment was mounted under the driving trailer. It was disbanded in 1964, its motor coach going to 4 EPB 5352, and (later) its DTS to 2 EPB 5710, again both as substitutions following mishaps.

The next new non-corridor units to be introduced were for main line semi-fast and stopping services, and were classified 2 HAP as they were equivalent to a 2 HAL but with electropneumatic brakes. The first 42 units, numbered 6001-6042, were constructed in 1957-58 and were ordered to replace HALs on the Maidstone and Gillingham lines and for the first stages of the Kent Coast electrification from Victoria to Dover and Ramsgate via Chatham. (6012-42 were actually funded out of the Gatwick Airport budget, but sent direct to the Eastern section.) Built to BR standard 1951-stock speci-

fication, each was formed of a motor brake second with an identical layout to the 2 EPBs, and a driving trailer composite with a five-bay second class saloon, two toilets, a three-compartment first class section and cab with entrance vestibule. This gave a seating capacity of 134 second and nineteen first. The toilets were arranged so that each class of accommodation had access to one, without allowing through passage between the classes. Electrical and control equipment of these units was identical to what had gone before, but gearing was of the express type to allow 90mph operation.

Further 2 HAPs to the same basic design were built between 1958 and 1963, mostly for the Kent Coast electrification. 6043-6105, built in 1958-59, were to 1957 phase I standards with a camshaft control system. The next batch, 6106-6146, which followed in 1961, had 1957 phase II bodywork construction, but retained phase I cab ends. Internally, the doors and windows had aluminium-strip surrounds and the toilet windows lacked ventilators. Those in the final batch were among the last new units built at Eastleigh, where

The penultimate 2 HAP to be completed, 6172, stands outside Eastleigh Works when brand new in 1963. It has 1957 phase II bodywork, but additionally was given heavy cast steel 'Commonwealth' trailer bogies to improve riding and had distinctive angled roof rainstrips peculiar to the final HAPs. By this time, first class accommodation was being denoted by a yellow stripe underneath the cantrail. *BR Southern Region Official*

carriage construction ceased in 1963. Numbered 6147-6173, they differed from the earlier batches in having late phase II cab ends with tapered windscreens and a less deep headcode panel, and distinctive high-level rainstrips mounted at an angle and running almost the full length of the coach roof. Due to poor riding of the earlier units at 90mph, 6104 upwards were given trailer bogies of the heavy cast-steel Commonwealth type with coil springing. 6147-6173 were used mainly at first on the Portsmouth Direct and Brighton lines, but by 1967 most had gravitated to the South Eastern.

Withdrawal of the London-area 2 NOLs in 1956 released a number of SR 62ft motor coach and driving trailer underframes with bogies, and these were used to construct 36 further 2 HAP units, numbered 5601-5636, also in 1957-58. Due to the underframe design these were given Bulleid-style bodywork, and the reclaimed 'Central' motor bogies were fitted with new EE 507EA motors with roller bearings, and express gearing for 90mph capability. They also reverted to contactor (rather than camshaft) control and were therefore

1951 stock. The motor coaches were identical to those in the SR-type 4 EPBs except that a solid partition divided the seating into two groups of four bays. The driving trailers were side-corridor vehicles superficially similar to those in post-war HALs 2693-2700. There was a toilet at the inner end, three first class compartments, four second class compartments plus a rather dingy coupé with six seats across the width of the coach, and finally the motorman's compartment and entrance vestibule. From the corridor side these distinctive vehicles resembled certain Bulleid hauled stock with large windows between the doors. Due to this more wasteful use of space, these units seated four second and one first fewer than their BR standard cousins. The external doors themselves, ostensibly of standard Bulleid pattern with toplight, were actually moulded by hand in Eastleigh carriage workshops from glass fibre-reinforced plastic (GRP) and were self-coloured green. 5601-5636 mainly worked on the Eastern section indiscriminately with the BR standard HAPs, but also appeared on services out of Waterloo from 1967.

The basic bodywork of a driving trailer composite from a Bulleid-type 56xx 2 HAP unit, viewed from the compartment side. Mounted on a 62ft underframe recovered from a withdrawn 2 NOL, it is seen in Eastleigh works yard in 1958. *F. W. Ivey*

SR-type 2 EPB 5667, built in 1959 with Bulleid bodywork on 62ft 2 NOL underframes, pauses at Datchet with a Windsor – Waterloo service on 18th April 1968. It carries the later BR green livery in which it was built, but has gained a small yellow panel and inverted black triangle on the motor coach front. *John Scrace*

When the remainder of the NOLs were withdrawn in 1958-59, their underframes were re-used under a further batch of 34 2 EPB units, the last to be constructed using Bulleid-style bodywork before the jigs were dismantled, fourteen years after they were first erected and ten years after nationalisation. Numbered 5651-5684, they were outshopped from Eastleigh in 1959, and were mechanically similar to the 5601-series 2 HAPs which preceded them except in having suburban (rather than express) gearing. An innovation for SR suburban stock was that they had entirely semi-saloon accommodation, with no compartments, the motor brake seconds being identical to those in the 56xx HAPs and the driving trailer second having nine bays (divided by partition into five and four) followed by the cab. This gave a seating total of 178. These units also had GRP doors. 5651-5684 were originally put on to the Waterloo – Windsor/Weybridge line, where they displaced 4 EPBs which had earlier ousted the 2 NOLs in May 1957. In Ian Allan 'ABC's of the period 5651-5684 were classified as '2 NOP', but Mechanical and Electrical Engineer's department listings always coded them 2 EPB. Although also appearing on various other SW suburban lines, they remained the mainstay of the Windsor/Weybridge service until July 1974, when the first twenty were transferred to Selhurst for use specifically on the Caterham/Tattenham Corner routes where their all-semi-saloon accommodation assisted conductor-guard operation. The rest followed in May 1981, from which time they could be seen on any Central division suburban working.

The last entirely non-corridor suburban units to be introduced were seventy new 4 EPB units, turned out from Eastleigh Works between 1960 and 1963. The first 56, numbered 5301-5356, were to replace the last pre-war suburban units, SUBs 4300-4354, and three accident losses. Oddly, the last unit to appear, in 1961, was actually 5302. To BR standard design with 1957-type equipment and phase I bodywork, the motor coaches of 5301-5356 were identical in layout to those of the 57xx 2 EPBs except that they only had one periscope. 5301 and 5302 were made up with new motor coaches and spare Bulleid-bodied trailers, one open and one compartment. The others were formed with two BR standard trailers of unusual internal layout, each having a five-bay saloon and five compartments. The seating capacity of 5303 upwards was 392, the pair of units with Bulleid trailers seating two fewer. Only the 'No.1 end' motor coach had a motor-generator and the 'No.2 end' vehicle the batteries. Exceptions were 5301 and 5302, which had both motor coaches fitted with motor generator and battery, as had all previous 4 EPB units. All except 5301 had air-horns (rather than whistles which had previously been standard) from new. Those on 5303-5307 were mounted internally just above the cab windscreens, but these proved too noisy for the crews and so were soon repositioned on the roofs, which then became the standard position. The motor coaches concerned had blanking-off plates where the horn apertures had been until withdrawal. From their introduction, these units were common-user with the rest of the EPB fleet. 5303-5312 and 5337-5344 entered traffic with express-ratio gearing (swapped from 'Hampshire' diesel-electric units), but over the years the relevant motor bogies were exchanged between units on overhaul.

The fourteen final 4 EPBs, to be constructed, 5357-5370, were turned out from Eastleigh in 1963 at the same time as the final HAPs and were originally intended for the South Western division. They had late phase II bodywork and roof-mounted horns from new. As with the earlier units, they soon caused problems on the SW, as their greater length compared with the SR-bodied units prevented them fitting in some berthing sidings. However, they regularly appeared on the Waterloo – Guildford via Cobham line until about 1972, when the whole fleet was concentrated on South Eastern and Central division suburban services. In 1965 the trailers of 5357 and 5358 were given coil-sprung B5S type bogies for use on Central Division main line peak services, including the 17.53 Victoria – Brighton, but by 1981 only the latter still had them, by which time it was allocated to Slade Green.

The history of the HAPs from 1969 is complex, and it is convenient to deal with the SR and BR-bodied types separately, starting with 5601-5636. In that year fourteen units were downgraded to second class only by painting out the first class designations, sewing up the armrests and sealing the toilets out of use. Diagrammed for SW suburban services, they were reclassified 2 SAP in June 1969. All reverted to composite status in May 1970. In May 1972 all 36 members of the class were transferred to Brighton specifically for use on the coastal routes to Portsmouth and Hastings, these services being relaunched to the public as *Coastway* at the time. During this period they were also occasionally formed in London trains on the Brighton and Mid-Sussex lines. In 1976 the entire fleet moved on to Selhurst to replace some 4 SUBs on Central division suburban services and were down-

classed to 2 SAP, some for the second time. Two units, 5601 and 5636, were disbanded, their motor coaches going to form a 'new' 4 EPB unit, and the following year a further pair, 5602/03, suffered the same fate. In both cases, the non-standard driving trailers were scrapped. 5624 was reformed as a hybrid SR/BR unit, with coach 65499 from 2 SAP 5917, coach 14544 being withdrawn and cut up at Micheldever carriage sidings in 1977. 5624 was finally withdrawn in August 1983.

These units generally worked in twos or threes, but solo working on the Wimbledon – West Croydon and South London lines was not unknown. As time went by, the former first class compartments were given second class seating on over-haul. In 1980 the EPB facelifting programme began in earnest and the SAPs were progressively withdrawn, although not before a few had gained blue/grey livery. As before, the motor coaches were used with more former SUB trailers to make additional 4 EPB units and the driving trailers were condemned. Without diagrammed workings after October 1982, all had gone by May 1983. An exception was 5629, which was converted into stores unit 019 to replace HAL-based 022.

Above From the final batch of BR standard 4 EPBs built in 1963 to 1957 phase II standards with external window frames, tapered windscreens and shallow headcode panel, 5364 stands at Whyteleafe South with the Caterham portion of the 14.20 from Charing Cross on 11th June 1976. It carries the overall rail blue livery with full yellow ends, universal on suburban stock from 1972 until 1980. *John Scrace*

Returning to the BR standard HAPs, with the introduction of new 4 VEPs on the South Eastern division, 43 more were allocated to Wimbledon in 1973-74 to join the ten already there, with the balance of the fleet remaining at Ramsgate. Nearly all the Wimbledon units were downgraded to 2 SAP status for suburban work in a similar manner to the SR-bodied units described above, but in this case they were renumbered from 5903 upwards. Their main use was on the Waterloo – Windsor/Weybridge route. Others were allocated to the Central division. Further BR standard units were subsequently converted to SAP status, the total reaching 51 by 1977. HAPs 6001-21/24-42 became SAPs 5901-40; later, 6043/44 became 5941/42; in 1967, 6045-53 became 5943-51. 5951 reverted to 6053 in October 1977.

With the introduction of sliding-door class 508 stock in 1980 the SAPs all reverted to HAPs with their first class accommodation and toilets reinstated, and most were re-allocated to Brighton for *Coastway* services. In May 1982 48 of these were reformed as permanently-coupled pairs with the motor coaches at the centre and reclassified 4 CAP (for Coastway HAP). The purpose of this exercise seems to have been to provide all stock working along the coast with luggage vans at the centre, as on 4 CIGs and VEPs, largely for the benefit of Post Office staff. Units with 1951-type equipment were numbered 3201-3213 and those with 1957-type, 3301-3311. By this time HAPs were appearing in blue/grey, but no attempt was made to pair like-liveried units when the CAPs were formed, and hence several were originally piebald. Apart from their use on *Coastway* duties the CAPs frequently strayed on to Central division main line services, regularly reaching London. An excess of first class seating soon saw the compartments at one end being downclassed.

With the exception of those modified to become CAPs and the few Wimbledon-based units, the BR standard 2 HAP fleet remained virtually intact on the South Eastern division, based at Ramsgate, until withdrawal commenced in January 1982. Paradoxically, the final phase II units of the 6147-6173 batch were taken out of service first. (6134 was withdrawn in January 1982 and most of the others in 1982/83.) As with all other Southern Region stock built in 1958-63, the bodywork of BR HAPs contained blue asbestos insulation and, following serious health concerns regarding this material, legislation was passed requiring its removal if a particular unit was to remain in service. With a decreasing requirement for non-gangwayed semi-fast units, particularly as such stock was now banned from the narrow-bore tunnels between Folkestone and Dover, it was deemed more economic to send them for scrap. Some had been stripped of asbestos from the driving van and cab areas in a special workshop set up in Strawberry Hill depot however, including those in the CAPs, and these remained in service after 1983. Before this, the transfer of all remaining HAPs to East Wimbledon had begun.

To revert to 1965, in that year it was necessary to provide more modern stock to replace steam-haulage on the non-electrified Reading – Redhill – Tonbridge cross-country line, and six three-coach diesel-electric multiple units were, for want of a better phrase, lashed-up using a power car and trailer from a disbanded 'Hastings' 6S diesel-electric unit

and a driving trailer second from a 2 EPB. As SR diesel units had buckeye couplers throughout, to simplify conversion the chosen vehicles were those from the 5701-5711 series which retained the necessary mountings on the inner headstocks. The units disbanded were 5701/04/08-11, and this left spare six BR standard EPB motor coaches with 1951 equipment. Four of these were then marshalled with spare Bulleid-bodied all-steel trailers to form two additional 4 EPBs, 5261 and 5262, while the others became accident replacements in existing units. As the motor coaches had 1951 equipment, these new units were numbered at the end of the 1951-type 4 EPB series, even though externally they were otherwise identical to 5301 and 5302. 5261 was formed with two compartment trailers but 5262 had the standard formation. Two further 1951-type 4 EPBs were formed later, both comprising the motor coaches from two withdrawn 56xx 2 SAP units, with two rewired 4 SUB trailers in 5263 and two 'orphaned' EPB trailers in 5264. 5263 was formed in 1976 and was allocated to Wimbledon, 5264 a year later and based at Slade Green.

Three vehicles of 5263 were then the subject of various refurbishment exercises at Eastleigh. One motor coach had its centre partition removed and was given fluorescent strip-lighting, while both trailers were given seats with reprofiled cushions (superficially resembling those in 4 VEP stock), new internal panelling, fluorescent lighting and public address, and one had new ceiling panels. All vehicles were given improved draught-proofing around the doors and new flooring. The unit was painted in blue/grey livery, the first SR suburban EMU to be so treated.

Following these experiments, a standard specification for a light refurbishment, officially termed 'facelifting', was drawn up. This was seen as a method of improving the quality of existing rolling stock at a time when there was insufficient finance available for much-needed new trains. With the work being split between Eastleigh and the former Lancashire and Yorkshire Railway shops at Horwich (near Bolton), the first unit entered works in 1980, and by September 1983 54 units had been dealt with. Of these, fourteen were formed from ex-2 SAP motor coaches and former SUB trailers, and the remainder made-up purely from EPB vehicles. In some cases compartment trailers in units not to be dealt with were swapped for open trailers from units being sent for facelift, so the unrefurbished unit was now all-saloon. The compartment trailers were opened out as part of the facelifting process anyway, which had the effect of removing from service vehicles with closed compartments, latterly more subject to vandalism and security risk.

Work involved in bringing EPB vehicles, including former SAP motor coaches and SUB trailers, to facelifted standards was as follows. All partitions were opened out so the entire unit was saloon, seat units from scrap SUB vehicles being used where necessary. Simple false ceilings from white plastic-surfaced laminate, with strip-lights and public address, were installed, and the seats reupholstered but otherwise left unchanged. Internal panelling was renovated or replaced, and other improvements were similar to those in 5263. Externally, vehicles were given cantrail-height gutters where they did not already have them, and all units were outshopped in blue/grey (apart from 5414 which ran in service all-blue for a few days). The first two production facelifted units, 5225 and 5143, initially kept their original numbers, but the type were soon renumbered into a new 54xx series, with the unit number repeated above each windscreen. The remaining unmodified MBSO of 5263, now renumbered 5401, was facelifted to the production standard. Seating capacity of the facelifted units was slightly reduced to 368. Facelifted units from 5450 upwards were outshopped without the false ceiling panels as a cost-cutting exercise, the PA and lighting being mounted instead on channelling fixed to the existing ceiling. All facelifted units were originally allocated to Selhurst for use on Central division suburban services. This was seen by senior management as a means of spreading out new and refurbished stock among the divisions, the logic being that, as the South Western had the new class 508 units and the South Eastern the refurbished CEPs, the Central division should have the facelifted EPBs.

In 1982 a start was made facelifting 53xx BR standard-type 4 EPBs in a similar manner to the SR units, and 24 had been done by September 1983. All had come from the original batch within the range 5303-5351, and were rebuilt at Eastleigh as they became due for general overhaul. They kept their original numbers but were transferred from Slade Green to Selhurst. As before, compartment and intermediate saloon partitions were removed to make the accommodation fully open, the necessary seating coming from withdrawn HAPs. This gave exactly the same seating capacity as the SR-bodied units. As on the later SR units, false ceilings were omitted as an economy measure, the PA and strip-lighting being installed instead on longitudinal channelling which ill-fitted the undulations of the original plywood ceiling panels. Unit 5349 was given trailer 70455 which had been experimentally rebuilt in Slade Green workshops in a more thorough manner following extensive damage in a bomb explosion in 1976. This vehicle had cream plastic internal panelling, a lowered ceiling, reprofiled seats with SUB-type ends and phase II-type external window frames.

The next group of units on which facelifting was carried out were the 56xx SR 2 EPBs, work starting at Eastleigh early in 1983. Alterations were similar to the 4 EPBs, but in the driving trailers the centre partition was converted into an ineffectual glazed screen to divide the smoking and non-smoking accommodation. These changes reduced the number of seats by four. Eight units had been outshopped by September, being renumbered from 6301 upwards in order of facelifting. 6307 and 6308 kept their original ceilings and the fluorescent lighting was mounted as on the four-car units from 5450. All remained on the Central division.

Returning to the majority of EPB stock which had not been facelifted, the position at the end of September 1983 was that all BR standard 4 EPBs remained on the South Eastern division and SR 4 EPBs were split between South Western and South Eastern. SR 2 EPBs were all on the Central division and BR standard 2 EPBs were mainly on the South Eastern, but with 21 allocated to the South Western and two to the Central. The ex-'Tyneside' units worked entirely on the South Western.

EXPRESS AND SEMI-FAST CORRIDOR STOCK BUILT OR INTRODUCED 1956-83

An important component of post-war plans for extension of the Southern Electric system was electrification of the Kent Coast lines, requiring the design of a new generation of EP-braked express multiple units, gangwayed throughout. With this in mind a small batch of six prototype units, including two with buffet cars, was ordered from Eastleigh Works as early as 1951. In the event the order was considered non-urgent and postponed year by year for various reasons, probably connected with sheet steel shortages and a more pressing need for new suburban stock. As explained in Chapter 3, the Kent Coast scheme was finally authorised in 1955 as part of the BR Modernisation Plan, and following this the six new express units, the first since 1938 except for the complete replacements for war damage losses in 1945/46, were outshopped during 1956.

Disappointingly conservative in concept, the new units were very similar in formation and interior layout to the pre-war 4 COR and 4 BUF types, but made use of modern BR Mark 1 coach design and EPB control and braking systems. Indeed the original classifications for these units were 4 COR(EPB) and 4 BUF(EPB), but these were soon shortened to the more digestible 4 CEP and 4 BEP. Four 4 CEPs and two 4 BEPs were originally built, numbered 7101-7104 and 7001-7002 respectively. They were the only BR-design gang-wayed EMUs to be outshopped in the early Southern Region malachite green livery with 'cycling lion' emblem. Following a test programme based at Peckham Rye, the units entered passenger service on the Brighton line. The two buffet cars were not actually delivered until July 1957, 7001 and 7002 running as three-coach units in the meantime.

All vehicles were built on 63ft 5in underframes and had BR standard bogies. Electrical equipment was of the same 1951 type as fitted to the 4 EPBs, but with express gearing for a 90mph maximum speed as in the HAPs. Bodywork was of the earlier design without external window frames, and these units were the sole express EMU stock built to this pattern. Their appearance was unimaginative in the extreme, the cab fronts being arrived at merely by superimposing two EPB cab windows, jumper cables and a roughly central head-code box on to a standard BR Mark 1 gangwayed coach end. Pullman-type gangways were fitted, so coupling between vehicles within a unit was by automatic buckeye for the first time on express units.

Formation of the CEPs comprised two open motor brake seconds sandwiching a side-corridor composite and a side-corridor second, both the latter having toilets. Seating capacity was exactly 200 second class, 24 first. The motor coaches consisted of motorman's and guard's compartments and a seven-bay saloon divided into two sections, with seating two+two on each side of a central gangway. As on the CORs, the motorman's compartment was on the left (as viewed from inside), and a door shut it off when not in use. The poor loading and unloading characteristics of the otherwise similar pre-war motor coaches having been noted, entrance was via end vestibules and also by doors let directly into the centre seating bay. Apart from brakes and electrical equipment, the

One of the four pre-production 4 CEPs, 7103, runs into the eastern side of Victoria with a test train in 1956. At this stage it was fitted with a standard Mark 1 gangway door, without a headcode panel, and hence the headcode had to be chalked on! *F. W. Ivey*

A second class saloon interior in one of the prototype CEP motor coaches, photographed when brand new and upholstered in the 'shallow V' patterned moquette, one of three BR patterns common at this time. Comfortable enough but already considered dated, the basic seat design was identical to that in locomotive-hauled tourist open seconds, and was firmly based on the pre-war LMS style. *BR Southern Region Official*

Brand new 4 CEP 7144 departs from London Bridge forming the 9am to Brighton on 13th May 1959. The production CEPs and BEPs were given 1957 phase I bodywork incorporating unpainted aluminium window frames with raised surrounds, both clearly visible. *J. H. Aston*

trailers were exactly equivalent to Mark 1 locomotive-hauled vehicles, and differed from their pre-war predecessors principally in having no external compartment doors. The trailer second had eight compartments with entrance vestibules at each end and the centre, and two toilets at one end. The trailer composite had four first class compartments and three second with a toilet at each end, entrances being at each end and between the two classes. The trailers were marshalled within unit so that the first class compartments were at the centre and the gangways were on opposite sides. Internal decor was also uninspiring, but longitudinal aluminium luggage racks in the motor coach saloons were a new idea.

Steam-era expresses on the Kent Coast lines had included Pullman cars to provide catering facilities and, as the buffet cars in the new electric stock would continue to be staffed by Pullman, that organisation was consulted when designing the layout and facilities to be included in the new vehicles. Internal arrangements comprised a three-bay unclassed saloon with eighteen loose seats, staff toilet, kitchen, bar counter and finally an open area with a column-mounted centre table and four more loose seats. (An almost identical layout was chosen for the buffet cars in the contemporary Hastings line 6B diesel units.) Kitchen equipment was all-electric, working at 200V from a motor-generator mounted on the underframe. The buffet car in the BEPs replaced the compartment trailer second vehicle in the CEPs, reducing the second class seating capacity by 64.

The 1956 prototypes were considered generally satisfactory and therefore became the forerunners of a large production 4 CEP and 4 BEP fleet constructed at Eastleigh for the two phases of the Kent Coast electrification, with unit numbers commencing from 7105 and 7003 respectively. 7003-7012 and 7105-7153 were produced in 1958-59 for phase I, but were delivered some time before being required and many were stored between Ardingly and Horsted Keynes in the meantime. 7013-7022 and 7154-7204 were for phase II and appeared in 1960-61, while 7205-7211 were additional units constructed in 1963. The various production batches differed from the prototypes and each other in a number of ways. Electrically, they were fitted with 1957-type camshaft control equipment. The windows were fitted externally in unpainted aluminium frames. Those on the first batch were initially double-glazed but, following problems with condensation between the inner and outer panes, were replaced by single panes. The second batch had single panes from new, while 7205 upwards had improved double-glazing. Like the last BR standard HAPs and EPBs, the final seven units also had tapered cab windscreens and a shallow headcode panel. The phase I units had leaf-sprung BR mark 3 or 4 trailer bogies but, as with the pre-war stock, these quickly deteriorated to give a very poor ride. In an attempt to improve matters, a number of modifications and experiments were carried out, and in the course of these many bogies were swapped between the CEP/BEP fleet and BR standard EPBs and HAPs.

The trailer bogies of the phase II units from 7154 and 7013 upwards were the Commonwealth coil-sprung type, heavy but giving a much-improved ride. The buffet cars of 7003-7012 were also given them in 1960-61, but those of 7001 and 7002 not until 1964 and about 1970 respectively. In the case of 7001, this followed a short period in 1963-64 when its buffet was mounted on experimental air-sprung B4 bogies, but these deteriorated very rapidly. MBS 61033 in unit 7101 was given an experimental Commonwealth motor bogie for a short trial period in 1961, but this never went into production for SR units. 4 BEP 7002 was equipped throughout with experimental Girling disc brakes between 1965 and 1970. 7205-7211 were the last new corridor units to be delivered from Eastleigh works.

Following comments regarding the drabness of the prototype interiors, the production CEPs and BEPs were subject to the attentions of the newly-formed BR Design Panel. Wood panelling was replaced by laminate in various pastel shades, while the seating was redesigned with improved headrests and armrests. Significantly, second class saloons were upholstered in the new grey-based Trojan material which, as mentioned elsewhere, subsequently became ubiquitous in Southern stock, of both pre-war and post-1945 types. The first class seats in units from 7013 and 7154 upwards were redesigned to recline slightly. The saloon accommodation in these units was undoubtedly the most comfortable of any BR-designed EMU, and was copied almost exactly in the 1964 Brighton line replacement stock.

Apart from the Kent Coast routes, on which they operated virtually all the express services, including Dover and Folkestone boat trains, from the inauguration of the two phases, the CEPs and BEPs also worked Central division Mid-Sussex services from Victoria to Bognor Regis/Portsmouth via Horsham from the start of 1964, displacing pre-war COR and BUF stock. From their introduction in 1956 they had also regularly appeared on the Brighton main line. Conversely, 7205-7211 started life working peak-hour South Western division services between Waterloo and Farnham/Portsmouth, but soon gravitated to the Central/South Eastern pool. A few CEPs received the overall blue livery from 1966, some with yellow panels and others with full yellow ends. Some received full yellow ends while still in green livery, but most were repainted from green with small warning panels straight into blue/grey with full yellow ends, and all had received this livery by 1971. The buffet car of 7022 was experimentally fitted with pressure ventilation equipment some time in the mid 1960s, and most of its opening windows were replaced with plain glass.

In 1963 a further new type of express stock was designed, intended initially to replace the obsolete pre-war 6 PUL and 6 PAN units on the Brighton line. To distinguish them from existing 4 CEP and 4 BEP stock, the new units were given the designations 4 CIG and 4 BIG. There remains some argument as to the origin of these codes; IG was the old LBSCR telegraphic code for Brighton, appropriate for the intended use of the stock, but the same initials also stood for 'intermediate guard', describing one of the salient differences of the new units in comparison with what had gone before. Following

Following the attentions of the newly-formed BR Design Panel, the accommodation in the production CEPs was thoroughly redesigned. This official view again shows a motor coach saloon, where varnished wooden surfaces have largely been replaced by plastic laminate or fabric. The seats are covered with the grey-based 'Trojan' tapestry, which was to become ubiquitous in SR electric stock over the following twenty years. *BR Southern Region Official*

the practice established in the design of ac multiple unit stock for other regions of BR, both motor bogies and guards' accommodation moved from the driving vehicles to one of the centre coaches. Thirty-six 4 CIG and eighteen 4 BIG units were originally ordered, numbered 7301-7336 and 7031-7048 respectively. As building of complete vehicles at Eastleigh had ended, they were constructed at York Carriage Works, being delivered between September 1964 and early 1966. The first CIGs entered passenger service on 29th May 1965, and from the following April they entirely displaced 6 PUL and PAN units from the Brighton line. Due to the inevitable late delivery of the buffet cars, some 4 BIGs originally ran as three-coach units and a number of 4 BEPs were temporarily drafted from the South Eastern division to provide catering on trains otherwise formed of CIGs.

Brighton replacement 4 BIG 7046 slows for the Haywards Heath stop leading an afternoon express from Victoria to Eastbourne and Ore on 18th September 1966. This first batch of CIGs and BIGs were the last SR EMUs to be delivered in green with the BR badge on the motor coach (second vehicle back). Obvious differences from the CEP and BEP stock include rounded edges to the cab fronts, unit-end jumper cables housed in recesses and first class accommodation directly behind the cab. *BR Southern region Official*

The CIGs and BIGs were widely criticised as being outdated from new as they were designed around BR Mark 1 coach standards at a time when the first integral bodied Mark 2 vehicles were appearing on locomotive-hauled (even steam) services elsewhere on the Southern Region. They were to phase II design standards but with an improved cab-end design moulded from steel-reinforced GRP. The edges of the cab were rounded off, there was no roof overhang and the jumper cables were tidily located in recesses below the windscreens. The gangway connections both at unit ends and between vehicles were shrouded with metal aprons, again giving a much neater appearance. These changes were perpetuated on all subsequent EP-braked corridor units built up to 1974. Formation of the CIGs comprised two driving trailer composites sandwiching a trailer second and a non-

driving motor brake second, accommodating 192 second and 42 first class passengers. In the BIG units the trailer second was replaced by a buffet car, reducing the second class seating capacity by 32. As mentioned elsewhere, these were the last units to be delivered new in green, and the BR coach badge was situated midway on the motor coach sides, even though it was a non-driving vehicle. All had small warning panels occupying the lower half of the gangway connection, but from an early date 7303 was given experimental wrap-around full yellow ends extending back as far as the front of the cab doors. From 1967 units were outshopped in blue/grey, and none ever appeared in overall blue.

Both motor bogies and most electrical equipment were located under the motor coach, units with this arrangement being termed 1963 stock. The motor bogies were the same mark 4 type as on the CEPs, but all trailer bogies were of the fabricated coil-sprung B5S type, developed from the loco-hauled B4 design specifically for use under SR multiple unit stock. These at last gave EMU vehicles a satisfactory ride, a world away from the bucking and swaying of the pre-war express stock which they replaced and the early CEPs. An odd innovation was the not entirely successful installation of electric parking brakes. Collector shoes were located on the trailer bogies at unit ends, not on the motor bogies, and were cantilevered out on arms from the main bogie frame rather than being hung from shoe-beams.

A further criticism of the design from the passenger's viewpoint concerned the fussy internal layout of the driving trailers, which smacked of 'design by committee', and in many ways the accommodation represented at best only a minor advance on the thirty year old stock they were replacing, the almost total lack of second class compartments being a particular gripe. The driving trailer composites had a cab and entrance vestibule followed by four compartments connected by side corridor, of which the compartment directly behind the cab had an external door. Each unit had one DTC with four first class compartments and one with only three, the remaining one nearest the centre being second. There followed a rather fussy second class half-compartment with four seats, then a three-bay second class saloon and finally two toilets. There were external doors to the half-compartment and last saloon bay. The trailer second had nine seating bays with end vestibules and an external door let into the centre bay, and the motor brake second was similar with two bays at one end replaced by a luggage van and guard's compartment. Internally, the seating and decor resembled the last of the CEPs. The buffet cars in the BIGs were similar in layout to the trailer seconds, but four bays were taken up by a buffet counter and kitchen, and tables were permanently fixed between the seats other than in the central door position.

The 4 CIG and 4 BIG designs became the standard second-generation BR express stock for the Central and South Western divisions of the Southern Region, and further examples were built in quantity at York between 1970 and 1972 to replace the COR, BUF and GRI stock on the Waterloo – Portsmouth and Reading lines and on Central division services. CIGs 7337-7366 and BIGs 7049-7058 were for Waterloo – Portsmouth services, CIGs 7367-7437 were for the Reading line and Central division, and 7438 was the replacement for a condemned CEP, but allocated to the Central division. Although of identical layout, these later units differed in detail from the original batches. Technically, the motor bogies were of the coil-sprung mark 6 type, and the electric parking brake was omitted. Internally, appointments were to more austere standards first used in the 1967 Bournemouth stock, with thinner, harder cushions and a general lack of side headrests and armrests in second class. All were delivered in blue/grey with full yellow ends. Those later CIGs allocated to the Central division displaced the last of the CORs and appeared indiscriminately with the earlier units on Brighton, Hastings, Littlehampton and Mid-Sussex services, often with Brighton-allocated VEP and BEP units.

The 1967 Bournemouth line electrification, described in Chapter 3, made new demands on the multiple unit rolling stock to be used, and these were met in a novel way. The requirement that through services between Waterloo and Weymouth should work electrically between London and Bournemouth and by diesel power westwards led to the development of a push-pull arrangement making further use of the flexibility of the 27-wire EPB control system. These arrangements involved the use of high-powered motor units working with trailer units, without motors but with end cabs, which could be hauled or propelled electrically by the motor units between London and Bournemouth and by diesel locomotives between Bournemouth and Weymouth. To cover initial traffic requirements eleven of the powered units, classified 4 REP and numbered 3001-3011, and 31 trailer units were provided. Of these 28 were of four-coach formation, classified 4 TC and numbered 401-428. The remainder were three-coach 3 TC units, 301-303, and there were also two spare TC vehicles. The purpose of the 3 TCs was to enable a complete train of TC stock, powered by a class 33 or 73 locomotive, to fit the twelve-coach length platforms at Waterloo. Formation of the 4 REPs comprised two driving motor seconds, a side-corridor trailer brake first and an RB buffet/restaurant car, providing 128 second class and 24 first class seats, plus 23 unclassified places in the catering vehicle. The 4 TCs were formed with two driving trailer seconds, a side-corridor trailer first and a side-corridor trailer brake second, while the 3 TCs lacked the corridor first. Seating capacity was thus 160 second and (in the 4 TCs only) 42 first.

In a misguided attempt to save costs, use was made of existing locomotive-hauled Mark 1 coaching stock to provide most of the vehicles for the REPs and TCs, only the motor coaches of the REPs being brand new. The first 4 TC and the centre trailers of the first REP were converted at Eastleigh as a costing exercise, but all other vehicles were constructed or rebuilt at York. The REP catering cars were fitted with electric cooking appliances and two staff toilets but otherwise retained their original layout, as did the TC centre trailers. The trailer brake firsts of the REPs were modified from side-corridor composites, the new guard's and luggage compartment taking the place of the former second class compartments and toilet. The driving trailer seconds of the TCs were altered from tourist open seconds, the motorman's cab replacing two toilets, while new passenger entrance doors were cut into the first seating bay. A significant number of the vehicles used had originally been built by outside contractors, including Metro-Cammell, BRCW and Charles Roberts & Co. Many of the TC trailer firsts were converted from the earliest batch of Mark 1 side-corridor firsts, dating from 1951 – these included the prototype, which became TFK 70865 in unit 422.

Externally, the vehicles resembled CIG stock with the same GRP cab ends and shrouded gangway connections. As mentioned elsewhere, the semi-matt paint scheme in which these units had been delivered weathered very badly, and the entire fleet had been repainted into blue/grey with full yellow ends by the end of 1970. Internally, the rebuilt vehicles had new seating and laminate internal panelling in shades of blue and light grey, and the REP motor coaches were finished in

The 1970 batch of 4 CIG units largely replaced pre-war COR stock on the Portsmouth direct, Brighton and Reading lines, and were delivered in blue/grey livery with full yellow ends. Unit 7421 approaches Wokingham with the 10.58 Waterloo – Reading service on 3rd July 1982. The internal appointments in these later units were rather more austere than in the 1964 examples.
Alex Dasi-Sutton

The first 4 REP high-powered tractor unit, 3001, poses for an official view when brand new. The cast aluminium 'double arrow' symbol under the cab side window was a feature of all units (REPs, TCs and VEPs) originally provided for the Bournemouth electrification scheme and delivered in overall blue. The ETH jumper under the nearside buffer, an unusual fitting for SR EMU stock, was required to heat TC units coupled to it.
BR Southern Region Official

the same style. First class seating was upholstered in the new British Rail charcoal grey check moquette and had adjustable bolster-like head cushions fitted with removable white nylon covers. Seating in the second class accommodation was finished in a new green/blue pattern, but the seats were thin and hard compared with what had gone before. Exceptionally, the TC open saloons retained their original seat units and had deeper headrests and thicker cushions in consequence. The catering vehicles had loose seats at tables and, as a full restaurant service was provided on many workings, seating bays in the adjacent motor coach were fitted with tables as a permanent arrangement.

Electrically the Bournemouth REP and TC fleet was classed as 1966 stock. Each REP motor coach had two mark 6 motor bogies each equipped with a pair of EE 546 traction motors rated at 365hp. These were specified by the BRB and were already in use (although more conservatively rated) on certain ac stock on other regions, as well as on the SRs own class JB (later 73/1) electro-diesel locomotives. This gave a total installed rating of nearly 3,000hp, enough to power twelve coaches (the REP and two TCs) on the Waterloo – Bournemouth stretch. A REP motor coach was electrically equivalent to a class JB, which could substitute if necessary. Each motor bogie had two collector shoes on each side, and power circuits were duplicated. Unlike 1963 stock, the Bournemouth units were all equipped with a power jumper under the nearside buffer and a receptacle under the offside, to allow the REP to provide electricity to the heating and auxiliary circuits of the TCs coupled to it. Trailer bogies on both REPs and TCs were of the coil-sprung B5S type.

The first three 4 TCs entered service on the Bournemouth line, powered by the SRs type 3 KA diesel-electric locomotives, as early as July 1966, and the first REPs commenced traffic operation in April 1967 shortly after completion of the whole route. Other workings by this time were diagrammed for TCs worked push-pull by electro-diesels. (See below for details of these locomotives.) Numbers of REPs and TCs gradually increased up to the official inauguration of the Bournemouth electrification that July, although it was not until well into 1968 that all were in traffic and running in a satisfactory manner. Significant mixing of vehicles resulted in many mis-formed units in the early days – for example some 4 TCs ran without trailer firsts for a short time due to the late delivery of these vehicles, or with REP buffet cars formed in them to provide catering accommodation on trains when there was a lack of available REP motor coaches.

Initially sufficient rolling stock was provided to work an hourly semi-fast train between Waterloo and Bournemouth, extended to Weymouth every other hour, and a two-hourly fast service, which ran through to Weymouth to provide the necessary sixty-minute interval service west of Bournemouth. Increasing patronage led to the introduction of an hourly Waterloo – Weymouth fast service from May 1974, and to provide the additional rolling stock for this expansion four more 4 REP units, numbered 3012-3015, and three 4 TC units, 432-434, were provided. TC 432 included TBSK 70843, provided as a spare vehicle in 1967. Additionally, the three existing 3 TC units were made-up to four coaches with an additional trailer first, and renumbered 429-431. As before, all trailer vehicles were rebuilt from existing Mark 1 vehicles

Prior to the full inauguration of electric services on the Bournemouth line, recently delivered 4 TC trailer unit 417, propelled by locomotive D6520, passes Lymington Junction after calling at Brockenhurst with the 10.43 Southampton Central – Bournemouth Central service on 31st March 1967. *John Scrace*

4 VEP 7703, from the original batch of twenty built for the Bournemouth electrification scheme, calls at the new Southampton Airport station leading a Bournemouth – Waterloo semi-fast service in October 1968. The first ten units unusually had blue-painted window frames rather than unpainted aluminium. *Colin Boocock*

at York, and the eight new REP motor coaches 62476-83 also built there were the very last vehicles to be constructed to the BR Mark 1 pattern, surely an indictment of the SRs ultra-conservative post-war rolling stock policy. The catering vehicles in 3012-3015 were slightly different from those in the first eleven REPs, being converted from RU unclassified restaurant cars, but seating was the same and no operating distinction was made between the two types.

For the Bournemouth line there was also a requirement for conventional electric stock to operate the Waterloo – Bournemouth stopping services, some of which attached or detached Alton or Portsmouth portions at Woking. To operate these services twenty four-coach units, classified 4 VEP and numbered 7701-7720, were provided. Their formation was the same as the CIGs, with a centrally-located motor coach, two driving trailers and an intermediate trailer, gangwayed throughout. The motor coaches were built at Derby Litchurch Lane and the trailers at York. While still basically following BR Mark 1 design and construction parameters, VEPs were designed for stopping services and had three+two seating in second class, with a side-door to each seating bay and luggage racks over the seat backs as in the EPBs and SUBs. This arrangement gave a seating capacity of 232 second and 48 first. The driving trailers had a cab identical to those of the CIGs, a four-bay second class open section, four first class compartments connected by side corridor, and a toilet. The trailer second had ten bays with no partition, and the motor coach only six bays and a huge luggage area. The interior ambience in the saloons was little different from a SUB, the seats being thinner and harder, and thus less comfortable; but between the doors were large intermediate aluminium-framed windows with sliding ventilators and orange curtains – both the ventilators and curtains were to become a maintenance liability and were eventually done away with. First

class compartments were identical to those in the REPs and TCs, except that each had its own external door. The electrical layout closely resembled the 1970 CIGs, but the EE 507EA motors were given a higher nominal rating of 275hp (rather than 250). External livery was the sprayed blue finish, with small yellow warning panels and cast 'double arrows' on the cab sides. 7701-7710 were outshopped with blue window frames but on the remainder they were left as bare metal.

The 4 VEP design was then constructed in quantity to replace the pre-war semi-fast stock on the Central and South Western divisions from 1968, and later units were all but identical to the first twenty. All vehicles in these later batches were built at York. 7721-7755 were delivered in 1968 mainly to replace the 4 LAVs on the Brighton main line, while 7756-7815 followed between late 1968 and early 1970 to replace remaining BILs and HALs on the coastal and Portsmouth Direct lines. All were delivered in the later glossy (brushed, rather than sprayed) overall blue livery with full yellow ends and unpainted aluminium window frames. These latter were fixed with steel bolts, giving rise to characteristic rust streaks almost from new. 7808 was experimentally outshopped new in blue/grey without the cast BR symbols. Production recommenced in 1972 and was completed in 1974, during which time two further batches entered service, all in blue/grey from the start. 7816-7853 replaced the last of the CORs on coastal services and also ousted SUBs from their brief 1973 sojurn on the Guildford New line via Cobham. Finally 7854-7894 were built because finance was available at the time rather than because they were really needed; originally allocated to Ramsgate for use on Kent Coast stopping services, they replaced HAPs (see above). The earlier batches were repainted into blue/grey as they passed through works, making them all match the true express stock with which they all too often worked indiscriminately.

An interesting interlude concerns units 7739/41/42 from the 1968 batch, which were disbanded before entering service. Instead, seven vehicles were reformed with a rewired RB loco-hauled catering car to form 8 VAB 8001, for use as a spare express unit on Bournemouth line fast services. Formed driving trailer composite + motor brake second + buffet car + motor brake second + driving trailer composite + driving trailer composite + motor brake second + driving trailer composite, the former VEP vehicles originally remained blue but the buffet was blue/grey, giving the unit a piebald appearance. The centre driving trailers were marshalled with their cabs adjacent. The purpose of providing three motor coaches was to give sufficient power to haul or propel a TC trailer unit, but in practice it usually worked coupled to another VEP which had its motors isolated. One motor coach adjacent to the buffet had its doors sealed and tables fitted to provide a dining saloon, with seating allocated two+one either side of the gangway. 8001 was disbanded in January 1975 following the delivery of additional REPs, by which time all its coaches were in blue and grey livery. Its coaches were reformed into VEPs 7741 and 7742. As various spare vehicles had been used to replace accident-damaged coaches in other units, 7739 could not be reinstated and hence never ran in service.

With the gradual sealing-up of VEP sliding window ventilators from about 1976 onwards, 7755 and 7756 had their entire windows replaced by plain sheet glass, greatly improving their appearance. 7755 was also fitted experimentally with luggage shelves in place of a few seats for use on Gatwick Airport services and, following this, a small fleet of twelve units was converted in 1978 specifically for the Victoria – Gatwick Airport run. Units 7788-7799 were renumbered 7901-7912, reclassified 4 VEG, fitted with luggage racks and obscured quarter-lights in place of the end seats in second class saloons (reducing capacity by twenty), and given a special 'airport' livery. Initially this was a red cantrail tape, but was soon changed to a green stripe in the same position together with branding below the windows at each driving end reading 'Rapid City Link Gatwick – London' and an aeroplane symbol. The VEGs also retained their orange curtains at a time when other VEPs were losing theirs. Regularly straying from their booked workings, VEGs were known to turn up on any Central division service diagrammed for VEPs, regularly reaching Portsmouth Harbour and Littlehampton. From mid 1983 VEG units were outshopped following overhaul in standard livery, in readiness for their conversion back to VEPs following introduction of improved stock on the dedicated airport services from May 1984.

In 1975, 4 CEP 7153 was selected for an experimental rebuild at Eastleigh Works with the aim of reorganising the internal layout to make it resemble more recent stock with the guard's accommodation at the centre, and also to modernise the seating in line with standards elsewhere in the country. It was recognised that comfort and ambience of SR express stock fell short of that on other regions, but equally it would be uneconomic to replace the mechanically-sound Kent Coast CEP and BEP fleet for a further twenty years. In the motor coaches a bay of seating replaced the former van area, while the compartment trailer second was converted into a saloon with two toilets at one end. In the composite the four first class compartments remained, but two of the second class compartments became the new guard's accommodation and van area, and the final second class compartment was given first class seating. Internally, all was new, with laminate panelling and 'InterCity 70' type seating (as in modern Mark 2e/f hauled stock) with moulded plastic shells, black foam armrests and removable cushion covers. Over-complicated ceiling panelling incorporating fluorescent strip-lighting and a PA system were fitted. Externally the gangway connections were shrouded in sheet metal to resemble those on the CIGs, but other than necessary window rearragements little else was changed. The rebuild was deemed a success and after some months on the Victoria – Gatwick Airport run 7153 returned to Ramsgate to sink into anonymity among the rest of the CEP fleet.

In 1979 the rebuilding of the entire 4 CEP and 4 BEP fleet, to a standard similar to 7153, commenced, the work being given to the former GWR workshops at Swindon which were otherwise idle. The rebuilt CEPs largely resembled the prototype, the main difference being the use of tinted windows with hopper-type ventilators, their lack of adjustment being unsuitable for express stock and soon the cause of considerable complaint. Internally, the peculiarly-shaped seat cushions in second class were ostensibly the result of a late specification change following an upholstery warehouse fire unconnected with BR. The single compartment adjacent to the brake was fitted out with second class seating, but still with only three seats per side. Seating capacity of the rebuilt units was virtually unchanged, with just two fewer second class seats. Mechanically, all non-motored bogies were of the Commonwealth type, in some cases recovered from withdrawn hauled stock, but the mark 4 motor bogies remained. Electrically, the circuits were altered to more closely resemble 1963 stock, and a VEP-type motorman's desk was fitted.

Initially, the rebuilt units were renumbered on leaving works with a six digit number incorporating the numerical classification 411 and three extra digits starting at 501. Most of the BEPs were converted into CEPs, their buffet cars being replaced by open seconds converted from hauled stock, and this gave a total of 121 CEPs together with two spare motor coaches. Fourteen former loco-hauled TSOs were converted for use in the CEP programme, all originally dating from the 1952-56 period. Phase I units were numbered from 411506 upwards and phase II units from 411608 downwards, both in order of conversion, while the numbers 411501-411505 were reserved for the five remaining prototypes (7102 having already been written-off) with 1951-type contactor control gear. The first production rebuild, 411506, was outshopped in December 1979 and by September 1983 virtually all had been done. After the first 27 had entered service, unit numbering reverted to the traditional four-digits, the initial '41' being omitted. The numbers 1609-1621 were allocated to additional phase II units.

With the CEP rebuilding scheme it was planned to abolish catering cars from the South Eastern division entirely, and the original intention was that all BEPs should become CEPs in the manner described already. However a later change of

4 CEP 7153 was rebuilt at Eastleigh in 1975, the main alteration being to move the guard's and luggage area to one of the centre vehicles, as on more recent express stock. The former van spaces behind the cabs were converted into passenger accommodation, as can be seen clearly in this view of 7153 emerging from Shakespeare Cliff tunnel at the head of a Victoria to Dover Marine boat train on 23rd July 1983. *Alex Dasi-Sutton*

plan resulted in a requirement for seven refurbished 4 BEPs for use on the Waterloo – Portsmouth Direct line, where they would work with 4 CIG stock and replace 4 BIGs which would be transferred to the Brighton line following asbestos stripping. The seven buffet cars selected for refurbishing all came from the phase II batch. Numbered 2301, the first rebuilt BEP re-entered traffic in March 1983 and by September three had been done, although 2303 did not actually go into traffic until the beginning of October. The motor coaches and trailer brake composite were the same as in the CEPs, and the buffet car was completely altered from its previous configuration. The new layout comprised a three-bay second class saloon with normal seating for 24 followed by a staff toilet and buffet compartment with counter. Finally, the buffet area had shelves along one side and a longitudinal bench seat with three tables along the other, all panelled in bright orange laminate. The buffet facilities included a microwave oven for the first time, although the initial range of available micro-waved snacks was quickly curtailed. 2303 was interesting in having late phase II motor coaches, with tapered windscreens, originally from CEP 7208.

As a result of a catering vehicle shortage on the Portsmouth line in 1983, two temporary eight-car units were made up for the summer timetable. Some years previously two 1962-vintage locomotive-hauled Mark 1 miniature buffet cars (RMB), 1872/73, had been fitted with EPB jumper cables and waist-level brake pipes, mainly to work between 4 TC units on excursions. By 1983 they had been parked out of use in Clapham Yard for some time. Resurrected with the minimum of attention, each was marshalled between a pair of 4 CIGs, one of which had its trailer second removed, to form an eight-coach unit classified 8 MIG. It was not possible to form these

buffet cars within a unit as the jumper cable arrangements between vehicles within a unit were different from those at the cab ends. Numbered 2601 and 2602 with crude hand-painted numerals, the former was made up of 7401+1872+7402, and the second 7403+1873+7404 – in both cases the TSO was removed from the even-numbered CIG. Both of these tempo-rary lash-ups were in traffic by mid May, but after only one summer's service they were disbanded and the CIGs returned to normal at the beginning of October. Not least this was because the lack of train heating jumpers on the CIGs meant that the buffets could not be heated.

Temporary buffet accommodation was also required on the Brighton line and this was provided by retaining four unrebuilt BEP buffet cars not required for the refurbishment programme and marshalling these in place of the TSO in four recently refurbished CEPs. Classified 4 TEP and numbered 2701-2704, only the first two were made up in the period under review. 2701 was formed at the beginning of August 1983 and consisted of 1556 plus buffet 69010 from 7011, while 2702 followed in mid-September and consisted of 1557 and buffet 69021 from 7022 – this latter was the experimentally air-conditioned vehicle.

The last reported unrebuilt CEP, 7106, was noted in traffic on 11th July 1983, and was sent to Swindon ten days later. Conversely the last two BEPs in original condition, 7018 and 7021, were still in service on the Central division in the middle of September, and these constituted the last unrefur-bished Kent Coast express units to remain in traffic. (When eventually disbanded they gave up their buffets to TEPs 2703 and 2704.) By the end of September about ten CEPs and four BEPs were awaiting return from Swindon Works following rebuilding.

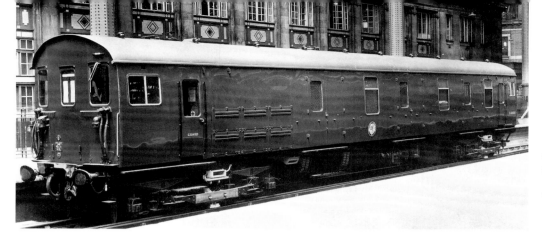

Motor Luggage Van (MLV) 68007 at Dover Marine in the early 1960s. The traction batteries, for operation over non-electrified quay lines, are located under the hatches behind the cab door, while the vacuum brake pipe may be seen below the left hand buffer. *Colin J Marsden Collection*

MOTOR AND TRAILER LUGGAGE VANS (MLV/TLV)

The ten motor luggage vans or MLVs, built at Eastleigh between 1959 and 1961, do not fit easily into either of the stock categories so far mentioned in this chapter, although contemporary with both. Constructed primarily to provide adequate luggage space on boat trains between London and Dover/Folkestone otherwise formed of 4 CEP and 4 BEP stock, they superficially resembled a BR standard Mark 1 full brake with a suburban-style cab at each end, and were on standard 63ft 5in EMU underframes. Carrying coach numbers only, 68001 and 68002 were provided for phase I and 68003-68010 for phase II and, although there were detail differences between the two batches, both had body sides with raised window frames and cab ends with parallel-sided windscreens and deep headcode panel. The electrical installation included 1957-type camshaft control equipment and two standard EE 507 motors with express gearing mounted on the bogie located at the No.1 end. Both bogies, of the standard mark 3B motor-bogie type, were equipped with shoegear. Internal layout comprised a cab at either end, a guard's compartment and large and small luggage areas; these had two and one double doors on each side, respectively. The guard's compartment was directly behind the cab at the 'No.1' end. Side windows were strengthened with steel mesh rather than bars, and the lack of end gangways gave greater security for bonded and registered mail. Livery of all MLVs when new was dark green with the carriage roundel centrally on the sides, but there were no numbers at unit ends. All ten were based at Ramsgate from their introduction.

The MLVs incorporated several interesting non-standard features to increase their versatility. Firstly, they were dual-braked and, as vacuum brakes remained standard on hauled stock at the time they were introduced, this latter feature enabled them to haul a short trailing load of 100 tons (reduced to fifty tons on the steeply-graded Folkestone Harbour branch). Power for the vacuum brake exhausters was normally provided by the motor-generator. Secondly, they were fitted with traction batteries to allow them to work over non-electrified quayside lines, albeit at slow speed. Mounted behind hatches on the body sides adjacent to the guard's compartment, they were charged while working off the third rail, current being supplied from an auxiliary generator coupled to the motor-generator. External charging points were also provided for the MLVs at Grosvenor Road sidings outside Victoria and at various other locations. These batteries

supplied current at 200V to the motors, compressors and vacuum brake exhausters. The pick-up shoes retracted automatically when battery power was selected by the motorman, in order to avoid clearance problems on non-electrified lines and to enable the vans to regain the conductor rail at locations where lead-in ramps were not provided. The shoes were raised and lowered pneumatically, using air from the compressors. The maximum time an MLV could work on battery power without recharging was about twenty minutes.

Apart from 68004, which ran with all-blue body sides for a short period, all ten motor luggage vans were repainted into blue/grey livery with full yellow ends between 1968 and 1970, the coach number then being repeated on the ends above the headcode. Apart from their use on boat trains, on which they invariably worked at the London end, they were additionally diagrammed for a few normal service trains carrying heavy mail traffic on the Kent Coast lines, and were also occasionally worked solo carrying mail both on the Central and South Eastern divisions.

Large amounts of luggage and bonded mail loaded the MLVs on some boat trains very heavily in the mid 1960s, requiring the use of two on some services. Apart from straining the available power supply this was considered wasteful, and a solution to the problem was found by providing six trailer luggage vans or TLVs. Numbered 68201-68206, they were converted from BR standard 58ft full-brakes at Selhurst in 1968. The gangway connections were sealed up but left in situ in case it was decided to convert them back to locomotive-hauled use later. Waist-level air-brake pipes and 27-wire jumpers were fitted on the offside only, so two could not be coupled together with through MU control. Inserted between an MLV and a 4 CEP at the London end of boat trains, all went into service while still painted maroon. As Kent Coast stock was in a mixture of green, all-blue and blue/grey liveries at this time, many such boat trains would have been distinctly colourful! All had been repainted into blue/grey by 1969. Remaining in traffic only until 1974, the TLVs were withdrawn partly due to a downturn in traffic and partly due to a Union dispute over whether they were defined for shunting purposes as EMUs or hauled stock. Following their use as match vehicles for delivery of the 1974 batch of Bournemouth line REP and TC stock from York, they finally became departmental stores vehicles on the Western Region in 1979 (renumbered ADB 975610-15, but not in order) at which point they drop out of our story.

LOCOMOTIVES

This section deals briefly with the four main line locomotive classes, one diesel-electric, one straight electric and two electro-diesel, introduced from 1958 as part of the modernisation of the Southern Region. Emphasis is placed on passenger train haulage and more particularly on their involvement with the EMU stock with which this book is largely concerned. Diesel shunters are not included.

For the two phases of the Kent Coast electrification scheme there was a requirement for a small fleet of highly-powered electric locomotives to cover newspaper, parcels and general freight duties on the electrified lines, as well as certain passenger trains not worked by multiple units. In the decade since the original Bulleid Co-Co locomotives had been built there had been major advances in electric locomotive design, enabling a significant power increase for a much reduced overall weight. An initial order for thirteen locomotives for phase I was increased to 24 to cover phase II also and the class, numbered from E5000 upwards, was delivered between 1958 and 1960. The doyen of the class, E5000, was later renumbered E5024.

The new locomotives were designed and built at the BR Works at Doncaster and were an amalgam of the 'booster' technology pioneered on the earlier Bulleid Co-Cos and more recent Swiss developments in lightweight bogie electric locomotives (such as the SBB Re4.4/1 class). Of Bo-Bo wheel arrangement, all electrical equipment was supplied by English Electric, four EE 532 traction motors giving a rating of 2,552hp, more than comparable with the most powerful steam locomotives they replaced. These motors were mounted on the bogie frames, power being transmitted to the wheels through the patented Brown-Boveri (BBC) spring drive. Bogies and drives were built in Switzerland by SLM, the latter under licence from BBC. Only one booster was fitted, and the controller had 33 notches of which 1-15 'bucked' and 16-29 'boosted' the line supply, while 30-33 were for weak-field. (Chapter 6 gives a fuller explanation of this system.) Both air and vacuum brakes were fitted, and maximum speed on passenger trains was 90mph. Following earlier experiments, 750V dc trolley wires were erected in many of the yards these locomotives were to use to alleviate the safety problems of ground-level conductor rails, and a central pantograph was therefore fitted which retracted into a roof recess when not in use.

The bodies of these smart-looking locomotives were just under 50ft in length with a BR Mark 1 coach profile and slightly sloping ends with radiused edges. The windscreens were grouped with a standard two-character roller blind headcode panel, which included letters as well as numbers for the operation of freight and parcels trains. Livery was mid-green (lighter than the 1957 EMU shade) with white windscreen surrounds and a white/red/white stripe along the body sides. Underframe and bogies were black, the central portion of the roof light grey, and buffer beams bright red.

The E5000 class, classified HA by the SR operating department, were all allocated from new to the electric locomotive shed built especially for them at Stewarts Lane, Battersea. The *Night Ferry*, with its through Wagons Lits sleeping cars

to Paris and Brussels, was hauled by these locomotives from 8th June 1959, a week before the official 'switch-on' of Kent Coast phase I, running between Victoria and the train ferry berth at Dover Marine via Chatham. Likewise, the *Golden Arrow* Pullman service was electrically hauled from the inauguration of phase II on 12th June 1961, routed via Tonbridge. Special insignia were provided for the locomotives on this duty and the usual performer, E5015, was maintained in an especially clean condition by Stewarts Lane staff. From 1964 the Bo-Bos shared with the Bulleid locomotives haulage of the Victoria – Newhaven boat train, although their lack of steam heating required them to work in tandem with a class 5 4-6-0 steam locomotive during winter months until electrically-heated coaching stock was introduced. Otherwise, their main duties were van and miscellaneous freight trains all over the South Eastern. They lost their central lining stripe on first repaint from about 1964 and some gained small yellow warning panels, not all the same size, at this time.

The Kent Coast electrification scheme envisaged complete elimination of steam traction from the Eastern section and diesel locomotives were therefore also required for various duties including freight, parcels and miscellaneous passenger workings. The BTC originally intended that the sizeable Southern Region demand for a medium powered diesel electric locomotive in the Type 3 power classification could be met by providing the English Electric Co-Co design (later class 37). However the SR Chief Civil Engineer, who still had a certain autonomy in these matters, refused to accept a six-axle design and would only countenance a Bo-Bo.

Birmingham Railway Carriage and Wagon Co. of Smethwick, a company which has featured previously in these pages, had already supplied to BR a Type 2 Bo-Bo design (later class 26). By using the same bodyshell but omitting the steam heating boiler, it was possible to fit an eight (rather than six) cylinder Sulzer engine of type 8LDA28 which, with four Crompton Parkinson type C171 traction motors, gave a Type 3 power rating of 1,550hp. Other alterations for SR purposes included the installation of electric train heating (ETH) and dual-braking – both non-standard features at the time, and the almost-flat cab ends were given standard two-character EMU roller-blind headcode panels between the windscreens. 'Blue star' multiple-unit equipment made multiple working within the class and with the majority of other BR main line diesel locomotives possible, but at this stage operation with electric stock was not envisaged.

98 locomotives of this basic type, numbered D6500-D6597, were delivered to the SR in 1960-61. Of the four batches the first two, comprising D6500-D6544 and D6545-D6565, were required for the elimination of steam working in Kent by the completion of phase II of the Kent Coast electrification. The third batch ordered became D6586-D6597, twelve locomotives constructed to the narrow Hastings line loading gauge, with bodies only 8ft 5in wide rather than the standard 9ft 3in. Serious design difficulties were encountered in squeezing equipment into the narrower bodyshell, and as a result they were the last batch to be delivered, after 'standard' D6566-D6585 which were intended for general use in Kent and

For a number of years following electrification, HA electric locomotive E5015 was kept especially clean by Stewarts Lane staff, specifically for use on the *Golden Arrow* Victoria – Dover (for Paris) Pullman boat train service. Carrying the appropriate headboard and flags, the 10am Down working is seen approaching Shortlands Junction on 27th August 1961, just two months after the start of electric working. Note the four wheeled van and two Bulleid corridor coaches between E5015 and the leading Pullman. *John Scrace*

The entire 2552hp output of the class HA electric locomotives was often required to haul the heavy *Night Ferry* service, with its through *Wagon Lits* sleeping cars between London and Paris/Brussels. On the morning of 4th August 1962 E5010 was in charge of the Victoria-bound working, photographed approaching Catford. *John Scrace*

In original green livery with grey lining and white cab-window surrounds, BRCW type 3 KA diesel-electric locomotive D6584 heads north along the West London line at Lillie Bridge on 5th June 1966 with a train of condemned PAN pantry cars and a solitary PUL Pullman composite, probably bound for King's scrapyard at Wymondham, Norfolk. *Brian Stephenson*

Sussex. All were delivered in the same livery of BR diesel green with light grey roof, white cab window surrounds and a light grey stripe around the entire body just above waist height. Below underframe level they were black, with red buffer beams. The standard locomotives, classified by the SR KA, were given the BR locomotive badge but, oddly, the Hastings line KB subtype had carriage roundels. Yellow warning panels covering the whole lower half of the ends were added from 1965, but a number of the class still lacked them three years later. Most were initially allocated to the new Hither Green diesel depot, but from May 1960 when the first was delivered until October 1967 the KBs were based at St Leonards West Marina.

The early locomotives were employed on miscellaneous duties in Kent and Sussex, including haulage of through passenger trains between London and the Kent Coast via Tonbridge prior to the switch on of phase II in 1962. After this there was a surplus due to a downturn in traffic and members of the class were moved to Eastleigh for the first time, after which they soon became regular performers on

Bournemouth line passenger diagrams. Following dieselisation of the Central division Oxted line in 1963, the class was used on certain peak-hour trains between Victoria or London Bridge and Tunbridge Wells – from September 1963 a regular duty involved hauling set 900 (later 701) formed of 2 BIL and 4 SUB EMU vehicles (see Chapter 4).

An acknowledged disadvantage of straight electric locomotives of the E5000 and 20001 types was their complete inability to operate over non-electrified lines and sidings, and therefore the idea of providing an auxiliary diesel engine for such occasions arose. Although various suggestions for such a dual-powered locomotive had been passed around even before 1939, it was not until 1956 that serious design work on what became known as an 'electro-diesel' began, and authority for the construction of six prototypes was granted in 1959. Designed at Brighton and built in the carriage works at Eastleigh, the first example emerged at the end of January 1962, and all six had entered service by the middle of November that year. They were numbered E6001-E6006 in order of delivery.

Although a new type, the electro-diesels, given the SR operating code JA, were really a combination of existing technology and few parts in them were untried. The slab sided box-like bodies were built to Restriction 0 to allow them to operate on the Hastings line, and the cabs had domed roofs influenced by the 5 BEL units, which the designers at Brighton observed passing their drawing office window several times each day. Bogies, of 8ft 9in wheelbase, were based on the Swiss type used on the HAs, but redesigned at Brighton. Significantly, the cab ends had the same fittings as contemporary EMUs, incorporating a two-character headcode panel, EPB-type waist-level control and brake hoses and buckeye coupler. There was an additional power jumper cable below the driver's windscreen. Unusually, saddle-shaped self-contained buffers of the type used on electric units were originally fitted, but these were later replaced by the standard oleo round type.

On the electrical side, all equipment was once more supplied by English Electric, power being provided by four 400hp traction motors of type EE 542A, nose-suspended in conventional SR fashion and controlled by camshaft-actuated resistances. The auxiliary diesel engine was an EE four-cylinder 4SRKT, this and the main generator being similar to those in the SR's fleet of diesel electric multiple units introduced from 1957. These arrangements gave 1,600hp on electric power, roughly equivalent to the KA diesel electrics, and 600hp on diesel. This was double that required for purely shunting purposes and for 'getting out of trouble', so more general use on diesel power was probably envisaged. As on the MLVs, the collector shoes were raised when working on auxiliary power. Maximum speed was officially 80mph, but 85mph could be reached in practice. Multiple-unit equipment enabled the class not only to multiple with any 'blue-star' equipped locomotive, including the KAs and KBs, but also with any electric unit fitted with EP brakes and 27-wire control, with operation from any driving cab in the train. Dual-braking was fitted and, if coupled between vacuum and air-braked stock, the JA could translate one system into the other. Many trials with this system were undertaken when the locomotives were new.

E6001 was outshopped in the same bright green as the E5000 class, with a light grey central roof panel and white cab-window surrounds. However there was no lining band, and the carriage roundel was used. As far as can be ascertained, it was the first item of SR rolling stock to be given a small yellow warning panel, but this was not approved at the time and was quickly replaced with an all-around light grey band at solebar level. The remaining five were given this revised livery from new, but the small warning panels reappeared on all from about 1965. The class shared the purpose-built facilities at Stewarts Lane and soon proved their worth, their diesel equipment proving invaluable during engineer's possessions as well as in non-electrified carriage sidings and yards. Their success paved the way for a production order for thirty more as early as June 1963, and soon afterwards a further thirteen were authorised in connection with the Bournemouth electrification.

Complete construction of the production electro-diesels,

classified JB and numbered E6007-E6049, was contracted out to English Electric. They were built at the Vulcan Foundry at Newton-le-Willows, and delivered between October 1965 and January 1967, all being worked down to the SR on their own diesel power. Although mostly the same as the prototypes, there were various detail differences, and as a result the two types were not supposed to operate in multiple. The power bogies were redesigned and different traction motors, type EE 546.1/B, fitted. These were geared for a 90mph maximum speed. The bogie design (with different springing) was also used on EMU stock introduced between 1966 and 1974, while the motors were the same as those in the 4 REPs. The unit-end power jumpers were left off. The first seven were delivered in the new British Rail blue with light grey solebar stripe, an almost white roof and small yellow warning panels, but lacked any evidence of ownership. Later examples omitted the solebar stripe but had the white 'double arrow' symbol on the sides, and this was later added to the other seven. All, including E6001-E6006, were repainted in the uninspiring overall blue with full yellow ends between 1968 and 1971, accentuating their slab-sided appearance.

The technical arrangements for the Bournemouth line electrification, authorised in 1964, already mentioned in this chapter and elsewhere, and an integral part of the operation was the haulage and propulsion of trailer units by diesel locomotives in the 'push-pull' mode between Bournemouth and Weymouth. To test this arrangement Eastleigh-based KA D6580 was converted in 1965 to run in multiple with EP-braked electric stock. Put simply, this involved fitting a converter which translated the four standard power settings of an EMU controller into four set engine speeds on the locomotive. Connected via the standard waist-level EPB 27-wire control cable, these alterations enabled the locomotive controls to operate the motors of a suitably-equipped electric unit and also control of the locomotive (including engine starting) from a remote EMU cab. The 6 TC six-coach control trailer unit made up from surplus pre-war express stock vehicles to work with D6580, numbered 601, is fully described in Chapter 5. For a short period this locomotive was even fitted with third-rail collector shoes, but alterations to allow its traction motors to draw current directly from the conductor rail were never carried out. Following some hair-raising but satisfactory testing at speeds of up to 85mph, D6580+601 went into service on Oxted line duties, and the locomotive was also a regular performer on the Bournemouth line prior to electrification. When altered, D6580 was given small EMU-style yellow warning panels.

Following the successful outcome of these tests, eighteen more of the class were converted at Eastleigh for push-pull working in 1966 and 1967. Those chosen, D6511/13/14/16/17/19-21/25/27-29/31-33/35/36/38, were all due for heavy overhaul at the time. Generally similar to D6580 with waist-level brake and control jumper cables, the production conversions were also fitted with buckeye couplers and rubbing plates, and the prototype was soon altered to conform. They were outshopped in rail blue with full yellow ends including the cab window surrounds, white lettering and the new 'double arrow' symbol.

E6001, the prototype class JA electro-diesel locomotive, stands outside Hither Green depot late in 1962. It is in as-built condition with EMU-type oval buffers, and livery is bright green with coaching stock badges and small yellow warning panels (which were later painted out). The domed cab roofs were apparently influenced by those of the *Brighton Belle* units. *Colin Boocock*

Photographs of D6580 experimentally modified for push-pull operation with 6 TC 601 and other EP-braked stock are very rare. In this view it is seen pausing at Basingstoke with a Waterloo – Bournemouth train on an unknown date in 1966. The combination of multiple unit jumpers, no buckeye coupling, green livery and EMU-style yellow warning panel was unique. *J. N. Faulkner*

Making use of its 650hp diesel engine prior to regaining the live rail at Northam, Class 74 HB electro-diesel E6104 departs from Southampton Eastern Docks with the empty stock of a boat train from Waterloo on 22nd May 1968. This was very much the type of working for which these powerful, but unreliable and short lived, locomotives were designed. *Southern Images / John H. Bird*

Apart from the JBs, the Bournemouth line electrification also required a small fleet of more powerful electro-diesel locomotives for heavier workings such as the Channel Islands boat train. Comparative costings were calculated at Eastleigh between building entirely new locomotives or converting HA straight electrics, some of which were now surplus as a result of dwindling freight traffic. These costings came out in favour of conversion, and hence ten of the class, E5003/5/6/15/16/17/19/21/23/24, were taken out of service for a complete rebuild at Crewe works in 1967-68. With one exception, those chosen were all due for a general overhaul anyway. The rebuilt locomotives were reclassified HB and numbered E6101-E6110.

Considerable difficulty was experienced in fitting all the additional equipment into the original HA bodyshells, and much rearrangement was necessary. They were firstly stripped down to leave only the underframe and cabs, and even the latter were redistributed randomly among the conversions. To help carry the additional weight of equipment, new load-bearing body sides were built on, with warren-girder trussing. The bogies (albeit with altered springing), traction motors and booster were retained, but the booster was relocated and its flywheel removed, the weight of the armatures being found sufficient to maintain momentum. The space left was occupied by two new traction motor blowers. Weight considerations precluded the use of the standard EE four-cylinder diesel engine used elsewhere, and instead the high-speed six-cylinder Paxman 'Ventura' of 650hp was fitted, driving a lightweight generator which supplied current to the booster set in the absence of the live rail. Even so, the axle loading reached the 21.75 ton maximum allowed on the SR. The engine silencer, radiator and cooling fan were located in the roof space previously occupied by the pantograph, and new translucent GRP roof panels fitted. Buckeye couplings and waist-level EPB type control/brake hoses were fitted, as on the JBs and push-pull fitted KAs with which the HBs could (in theory at least) operate in multiple.

The most significant advance in these locomotives was the use of electronic components in the control system, both to save weight and provide improved control response for 90mph schedules on the Bournemouth line. Rather than having conventional resistances to control booster excitation, thyristors were utilised, giving infinitely variable power gradation dependent on controller position. It was of course necessary also to provide four fixed controller positions for working in multiple with TC and EMU stock. Furthermore a primitive form of computer logic was used to control wheelslip. This electronic equipment was organised on modules which could be removed and replaced in the event of a defect. The HBs were one of the earliest applications of electronics on Britain's railways and paid the price in terms of reduced reliability, a problem which was to beset these otherwise powerful and useful machines throughout their short working lives.

The HBs were all outshopped in rail blue with full yellow ends. None was ready for the start of the Bournemouth electrification, E6102 being delivered in November 1967 and the rest following in the first six months of 1968. Based at Eastleigh, they spent their first few months on trial, often in company with the spare 4 TC driving trailer, and their only use in traffic was on ECS duties between Clapham Yard and Waterloo. They finally entered revenue-earning service on 6th May 1968, working mainly on boat trains between Waterloo and Southampton Docks or Weymouth, although the Weymouth trains generally changed over to a diesel at Bournemouth for the final non-electrified section. They also worked van trains from Poole and Eastleigh and continued to fill-in on ECS turns, but at this time they were not allowed on freight and did not usually operate during rush hours due to likely failure and consequent disruption. Reliability was at first appalling with many parts subject to failure, one of the main problems being caused by overheating crystals in the logic circuits. With familiarity its availability improved, and by 1974 the failure rate was down to one tenth of that in 1968. By this time the HBs were also working freight services, particularly transfer freights between the SR South Western division and the Western Region at Acton, travelling via the non-electrified West London line. The many steep banks on this route were a struggle for the 650hp diesel and such trains were frequently slowed to a crawl.

Blue livery gradually spread to remaining unconverted members of the HA electric and KA/KB diesel-electric classes, and a number ran for a time in green with full yellow ends. From 1968 the D prefix was dropped from diesel locomotive numbers, and at the same time a new numerical system of classification came into use. There was more than one attempt at this, and it was not until 1974 that final class numbers were decided upon. The standard KA locomotives became class 33/0, the push-pull fitted examples 33/1 and the Hastings-gauge KB examples 33/2. At the same time five-digit numbers came into use, the three types of class 33 being renumbered 33001-33065, 33101-33119 and 33201-33212 respectively in order of their original numbers. Of the electric and electro-diesel classes, the remaining HAs became class 71 numbered 71001-71014, the JAs class 73/0 73001-73006, the JBs class 73/1 73101-73142 and the HBs class 74 74001-74010.

A decreasing workload resulted in the early withdrawal of remaining members of class 71, while continuing unreliability resulted in the eradication of class 74, neither type outlasting the 1970s. In both cases their work was taken over by the more flexible classes 33 and 73. The premier passenger working of the HAs, the *Golden Arrow* Pullman, had already finished in September 1972. The entire class was taken out of service from 23rd September 1976 and placed in store at Ashford, Hither Green and Stewarts Lane. Retained for a time in case of future traffic increases, none ever turned a wheel in BR revenue-earning service again, although they were not finally withdrawn on paper until November 1977. The first class 74 to be withdrawn, 74006, had been condemned in June 1976 following fire damage, 74002 went in July 1977 and the rest followed at the end of that same year. A farewell railtour, utilising 74003 and TC stock, had been run on 3rd November. In the case of both classes many locomotives remained dumped at various SR locations for some months before being sold for scrap, Birds at Long Marston and Cashmores of Newport being the main dealers involved.

71001, the earliest of the HA class to remain intact, was retained for the National Collection, restored to original green livery as E5001 at Doncaster in 1978, and placed on display at the NRM, York. In 1992 it was given a full mechanical and electrical overhaul at Chart Leacon and was then used for various railtours and other special trains around the SR until 1995. Following a period in store at St Leonards, it was inspected at Stewarts Lane in 2001 with a view to returning it to main line service once more, specifically for hauling the *Venice Simplon Orient Express* Pullmans. Nothing came of this, but in 2006 E5001 was placed on permanent display at 'Locomotion', the NRM's museum at Shildon, County Durham, where it keeps company with 2 BIL 2090 (see Chapter 4).

Passenger workings for class 33 continued to expand, and only an outline is given here. In October 1971 the class took over the Waterloo – Salisbury – Exeter workings from the unreliable WR *Warship* class, remaining on these services until replaced by class 50 from May 1980. From this date they took over haulage of the entire Portsmouth Harbour – Bristol – Cardiff service, which was soon increased to a regular hourly interval. As extensions of their diagrams on these services, they worked further into Wales, and between Cardiff and Crewe, well away from SR territory, from May 1982. Other operations included certain peak-hour Oxted line services to East Grinstead and Uckfield, odd trains on the Reading – Redhill – Tonbridge cross-country line, and on the then unadvertised Clapham Junction – Kensington Olympia rush-hour shuttle. Class 33/1 continued to work the Bournemouth – Weymouth push-pull services, and also the Waterloo – Weymouth boat train which worked through the streets of Weymouth to reach the Quay station. After the demise of the 71s, classes 33 and 73 shared haulage of the *Night Ferry* until its own withdrawal at the end of October 1980.

Following the relaxation of the BR rule banning the naming of locomotives which had been in force throughout the 1970s, a number of members of classes 33/0 and 73/1 were named between 1980 and 1983. Nameplates were all in cast aluminium with polished metal lettering and border on a red background. Below is a list of allocated names:

Number	Name	Date of Naming
33 008	*Eastleigh*	11th April 1980
33 025	*Sultan*	6th August 1981
33 027	*Earl Mountbatten of Burma*	2nd September 1980
33 052	*Ashford*	15th May 1980
33 056	*The Burma Star*	2nd September 1980
73 101	*Brighton Evening Argus*	3rd December 1980
73 121	*Croydon 1883-1983*	September 1983
73 129	*City of Winchester*	1st December 1982
73 142	*Broadlands*	25th December 1980

Isle of Wight 3 TIS EMU 037 standing in platform 4 (one of the District Line bays) at Wimbledon during its transfer from LT Acton Works to Stewarts Lane in 1966. The former 'standard' tube stock vehicles have been stripped of paint and converted from LT fourth-rail to the standard SR third-rail system at Acton, and will be painted in the new BR blue livery with full yellow ends at Stewarts Lane. *J. N. Faulkner*

FORMER TUBE STOCK FOR THE ISLE OF WIGHT

As far as the Southern (Railway and Region) was concerned, a unique feature of the 1967 electrification of the isolated Ryde Pier Head – Shanklin line on the Isle of Wight (IoW) was that financial constraints necessitated the acquisition of second-hand EMU vehicles, in this case from London Transport. The 43 cars eventually purchased were from the pre-1938 tube stock fleet, whose history has been covered in detail elsewhere (see Bibliography). Roughly contemporary with the first generation of SR electric suburban stock, the so-called 'Standard' tube stock fleet was placed into service in the 1923-34 period, eventually totalling 1,466 vehicles. The first production tube cars to have air-operated sliding doors, they replaced the pre-1914 gate-ended stock built for the opening of the deep-level tubes, and were also required

for extension of the tube lines into the suburbs. A number of car builders were involved in construction of the 'Standard' tube stock fleet (including some involved in outside-contract work on SR electric rolling stock during the same period) and this, together with various improvements over the eleven years of production, led to innumerable detail design differences between the various batches. However, there were many features in common and a general description can therefore be given.

Three types of car were produced: driving motor cars, trailers and control trailers (driving trailers in SR parlance). All were just over 50ft in length, motor cars being slightly longer than trailers and later batches longer than earlier. Construction consisted of a steel underframe with bodywork of steel panels on a hardwood frame. Motor cars had a single motor bogie at the driving end and the underframe was cranked up over it to allow space for the traction motors and larger diameter driving wheels. Above the motor bogie an equipment compartment was located, containing the control contactors and resistance grids. Non self-lapping electro-pneumatic brakes were fitted. Motor cars had a wide pair of doors at the centre and a guard's position at the non-driving end, while trailers had two slightly narrower door pairs each side. Except over the sliding door positions, the roof was formed into a shallow clerestory, and the cab windscreens were arched at the top. Internally, seating was a mixture of transverse and longitudinal, giving a much lower capacity than conventional SR slam-door stock but increased standing room.

Concern regarding the advanced age of existing steam locomotives and coaches on the IoW, all of which were of pre-Grouping origin, had led the SR to commence the procurement of redundant LT tube cars for possible use on the Island as early as 1964. At this time the obsolete 'Standard' stock was being rapidly withdrawn by LT, and was particularly suitable for the IoW because restricted clearances through Ryde tunnel precluded the use of normal-sized vehicles. By July 1965, 44 cars were held at Micheldever and a further 29 on LT premises at Ruislip. Following the October 1965 announcement that the Ryde Pier Head – Shanklin line was to be electrified, 43 cars were eventually retained to work the line, enough for six seven-coach trains with one spare motor car. Of these, 25 came from the Micheldever batch, eleven from those already purchased but still at Ruislip, and seven directly from the Northern City line, the last LT line on which 'Standard' stock worked in passenger service, as withdrawn. These latter vehicles, all driving motors, were from the final 1931/34 batches of this stock and were exchanged for older cars previously purchased.

The tube cars were firstly given a thorough mechanical and electrical overhaul at LT's Acton Works, where modifications were also carried out to convert them from the Underground fourth rail system to the standard SR third rail arrangement with running-rail return. They were then worked to Stewarts Lane for repainting in the new standard BR suburban livery of overall blue with white lettering, yellow ends and brown underframes and bogies. Some seating was replaced by luggage racks, but vehicles were not re-upholstered except where necessary, and they retained leather armrests on the longitudinal seats. The vehicles were formed up into six four-car and six three-car units, given the SR codes 4 VEC and 3 TIS respectively. ('Vectis' was the Roman name for the Island.) The 4 VEC units, numbered 041-046, were made up of two driving motor cars sandwiching two trailers; in the first four units one of these trailers was a former control trailer with driving equipment decommissioned and its cab end painted blue. 3 TIS units 031-036 were formed motor car + trailer + driving trailer, but in this case the driving controls in the latter were operational and the cab end was painted yellow in consequence. However, TIS units were not normally allowed to work solo outside depot confines due to a lack of collector shoes on the driving trailer and consequent risk of gapping.

Following completion, the first of the 'new' Isle of Wight electric stock was tested on the South Western main line between Wimbledon and Woking, and then transferred to Fratton for crew training on the Portsmouth Direct line as far up as Haslemere. From Fratton, vehicles were then individually shipped over to the island, using a Pickford's low-loader and the Portsmouth – Fishbourne car ferry. The first vehicle to be taken over was a driving trailer on 1st September 1966. Hauled by *Calbourne*, one of the Island's remaining O2 0-4-4 steam locomotives, it ran a trial return trip between Ryde and Shanklin on 4th September, mainly to demonstrate to the Transport Minister the effective difference in platform heights between existing coaches and the tube cars. For this demonstration, the Westinghouse brake pump of the locomotive was used to provide the necessary compressed air to operate the sliding doors. Three complete 4 VECs and one 3 TIS were taken over in the last seven weeks of 1966, the remainder arriving the following year, the last in May. On arrival, cars were rerailed using a special unloading ramp at Ryde St Johns Road, following which they were marshalled up into their correct unit formations by steam loco. As recounted in an earlier chapter, electric services on the Island commenced on 20th March 1967.

Unexpected problems with severe wheel-flange and rail wear surfaced virtually as soon as the new service started, leading to the hurried installation of check rails and flange lubricators by September 1967. At the end of the year motor coach S15S (from unit 042) was damaged beyond repair in a depot incident, but for various reasons there was some delay before a substitute could be obtained, and in the meantime there were no spare vehicles on summer Saturdays. It was eventually replaced using a surplus pilot motor car from the LT service stock fleet which, following overhaul and repainting at Acton Works, was sent to the island by road. The 'new' S15S arrived in March 1971 and entered service that July.

Unsurprisingly, a number of vehicle withdrawals resulting from incidents, or simply old age, gradually reduced the rolling stock fleet on the IoW, the total having dropped to 37 vehicles by May 1982. Starting in 1976, vehicles were given light grey sliding doors on repaint, and in early 1982 a start was made on painting remaining units in blue/grey livery, with black patches around the cab windows and 'Isle of Wight' lettering on the car sides. Internally, the armrests gradually disappeared and the seating was re-upholstered, firstly into the BR 'blue check' pattern and later using the LT orange/yellow/black design, the latter (together with other internal improvements) paid for by a £1,500 grant from the IoWCC. By this time a number of units had been reformed and ad hoc formations, in order to keep cars in traffic, were frequent. The official situation at the end of September 1983 was that there were five 4 VEC (now class 485) and five 3 TIS (class 486) units, of which one (036) had two normal trailers and hence no cab at the Ryde end. Additionally, there was one spare motor car and one trailer. Although the most elderly cars on the island were virtually sixty years old by this time, there were no definite plans for future stock replacement, the advantages of the existing units then being thought to far outweigh those of any possible successors.

BR DESIGN SLIDING DOOR STOCK

Although modern suburban electric units with sliding doors had been introduced in the Liverpool area in 1938-39, on the Liverpool Street – Shenfield services in 1948, and in the Glasgow area in 1961-62, elsewhere BR remained firmly wedded to the outdated slam-door arrangement influenced by the staunchly conservative SR engineering establishment. As described above, this policy resulted in brand new 4 EPBs with closed compartments and bare-bulb lighting being turned out from Eastleigh Works as late as 1963. While in mainland Europe power-operated sliding or plug doors were already becoming the norm, it was not until 1965 that BR belatedly commenced design work for a new standard inner-suburban EMU with automatic sliding doors, intended for eventual future replacement of the vast slam-door fleets on the Southern and other regions. Following some more outlandish sketches, including an idea for a double-decked train with short vehicles articulated between single axles, what emerged from deliberations at Derby was a sliding door bodyshell not dissimilar to the stock used on LT surface lines. A wooden mock up of a complete coach body for the proposed design, including front end and cab layout, was erected at Doncaster. This was used, with an existing slam-door vehicle for comparison, for loading and unloading tests undertaken in simulated rush-hour conditions using 300 volunteers from the Works. Following these tests the construction of three prototype electric units with sliding doors, two four-coach and one two-coach, was authorised, for extensive evaluation on the SR.

The three prototype units, officially labelled 'High Density Stock' but also given the SR-style designations 4 PEP and 2 PEP, were built at the British Rail Engineering workshops at York in 1970-72. (Early publicity also referred to them as PER, apparently for 'Prototype Electro Rheostatic', but this was dismissed as insufficiently sexy!) The first to be completed, 4 PEP 4001, was delivered to the Southern in May 1971, but was not unveiled to the Press until the following 14th September. The second four-car unit 4002, and the single 2 PEP 2001, followed early in 1972. This number and length of prototype units was selected to enable the formation of a ten-car train for testing in rush-hour conditions on the South Eastern division's Dartford lines. As the PEPs were delivered, they were based at the old LSWR electric depot at Wimbledon, Durnsford Road, for testing, initially on the quiet section between Farnham and Alton.

Above 4 PEP prototype unit 4001, entering Waterloo on its first visit for clearance tests on 22nd November 1971. These units took numbers originally allocated to the 4DD units. In both appearance and specification they were quite unlike anything seen on the Southern before. *John Scrace*

Mechanically and electrically, the PEP prototypes broke new ground in almost every area of SR electric multiple unit design. Of integral construction without a separate underframe, the car bodies were formed of aluminium sheet on a steel framework, with alloy castings around the door openings and ends. 4001 and 4002 were painted in the standard blue livery, but 2001 was left unpainted to test the bare aluminium finish and consequently was given red lettering, including the 'double arrow' symbol. The coach profile was entirely new with a roof considerably flatter than on Mark 1 stock and sides which were straight from the waist upwards but curved sharply inwards below. The yellow driving ends were slightly sloped, and the small windscreens appeared larger due to the addition of black patches around them. All vehicles had three door openings per side. The driving cars had a wide single-leaf door behind the cab (for the use of the crew) and two twin-leaf passenger doors, while the intermediate cars had three twin-leaf doors. The doors were air operated and had a peculiar 'passenger-open' feature, whereby a door had to be physically pulled a short distance before the automatic mechanism took over to complete the sequence. The units were gangwayed except at driving ends, the passage between coaches consisting of a yellow GRP box attached to the vehicle ends by rubber diaphragms. The cabs had inset emergency-only centre doors which were equipped with a two-digit roller blind headcode panel.

Electrical equipment and running gear were equally revolutionary. Although maximum speed was the standard suburban 75mph, to provide a higher rate of acceleration all axles were powered, each being geared to an EE 100hp motor. Conventional camshaft-activated resistance speed control was utilised, but this was combined with an electronic logic system whereby a potentiometer driven by the camshaft produced an electrical signal proportional to the camshaft position, and this signal was then interpreted by the logic circuitry and appropriate switching activated. Electro-pneumatic brakes were fitted, but the PEPs also had rheostatic brakes for additional slowing down from speed, again controlled by camshaft. The waste heat generated was then used to heat the passenger saloons. Control circuits worked at 110V (rather than the previous SR standard 70V), supplied from a motor-alternator located under every second vehicle and which also provided ac current to power interior lighting. Simple pivoted bars connected vehicles within each unit, but at the cab ends fully-automatic Scharfenberg couplers were fitted. These incorporated all mechanical, electrical and air connections in one unit, and coupling and uncoupling were actuated electrically from inside the cab. The coupler also took full buffing loads, there being no buffer beam or separate side buffers.

Two new types of bogie were tried out on the PEPs. Those underneath 4001 and 4002, classified DOC1, had frames fabricated from welded steel sheet, with primary suspension provided by coil-sprung radius arms pivoted on bonded rubber bushes and secondary suspension by a swing bolster. 2001 was equipped with even simpler bogies with trough-shaped steel side frames and air-bag secondary suspension, backed up by rubber springs to take the body weight in the event of

a failure.[23] The active air suspension system was designed to maintain the distance between coach body and rail whatever the loading, air from the compressors being pumped into, or released from, the air bags via a system of valves to achieve this. Originally known as the 'Air Flexicoil' design and later given the designation BP8, this type of bogie became the preferred design and developments of it were used on all subsequent BR sliding door multiple unit stock up to 1992, including the production classes 508 and 455 detailed below. Both bogie types were fitted with calliper-operated disc brakes. Shoe gear, of the type fitted to 1966 stock, was fitted to the bogies directly beneath the driving cabs, and also to the two central bogies of 4001 and 4002.

Internally too, PEPs represented a clean break with the past, being all too obviously designed with short distance commuting in mind. The hard low-backed bus-style seating had thin individual cushions fitted with removable covers for easy cleaning, was arranged with only two seats each side of a wide central gangway, and many seat pairs were arranged face to back. These arrangements provided greater standing space at the expense of seating capacity, and to add to the 'rapid transit' ambience, the ceilings had hanging handholds, exactly as on London Underground trains. Lighting was by fluorescent tubes recessed in the ceiling, and the GRP or laminate internal panelling was in muted shades of grey other than at the doorway positions where bright yellow predominated. An air-conditioning system was initially fitted in 4001, forced air ventilation being admitted into the interior through louvres in the seat supports and door draught screens, warmed if necessary by waste heat generated by the rheostatic braking. In practice, these ventilation arrangements proved inadequate, and the plain double-glazed windows originally fitted had to be given conventional sliding glass panels before the unit carried passengers. 4002 and 2001 were also given these revised windows, which had a horizontal bar across the opening portion, before entering passenger service. However, they could not be fitted directly behind the cabs as the windows here formed part of the door pockets. It was apparently intended that various other internal layouts would be tried out, including longitudinal seating, but this never happened.

Following extensive testing, public services using the new stock commenced on 4th June 1973 when, following a press trip, 4001 entered service on the 11.43 Hampton Court to Waterloo. For most of their time in passenger service, which lasted until December 1976, the three units were restricted to South Western division inner-suburban workings between Waterloo and Chessington South, Shepperton and Hampton Court, due (as much as anything) to restricted clearances on other SW suburban routes. However, the complete ten-car train spent six unhappy weeks in the summer of 1973 on South Eastern rush hour services, working selected trains

---

23 Prior to introduction of the PEPs, prototype DOC1 bogies had been tried out underneath test unit 051, formed from two motor coaches and one driving trailer of redundant Eastleigh-built London Midland Region London area dc stock.

between Charing Cross/Cannon Street and Dartford via both the Sidcup and Bexleyheath routes, and also to Bromley North. Shorter formations were also sometimes used, and they were berthed at Slade Green when not in use. The new features of the PEPs did not find favour with the commuters of North Kent, and they were thankfully removed prior to the end of their officially allotted time after 4001+4002 had failed one evening, completely blocking the Sidcup line and resisting rescue due to their non-standard couplings.

Resulting from these trials, which included customer surveys on many timetabled workings, and following wide-spread protests from (among others) local user groups and MPs, it was concluded that several aspects of the PEP design, which was only ever intended to be experimental, were unsat-isfactory. In particular, the internal two+two layout provided insufficient seating capacity, and the seats themselves were too small and uncomfortable for outer-suburban journeys. The three door-pairs each side, while allowing speedy entrance and exit, also caused too much cold air to enter the train when standing in stations. Thus it was decided that production builds should have three+two seating and only two door-pairs per side. Unfortunately, the inadequate seats remained.

In the latter part of 1973 one driving car from 2001 was swapped for a similar vehicle from 4001, the resulting 2 PEP having one blue vehicle with DOC1 bogies and one unpainted vehicle with air-bag bogies. This was the first of the PEP trio to be taken out of service, and in 1974 it left the SR. (Following transfer to the Railway Technical centre at Derby it was given a blue pantograph-equipped centre trailer, re-equipped to work off 25kV ac overhead, and renumbered as depart-mental test unit 920 001. It subsequently served as prototype for both the Great Northern class 313 and Glasgow class 314 fleets, the first production units based on the PEP proto-types, and following some time out of use was eventually scrapped in 1987.) 4001 and 4002 also entered departmental service following withdrawal from passenger service at the end of 1976, but their purpose was not so clear cut. Given departmental numbers 056 and 057 respectively (although for some years they did not carry these), they spent periods at Derby Research Centre and also on the SR based at the Strawberry Hill research facility or at East Wimbledon. 057 (4002) saw the more use, being employed in testing various items of new or experimental equipment such as the BP25 bogie, and continued to be seen around the Region. In 1980 it was experimentally repainted in red and grey with upswept stripes across the cab sides, a scheme which was to strongly influence later BR sector liveries. Dumped out of service in Clapham Yard in March 1983 after arriving under its own power, 057 was eventually hauled off for scrapping in 1989. 056 (4001) was unsuccessfully tried out as a depot shunter at East Wimbledon, but spent its last days mouldering at Derby prior to being broken up.

The production suburban EMUs derived from the PEP prototypes for the SR were classified 508, an initial order for 58 four-coach units being authorised in 1977 as the first tranche of SUB replacement stock for use on the South Western division. This was cut down to 43 units as an economy measure in September 1978. Once more constructed at BREL York Works, they constituted the fourth production variant of the new BR standard inner suburban multiple unit design, following on from the dual-voltage class 313, ac-only 314, and dc-only class 507 types. It has been suggested that class 508 had originally been intended as further three-car units for Liverpool-area electrified lines, to join the almost identical class 507 fleet already there, but due to an urgent need for new stock on the SR they were built with an extra trailer each and diverted south. As explained below, they proved unsuccessful in service conditions on the SR and were eventually transferred to Merseyside, but had they proved satisfactory there is no evidence to suggest that they would ever have moved north. Indeed, an order was placed in 1980 for a further 358 vehicles of the same type for the SR, but these were instead delivered as the rather different class 455, described below.

Formation of the class 508 units, numbered 508001-508043, comprised two driving motor cars, each with all four axles powered, and two trailers. There were no van areas, and total seating capacity was 320. The cars had integral bodies of steel-framed alloy construction similar to the PEPs, with the same, almost flat roofed, profile, but all had only two pairs of double-leaf sliding doors for passenger use each side. The motor cars had an additional single-leaf sliding door each side, opening into a roomy vestibule behind the cab. The GRP driving ends were upright with a recessed emergency end door, but lacked a headcode panel. Instead, roller-blind destination and route indicators, with black lettering on a white background, were located above each windscreen. Livery was the by then standard BR blue/grey, and the yellow ends had the same black patches as the PEPs. The windows were double-glazed with tinted glass, and had single 'hopper' opening ventilators at the tops, as on the refurbished CEPs (see above). Internal arrangements and decor mainly resem-bled the PEPs, but with all seats facing and arranged three+two across with an off-centre gangway except at door pocket and coach end positions where it was two+two. Strangely, the two trailers were asymmetric, with an addi-tional inward-facing single seat on each side adjacent to one of the door positions. Pressure ventilation was fitted. Units were equipped with passenger operated push-buttons for door opening and closing, locked and released by the guard who could also close all doors from a master control panel when the train was ready to depart. Orange indicator lights on the coach sides showed when the door push buttons were activated.

Traction motors were of the GEC G310AZ type, rated at 111hp (82.5kW) and geared for a 75mph maximum speed, controlled by conventional camshafts and resistances. Bogies were of the BX1 type with air-bag secondary suspension, developed from the BP8 type used under PEP 2001. Rheostatic and air-operated disc brakes were fitted, the latter controlled by the 'Westcode' electro-pneumatic system. Additionally, anti-wheelslip protection equipment was installed, which was soon to prove troublesome. Control and other auxiliary circuits again worked at 110V, supplied from a motor-alter-nator and rectifier. A further new type of coupling was used

Clearly intended to emulate a London Transport Underground car, the PEP prototypes had two+two low-backed seating with wide centre gangway and flexible handgrips for standing passengers. Taken when brand new on 18th July 1971, this interior view of a driving motor coach of 4001 (looking back from the cab) shows the plain glass side windows originally fitted: air conditioning was through vents visible in the seat supports. *BR Southern Region Official*

to couple units, of American origin and known as the Tightlock. (Although almost universal in continental Europe and even used on trams, the PEP's Scharfenberg type was considered too expensive for series production.) Superficially similar to the traditional buckeye, a single box was mounted underneath incorporating all electrical and air connections, which mated automatically when the coupler was engaged. Needless to say, class 508 was a coupling class in its own right as far as the SR was concerned. Problems experienced when attempting to attach or detach on a curve (as on some of Waterloo's suburban platforms) led to many restrictions, and for much of their short stay on the SR coupling and uncoupling were only permitted on depot. Couplings and gangway connections between vehicles in a unit were as on the PEPs. Different items of equipment were mounted underneath each vehicle, so it was necessary to distinguish both motor and trailer cars as types A and B. For example the battery and motor alternator were mounted on the type B motor car, while the compressor (to supply air for brakes, suspension and doors) was mounted on the type A trailer.

New class 508 units were delivered from York to the SR via Temple Mills, their non-standard couplings necessitating the use of pairs of special match wagons. They were commissioned at Strawberry Hill before entering service based at East Wimbledon Depot, where side pits had to be provided to allow access by fork-lift truck to the heavy underslung equipment. At one period units were arriving on the Southern at a faster rate than commisioning staff could deal with them, and a number had to be temporarily stored at Basingstoke. The last of these, together with the final deliveries direct from York, had arrived at East Wimbledon by the beginning of May 1980. Due to an initial lack of spares 508005 was cannibalised to keep the remainder of the fleet working, while 508002 was used for extended brake testing. As a result this pair were the last to enter passenger service, in March 1981 and December 1982 respectively. The first passenger

workings for the class had commenced on Monday 7th January 1980, covering services to Shepperton and Hampton Court. At first there were various route and speed restrictions due to their non-standard profile, but these were gradually eased, culminating in runs to Horsham via Dorking from the May 1982 timetable change. At the peak of their operations, class 508 units were operating over virtually all South Western suburban routes.

As we have seen, the class 508 fleet incorporated many features and systems new to the SR, including motors, controls, brakes and couplings, whilst virtually every part was non-standard to the 1951-66 stocks. In addition, the class suffered from a large number of faults, apart from the coupling problems already mentioned. These factors combined to turn the SR engineering establishment, used to the rugged and reliable SUB and EPB stock, against them immediately from their introduction. In particular, problems with the anti-wheelslip equipment came to a head in the autumn of 1981, when the class had to be temporarily withdrawn en masse from 2nd November as crews considered them unsafe to drive in autumn leaf-fall conditions. Although these difficulties were in time overcome, it was soon decided that the class 508 fleet should after all be reallocated to the Liverpool area as soon as further new stock, to a revised design ostensibly more suited to SR operating conditions, had been delivered. Transfer to Birkenhead North depot for modifications prior to entering service on Merseyrail's Northern Line commenced in April 1982, with 508042 and 508043 being the first to go. Only three coaches from each unit actually went to Liverpool, the remaining trailer being removed and stored for subsequent use in later new SR suburban stock. By September 1983 about half the 43 strong fleet had been transferred. (To complete the story, the last scheduled working of class 508 on the SR took place on Friday 7th December 1984, when 508005+508025 formed the 18.02 Waterloo to Dorking service.)

In 1980 there was a change of policy within the British Railways Board with regard to the design and construction of future suburban electric stock, when many of the significant new design features introduced in the PEPs and incorporated into class 508 were abandoned. Firstly, there was a reversion to steel for bodywork construction, based on the highly successful BR Mark 3 main line design but shortened to 20m and with intermediate sliding doors to give the same basic coach layout as previously. This design was very strong, considerably cheaper than aluminium at first cost and almost as light. Secondly, there was a return to the electrical layout of previous SR EMU stock, with a single intermediate motor coach equipped with four larger motors. The new bodywork design was actually first tried out on a pair of experimental diesel-electric units, but the first electric production variant was the outer-suburban ac class 317 for the St Pancras – Bedford electrification. While entry of these units into traffic was delayed until 1984 by a trade union dispute over driver-only operation, experience with them led to various minor bodywork changes in the SR units.

The Southern Region version of the revised BR standard suburban multiple unit was initially classified 510, but this was changed to 455 before the first was delivered. 74 new four-coach units of this type were initially ordered, followed by a further 43 and later a final twenty, all to be constructed at York. Formation of the class 455 units, which at first glance appeared superficially similar to the 508s, comprised two driving trailer seconds, a non-driving motor second with all axles powered, and a trailer second. The first batch was numbered from 5801 upwards, and all were outshopped in blue/grey with yellow ends and black windscreen patches. About the only features remaining from the PEPs were the brake control system, bogies with air-bag suspension and disc brakes, the gangways between intermediate coaches, and the inadequate low-backed seating.

Bodywork was of a new profile, taller and more curved at the roof, which had distinctive horizontal ribbing along its length. The driving ends incorporated a proper gangway connection with rubber shrouding, but this was not intended for through passage by passengers. The roof above the cab incorporated a sloping flat section above each windscreen either side of a curious raised 'box' housing the AWS equipment, the whole appearing singularly ugly and characterless. Forced-air ventilation was provided, with fans (mounted above a lowered ceiling at car ends) sucking in air through body side louvres and blowing it into the saloons through ceiling grilles. The side windows had their opening 'hopper' ventilators divided into two sections. Internal layout was very similar to class 508, giving a seating capacity of 356, and door control arrangements were identical. There can be no doubt that the first class 455 units represented the very nadir of BR EMU design and construction, crude and unsympathetic design being allied to unbelievably poor standards of fitting and workmanship. Apart from the peculiar front end arrangements, many of the faults concerned interior fitments, and were all too obvious to the curious passenger. The worst features included the pressed-steel luggage racks, bent ceiling grilles and the fit of internal panelling around the windows.

The initial batch of class 455s was equipped with existing type 507 traction motors, recovered from withdrawn SUB and HAP units and re-engineered to the latest specification using metric measurements for the first time. Maximum speed was again 75mph. Conventional camshaft control gear, similar to the SR 1963 arrangement, was used, but working at 110V supplied from a motor-alternator and battery mounted under the motor coach. Apart from supplying the control circuits via a transformer and rectifier, this also provided current at 415V 50Hz ac to power the fluorescent lighting, heating, ventilation fans and headlamps. The electro-pneumatic brakes were again controlled by the 'Westcode' system with disc pads on the bogies, but the rheostatic braking option was omitted. Compressors to supply air for the brakes and doors were mounted under all three trailers. Unpowered bogies were similar to previous types with air-bag suspension and designated type BT13, but motor bogies had heavier frames and various other modifications and were classified type BP20. Tightlock couplings at unit ends no longer incorporated integral control and air connections, conventional waist-level jumper cables being utilised instead, obviating the need for the restrictions which bedevilled class 508 on the SR. These comprised a 42-wire control jumper on the offside and repeated main reservoir air hoses on each side near the outer edge. Coupling and uncoupling was carried out electrically using buttons in the cab. These changes once more made class 455 a coupling class on its own, so in the early summer of 1983 the South Western division was running four different and incompatible types of stock on its suburban services (SUB, EPB, 508 and 455).

The first class 455 unit was substantially ready at York Works by September 1982. Following completion, the initial eleven units were sent to Wolverton for various electrical alterations to be carried out, including the installation of a wheelslip protection override system, but York completed later units to the revised specification. Unit 5805, then the only example in a fit state, was hauled down to the SR for an inspection at Waterloo on 16th November, but then returned to Wolverton. The first permanent arrivals took place on 20th December for commissioning at Strawberry Hill but, due to a staff dispute, crew training did not start until 26th February 1983. From that date regular ECS runs were operated between Waterloo and Shepperton on Tuesdays, Thursdays and Saturdays. The class finally commenced passenger service out of Waterloo on 28th March, with a single eight-car diagram covering services to Chessington, Shepperton and Hampton Court. Further diagrams were introduced on 11th April and 3rd May, by which time units were being delivered at a rate of about two per week. From the 16th May 1983 timetable revision, fifteen units were required for traffic out of the 21 by then delivered, when in addition to routes already mentioned they worked on the Kingston and Hounslow loops and to Effingham Junction via Epsom. Use of class 455 gradually increased through the summer as further new units were delivered, displacing not only the last of the 4 SUBs, but also enabling transfer of class 508 units to Merseyside to begin in earnest. By the time the final SUB had been withdrawn, units up to about 5835 were in traffic.

Class 508 unit 508 040 approaches Ashtead with a morning peak Effingham Junction to Waterloo service on 31st August 1982. Although clearly derived from the PEP prototypes, obvious differences include a more upright cab end, tightlock couplers, destination blinds in place of the time-honoured headcode panel, and hopper-type window ventilators. *David Brown*

The class 455 units were the last entirely new design of Southern EMU to be introduced during the period covered in this book. Although superficially similar to class 508 which immediately preceded them, they differed in virtually all respects, particularly in reverting to all-steel bodywork and a single intermediate motor coach. The peculiar design treatment of the cab front was particularly criticised. 5812 passes Ashtead substation, one of those built for the 'Change of Frequency Scheme', with the 16.12 Waterloo – Effingham Junction service on 31st May 1983. *David Brown*

CHAPTER 8:
EPILOGUE – THE SCENE IN 1983

The summer of 1983 represented a period of unprecedented variety in the types of electric multiple unit in use on the Southern Region, which was arguably at its most interesting since the withdrawal of the original SR main line express and semi-fast stock in the 1964-72 period. The following paragraphs therefore give a survey of what could be seen and travelled in on the different divisions at the start of the summer timetable in May of that year.

On the South Eastern division, suburban services were almost without exception worked by non-facelifted EPB stock. 4 EPBs used included both SR and BR standard varieties, as well as the four non-standard units 5261-5262 and 5301-5302 with BR standard motor coaches and Bulleid trailers. The 2 EPBs used were all BR standard examples of the '5701' type with eight-bay motor coaches. Apart from making up ten-coach peak formations (which ran all day in some cases), they were also used singly on Grove Park – Bromley North and Elmers End – Addiscombe branch shuttles. SE suburban commuters endured gloomy conditions with bare-bulb tungsten lighting and dusty grey Trojan seating, although even in 1983 the earlier yellow/black and red/black 'tiger stripes' persisted in a few vehicles. Almost all units retained some compartment accommodation. Main line services were worked by a mixture of non-corridor 2 HAP and gangwayed 4 VEP and 4 CEP stock, virtually all of the latter having been refurbished with new interiors by this time. HAPs tended to work services between Victoria and Maidstone East and on Kent branches such as Strood – Paddock Wood and Sittingbourne – Sheerness, but still turned up daily on stopping services running the full distance between London and Dover or Thanet. CEPs and VEPs were seemingly used almost indiscriminately on the longer distance services, all BEPs having been disbanded or transferred away by this time. Boat trains were generally formed 12 CEP, often with an MLV added at the London end. Comfort in HAPs was no better than the suburban EPBs. Although riding more smoothly, VEPs were hardly an improvement, while in the rebuilt CEPs the combination of oddly-shaped seat cushions and draughty 'hopper' ventilators were disliked by many passengers who avoided them where possible, despite a much lighter general ambience.

EPB stock also had a virtual monopoly of suburban services on the Central division. All 4 EPBs were facelifted examples with much brighter interiors, including about fifty SR-bodied units of class 415/4 and 24 BR standard units of class 415/6. A few SR-bodied 2 EPBs had also been facelifted, but the majority remained in original condition, as did the pair of BR standard units (5753/54) normally seen on the

Wimbledon – West Croydon or Tattenham Corner lines. 4 SUBs still operated a small number of services at this time, working out as far as Coulsdon North and Horsham via Dorking. On the main lines, services were mainly handled by 4 CIG, 4 BIG and 4 VEP stock and, as on the South Eastern, both types of non-buffet unit often appeared indiscriminately on express, semi-fast and stopping trains. A few unrefurbished 4 BEP units, the last of their breed, were also in use on the Brighton line. Along the coast, from Brighton to Portsmouth Harbour and Ore, 4 CAP units worked many of the services, but corridor stock also often appeared and conversely CAP stock worked to and from London on a daily basis. Similarly, although the 4 VEG units were officially dedicated to the Victoria – Gatwick Airport – Horsham services, they too could turn up on occasion on virtually any main line working.

By far the widest variety of suburban stock could be seen on the South Western division suburban lines out of Waterloo. Slam-door stock in use comprised remaining 4 SUBs, non-facelifted SR 4 EPBs and BR standard 2 EPBs including the 'Tyneside' examples, while sliding-door stock comprised the entire fleet of 43 class 508 units and the first examples of class 455 then entering service. Complex diagramming meant that any of these types could be seen on most suburban routes, although SUBs did not normally venture west of Twickenham on the Windsor lines. The Staines – Weybridge route, at this time running as a shuttle, was worked by a single 2 EPB unit. The outer-suburban line from Waterloo to Guildford via Cobham, on which first class accommodation was advertised, was operated mainly by 4 VEP and 2 HAP units, often in multiple with a 4 EPB, but express 4 CIGs also regularly appeared. Strangely, the odd SUB occasionally turned up at this time, not having been seen regularly on this route (apart from a short interlude in 1973) since 1952. Other longer distance outer-suburban and main line stopping services were also worked by VEP, CIG and HAP stock, often indiscriminately. Thus, even at this late date, an unlucky passenger could travel from London to Portsmouth in the dingy and rough-riding motor coach of a 2 HAP, bereft of toilet facilities.

On its electrified main lines to the coast, the South Western also utilised a greater range of rolling stock types than the other divisions at this time. The hourly express and semi-fast services on the Waterloo – Bournemouth route were worked by the specialised 4 REP and 4 TC stock, with the latter continuing to Weymouth behind push-pull equipped class 33/1 diesels. For variety, an interesting vehicle in which to travel at this time was DTS 76331 formed in TC unit 417,

which was formerly a spare vehicle and had been experimentally modernised internally with fluorescent lighting and new Mark 2-style seating. TCs and class 33/1s also worked push-pull from Waterloo to Salisbury, not electrified beyond Basingstoke. A few particularly interesting peak-hour workings on this route included a portion to/from Eastleigh or beyond, formed of VEP stock, detached or attached at Basingstoke, but between there and London worked in multiple with the locomotive and TC unit, making full use of the versatile 27-wire EPB control system. On the Portsmouth Direct line most services were worked by 4 CIG stock but with no fewer than three types of catering unit. Most of the 4 BIGs, introduced on this line in 1970, were still allocated to the South Western at this time, but the first refurbished 4 BEP, 2301, was by now in traffic. The two temporary 8 MIGs 2601/02 were in use by the end of May. This temporary surfeit of catering units led on at least one occasion to an evening peak Waterloo to Portsmouth fast service being formed with a 4 BIG and the (then unique) 4 BEP, although presumably only one of the buffet cars was open.

Finally, we return to the footbridge on the Epsom to Leatherhead line immediately to the south of Ashtead station, a location first mentioned in the General Introduction in Volume 1. With services passing including Central division workings between Victoria or London Bridge and Dorking, Horsham or Effingham Junction, and South Western division trains from Waterloo to the same destinations, virtually the entire range of Southern Region suburban stock then in traffic could be seen in the early evening peak period between about 16.30 and 18.30. In the early summer of 1983, types to be seen included 4 SUBs, SR 4 EPBs of both original and facelifted varieties, facelifted BR standard 4 EPBs, BR standard 2 EPBs of both types, SR 2 EPBs including the first facelifted examples, and classes 508 and 455. With their four different and incompatible coupling and control systems, such variety would not have impressed Raworth and Bulleid in their quest for greater standardisation forty years earlier. Conversely, they would have been happier in the knowledge that (with the exception of the 508s, soon to be removed from the SR anyway) all the stock mentioned was equipped with versions of the English Electric type 507 traction motor.

Above 'All change'. On the afternoon of Sunday 31st July 1983, during the last summer of the period covered by this book, second and third generation SR suburban units rub shoulders in Dorking carriage sidings, awaiting the Monday morning rush hour. On the left, brand new class 455 units 5822 and 5825 will work services to Waterloo. Beside them 4 SUB 4721, in its final weeks of service, and 'facelifted' BR standard 4 EPB 5318 will form Victoria trains. *David Brown*

Left 4 REP tractor unit 3004, with two 4 TC trailer units in tow, approaches Christchurch with a Bournemouth – Waterloo semi-fast service on 11th June 1983. All units carry the final British Rail corporate blue and grey livery with full yellow ends. The units themselves were nearing the ends of their working life although their traction motors would, in Southern tradition, live on in their class 442 successors. *Colin Boocock*

APPENDIX 1

Summary of Southern Electric rolling stock types introduced 1951-83

SR Class	BR Class No.	No. Series	Introduced	Comments
4 EPB*	415/1	5001-5053 (1)	1951	SR type on reclaimed underframes, originally with 'Eastern' motor bogies
4 EPB*	415/1	5101-5262 (1,2)		Same as 5001-5053, but with 'Central' motor bogies
2 EPB	416/2	5701-5779, 5800	1954	BR standard type
2 EPB	416/2	5781-5795 (3)	1954	'Tyneside' type with larger brake van
4 CEP*	411	7101-7211 (4)	1956	BR standard type express stock
4 BEP*	410	7001-7022 (4)	1956	CEP with buffet car
2 HAP	414	6001-6173 (5)	1957	BR standard type
2 HAP*	414	5601-5636 (6)	1957	SR type
MLV	419	68001-68010	1959	Motor Luggage Van for Kent Coast boat trains
2 EPB*	416/1	5651-5684 (7)	1959	SR type. All open
4 EPB*	415/3	5301-5370 (8)	1960	BR standard type
4 CIG	421	7301-7438	1964	Express stock with intermediate motor coach
4 BIG	420	7031-7058	1964	CIG with buffet car
4 VEC	485	041-046	1967	Former LT pre-1938 tube stock for Isle of Wight
3 TIS	486	031-037	1967	As above
4 REP	430	3001-3015	1967	Motor units for Bournemouth line
4 TC	491	401-434	1967	Trailer sets for Bournemouth line
4 VEP	423	7701-7894	1967	BR standard gangwayed semi-fast units
TLV		68201-06 (9)	1968	Trailer Luggage Vans
8 VAB		8001 (10)	1968	Spare express unit for Bournemouth line
2 SAP	418	5601-5636 (6)	1969	Downclassed SR 2 HAP
4 PEP	445	4001-4002	1971	Prototype high-density sliding door stock
2 PEP	445	2001	1972	As above
2 SAP	418	5901-5951 (5)	1974	Downclassed BR 2 HAP
4 EPB*	415/1	5263-5264	1976/77	Additional SR type (11)
	508	508 001-043	1979	High-density sliding door stock based on PEP prototypes
4 VEG		7901-7912	1978	Modified VEP for Gatwick Airport services
4 CAP	413	3201-3213 (5)	1982	Permanently-coupled
		3301-3311		pairs of 2 HAP units
	455/8	5801-5850	1982	Production high-density sliding door stock (12)
8 MIG		2601-2602	1983	Temporary catering units for Portsmouth line (13)
4 TEP	482/7	2701-2702	1983	Temporary catering units for Central division (14)

*Facelifted or refurbished during the period under review.

(1)   Class in process of being facelifted in 1983 (class 415/4) and renumbered in series from 5402 upwards.

(2)   5261/62 formed using BR standard motor coaches with 1951 equipment from disbanded 2 EPB units, and spare SR-design trailers.

(3)   Built for Newcastle – South Shields line 1954/55, transferred to SR 1963.

(4)   Classes in process of being refurbished in 1983 and renumbered in series from 1501 upwards. Most 4 BEPs refurbished as 4 CEPs but seven retained, renumbered in series from 2701 upwards (class 412).

(5)   Some temporarily downgraded to 2 SAP (second class only) 1974-79. Some permanently paired as 4 CAP (class 413) from 1982.

(6)   Fourteen temporarily downgraded to 2 SAP in 1969-70, then all permanently from 1976. Withdrawn 1980-83. Most motor coaches facelifted and reformed in 4 EPBs (class 415/4).

(7)   In process of being facelifted in 1983 (class 416/3), renumbered in series from 6301 upwards.

(8)   5301/02 were formed with spare SR-design trailers. Class in process of being facelifted in 1983 (class 415/6), but not yet renumbered.

(9)   Converted from former loco-hauled BR standard 57ft full brakes to provide additional luggage space on Kent Coast boat trains. Withdrawn 1974.

(10)   Formed of vehicles from three new 4 VEP units plus a rewired former loco-hauled buffet car. Disbanded in 1974.

(11)   5263/64 were formed from SR 2 SAP motor coaches and spare SR-design trailers. 5263 became prototype facelifted 4 EPB, and was subsequently renumbered 5401.

(12)   Production of class 455/8 units continued beyond the cut-off date of this book, eventually reaching 74 units, numbered 5801-5874.

(13)   Formed of vehicles from two 4 CIG units plus miniature buffet car (RMB) previously wired for EPB EMU operation. Disbanded in September 1983.

(14)   Reformed from refurbished 4 CEPs with unrefurbished BEP buffet. Two further 4 TEP units, 2703-2704, were formed after September 1983.

APPENDIX 2

Original allocations of carriages to 2-coach and 4-coach suburban units built between 1941 and 1959, and to main line units built between 1932 and 1948.

Subsequent changes (principally in main line stock after 1963) involve lengthy and complex tabulation. Some have been included in the chapter texts where appropriate, but the complete lists are beyond the practicable scale of this history.

Accident and war losses are listed, with dates and locations, where known.

The general withdrawal of stock built before 1982 is dealt with in the main text. The later history and withdrawal of '1951' and later stock occurred after the period covered by this book.

Motor third brakes

8616-8655	4735-4754 (pair to each unit). Losses: 8621 (4737) accident Wimbledon Park Sidings 24/6/71; 8636/37 (4745) shunting accident Dorking North 3/9/73; 8643 (4748) accident Selhurst depot 27/3/74.

Thirds (one to each unit, in numerical order, except where noted otherwise)

8901-8946	4621-4666 (saloons). Losses: 8919 (4639) fire, Effingham Junc depot, 24/11/73; 8922 (4642) accident New Cross Gate 15/3/73; 8932 (4652) accident Waterloo 11/4/61
8947-9034	4667-4754 (10-comp). Losses: 8947 (4667) accident Wimbledon Park sidings 24/11/70; 9017 (4737) accident Wimbledon Park Sidings 24/6/71; 9025 (4745) shunting accident Dorking North 3/9/73
10001-10020	3001-20 (built as 2001-20). Loss: 10004 (3014) accident Eastbourne 25/8/58
10021-10054	3021-37 (two each unit) (built as 2021-37). Loss: 10039 (3030) war, Brighton 25/5/43
10055-10083	3101-3129
10084-10109	3130-3155. War losses: 10071 (3117) and 10073 (3119) Portsmouth Hbr 10/1/41; 10091 (3137) Portsmouth Hbr 13/8/40; 10098 (3144) Fratton depot 26/4/41
10071/73/91/98	3117/19/37/56 replacements of war losses
10110-10112	3158/44/57
10113-10115	3041-3043 thirds (later seconds) ex firsts 12254/59/53 derated 1946
10121-10143	4277-4299 (saloons). Loss: 10126 (4282) accident Durnsford Rd depot, 8/67
10144-10166	4277-4299 (10-comp). Loss: 10166 (4299) fire, Effingham Junc depot 24/11/73
10167-69	(10-comp) note (l)
10170-10229	(10-comp) note (l)
10230-10345	(10-comp) note (m). Losses: 10241 (4745) shunting accident Dorking North 3/9/73; 10291 (4667) accident Wimbledon Park sidings 24/11/70; 10312 (4607) accident Wimbledon Pk Sidings 4/12/73
10346-10400	(10-comp) note (n)
10419-10428	4101-4110
10429-10438	4111-4120
10439-10448	4121-4130 (semi-saloon)
10449-10471	(10-comp) note (p)
10472-10481	4378-4387 (10-comp). Loss: 10475 (4381) fire, Effingham Junc depot 24/11/73

Motor third brakes (one to each unit, in numerical order, except where noted otherwise)

10497-10500	2954-2955 (pairs)
10501-10566	2921-2953 (pairs). Loss: 10511 (2926) accident South Croydon 24/10/47
10567	2010 (built as 1890, then renumbered 1900)
10568-10576	2001-2009 (built as 1891-99)
10577-10612	2011-2046 (built as 1901-20/54-69). Losses: 10580 (2014) war, Brighton 25/5/43 (underframe salvaged, to 12855); 10594 (2028) accident Waterloo 10/66

10613-10614	2047-2048 (built as 1970/71)
10615-10682	2049-2116. Losses: 10654 (2088) accident Barnham 1/8/62; 10668 (2102) war, Portsmouth Hbr 12/8/40
10683-10718	2117-2152. Losses: 10685 (2119) war, Peckham Rye, 27/12/44; 10697 (2131) war, Portsmouth Hbr 12/8/40
10719-10794	2601-2676. Loss: 10771 (2653) Aldershot 2/69
10795-10810	2677-2692. Loss: 10798 (2680); accident Chatham 5/4/56, stored Hassocks until 4/60, then to Eastleigh, leading end of underframe grafted on to 10895 of 4355 (ex accident Herne Hill 1/4/60); 10895 returned to traffic 7/60
10811-10817	2693-2699
10829-10848	4378-4387 (in pairs). Losses: 10835/36 (4381) fire, Effingham Junc depot 24/11/73; 10839 (4383) accident Durnsford Rd depot 11/1/72
10849-10894	4277-4299 (in pairs). Losses: 10859 (4282) accident Durnsford Rd depot 8/67; 10868 (4286), fire Coulsdon North 8/70; 10894 (4299) fire Effingham Junc depot 24/11/73
10895-10940	4355-4377 (in pairs). Losses: 10905 (4360) accident /64 (location not known); 10916 (4365) Wimbledon Stn 15/2/68; 10921 (4368) accident Whitton Junc 17/8/67
10941-10960	4101-4110 (in pairs)
10961-10980	4111-4120 (in pairs). Loss: 10980 (4120) accident /61 (?depot)
10981-11000	4121-4130 (in pairs)
11001-11002	Prototype cars in 2001, to traffic in 2041/42, then 3041/42
11003-11042	3002-07/09-20/41-43 (in pairs) (built as 2002-07/09-20 and 2041-43). Losses: 11017 (3009) accident (Brighton sidings?) 10/9/64; 11027 (3014) accident Eastbourne 25/8/58
11043-11044	Production series coaches for 3001 (built as 2001)
11045-11046	3008 (built as 2008)
11047-11080	3021-3037 (in pairs) (built as 2021-37)
11081-11138	3101-3129 (in pairs). Losses: 11082 (3101) war, Wimbledon Park sidings 29/6/44 (underframe salvaged, to 11212(3147) in 1956; 11113/14 (3117) and 11117/18 (3119) war, Portsmouth Hbr night of 10-11/1/41.
11139-11176	3054-3072 (in pairs). Losses: 11151/52 (3060) war, Portsmouth Hbr night of 10-11/1/41; 11157 (3063) war, Wimbledon Park sidings, 29/6/44
11177-11228	3130-3155 (in pairs). Losses: 11181 (3132) war, Portsmouth Hbr night of 10-11/1/41 (wreck retrieved from harbour 1946). 11186 (3134) accident Drayton Crossing 8/2/63; 11192 (3137) war, Portsmouth Hbr 13/8/40; 11205 (3144) war, Fratton depot 26/4/41; 11213 (3074) accident (Brighton sidings?) 10/9/64
11229-11254	3073-3085 (in pairs). Loss: 11242 (3079) accident New Cross Gate sidings 27/9/62
110/111/112xx	War loss replacements: nos. 11082, 11113/14/17/18/51/52/57/81/92, 11205 – alloc. to units 3137/37/17/19/17/57/57/44/32/19/44 respectively
11301-11370	4621-4655 (in pairs). Losses: 11302 (4621) fire 1972 (location not known); 11309 (4625) fire, Selhurst depot c5/71; 11314 (4627) accident Wimbledon Stn 15/2/68; 11330 (4635) accident Horsham siding, 12/7/73; 11340 (4639) fire, Effingham Junc depot 24/11/73; 11344 (4642) accident New Cross Gate 15/3/73; 11364 (4652) accident Waterloo 11/4/61
11371-11378	4656-4659 (in pairs). Loss: 11381 (4661) accident (shunting) Dorking North 3/9/73
11379-11392	4660-4666 (in pairs)

Thirds (built to composite dimensions; one to each unit)

11448-11470	note (r)
11471-11480	4101-4110. Loss: 11478 (4108), 1/61 (?depot)
11481-11490	4111-4120
11491-11500	4121-4130

Composites

11501-11534	2921-2953 (one each unit) (built as 1921-53)
11534-11535	2954-2955

Lavatory and corridor composites

11751-11790	3001-3020 (two each unit) (built as 2001-20)
11791-11819	3101-3129 (one each unit). War losses: 11807 (3117) and 11809 (3119) Portsmouth Hbr, night of 10-11/1/41; 11827 (3137) Portsmouth Hbr 13/8/40; 11834 (3144) Fratton depot 26/4/41
11807/09/27/34	3156/17/37/44 replacements of war losses
11820-11845	3130-3155 (one each unit)
11846-11858	3073-3085 (one each unit)
11859	3119 (war loss replacement)
11860	3157 built numbered 12234 restaurant first, altered to compartment composite by 1957
11861	12232 officially derated 1946 to non-dining composite but not altered externally. Written off c2/64; to use as office on siding at Brockenhurst 8/66, to Micheldever sidings 5/68 and scrapped
11862-11867	3041/41/42/42/43/43 composites ex firsts 12255/52/58/57/51/56, derated 1946
11999-12000	2954-2955 (one each unit)
12001-12033	2921-2953 (one each unit) (built as 1921-1953). Loss: 12001 (2926) Brighton 19/9/61

Driving trailer lavatory composites (one to each unit)

12034-12069	2011-2046. Loss: 12037 (2014) war Brighton 25/5/43
12070-12071	2047-2048
12072-12100	2049-2077. Losses: 12079 (2056) accident Brighton, 31/12/46; 12082 (2059) accident Durnsford Rd depot 24/10/66; 12092 (2069) accident Ford, 5/8/51
12101	2010 (built as 1890, then renumbered 1900)
12102-12110	2001-2009 (built as 1891-99)
12111-12149	2078-2116. Losses: 12121 (2088) accident (fire) Littlehampton /50 (underframe salvaged, used for 12854); 12129 (2096) accident Brighton 23/6/69 replaced by 12101; 12133 (2100) accident Ford, 5/8/51, underframe salvaged, used for 12856; 12135 (2102), war, Portsmouth Hbr 12/8/40; 12138 (2105) accident East Preston Crossing, 22/9/65
12150-12185	2117-2152. Losses: 12156 (2123) accident 1967 (?depot); 12166 (2133) accident Guildford 8/11/52
12186-12231	2601-2646. Losses: 12211 (2626) accident Vauxhall 29/9/66; 12231 (2646) accident 16/11/47 (?depot)

Restaurant firsts

12232-12250	3054-3072 (not in numerical order). Loss: 12249 (3060) war, Portsmouth Hbr night of 10-11/1/41

Firsts

12251-12259	3041-3043 (three to each unit) (built as 2041-43). Loss: 12234 (3058) war, Hampton Court 8/12/40
12251-59	derated to composite and renumbered c.1946 to 11866, 11867, 10115, 10113, 11862/63/64/65, 10114
12260-12276	3021-3037 (built as 2021-37)

Thirds (saloons)

12351-12360	4378-4387. Loss: 12363 (4623) accident Effingham Junc 1/7/72
12361-12395	4621-4655
12396-12399	4656-4659
12400-12406	4660-4666

Pantry firsts

12501-12517	3021-3037 (built as 2021-37)

Buffets

12518-12530	3073-3085. Losses: 12518 (3073) war, Streatham Hill 27/9/40; 12524 (3079) accident New Cross Gate sidings 10/9/64

Restaurant kitchen thirds

12601-12619	3054-3072 (12601-19 not allocated in numerical order; 12613 fire damage 2/54, altered to buffet, dia 2602, on repairs budget, 1955; 12602/05/09 altered to griddle cars, dia 2572, 1961/2). Losses: 12606 (3058) war, Hampton Court 8/12/40; 12617 (3063) Wimbledon Park sidings 29/6/44

Motor third brakes

12650-12664	4601-4607 (in pairs), and 4590 note (s). Loss: 12663 (4607) accident Wimbledon Park sidings 4/12/73
12665-12750	4667-4709 (in pairs). Losses: 12666 (4667) accident Wimbledon Park sidings 24/11/70; 12737 (4703) accident Wimbledon Park sidings 24/11/70; 12748 (4708) accident Wimbledon Park sidings 14/9/72
12751-12800	4710-4734 (in pairs). Losses: 12751 (4710) accident New Cross Gate c.1976; 12775 (4722) accident Durnsford Road depot 3/71; 12790 (4729) accident Wimbledon Park sidings 3/10/73

Driving trailer composites (one to each unit)

12801-12846	2647-2692. Losses: 12807 (2088; formerly in 2653) accident Barnham 1/8/62; 12834 (2680) accident Chatham 5/4/56; 12842 (2688) accident Ascot, 2/68
12847-12853	2693-2699. Loss: 12850 (2696) circa 9/69, location not known
12854	2653 (underframe salvaged from 12121)
12855-12858	2700, 2133, 2100, 2069 (underframes: 12855 salvaged from 12037; 12856 salvaged from 12133; 12857/58 new)

Motor third brakes (double deck) (pairs)

13001-13004	4001-4002

Thirds (double deck) (pairs)

13501-13504	4001-4002

Motor third brakes (all allocated in pairs except 14521-14570, which were one each unit). (Those completed mid 1956-1959 were second class).

14001-14030	5001-5015
14031-14066	5016-5034. Losses: 14041 (5021) accident Crayford 17/2/59; 14045 (5023) accident Maze Hill 4/7/58
14067-14106	5034-5053. Losses: 14093 (5047) written off 1978
14201-14210	5101-5105
14211-14310	5106-5155. Losses: 14259 (5130) fire, Effingham Junc depot 4/11/73; 14281 (5141) accident Wimbledon Park sidings 14/7/61
14311-14410	5156-5205. Losses: 14334 (5167) accident Selhurst depot c.1/70; 14406 (5203) accident Selhurst depot c.6/80; 14408 (5204) accident St John's 4/12/57
14411-14430	5206-5215
14431-14520	5216-5260. Losses: 14440 (5220) accident (SE division, ?depot), 12/10/72; 14450 (5225) accident Staines 9/8/57; 14479 (5240) fire Cannon Street 19/6/72; 14489 (5245) accident Wimbledon Park sidings 14/7/61; 14507 (5254) accident Borough Market Junction 17/2/70
14521-14556	5601-5636
14557-14570	5651-5684

Thirds (all batches shown here, one car per unit; all cars 10-compartment except 15101-58, 15234-83, 1533-83, 15394-403, which were saloons), and 15005/38/80, which were designed as 9-compartment composites. (Those completed mid 1956-1959 were second class).

15001-15033	5001-5033 15001-4/6-33 renumbered and rewired ex 101/102/103/104xx; 15005 ex 11454; all under HO 3798 and 3799, of 29/5/51; dia nos. retained. Loss: 15008 (5008) body rust, scrapped 1959
15034-15078	5216-5260 15034-37/39 as 15001 etc; 15038 ex 11451; all under HO 4174, 11/12/55
15079-15084	5302, 5008, 5261(2), 5262, 5115 renumbered and rewired ex 101/102/103xx (15080/84 ex 11456/85) in reforming operations. 11485 originally in 4115, then trailer set 900, then as 15080 to 5008
15101-15115	5001-5015
15116-15133	5016-5033
15134-15153	5034-5053
15154-15158	5101-5105. Loss: 15156 (5103) fire Stewarts Lane 9/4/71
15159-15178	5034-5053. Loss: 15172 (5047) written off 1978
15179-15183	5101-5105
15184-15233	5106-5155. Losses: 15200 (5122) fire Stewarts Lane 9/4/71; 15228 (5150) corrosion write-off /61 (replaced by second 15228 ex 10394)
15234-15283	5106-5155. Losses: 15250 (5122) fire Stewarts Lane 9/4/71; 15278 (5150) corrosion write-off /61 (replaced by second 15278 ex 12392)
15284-15333	5156-5205. Losses: 15300 (5172) accident SE division c12/68 (?depot); 15332 (5204) accident St John's 4/12/57
15334-15383	5156-5205. Loss: 15382 (5204) accident St Johns 4/12/57
15384-15393	5206-5215
15394-15403	5206-5215
15404-15448	5216-5260
15449-15481	4 SUB thirds in 10xxx refitted as saloons and renumbered for units in series between 5412 and 5454 (not in numerical order)

Driving trailer composites

16001-16036	5601-5636

Driving trailer seconds

16101-16134	5651-5684

Notes:

(l) ordered nominally for augmentation units 4517-4579; 40 allocated new to 45xx; 20 allocated to units in batch 4355-4377.

(m) ordered for augmentation units 4401-4516; allocated to 3-car units in random order; many reallocated during first year of traffic due to alterations for bogie clearances

(n) ordered for augmentation units 4300-54; allocated to 3-car units in random order

(p) 10449-10471 ordered for units 4355-4377; 14 allocated new to augmentation units in 45xx; 9 to 4355 batch

(r) 11448-1470 ordered for units 4355; 9 allocated new to augmentation units 4610/14/13/05/03/01/06/04, then to units in 45xx; 14 to 4355 batch

(s) 12664 new 4/50, to 4590 until 9/54, then refurbished and to 2700

(t) 12855 new to 2700 (disbanded 3/68) then to 2688, then to 2696 in 10/69

APPENDIX 3

Summary of carriage numbers, with HO Order, Diagram and Unit Numbers for Second Generation suburban stock (1939-59) and First Generation main line stock (1932-55)

Carriage renumberings up to 1983 included; reallocations and formation changes not included.
Note that from 1949, 'old' numbers in 8xxx were re-issued for new or rebuilt suburban vehicles.
Pullman cars (units 2001-20/41-43/51-53, later 3001, etc.) built 1932, are not included below.

Carriage numbers	SR Order No./Date	SR Dia No.	Completed	Unit Nos.
Motor third brakes				
8616-8655	HO 3638 – 16/1/50	2126	7-11/51	4735-4754
8656-8673**	-	-	-	-

** carriage numbers intended for 5001-5009; 8656-59 renumbered to 14001-04 after leaving Eastleigh carriage works; 8660-73 renumbered before leaving carriage works paint shop. See 14001-14018

Thirds				
8901-8935	HO 3504 – 7/9/48	2018	5/49 -1/50	4621-4655
8936-8939	HO 3505 – 7/9/48	2018	1 -2/50	4656-4659
8940-8946	HO 3506 – 7/9/48	2018	2 -3/50	4660-4666
8947-8989	HO 3617 – 2/11/49	2018	5 – 12/50	4667-4709
8990-9034	HO 3638 – 16/1/50	2018	12/50 -11/51	4710-4754
9035-9043**	-	-	-	-

** carriage numbers intended for 5001-09; 9035-38 renumbered to 15101-04 after leaving Eastleigh carriage works; 9039-43 renumbered before leaving carriage works paint shop. See 15101-09

Carriage numbers	SR Order No./Date	SR Dia No.	Completed	Unit Nos.
10001-10020	HO 570 – 16/5/30	2006	9-12/32	3001-20
not allocated to units in numerical order				(built as 2001-20)
10021-10054	HO 805 – 23/3/34	2010	3–6/35	3021-37
				(built as 2021-37)
10055-10083	HO 926 – 14/5/36	2009	2-4/37	3101-3129
10084-10109	HO 950 6/11/36	2009	1-4/38	3130-3155
10071/73/91/98	HO 3078 – 2/11/44	2009	c.10/46	3117/19/37/56
war loss replacements				
10110-10112	HO 3078 – 2/11/44	2009	10/46	3158/44/57
10113-10115		2016 ex-2504		3041-3043
ex firsts 12254/59/53 derated 1946				
10121-10143	HO 3464 – 24/11/47	2018	12/48-4/49	4277-4299
10144-10166	HO 3464 – 24/11/47	2013	12/48-12/49	4277-4299
10167-10169	HO 4796 – 23/5/47	2013	1/48	note (l)
10170-10229	HO 3463 – 24/11/47	2013	1/48-7/48	note (l)
10230-10345	HO 3351 – 2/4/46	2013	10/46-5/47	note (m)
10346-10400	HO 1094 – 16/5/39	2013	6/45-4/46	note (n)
10419-10428	HO 1060 – 28/11/38	2012	c.9/41 (10419)	4101
			c.12/44-4/45	4102-4110
10429-10438	HO 1060 – 28/11/38	2014	4-7/46	4111-4120
10439-10448	HO 1060 – 28/11/38	2015	8-10/46	4121-4130
10449-10471	HO 3231 – 5/5/45	2014	8/47	note (p)
10472-10481	HO 3384 – 23/5/47	2018	9-11/48	4378-4387
Motor third brakes				
10497-10500	HO 1057 – 28/11/38	2117	c.2/40 and c.5/40	2954-2955
10501-10566	HO 569 – 16/5/30	2106	1932	2921-2953
				(built as 1921-53)
10567	HO 806 – 23/3/34	2111	c.2/35	2010
				(built as 1890, then renumbered 1900)
10568-10576	HO 806 – 23/3/34	2111	c.3/35	2001-09
				(built as 1891-99)
10577-10612	HO 898 – 8/1/36	2115	c.8-12/36	2011-2046
				(built as 1901-20/54-69)

10613-10614	HO 903 – 27/1/36	2115	c.2/36-1/37	2047-2048
				(built as 1970/71)
10615-10682	HO 949 – 6/11/39	2115	6-12/37	2049-2116
10683-10718	HO 948 – 6/11/36	2115	8- 11/38	2117-2152
10719-10794	HO 1023 – 29/4/38	2116	c.1-7/39	2601-2676
10795-10810	HO 1058 – 28/11/38	2116	c.11/39-c.3/40	2677-2692
10811-10817	HO 3230 – 5/5/45 and 28/5/47	2121	11-12/48	2693-2699
10829-10848	HO 3384 – and 3385 – 23/5/47	2126	9-11/48	4378-4387
10849-10894	HO 3464 – 23/11/47	2126	12/48-4/49	4277-4299
10895-10940	HO 3231 – 5/5/45	2119	9/47-6/48	4355-4377

ex works in reverse order ie 4377-55

10941-10960	HO 1060 – 28/11/38	2118	c.9/41 (10941/2)	4101
			c.12/44-4/45	4102-4110
10961-10980	HO 1060 – 28/11/38	2119	4-7/46	4111-4120
10981-11000	HO 1060 – 28/11/38	2120	8-10/46	4121-4130
11001-11002	External contract	2108-2109	1931	Test unit '2001'

prototype cars; to traffic 1/33 in units 2041/42 (3041/42)

11003-11042	External contract 5/30	2107	10-12/32	3002-07/09-20/41-43
				(built as 3002-07/09-20/41-43)
11043-11044	External contract 5/30	2107	1932	3001 (built as 2001)
11045-11046	External contract 5/30	2107	1932	3008
				(built as 2008)
11047-11080	External contract 3/34	2112	3-6/35	3021-3037

not allocated to units in numerical order (built as 2021-37)

11081-11138	HO 924 – 14//5/36	2114	2-4/37	3101-3129
11139-11176	HO 924 – 14/5/36	2114	4-c.5/37	3054-3072
11177-11228	HO 950 – 6/11/36	2114	1-4/38	3073-3085
11229-11254	HO 951 – 6/11/36	2114	5-6/38	3073-3085
110/111/112xx	HO 3075 – 2/11/44	2114	7-11/46	

nos. 11082, 11113/14/17/18/51/52/57/81/92, 11205   3137/37/17/19/17/57/57/
11 war loss replacements   44/32/19/44 respectively

11301-11370	HO 3504 – 7/9/48	2126	5/49-1/50	4621-4655
11371-11378	HO 3505 – 7/9/48	2126	1-2/50	4656-4659
11379-11392	HO 3506 – 7/9/48	2126	2-3/50	4660-4666

Thirds (built to composite dimensions)

11448-11470	HO 3231 5/5/45	2314	c.8/47-9/47	note (r)
11471-11480	HO 1060 28/11/38	2312	c.9/41 (11471)	4101
			c.12/44-4/45	4102-4110
11481-11490	HO 1060 28/11/38	2314	4-7/46	4111-4120
11491-11500	HO 1060 28/11/38	2314	8-10/46	4121-4130

Composites

| 11501-11533 | HO 569 16/5/30 | 2305 | 1932 | 2921-53 |

11501-20 not allocated to units in numerical order (built as 1921-53)

| 11534-11535 | HO 1057 28/11/38 | 2311 | c.2 and c.5/40 | 2954-2955 |

Lavatory and corridor composites

| 11751-11790 | HO 570 16/5/30 | 2307 | 9-12/32 | 3001-3020 |

not allocated to units in numerical order (built as 2001-20)

| 11791-11819 | HO 925 14/5/36 | 2309 | 2-4/37 | 3101-3129 |
| 11807/09/27/34 | HO 3079 2/11/44 | 2309 | /46 | 3156/17/37/44 |

war loss replacements

11820-11845	HO 951 6/11/36	2309	1-4/38	3130-3155
11846-11858	HO 951 6/11/36	2309	5-6/38	3073-3085
11859	HO 3079 2/11/44	2309	/46	3119
11860	HO 3079 2/11/44	2309	10/46	3157

built as no. 12234 to dia. 2571, altered to compartment composite by 1957

| 11861 | Order details not known | | | 3158 |

built as 12232 to dia. 2571 in 1937; derated during war to non-dining composite but externally unaltered

				3041-3043
11862-11867				
derated firsts ex 12255/56/58/57/51/52				
11999-12000	HO 1057 28/11/38	2310	c.2/40 and c.5/40	2954-2955
12001-12033	HO 569 16/5/30	2306	1932	2921-2953
12001-20 not allocated to units in numerical order				(built as 1921-1953)

Driving trailer lavatory composites

12034-12069	HO 898 8/1/36	2701	c.8-12/36	2011-2046
12070-12071	HO 903 27/1/36	2701	c.12/36, 1/37	2047-2048
12072-12100	HO 949 6/11/39	2701	6-10/37	2049-2077
12101	HO 806 23/3/34	2700	c.2/35	2010
			(built as 1890, then renumbered 1900)	
12102-12110	HO 806 23/3/34	2700	c.3/35	2001-2009
				(built as 1891-99)
12111-12149	HO 949 6/11/36	2701	10-12/37	2078-2116
12150-12185	HO 948 6/11/36	2701	8-11/38	2117-2152
12186-12231	HO 1023 29/4/38	2702	c.1-c.5/39	2601-2646

Restaurant firsts

12232-12250	External contract and	2571	by 7/37	3054-3072
not allocated to units in numerical order	HO 931 9/6/36			

Firsts

12251-12259	HO 571 16/5/30	2504	11-12/32	3041-3043
derated and renumbered 1946 to 11866/67, 10115, 10113, 11862-65, 10114				(built as 2041-43)
12260-12276	HO 805 23/3/34	2506	3-6/35	3021-3037
				(built as 2021-37)

Thirds

12351-12360	HO 3384, 3385 23/5/47	2018	9-11/48	4378-4387
12361-12395	HO 3504 7/9/48	2018	5/49-1/50	4621-4655
12396-12399	HO 3505 7/9/48	2018	1/50	4656-4659
12400-12406	HO 3506 7/9/48	2018	2-3/50	4660-4666

Pantry firsts

12501-12517	HO 805 23/3/34	2600	3-6/35	3021-3037
				(built as 2021-37)

Buffets

12518-12530	HO 951 6/11/36	2601	6-7/38	3073-3085

Restaurant kitchen thirds

12601-12619	External contract and HO 9322505		by 7/37	3054-3072

not allocated to units in numerical order; 12613 altered to buffet, dia 2602, on repairs budget, 1955; 12602/05/09 altered to griddle cars, dia 2572 (HO 4855 of 10/10/60); to traffic 1962

Motor third brakes

12650-12664	HO 3618 2/11/49	2126	4/50	4601-4607
				and 4590 note (s)
12665-12750	HO 3617 2/11/49	2126	5-12/50	4667-4709
12751-12800	ho 3638 16/1/50	2126	12/50-11/51	4710-4734

Driving trailer composites

12801-12846	HO 1023 29/4/38	2702	c.5-c.12/39	2647-2692
12847-12853	HO 3230 and 3232 5/5/45 amended 28/5/47	2321 amended to 2705	11-12/48	2693-2699
12854	HO 3618 2/11/49	2705	12/50	2653
12855-12858	HO 4009 2/7/53	2705	1/55	

mishap replacements allocated to 2700 (note t), 2133, 2100, 2069 respectively

Motor third brakes (double deck)

13001-13004	HO 3529 9/2/49	2128	9/49	4001-4002
				(4901-4902 from 1970)

Thirds (double deck)

13501-13504	HO 3529 9/2/49	2020, 2021	9/49	4001-4002

standard suburban buffing arrangements, hence two dia. nos. (4901-4902 from 1970)

Motor third brakes

14001-14030	HO 3638 16/1/50	2129	11/51-9/52	5001-5015
14031-14066	HO 3756 2/2/51	2129	4-9/53	5016-5034
14067-14106	HO 3757 2/2/51	2129	9/53-2/54	5034-5053
14201-14210	HO 3757 2/2/51	2129	11/53-1/54	5101-5105
14211-14310	HO 4016 14/7/53	2129	2/54-2/55	5106-5155
14311-14410	HO 4099 30/3/54	2129	2/55-1/56	5156-5205
14411-14430	HO 4172 11/2/55	2129	2-4/56	5206-5215
14431-14520	HO 4173 11/2/55	2129	4/56-3/57	5216-5260
14521-14556	HO 4281 12/4/56	2129	2-10/58	5601-5636
14557-14570	HO 4281 12/4/56	2129	9-12/59	5651-5684

Thirds
Note: dia. 2015 are compartment thirds; dia. 2018 are saloon thirds; dia. 2314 are 'pseudo'-composites*

15001-15033	HO 3798/99 29/5/51			5001-5033

15001-4/6-33 rewired and renumbered ex 101/102/103/104xx, 15005 ex 11454*; diagram numbers retained

15034-15078	HO 4174 11/12/55		4/56-3/57	5216-5260

15034-37/39 as 15001 etc; 15038 ex 11451*; diagram numbers retained

15079-15084

renumbered and rewired ex 101/102/103xx (15080/84 ex 11456/85*); used in reforming operations
diagram numbers retained; to units 5302, 5008, 5261(2), 5262, 5115

15101-15115	HO 3638 16/1/50	2018	11/51-9/52	5001-5015
15116-15133	HO 3756 2/2/51	2018	4-9/53	5016-5033
15134-15153	HO 3757 2/2/51	2018	9/53-2/54	5034-5053
15154-15158	HO 3757 2/2/51	2018	11/53-1/54	5101-5105
15159-15178	HO 3757 2/2/51	2015	9/53-2/54	5034-5053
15179-15183	HO 3757 2/2/51	2015	11/53-1/54	5101-5105
15184-15233	HO 4016 14/7/53	2015	2/54-2/55	5106-5155
15234-15283	HO 4099 30/3/54	2018	2/54-2/55	5106-5155
15284-15333	HO 4099 30/3/54	2015	2/55-1/56	5156-5205
15334-15383	HO 4099 30/3/54	2018	2/55-1/56	5156-5205
15384-15393	HO 4172 11/2/55	2015	2-4/56	5206-5215
15394-15403	HO 4172 11/2/55	2018	2-4/56	5206-5215
15404-15448	HO 4173 11/2/55	2018	4/56-3/57	5216-5260
15449/50	No ordering data known			5263

interior alterations, rewired and renumbered ex 10440 and 10337 as prototypes for EPB 'facelifting' scheme

Driving trailer composites

16001-16036	HO 4281 12/4/56	2703	2-10/58	5601-5636

Driving trailer thirds

16101-16134	HO 4281 12/4/56	2704	9-12/59	5651-5684

Notes:

(l) 10167-10229 ordered nominally for augmentation units 4517-4579; 40 allocated new to 45xx; 20 allocated to units in batch 4355-4377

(m) 10230-10345 ordered for augmentation units 4401-4516; allocated to 3-car units in random order; many reallocated during first year of traffic due to necessary alterations for bogie clearances

(n) 10346-10400 ordered for augmentation units 4300-54; allocated to 3-car units in random order

(p) 10449-10471 ordered for units 4355-4377; 14 allocated new to augmentation units in 45xx; 9 to 4355 batch

(r) 11448-1470 ordered for units 4355; 9 allocated new to augmentation units 4610/14/13/05/03/01/06/04, then to units in 45xx; 14 to 4355 batch

(s) 12664 new 4/50, to 4590 until 9/54, then refurbished and to 2700, altered to dia 2126A (ie, double periscope fitted in van)

(t) 12855 new to 2700 (disbanded 3/68) then to 2688, then to 2696 in 10/69

APPENDIX 4

Southern Railway-design 1932-59 Main Line and 1941-59 suburban stock: Summary of initial allocations of coaches to units

Main line unit numbers listed are post-1937 renumbering.

All coaches were allocated in numerical order except where otherwise shown.

Except for the compartment trailers reallocated from augmented 4 SUB units in 1950-57, 4 SUB and 4 EPB units formed or reformed at later dates from displaced or spare coaches from existing units which were disbanded are not listed here.

2 BIL

2001-2010	motor third brake 10568-76/87; driving trailer composite 12102-10/01
2011-2152	motor third brake 10577-10718; driving trailer composites 12034-12100/11-185

2 HAL

2601-2699	motor third brake 10719-10817; driving trailer composites 12186-12231, 12801-53
2700	motor third brake 12664; driving trailer composite 12855

4 LAV

2921-2953	motor third brake 10501-66 in pairs
	corridor composite trailers 12001-33, allocated in the order: 12002/04/13/05/03/01/06/12/07/08, 12020/10/16/11/14/19/09/17/15/18, 12021-33;
	compartment composite trailers 11501-33, allocated in the order: 11501/02/17/06/10/09/04/08/03/18, 11520/07/16/14/13/15/19/11/05/12, 11521-33
2954/55	motor third brake 10497-10500 in pairs; corridor composite trailers 11199, 12000;
	compartment composite trailers 11534/34

6 PUL and 6 CIT

3001-3020 and 3041-3043

motor third brake:	3001-05: 11043/44; 11003/04; 11005/06; 11007/08; 11009/10;
	3006-10: 11011/12; 11013/14; 11045/46; 11017/18; 11019/20;
	3011-15: 11021/22; 11023/24; 11025/26; 11027/28; 11029/30;
	3016-20: 11031/32; 11033/34; 11035/36; 11037/38; 11039/40;
	3041-43: 11001/41; 11002/42; 11015/16
corridor third:	3001-10: 10017/02/03/06/08/11/13/19/10/16;
	3011-20: 10018/20/01/04/05/07/09/12/15/14
corridor composites:	3001-05: 11783/84; 11753/54; 11755/56; 11761/62; 11765/66;
	3006-10: 11771/72; 11775/76; 11787/88; 11769/70; 11781/82;
	3011-15: 11785/86; 11789/90; 11751/52; 11757/58; 11759/60;
	3016-20: 11763/64; 11767/68; 11773/74; 11779/80; 11777/78
corridor firsts:	in the order, 2nd, 3rd and 5th cars in each unit:
	3041-43: 12254/55/56; 12259/58/57; 12253/51/52

Pullman cars: see main text.

5 BEL

3051-3053	see main text.

4 RES

3054-3072	motor third brake:	11139-76 in pairs
	restaurant firsts:	3054-63: 12248/46/45/47/34/50/49/33/35/32;
		3064-72: 12236/37/38/39/40/41/42/43/44
	restaurant kitchen third:	3054-63: 12619/10/09/11/06/12/15/07/16/17;
		3064-72: 12601/05/04/08/02/03/14/18/13

4 BUF

3073-3085	motor third brake:	11229-54 in pairs
	corridor composites:	11846-58
	buffet cars:	12518-30

4 COR

3101-3129	motor third brake:	11081-11138 in pairs
	corridor third:	10055-83
	corridor composites:	11791-11819
3130-3155	motor third brake:	11177-11228 in pairs
	corridor third:	10084-10109
	corridor composites:	11820-45

4 DD

4001-4002	motor third brake: 13001-04 in pairs;
	trailer third: 13501-04 in pairs

4 SUB

4101-4130	motor third brake:	10941-11000 in pairs
	trailer third:	10419-48
	trailer "composite" compartment (third class trim) 11471-11500	
	(formation: odd motor – trailer third – trailer "composite" – even motor)	
4277-4299	motor third brake:	10849-94 in pairs
	trailer third saloon:	10121-43
	trailer third compartment:	10144-66
4355-4377	motor third brake:	10895-10940 in pairs

trailer third compartment (101xx/2xx/4xx), trailer third saloon (10463 in 4377);
and trailer "composite" compartments (third class trim) (114xx):

4355-59	10220/21; 10218/19; 10216/17; 10214/15; 10209/10;
4360-64	10207/08; 10205/06; 10199/200; 10197/98; 10196/11461;
4365-69	10173/11462; 10172/11469; 10171/11470; 10170/11468; 10464/11466;
4370-77	10461/11467; 10462/11463; 10465/11464; 10455/11465; 10454/11460; 10457/11459; 10458/11458; 10463/11457

4378-4387	motor third brake saloon:	10829-848 in pairs
	trailer third saloon:	12351-60
	trailer third compartment:	10472-81

4601-4607	motor brake third saloon:	12650-63 in pairs
	trailer third compartment:	10240/45; 10242/76; 10287/97; 10265/325; 10337/259; 10237/348; 10312/373

4621-66	motor third brake saloon:	11301-92 in pairs
	trailer third saloon:	12361-406
	trailer third compartment:	8901-46

Note: coaches built for 4621-66 had reconditioned underframes, except coaches 8918/19/21/23/25-33/36-46, 12378/79/81/83/85-91/93/96-12406 and 11386-92 which had new underframes

4667-4734	motor third brake saloon:	12665-12800 in pairs
	trailer third saloon:	8947-9014
	trailer third compartment:	
	4667-4680:	10291/264/261/249/279/320/344/296/258/230/247/323/318/304;
	4681-4690:	10321/293/290/270/314/274/267, 11450, 10301/282;
	4691-4700:	10303/232/327/263/334, 11448, 10286/329/236/250;
	4701-4710:	10305/331/311/295/271/231/343/317/233/342;
	4711-4720:	10330/294/256/324/307/300/306/252/243/340;
	4721-4730:	10339/341, 11455, 10284/235/336/315, 11449, 10393/262;
	4731-4734:	10252/239, 11453, 10338

4735-4754	motor third brake saloon:	8616-8655 in pairs
	trailer third saloon:	9015-9034
	trailer third compartment:	

4735-4744: 10234/181/308/310, 11452, 10255/288/319/273/313;
4745-4754: 10241/316/269/213/268/302/244/326/257

Note: motor third brake and trailer third saloon built for 4667-4754 had reconditioned underframes, except for 8654/55 and 8967 which had new underframes

Trailer third compartment coaches were built 1946-48 for augmented units, repainted but not internally refurbished for 4667-4754. 114xx were compartment composite layout internally

5001-5033	motor third brake saloon:	14001-14066 in pairs
	trailer third saloon:	15101-15133
	trailer third compartment:	15001-15033 (15005 compartment composite layout)

5034-5053	motor third brake saloon:	14067-14106 in pairs
	trailer third saloon:	15134-15153
	trailer third compartment:	15159-78

5101-5105	motor third brake saloon:	14201-14210
	trailer third saloon:	15179-15183
	trailer third compartment:	15154-15158

5106-5155	motor third brake saloon:	14211-14310
	trailer third saloon:	15234-15283
	trailer third compartment:	15184-15233

5156-5205	motor third brake saloon:	14311-14410
	trailer third saloon:	15334-15383
	trailer third compartment:	15284-15333
5206-5215	motor third brake saloon:	14411-14430
	trailer third saloon:	15394-15403
	trailer third compartment:	15384-15393
5216-5260	motor second brake saloon:	14431-14520
	trailer second saloon:	15404-15448
	trailer second compartment:	15034-15078
5601-5636	motor second brake semi-saloon:	14521-14556
	driving trailer composite:	16001-16036
5651-5684	motor second brake semi-saloon:	14557-14590
	driving trailer second:	16101-16134

BIBLIOGRAPHY

Under the 'General' section and each chapter heading, books are listed first, followed by magazine articles, and then any unpublished manuscripts used during research for this book. Both books and magazines are listed in order of publication date (where known). Most of the books are now out of print, but because of their availability from remainder or second-hand sources through internet agencies, ISBN numbers have been included where known.

NOTES AND ABBREVIATIONS
(M):- After the author's name, indicates a magazine article.
LR:- Live Rail, the bi-monthly magazine of the Southern Electric Group.
RG:- Railway Gazette.
RM:- Railway Magazine.
RSE:- Railways South East, published twice-yearly 1988-93.
RW:- Railway World.

GENERAL
Various editions of Locomotives and Other Motive Power – Combined Volume compiled by D. Percival and A. Williams. Ian Allan 1966-1983
London's Local Railways by Alan A. Jackson. Second Edition, 1999 Capital Transport (1 85414 209 7)
Sir Herbert Walker's Southern Railway by C. F. Klapper. Ian Allan 1973. (0 7110 0478 1)
Southern Electric 1909-1979 by G. T. Moody. Ian Allan 1979. (0 7110 0924 4)
Southern Railway Handbook by B. K. Cooper. Ian Allan 1983. (7110 1291 1)
DMU and EMU Disposal by Ashley Butlin. Coorlea Publishing, 1988. (0 9480 6908 2)
Southern Electric: A View From the Past by Graham Waterer. Ian Allan 1998 (0 7110 2621 1)

VOLUME 1

GENERAL INTRODUCTION
Maunsell's S.R. Steam Carriage Stock by David Gould. The Oakwood Press 1990. (0 8536 1401 6)
An Illustrated History of Southern Coaches. Mike King. Oxford Publishing Co 2003. (0 8609 3570 4)

CHAPTER 1: PRE-GROUPING ELECTRIFICATION SCHEMES
The London Brighton and South Coast Railway Volume 3 – Completion and Maturity by J. T. Howard Turner. Batsford 1979. (0 7134 1389 1)
The LSWR in the Twentieth Century by J. N. Faulkner and R. A. Williams. David & Charles 1988. (0 7153 8927 0)
The Electrification of a Portion of the Suburban System of the London, Brighton and South Coast Railway by Philip Dawson. Minutes of Proceedings of the Institute of Civil Engineers, Volume CLXXXVI, 1911

The Electrification of the L.B.&S.C. Ry. Suburban System by Montague F. Long. Paper No.9, The Institution of Locomotive Engineers 1912
Memories of the 'Elevated Electric' by Lawrence R. Burness. (M) LR 51, November 1979
The South Western Electric 1912-23 by David Brown. (M) LR 81/82, October/December 1984
The Triumph of the Third Rail by J. N. Faulkner. (M) RSE 2, Summer 1988
Cheam, Sutton and the 'Elevated Electric' by Adam Sharr. (M) LR 120, April 1991
Cheam, Sutton and the 'Elevated Electric' – A Postscript. (M) LR 121, June 1991

CHAPTER 2: ELECTRIFICATION AND EXPANSION IN THE SUBURBAN AREA 1923-39
Semi-Detached London by Alan A. Jackson. Wild Swan 1991.
History of Southern Electric System Volume 2 by L. A. Mack and others. Unpublished manuscript c.1983
The Chessington Rollercoaster by Adam Sharr. (M) LR 126, April 1992

CHAPTER 4: THE LBSCR AND SR ELEVATED ELECTRIC STOCK 1909-29
The Electrification of a Portion of the Suburban System of the London, Brighton and South Coast Railway by Philip Dawson. Minutes of Proceedings of the Institute of Civil Engineers, Volume CLXXXVI, 1911
Service Stock of the Southern Railway by R. W. Kidner. The Oakwood Press 1993. (0 8536 1429 6)

CHAPTER 5: LSWR AND SR DC SUBURBAN STOCK INTRODUCED 1914-38
Bogie Carriages of the London, Brighton and South Coast Railway by David Gould. The Oakwood Press 1995. (0 8536 1470 9)
LSWR Suburban Electric Stock by David Brown. (M) LR 83-85, February/April/June 1985
Splicing SE&CR Bodies at Ashford, 1924-1928 by H. C. Hughes. (M) RSE Vol.2 No.4, Summer 1991
Steam to Electric – LSWR Style by H. C. Hughes. (M) RSE Vol.3 No.2. Summer 1992
Southern Electric – The First Generation Suburban Stock. Unpublished manuscript by Richard Bell, 1989

CHAPTER 6: THE 4 SUB UNITS 1939-83
Model Railway Constructor Handbook 1: Bulleid Coaches in 4mm Scale by S. W. Stevens-Stratton. Ian Allan 1983
The '4 Sub' Story by Bryan Rayner and David Brown. Southern Electric Group 1983. (0 906 8809 8)9
Sidelights on the Second Generation 'Sub's by SCWS. (M) LR 81, October 1984
More on the '4 Sub's – Extracts of letter from A. T. H. Tayler. (M) LR 83, February 1985

This posed photograph showing passengers inside prototype Brighton express motor third brake 11001 was taken in October 1931, probably in the sidings at Durnsford Road, Wimbledon.
Charles Brown Collection (RAF Museum)